Microsoft® Power Platform™

for dummies®
A Wiley Brand

Microsoft® Power Platform™

by Jack Hyman

for dummies®
A Wiley Brand

Microsoft® Power Platform™ For Dummies®

Published by: **John Wiley & Sons, Inc.,** 111 River Street, Hoboken, NJ 07030-5774, www.wiley.com

Published simultaneously in Canada

For general information on our other products and services, please contact our Customer Care Department within the U.S. at 877-762-2974, outside the U.S. at 317-572-3993, or fax 317-572-4002. For technical support, please visit https://hub.wiley.com/community/support/dummies.

Wiley publishes in a variety of print and electronic formats and by print-on-demand. Some material included with standard print versions of this book may not be included in e-books or in print-on-demand. If this book refers to media that is not included in the version you purchased, you may download this material at http://booksupport.wiley.com. For more information about Wiley products, visit www.wiley.com.

Library of Congress Control Number is available from the publisher.

ISBN 978-1-394-27700-1 (pbk); ISBN 978-1-394-27702-5 (ePDF); ISBN 978-1-394-27701-8 (epub)

SKY10090320_110824

Contents at a Glance

Table of Contents

Introduction

Microsoft Power Platform enables organizations to reimagine the way they develop and deliver business solutions. Microsoft designed the Power Platform suite of tools so that any user, from the business analyst to the senior developer, can create data-driven solutions rapidly. This way, users of all skill levels throughout an organization can build solutions to analyze data, automate processes, create autonomous agents, and more. Meanwhile, seasoned developers can shift their attention to more robust efforts that require more analytical focus. This is all made possible by the powerful, low-code applications and services provided in the Power Platform suite.

This book explains the capabilities of each component of Power Platform, and shows how to set up the environment to get the most from the available applications. Here is a quick rundown of the Power Platform applications covered in this book, and a brief description of what each application does:

- **Power Apps (canvas and model-driven):** Enables users to build custom applications that are highly graphical or data-driven.
- **Power BI:** Business intelligence and data analysis functionality.
- **Power Automate:** Workflow automation.
- **Dataverse:** Web-based data transformation.
- **Power Pages:** Data-driven, low-code website development.
- **CoPilot for Power Platform:** Virtual agent creation.

This book is designed to be your compass in navigating the expansive world of Microsoft Power Platform, providing you with the knowledge and skills needed to leverage its full potential. While by no means will you learn everything you need to get your black belt, *Microsoft Power Platform For Dummies* gives you the essentials you need to produce applications, data products, and workflow automation at speed and scale.

About This Book

Microsoft Power Platform is a suite of low-code solutions that provide a secure and trusted framework, powered by Microsoft Cloud services, to work with other Microsoft products, such as Azure, Dynamics 365, and Microsoft 365. Most users leveraging the Power Platform do not require extensive technical skills, although some features do require a bit more hands-on-the-key knowledge. *Microsoft Power Platform For Dummies* is intended for the following users:

- **Business analysts:** These users leverage Power BI for analyzing data, creating reports, and deriving insights to make informed decisions. They also use Power Apps to build custom business applications without needing to write code.
- **IT professionals:** IT users are those who aren't developers but fill roles such as business, data, and security engineers. Each of these roles uses the Power Platform for automating business processes, managing data and app environments, applying authentication and authorization to applications, enforcing data governance, and integrating with existing systems using Power Automate and Power Apps.
- **Developers:** There are two types of developers in the Power Platform community, *citizen developers* (beginning-to-intermediate developers) and *professional developers* (probably have a computer science degree).
  - **Citizen developers** are apt to design applications requiring little to no-code, using Power App Canvas features. These users are also more inclined to build less sophisticated reports and apply the workflows in their quest to rapidly deploy a solution.
  - **Professional developers** extend the capabilities of the Power Platform by creating custom connectors, integrating with external data sources, and using Azure functions for more complex workflows or processes. Professional developers traditionally have skills as .NET or web developers, so their experience in deploying web applications extends the power of the platform.
- **Data scientists and analysts:** Users whose job it is to transform data into actionable insights use Power BI along with AI-based solutions such as Fabric and Copilot to create comprehensive data models, perform analytics, and share insights across the organization. The result of the data professionals' work are power reports, dashboards, and KPIs for dissemination within a solution. Their work can be standalone as well.
- **End users:** When the application is complete, end users benefit from the applications and automation orchestrated across each Power Platform application. End users gain access to custom-built apps for daily tasks, access reports, and dashboards leveraging Power BI for insights independently or embedded in an app. Also, end users are beneficiaries of automated workflows that simplify processes whether the automation is desktop-based or in the cloud.

- **Administrators:** Unlike developers who create and manage the applications, the administrator must ensure that the applications in the cloud apply the appropriate compliance, security, and data resources. Administrators oversee deployments of applications across one or more tenants, work to ensure authentication and authorization rights propagate from Microsoft 365 and Dynamics 365, and monitor the health of the application environment.

This book provides something for everyone, but the focus is on the true "power user" who has beginning-to-intermediate technical skills and wants to learn to develop solutions, analyze data, or administer the application.

Throughout the book, certain conventions have been used as a way to help power you through your journey.

- **Bold text** means that you're meant to type the text just as it appears in the book. The exception is when you're working through a steps list: Because each step is bold, the text to type is not bold.
- Web addresses and code snippets appear in `monofont`. If you are reading the digital edition of *Power Platform for Dummies,* you can click on these links, and they will take you to the intended URL in a jiffy.
- There are a few times when command sequences are presented using Power Platform's low-code language, Power Fx. In those cases, you'll sequence these steps similar to Tables ⇨ New Table ⇨ Create A New Table to create a new table in Dataverse from the Power Apps Maker Portal.
- Several images include black arrows, incorporate rectangles around a screen segment, or have a letter pointing to one or more application functions. This is done to help guide you to specific references made in the text.

To make the content more accessible, this book is divided into five parts:

- **Part 1, "Grasping Power Platform Foundations,"** is your entry point into learning the Power Platform. In Chapter 1, you explore terminology, and Chapters 2 and 3 cover administration and data concepts that are essential to building solutions.
- **Part 2, "Getting Your Power Apps Hat On,"** is your crash course into building canvas apps, model-driven apps, and portals, all built using a common construct, Power Apps.
- **Part 3, "Telling the Data Story with Power BI,"** takes you on a journey from data exploration and cleansing to visualization and sharing using Microsoft enterprise data analytics solution, Power BI.

- **Part 4, "Simplifying Workflows with Automation,"** introduces cloud and desktop workflow automation leveraging Power Automate. You'll get hands-on practice with basic exercises utilizing triggers, actions, flows (automated, instant, and scheduled), connectors, conditions, loops, and expressions, all of which are used to automate workflows between apps and services.
- **Part 5, "The Part of Tens,"** describes best practices and third-party resources many of the industry pros use when seeking help.

Foolish Assumptions

Diving into Microsoft Power Platform can be a bit intimidating at first because of its sprawling capabilities. Microsoft has designed the Power Platform to be a comprehensive suite for business analytics, app development, and process automation, with the goal that all users can engage with the platform. Reality check: There are many nuances that a newbie will not be able to handle out of the gate. Because the aim is to go beyond creating simple apps, workflows, and data insights, the breadth of Power Platform's offerings requires a bit of technical prowess and will sometimes feel daunting.

This book is crafted to guide end users through the critical features of the Power Platform, without assuming prior expertise or deep technical knowledge. This book is not a guide aimed at certification seekers or those looking to delve into the depths of platform administration or advanced development techniques. This is a true foundational concept book. For those areas, there are other resources more specifically suited to those purposes on the market. In *Microsoft Power Platform For Dummies*, I'll point you toward the official Microsoft documentation and other resources, when appropriate, where you can expand your understanding of specific technical details as needed. Remember, this book should serve as a roadmap for the beginning-to-intermediate developer wanting to get a taste of each major feature across the Power Platform. Also, the platform is ever-evolving; what is presented in the first edition of Power Platform for Dummies may vary slightly from your current user experience using each of the tools. Why is that? Microsoft is making updates to the user experience and functionality almost weekly (although sometimes it can even be more frequent), especially as they infuse Microsoft Copilot throughout the product. So, please don't be alarmed by the slight variations.

To ensure that you can follow along and make the most out of this book, I've based our journey on a few key assumptions about your starting point:

- **Access to Power Platform tools:** I assume that you've purchased a copy of Microsoft 365, which comes with many of the Power Platform suite applications, including Power Apps, Power Automate, and Power BI. To get more of the advanced features, I recommend procuring the Per User Premium licenses. While certain aspects of these tools are available for free, such as Power BI Desktop, comprehensive use of the platform often requires a paid subscription.
- **Internet connectivity:** This might seem straightforward, but it's crucial. All components of the Power Platform require an internet connection, as Power Platform is 100 percent cloud-based.
- **Engagement with a meaningful project:** The assumption here is that you have a project or a dataset that is significant and relevant to your work or interests. Throughout the book, I provide a thematic example and cite sample datasets. However, applying what you learn to your own real-world experiences greatly enhances your understanding and skills. A meaningful project should involve a dataset that is complex enough to challenge you but not so vast as to be unmanageable for learning purposes.
- **Basic understanding of your business processes:** I assume you have a basic understanding of the business processes you want to improve or automate. Power Platform is most powerful when applied to real-world scenarios, and having a grasp of the processes you want to enhance will greatly aid in learning to use the platform effectively.

If you are equipped with these foundational tools and knowledge, you will be better positioned to explore the more complex functionalities of Power Platform, turning the seemingly daunting into powerful solutions.

Icons Used in This Book

Throughout *Microsoft Power Platform For Dummies*, you see some icons along the way. Here's what they mean:

TIP

Tips help you identify shortcuts or ways to expedite the development and delivery of Power Platform solutions.

REMEMBER

Remember icons help you identify the big concepts that you need to understand to be proficient in the use of Microsoft Power Platform. Consider these the equivalent of a foundation in the house.

TECHNICAL STUFF

The Technical Stuff icon calls attention to technical configurations, settings, or features that go beyond the low-code advertising Microsoft promotes with Power Platform.

WARNING

Don't panic when you see the Warning icon. These warnings point out technical issues that may require closer attention on your part.

ON THE WEB

When a resource is available on the Web, particularly an indispensable one from Microsoft, you'll find a link recommending you check it out. Many of these links provide access to resources and code snippets that simply cannot be put in a *For Dummies* book.

Beyond the Book

In addition to the content you're reading in this book, you have access to a free Microsoft Power Platform Cheat Sheet. Similar to the structure of the book, the Cheat Sheet contains sections for Dataverse, Power Apps, Power Pages, Power BI, Power Automate, and Copilot for the Power Platform. To find the Cheat Sheet, go to `www.dummies.com` and enter **Microsoft Power Platform For Dummies** in the Search box.

Throughout this book, you are also directed to publicly available datasets and free utilities that can help accelerate your delivery of Power Platform solutions.

Where to Go From Here

Power Platform is meant to work as a complete solution, meaning all the applications support one another, but as you can guess, most users don't use it that way. That's why you can start at any chapter in this book, and you will be just fine. If you want to focus on data analytics only, head over to Part 3. If your mission is to learn about data-driven website development, see Chapter 8. The book has been written using a building blocks mentality, but if you need to jump around, go ahead and have fun. You won't be missing anything!

1

Grasping Power Platform Foundations

IN THIS PART . . .

Assess what you and your business can achieve with Power Platform.

Explore the Power Platform admin center and Power Apps Maker Portal.

Use Microsoft Dataverse to organize and secure large datasets, and create business process flows for model-driven apps.

IN THIS CHAPTER

» Recognizing the business value of Microsoft Power Platform

» Identifying the key components of Power Platform

Chapter 1
Touring the Power Platform

Until recently, only skilled technicians could develop software, provide data analytics, automate workflows, and work with artificial intelligence. Now, business technology tools, such as the tools that make up the Microsoft Power Platform suite, can help users of just about any skill level perform application development and data analysis. With these tools, you can develop enterprise solutions by using simple drag-and-drop interfaces — the tools do all the coding magic behind the scenes.

This chapter provides an overview of the capabilities included in Microsoft Power Platform. I discuss the benefits that Microsoft Power Platform's highly adaptable and open platform offers. The platform greatly simplifies business operations and allows for significant integration opportunities, not just across Microsoft applications, but for a broad range of enterprise vendors outside the Microsoft ecosystem.

Grasping the Power of Power Platform

Microsoft Power Platform is a suite of Microsoft tools that enables users of all skill levels to rapidly develop applications. You don't need to be a programmer to use these tools. You simply need to know how all the tools work together and have a strong sense of logical reasoning that you can apply.

Now, you might be wondering what I mean by a *suite*. Well, Power Platform includes a collection of tools within a single application: tools for application development, enterprise data analytics, workflow automation, virtual agent design, data connection deployment, and data platform design. The Microsoft 365 suite also bundles a collection of tools together: Word for document management, Excel for data analysis, PowerPoint for presentations, and Access for consumer-oriented database management.

Table 1-1 lists each tool included in Microsoft Power Platform and briefly describes its purpose. The section "Zooming into the Platform Features," later in this chapter, discusses each of Power Platform's tools, or *components*, in more detail.

TABLE 1-1 Microsoft Power Platform Tool Capabilities

Tool	Purpose
Power Apps	Low-code development tool to create custom business applications. Makes app creation more accessible and less time-consuming.
Power BI	A sophisticated tool for data visualization and business analytics. Users can create comprehensive reports and dashboards with a variety of charts and visuals.
Power Automate	Robust business process automation tool for the desktop and cloud, with a focus on operational efficiency.
Power Pages	A web design tool that you can use to create professional websites or public-facing portals without having to use code. Integrates with Power Apps, Power Automate, and Power BI.
Dataverse	A cloud-based data repository that enables users to store and manage data used by business applications such as Power Platform and Dynamics 365.

Benefiting from a low-code, no-code solution

Low-code, no-code development means that a developer, either professional or amateur, can design and develop a product for the Web by using a set of intuitive drag-and-drop tools that reduce or even eliminate the need for code. Sure, you need to bring your objects together on the application or *report canvas*, the area in which you design the low-code capability, by referencing specific parameters (using short *references* or code snippets). But by no means do you have to write a novella's worth of code just so a user can click a button or activate a drop-down menu. Those days are long gone.

REMEMBER

Unlike your traditional coders, Power Platform developers fall into two types — citizen developers and professional developers:

- **Citizen developer:** Knows enough to be dangerous when it comes to web development and their business, but has no professional training in developing complete software applications.
- **Professional developer:** Has many years of experience with programming languages that are available in Microsoft Visual Studio and understands more than just drag-and-drop capabilities. Professional developers are familiar with more than one programming language (such as C# and PowerShell) and frameworks (such as .NET Framework and ASP.NET).

Low-code platforms

Low-code platforms, such as Power Platform, provide pre-built components, templates, and drag-and-drop tools so that developers can reduce the amount of hand-coding they need to input to develop applications. Notice that I say reduce — you still likely need to do some hand-coding, even when you work in a highly visual environment for creating your end product, not just a glorified code editor.

If you work in the visual development environment of a low-code platform, you can drag and drop application components, such as check boxes, drop-down menus, labels, or galleries; connect them by using predefined workflows, data connections, or custom formulas; and configure each component's properties via logical units. Most developers do find, however, that they have to do some hand-coding to incorporate complex functionality or logic. More complicated coding practices might include using multistep logic, such as if-else or do-while logic.

Low-code platforms can help you with rapid development when you need to scale over time. Whether you're a professional developer who has decades of experience or an industry professional who needs to quickly create functional solutions, these platforms can assist. For example, industry professionals commonly want to convert a legacy .NET application into a model-driven Power Apps app. The datastore for the .NET app often takes the form of an Access or SQL Server database, which is then migrated to Dataverse. Although this process may seem straightforward, it often requires careful execution to ensure flawless conversion.

No-code platforms

No-code platforms eliminate the need for you, as the developer, to do any hand-coding, period. You don't need programming skills to use these platforms. You simply drag, drop, and click, using a visual interface. No-code platforms offer pre-built templates that offer a wide array of out-of-the-box interfaces to help users configure applications. If you've ever used Microsoft Word (who hasn't?), created a table, and then saved your document as an HTML, you've effectively created a no-code document — ta-da!

Unlike low-code platforms (see the preceding section), where you might need to have some development skills to use them — hence users may shy away from those tools — no-code platforms enable just about anyone to get involved in the application development, data analytics, and workflow automation lifecycle. You just need to have an idea, generally know where to place the content, and then click a Save button. Essentially, most users who leverage a canvas app (which you can read about in the section "Power Apps," later in this chapter) follow that process in conjunction with the help of Microsoft 365 applications such as Excel (Microsoft's spreadsheet program), PowerPoint (its presentation program), and SharePoint (an online collaboration and content management offering).

Connecting with the Microsoft ecosystem and beyond

Microsoft made sure that every application in its enterprise lineup works with Microsoft Power Platform, and you can use them all without having the skills of a lifelong coder.

And believe me, Microsoft isn't alone in its quest to move away from requiring users to have deep technical know-how. The industry is leaning overall toward a focus on allowing business users to be more efficient in their ability to develop applications, analyze data, and automate their business operations. In its marketing, Microsoft showcases hundreds of ways that businesses can effectively use Microsoft products, but here are three takeaways I think are worth pointing out:

- **Business application productivity:** With Power Platform, you can easily integrate with Microsoft 365 (formerly Office 365) applications such as Word (Microsoft's word processor), Excel (its spreadsheet software), PowerPoint (presentation software), Outlook (its e-mail service), and SharePoint (Microsoft's spot for online content storage) to create business workflows, analyze data created from defined lists, or create small applications from structured datasets.

  For example, you can go to the Automate menu in Excel to trigger Workflows or the Integrate menu in SharePoint to execute Power Platform functionality with one click. It's that easy.

- **Enterprise applications:** Dynamics 365 is Microsoft's suite of enterprise resource planning (ERP) and customer relationship management (CRM) applications. A developer can create customer forms for either the ERP or CRM application suite, establish business workflows when a user enters specific data into the system, or curate highly graphical reporting to augment data stored in the applications without much programmatic effort.
- **Cloud computing connectivity:** Power Platform utilizes Microsoft's cloud platform, Azure, for advanced features. For example, Azure Logic Apps supports the creation of advanced workflow automation, and Azure AI services enhance intelligent application capabilities, including integration with Microsoft Copilot (Microsoft's AI-powered digital assistant).

TECHNICAL STUFF

Microsoft offers one of the most comprehensive security, compliance, and governance solution sets. Applications built by using Power Platform benefit from Azure's robust security features, including those that are low-code and no-code (which I talk about in the section "Benefiting from a low-code, no-code solution," earlier in this chapter). Additionally, administrators of Power Platform applications can govern and monitor their applications by using a wide range of compliance and governance tools built right into the Microsoft 365 console.

Zooming into the Platform Features

Microsoft Power Platform, as illustrated in Figure 1-1, provides a unified application platform designed to streamline business processes, improve data visualization, and simplify application development within the Microsoft ecosystem. The top row displays each of the Power Platform applications. These applications can connect to other data sources in one of three ways:

- Connecting to Microsoft and third-party data connectors to push and pull data
- Using Microsoft's own Dataverse data repository
- Integrating with one or more Microsoft AI services, such as Copilot, to assist users in automating workflows, generating insights, and building applications more efficiently through natural language interactions

All of these Power Platform applications require access to data for them to work successfully.

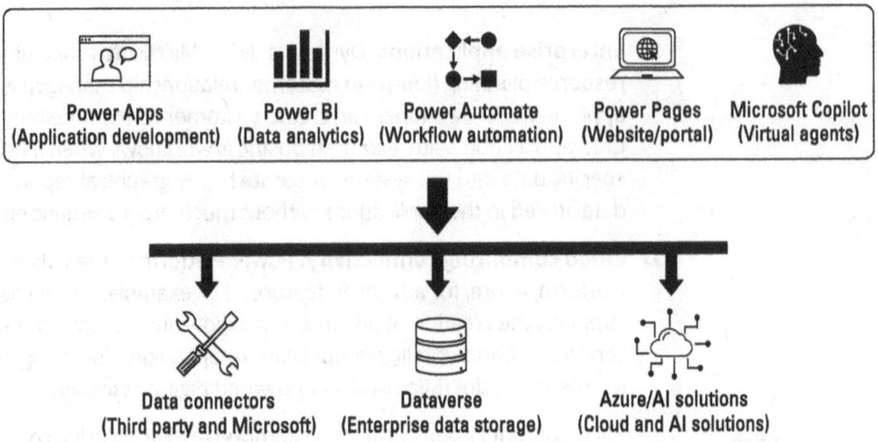

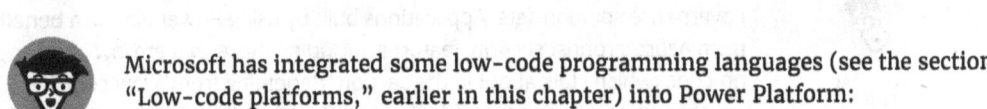

FIGURE 1-1: Microsoft Power Platform components and capabilities.

TECHNICAL STUFF

Microsoft has integrated some low-code programming languages (see the section "Low-code platforms," earlier in this chapter) into Power Platform:

- **Power Fx (Power Platform's low-code programming language):** Allows users to define logic and automate functionality across the platform by using simple, Excel-like formulas to manipulate data, trigger actions, and call parameters.
- **DAX (Data Analysis Expressions):** Used specifically in Power BI (discussed in Part 3 of this book), DAX is a collection of functions and operators that you can combine to create formulas and expressions for performing advanced data analysis and reporting. It allows users to manipulate and analyze data within Power BI, enhancing reporting capabilities.

Microsoft Power Platform applications allow access to almost every enterprise relational database player in the market; not just Power BI, but also SQL Server, Oracle, DB2, MySQL, PostgreSQL, Sybase, and Amazon Redshift, to name a few.

Power Apps

The cornerstone of Power Platform is the Power Apps tool, which enables users to build custom apps without requiring traditional coding. By using the Power Apps tool, you can speed up the delivery of customized applications at a fraction of the cost of traditional development because you don't need a team of data and design experts. I talk about Power Pages, the external portal functionality that you can derive from Power Apps, in the section "Power Pages," later in this chapter, and in Part 2 of this book.

You can use Microsoft Power Apps to design forms in applications such as SharePoint (Microsoft's online collaboration and content management platform) and Microsoft Dynamics 365 (the suite of enterprise resource planning [ERP] and customer relationship management [CRM] applications). It's also a standalone application in the Microsoft Power Platform, where you can design forms to capture and manage data, automate processes, or integrate with other systems. Power Apps allows you to rapidly develop custom applications or, to a lesser degree, forms in other Microsoft enterprise applications, without requiring much code.

You can use Power Apps to create two types of apps:

» **Canvas apps:** Allow a designer to start with a blank canvas and craft a highly graphical interface by bringing icons, blocks, text fields, labels, and interactive components onto the screen. You drag and drop the components onto the page to create the layout that you want for the application, whether you make it highly sophisticated or as simple as the Compensation Calculator shown in Figure 1-2.

FIGURE 1-2: The Compensation Calculator application created with the canvas app.

When creating a canvas app, you need to be familiar with how to configure the parameters for the elements so that they display the output you want. The calculator illustrated in Figure 1-2 has three data entry elements: OTE (meaning *on-target earnings*), Incentive %, and Multiple (by how many times what the rep brings in exceeds the rep's salary; for example, 10 times their base salary). Based on the data entered, the three calculated fields or columns (Salary, Sales Target, Sales Target Goal) display the output for a sales rep's compensation.

- **Model-driven apps:** Uses a structured data source, such as Dataverse, exclusively to create a form-based experience. You can't change the design unless you use custom controls or JavaScript (which requires some coding experience). That rigidity allows for a consistent look and feel, but also better data quality because the inflexible data structure allows for any user — whether end-user, power user, or developer — to manipulate the data in complex scenarios. If you want to streamline data for business operations, enhance productivity, and focus on data quality by using a consistent form and view-based approach, use model-driven applications.

The form in Figure 1-3 is a highly structured form requiring a user to enter very specific data for an Active Job Opportunity. You could format some fields as drop-downs and allow others to require text entry. The very nature of the data entry allows for repeatable analysis if someone wants to conduct data analysis later on by using a data analytics application, such as Power BI. Figure 1-4 displays a synopsis of two form inputs, presenting the view of the model-driven application for the two job opportunities that a user entered in the system (which an HR professional might do).

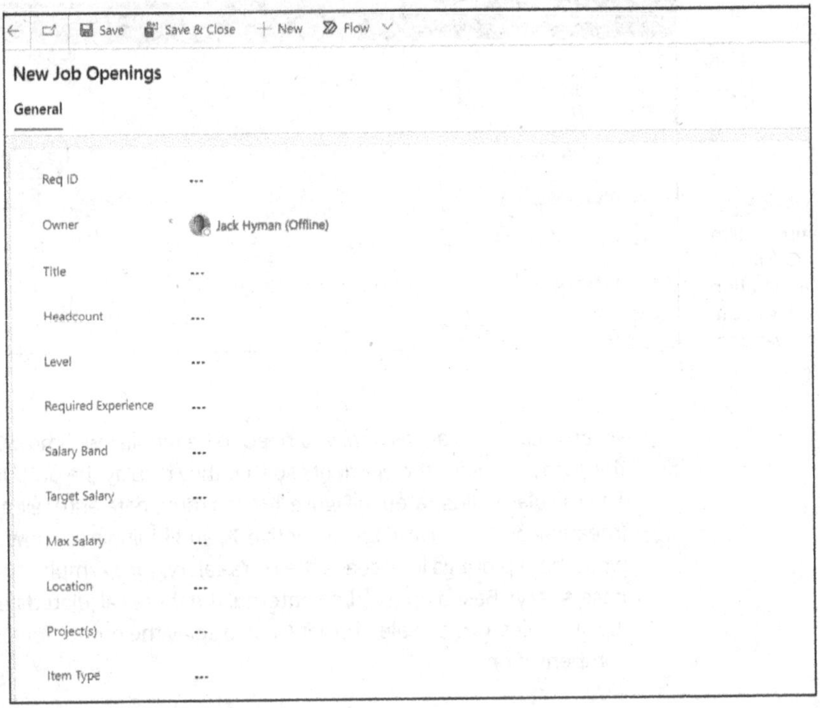

FIGURE 1-3: A model-driven app form created by using Power Apps.

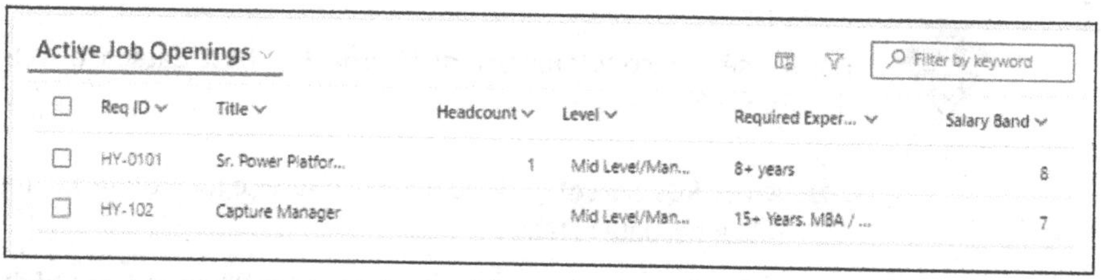

FIGURE 1-4: The view created by a model-driven app in Power Apps.

Dataverse

Microsoft has built all the Power Platform applications around one or more data platforms, with Microsoft's Dataverse being the most commonly used. Dataverse, formerly known as Common Data Services, combines the best of many database platforms that you're probably familiar with, such as Microsoft Access, SQL Server, and even non-relational databases such as NoSQL.

Microsoft Dataverse isn't a relational database; rather, it's a cloud-based storage platform that allows users to store their data and digital assets from two major Microsoft enterprise platforms: Microsoft Power Platform and Dynamics 365 (which I talk about in Chapter 3). Dataverse provides a unified and scalable service-and-app platform where users can securely store and manage their data across business applications. You can create a variety of data solutions, such as tables, views, and form types, without being an expert database administrator or having the infrastructure setup know-how. Microsoft provides Power Apps users with a handful of pre-built example Dataverse tables, such as the Account Table shown in Figure 1-5.

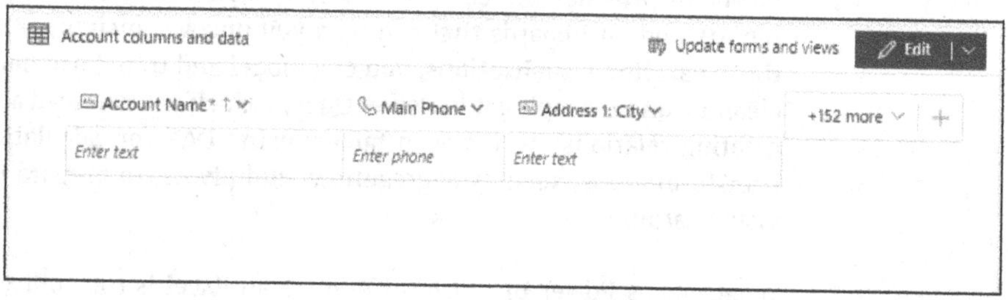

FIGURE 1-5: An example of a Dataverse table.

TIP

The knowledge that you need to set up a Microsoft Access database is about the same as what you need to work with Dataverse, except that Dataverse requires far more structure.

TECHNICAL STUFF

Dataverse is a conglomerate of Microsoft's best database technologies. It stores data types in

- **Azure SQL Server:** A cloud database service for storing and managing relational data in tables
- **Azure Storage:** A cloud service for storing different types of data, such as files, *blobs* (Binary Large Objects), and tables
- **Cosmos DB:** A non-relational (NoSQL) database that scales globally and provides fast access to data
- **Azure Data Lake:** A cloud storage service designed for storing large amounts of structured and unstructured data for analysis
- **Cognitive Search:** An AI-powered service that processes and analyzes large datasets (including those from Azure Data Lake and Dataverse) by using machine learning models to improve data indexing, retrieval, and insights

Power BI

If you're working with data-driven processes, you need to understand and accurately visualize data, as well as transform and model that data so that the results are clear and accurate. *Visualizing* data means showing it in charts or graphs, while *modeling* data means organizing it into tables and successfully connecting those tables together, if appropriate, by establishing relationships.

Power BI provides the comprehensive analytics toolset that you need to create reports and dashboards that can help you uncover insights. But, before creating those dazzling visualizations, you can model and transform data by importing it; cleaning and reshaping it in Power Query (which you can read about in Chapter 9); creating relationships between tables; using DAX for calculations; and applying transformations, such as aggregations and pivots, to prepare it for analysis and visualization.

What makes Power BI much different than Excel is the ability to integrate with other Power Platform components, of course, as well as with more than 100 external data sources that aren't Microsoft branded. Power BI can help your organization foster a data-centric culture. You can get a zest of what Power BI is in Part 3 of this book — but to get a full crash course, check out *Microsoft Power BI For Dummies*, by yours truly (Wiley).

You can use Power BI to analyze and visualize data, whether you collect it in Power Apps or provide it from other data sources. A single user can evaluate insights of one dataset, derived from an online data source or a simple CSV or XLS file, by using Power BI Desktop. That same user can also access the report produced and its accompanying data when published and shared across an organization through Power BI Services. If you want to surface the data outside of Power BI, you have plenty of options, as well. The most common involves using Embedded Power BI reporting in applications such as Power Apps, or using the Azure-based Power BI embedded data service.

With one or more of the Power BI offerings, users can quickly transform data from simple or complex data models into interactive reports, dashboards, and key performance indicators. Power BI has several options to choose from:

- **Power BI Desktop:** A free desktop application that allows you to connect to a data source, either on a user's desktop or online, to perform data transformations, define the underlying data model, and design reports that visualize insights. End-users can create and analyze most reports independently, enabling them to share and collaborate with others efficiently.
- **Power BI Services:** The online SaaS (Software as a Service) offering of Power BI includes various licensing options, such as Professional and Premium, with the primary differences being the number of dataset refreshes allowed per hour and the storage capacity available per user. You can use Power BI Services to share, collaborate, and distribute reports and dashboards across an organization in a cloud environment.
- **Power BI Report Server:** Unlike Power BI Online, Power BI Report Server is an on-premises solution that allows you to store, manage, and distribute Power BI reports, paginated reports, mobile reports, and traditional SQL Server Reporting Services (SSRS) reports. Report Server also provides a secure environment for hosting reports locally, without relying on the cloud, while offering the flexibility to transition to the cloud with Power BI Service if and when you want to.

Power Automate

Power Automate allows you to create autonomous workflows between apps, data, and third-party services in Power Platform, which can help you streamline business processes and reduce manual tasks. You can use Power Automate for simple notifications and data collection tasks, or to address complex business processes involving multiple steps and conditions. And you don't need a computer science degree to do any of this — Power Automate facilitates the entire process. You simply need to understand the logic behind a business process and data target that flows through the system.

You might also hear Power Automate referred to as a *robotics process automation platform*. That's accurate, as well. With Power Automate, you can create automated workflows between applications and services, in support of data synchronization, file synchronization, and alert notifications; and you don't even have to do any coding. The primary function of Power Automate is to reduce coding for repetitive tasks and processes so that individuals and organizations can more efficiently automate routine operations across applications, inside and outside of the Microsoft ecosystem. Flows come in many varieties, as noted in Table 1-2.

TABLE 1-2 Flow Types Available in Power Automate

Flow Name	What It Does
Cloud Flows	Creates a triggered event, such as the arrival of an e-mail from a specific person or the mention of a person in a social media posting.
Instant Flows	Initiate a flow based on a user's interaction with a button. You can automate this type of flow for repetitive tasks that a user performs from a desktop or mobile device.
Scheduled Flows	For activities based on a schedule, such as a daily data upload. For example, you might use this flow to upload a file to SharePoint from a defined location.

TECHNICAL STUFF

You may also hear about two other types of flows in Power Automate: Desktop Flows and Business Process Flows. Desktop Flows focus on automating tasks that occur on the web or directly on a desktop, responding almost instantly to user inputs. Business Process Flows, on the other hand, are structured around predefined steps that guide users through a series of tasks to achieve specific outcomes, ensuring consistency and adherence to processes.

For more about Power Automate, check out Part 4 of this book.

Power Pages

Microsoft Power Pages is a low-code (see the section "Low-code platforms," earlier in this chapter), secure, Software as a Service (SaaS) platform designed for creating, hosting, and managing external-facing business websites. Formerly known as Power Apps Portal, Power Pages provides tools that simplify the web development process so that you don't need to know web-based programming languages to design, configure, and deploy websites that are compatible with various web browsers and devices.

Power Pages includes customizable templates, a design studio for visual editing, and an *integrated learning hub* (a how-to set of educational tools so that you can build that killer website), which together support the efficient creation of websites tailored to specific business needs. You can also integrate other Microsoft Power Platform assets into a Power Pages website, using your existing security credentials from Microsoft Entra (formerly Azure Active Directory).

Power Pages allows for the construction of websites that

- » Use shared business data stored in Microsoft Dataverse (see the section "Dataverse," earlier in this chapter, for a discussion of this storage platform)
- » Develop built-in apps through Power Apps (see the section "Power Apps," earlier in this chapter)
- » Create workflows in Power Automate (flip back to the preceding section)
- » Integrate intelligent virtual agents, which Microsoft refers to as *Copilots*
- » Draft reports by using Power BI (check out the section "Power BI," earlier in this chapter).

The integration of Power Pages with Microsoft Dataverse facilitates a unified development process and ensures data consistency across various applications and services. You can build dynamic, data-driven websites that can support various external business functions through credential-based access.

IN THIS CHAPTER

- » Working with the key components of the Power Platform admin center
- » Figuring out what the Power Apps Maker Portal can do
- » Keeping your Power Platform universe safe and secure

Chapter 2

Framing the Power Platform Solution

With most Microsoft products, you double-click the product's icon, the corresponding application launches, and you can start working pretty much right away. Because the application functions as a platform, its interface is your entire home base. Power Platform works a little differently in this regard.

Working with Power Platform is like building an apartment complex. Each application is like a room, and these rooms (the apps you create with Power Apps) are part of an apartment (solution). The entire building (environment) hosts one or more of these apartments. You can customize each room with different features, such as reports in Power BI, workflows in Power Automate, and tables in Dataverse, similar to how you choose the decor for your apartment rooms.

This chapter shows how to navigate the Power Platform admin center and introduces the Power Apps Maker Portal, the glue that brings together a Power Platform solution.

Taking Control in the Power Platform Admin Center

When you begin your adventure into the land of Power Platform, first head to the admin center, where you can set up your environment (or environments, if you're managing more than one) based on your required specifications.

The admin center provides a unified portal experience where administrators can manage one or more environments. You can use this console to change global settings across the Power Platform. You also can use it to configure each environment's unique settings for applications, including Power Apps, Power Automate, Power Pages, and Microsoft Copilot Studio (which I don't cover in this book). The underlying platform has global features that support each environment, and each environment contains one or more applications, as shown in Figure 2-1.

Power Platform shares its admin center with Dynamics 365 to manage key administrative tasks such as security, billing, and data integration. This centralized hub allows administrators to handle user roles, license management, and data synchronization across both platforms efficiently.

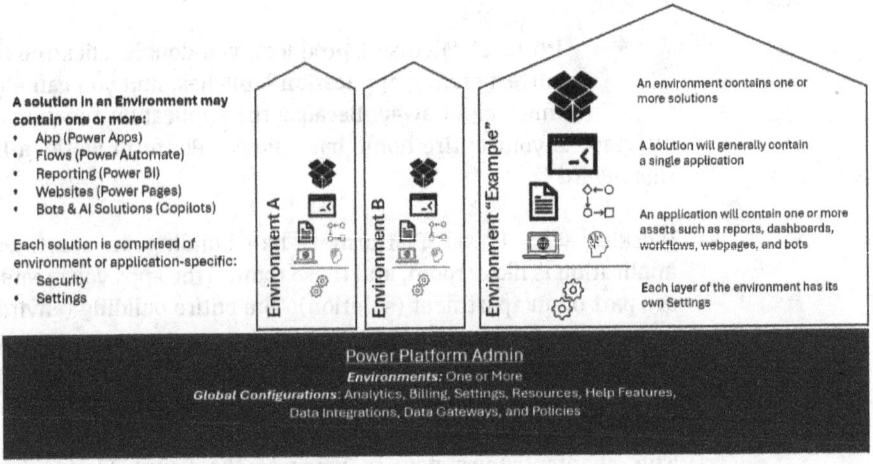

FIGURE 2-1: The nuts and bolts of Power Platform architecture.

To access the admin center for Power Platform, follow these steps:

1. **Go to `http://login.microsoft.com` and log in to your account by entering your username and password in the text boxes; then click Next.**

2. **Navigate to `http://admin.powerplatform.microsoft.com`.**

   You may be prompted to re-enter your credentials, either using the same username and password or a user account in the format *<username>*@*<domainname>*`.onmicrosoft.com`.

   Your Power Platform admin center opens, showing the navigation bar on the left, as well as the service health of the environment and recommended documentation in the center panel.

The only Power Platform component that you can't access through the admin console is Power BI; for that, you have to go to the Power BI admin portal. And Microsoft certainly has good reasons for this division. When you use Power BI, you, as a developer, must control the data output after you develop it. All the functions managed in the Power Platform admin center focus on development. On the other hand, the Power BI admin portal is separate because it manages specific settings for Power BI, including data governance, capacity management, workspace controls, and report usage monitoring. These unique features require a dedicated portal distinct from the broader Power Platform admin center.

ON THE WEB

You can access the admin portal for Power BI through `https://app.powerbi.com`.

REMEMBER

Power Platform shares the same underlying security and data architecture as Microsoft Dynamics 365, which is Dataverse. Therefore, don't be surprised to see references to applications such as Dynamics 365 Sales, Customer Service, Field Services, or Marketing within your Power Platform admin center, assuming you've also configured these applications.

Exploring Core Power Platform Admin Center Capabilities

Before diving headlong into a detailed discussion of the Power Platform admin center sections, I want to offer an overview of the basic purpose of the core sections that appear in the navigation pane. Figure 2-2 shows the pane, and Table 2-1 describes each core section that appears on it.

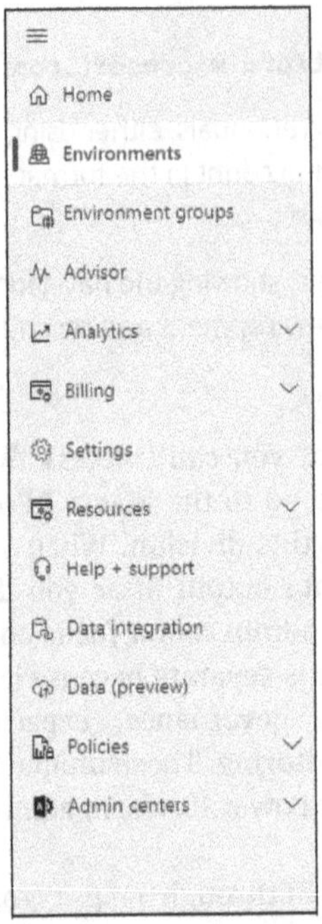

FIGURE 2-2: The Power Platform admin center's navigation pane.

TABLE 2-1 **Power Platform Admin Center Capabilities**

Section	Purpose
Environments	View, create, and manage the environments within the Power Platform. Select an environment to view its details, which include solution-specific settings.
Environment Groups	Manage a list of independent environments by structuring them into groups.
Advisor	Use a recommendation engine to help you optimize your Power Platform tenant.
Analytics	Get a detailed view of key metrics related to the health and performance of environments, particularly within Dataverse. Analytics tracks data including capacity usage, system performance, API calls, and operational efficiency.
Billing	View and manage licensing consumption if you or your organization procure premium licensing for your Power Platform configuration.
Settings	Modify global and environment-specific settings. You can also drill down to environment, sometimes referred to as *tenant*, settings.
Resources	Centrally manage and monitor assets such as Power Apps apps, Power Automate flows, Dataverse databases, and data connections.
Help + Support	Access free help and paid support. You can use the Help section to access the free technical documentation on Microsoft's website. You also can use this section to place a support request (through a paid support subscription).

Section	Purpose
Data Integration	Connect with various data sources. Data integrations between applications that use services such as Power Automate, Power Apps, and Dataverse; as well as two-way communication with Dynamics 365.
Data	Configure data gateways. You may need to create an on-premises or cloud-based data gateway for one or more of your Power Platform applications.
Policies	Manage all platform-related policy actions. The Policies section provides a centralized location for managing application-specific and global policies covering data, billing, and access control.
Admin Centers	A place to access other admin centers relevant to Power Platform, including the Power BI Admin Portal.

Environments

An *environment* in Power Platform is like a container where you store, manage, and share your organization's data, apps, chatbots, and workflows, helping to separate apps based on their roles, security needs, or user groups. Power Apps initially creates a default environment for every tenant, which all users can access to start using the platform. But while you develop apps, the configuration of environments varies based on the specific purpose and requirements of each app. Figure 2-3 shows an admin center Environments interface.

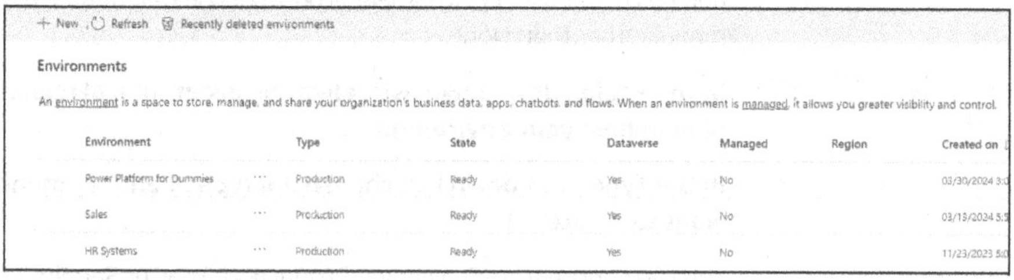

FIGURE 2-3: An Environments interface in the Power Platform admin center.

When you set up an environment, you must first decide whether you want that environment to be database-dependent. The data you use may be part of an environment, stored on Dataverse (the Power Platform version of a database), or from an external source (such as Microsoft Azure SQL Server).

For example, use a database such as Dataverse when you want to enable complex applications that have a complex data architecture and rich security design. All Dynamics 365 applications fall into this bucket, as do model-driven apps. In contrast, for lightweight apps that have simpler data needs, you can more easily use a document such as an Excel spreadsheet or SharePoint list because they set up simply, require less maintenance, and don't need the advanced capabilities that Dataverse offers.

If you want to establish a data-driven environment, you need a Power Platform license or to be a global administrator in your Microsoft 365 environment. You also must have at least 1GB of Dataverse capacity available. Although Power Platform allows you to create free apps with your standard Microsoft 365 license, Dataverse is a premium product and charges by the capacity (think of megabytes and gigabytes). Your use of data storage can add up quickly.

To create a Dataverse-based Power Platform environment, follow these steps:

1. **In the navigation pane of the Power Platform admin center, select Environments.**

   I explain how to access the admin center in the section "Taking Control in the Power Platform Admin Center," earlier in this chapter.

   The Environments interface appears.

2. **In the top-left of the interface, click New.**

   The New Environment pane appears (see Figure 2-4).

3. **Enter a name for your environment in the Name text box.**
4. **From the Group drop-down list, select the group that you want to assign the environment to.**

   To follow along with my example environment, select None. If your organization has created an environment group, choose that option in this drop-down menu, rather than None.

5. **In the Region drop-down list, select the geographical region where you plan to host your environment.**
6. **In the Type drop-down list, choose the type of environment that you want to create.**

   You can choose from Developer, Production, Trial, or Sandbox.

7. **Provide a description of what you plan to use the environment for in the Purpose text box.**
8. **Click the Add a Dataverse Data Store and toggle to choose Yes.**

   This option Yes creates a Dataverse instance for that environment. If you set this option to No, you have to rely on another data source, such as SharePoint.

9. **Set the Pay-As-You-Go with Azure? toggle to Yes if you want to link the environment to an Azure subscription when it comes time to pay for your Dataverse and cloud storage services.**

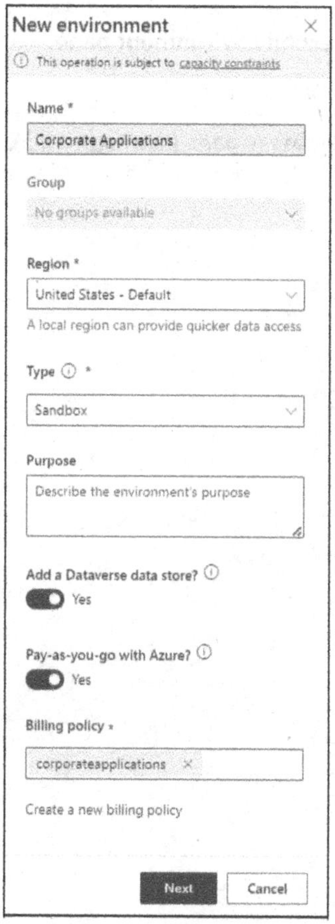

FIGURE 2-4: The New Environment pane for Corporate Applications.

If you select No to Pay As You Go in Power Platform, you use the standard capacity-based billing model, requiring you to own the appropriate licenses and manually manage your storage capacity. Such restrictions come with far less flexibility and potentially higher upfront costs.

10. **Select an option from the Billing Policy drop-down list to specify which billing policy you want to use.**

ON THE WEB

If you haven't created an Azure Billing Policy before or, for that matter, don't have an Azure account, this step can get a bit complicated. For guidance on how to handle billing policy setup, go to `http://learn.microsoft.com` and enter "set up pay as you go" in the Search text box; the results page offers you the latest info direct from Microsoft.

11. **Click Next to proceed to the second Environment pane.**

On this page, you can configure Dataverse.

12. **Click Next to open the Add Dataverse pane (see Figure 2-5).**

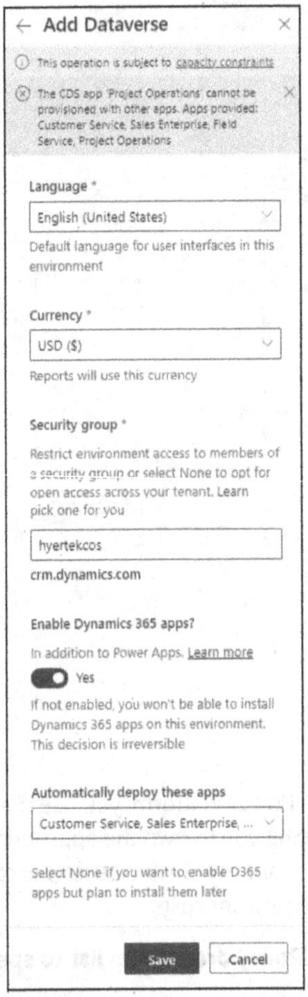

Add Dataverse
This operation is subject to capacity constraints
The CDS app 'Project Operations' cannot be provisioned with other apps. Apps provided: Customer Service, Sales Enterprise, Field Service, Project Operations
Language *
English (United States)
Default language for user interfaces in this environment
Currency *
USD ($)
Reports will use this currency
Security group *
Restrict environment access to members of a security group or select None to opt for open access across your tenant. Learn pick one for you
hyertekcos
crm.dynamics.com
Enable Dynamics 365 apps?
In addition to Power Apps. Learn more
Yes
If not enabled, you won't be able to install Dynamics 365 apps on this environment. This decision is irreversible
Automatically deploy these apps
Customer Service, Sales Enterprise, ...
Select None if you want to enable D365 apps but plan to install them later
Save
Cancel

FIGURE 2-5: The Add Dataverse options pane.

13. **Select the default language for the environment from the Language drop-down list.**

14. **From the Currency drop-down list, select the base currency that you want to use for financial reporting in this environment.**

15. **Click the plus sign (+), and then select an option from the Security Group available in Microsoft Entra.**

You can assign a security group to restrict access, or select None to allow open access.

16. **Enter your organization's name in the URL text box to generate a unique URL for your environment, and click Here under the URL.**

17. **Toggle the Enable Dynamics 365 Apps option to Yes to deploy Dynamics 365 apps.**

18. **In the Automatically Deploy These Apps drop-down list, select which apps to deploy, if you have the necessary licenses.**

    For example, you can select one or more of the following: Dynamics 365 Sales, Field Service, Project, or Guides. This drop-down list is generated based on what you've purchased, as well as what your administrator has assigned you a license to access.

19. **Save your new environment by clicking Save.**

    Your environment is generally available to use within 30 minutes. (It all depends on how Microsoft works, not you.)

WARNING

You have a single opportunity to include Dynamics 365 applications in your Dataverse environment: when you first set up the environment. Make sure that you have the right licensing in place at the onset because you can't go back and add new Dynamics 365 applications, or even reverse your integration of Dynamics 365, after you build an environment.

Analytics

The Analytics section of the Power Platform admin center helps administrators and developers understand usage, showing how often and in what ways users work with the resources. You can also use Analytics to help track errors and exceptions, allowing administrators to identify and troubleshoot issues so that they can help ensure smooth operation and minimize user outages.

Analytics also play a vital role in a number of Power Platform administrative tasks, helping administrators in

- **Performance management:** Identify performance bottlenecks so that you can address them to improve efficiency and user experience.
- **Policy enforcement:** Governance, pointing to targeted policies and control access, ensuring compliance with organizational standards.
- **Change management:** Adapt applications to changing management practices by illustrating changes to user or system behavior, such as performance bottlenecks.

The Power Platform application can create several report types: Dataverse, Power Automate, Power Apps, and Data Export. Figure 2-6 shows a Dataverse Analytics report.

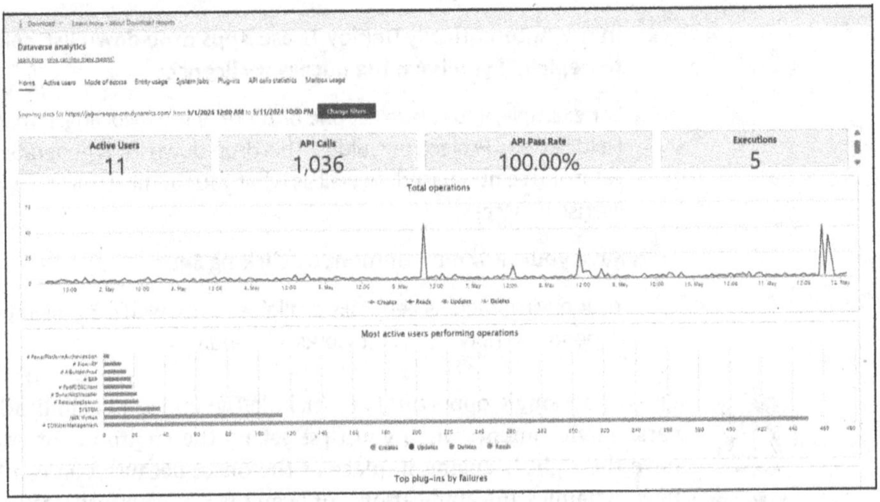

FIGURE 2-6: A Dataverse Analytics report.

To access Analytics in the Power Platform, after logging into the admin center (which you can read about in the section "Taking Control in the Power Platform Admin Center," earlier in this chapter), follow these steps:

1. **From the Environment Selector at the top of the screen, select the environment for which you want to view analytics, if necessary.**

   In the case of multiple environments, selecting the environment for which you want to view analytics opens the Power Platform Analytics dashboard from that environment. If you have only one environment, the Analytics interface opens in the core environment that you want to configure.

2. **Click Analytics in the navigation pane on the left side of the admin center.**

   The Analytics dashboard opens.

3. **In the Navigation pane, select the Analytics reporting tab applicable to your business need.**

   Review one or more reports, based on what you want to review. The report options include Dataverse, Power Automate, Power Apps, and Data Export.

Billing

Microsoft offers the Billing tab as a way for you to better understand how you're managing your licensing pool, not necessarily how much you're spending on all of those licenses. A system administrator usually assigns each user a license when the administrator initially configures their Microsoft Entra ID account.

If you want to see more granular data about a particular application and its consumption, you can drill down into any of the areas, available under the Billing tab, by clicking on one of the three tabs in the main window:

- **Summary:** Provides a summary of each environment in a tenant that requires licensing attention.
- **Environment:** Displays the licensing allocation for each environment within the tenant.
- **Intelligent Recommendations:** Suggests people in the organization who might benefit from having a Power Platform Premium License.

Settings

In Power Platform, a *tenant* is like an entire apartment building, which covers all the environments (apartments) within a single organization. For example, ABC Corporation is the tenant. Within ABC Corporation, they might have four environments: Sales, Accounting, Operations, and Human Resources. Each environment is a separate apartment within the building, with its own set of Power Platform licenses, data, and resources. Just like residents in an apartment have access only to their apartment and common areas, users assigned to a specific environment can create apps, workflows, and analytics only within that environment, not across the whole tenant (or apartment building).

Here's the catch when you head over to Settings: Tenant settings are like making building-wide regulations that impact every apartment (environment) in the building (tenant), not just one. These settings affect services and data management across all environments, ensuring consistent governance and control across the entire organization.

You have access to 25-plus settings that can impact the entire tenant. Some settings relate to managed environments, while others apply to both managed and unmanaged environments.

ON THE WEB

The list of tenant settings in Microsoft Power Platform is constantly changing. To stay up to date on the latest tenant settings and how to best configure each, head over to `http://learn.microsoft.com` and enter **Power Platform tenant settings** in the Search text box. Look for the latest list in the results that appear.

To access and manage the Tenant Settings shown in Figure 2-7, first log into your Power Platform admin center (flip back to the section "Taking Control in the Power Platform Admin Center," earlier in this chapter, for the details). In the left-hand navigation pane of the admin center, click Settings.

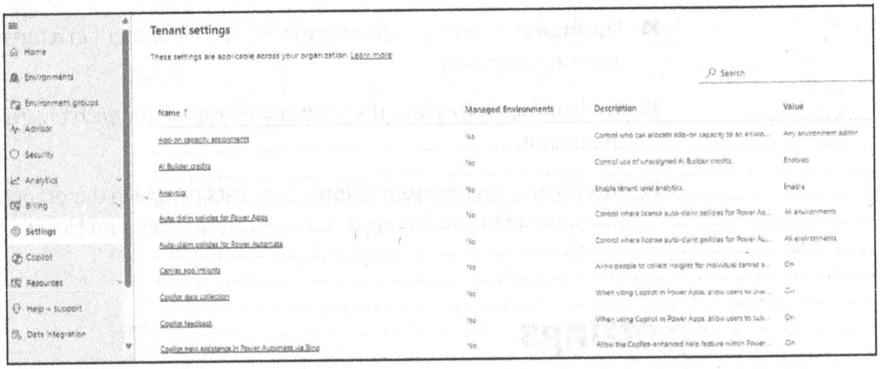

FIGURE 2-7: The Power Platform admin center allows access to Tenant Settings.

The Settings panel opens. This panel allows you to manage settings that affect all environments within your tenant. Your administrative account needs to have permissions that allow you to manage tenant-level settings.

Tenant-level settings only apply to managed environments. A *managed environment* in Microsoft's Power Platform provides enhanced governance, monitoring, and management capabilities, especially in larger organizations, where many stakeholders use a single platform. In a managed environment, only admins can manage and oversee the deployment, usage, and performance of Power Platform components such as Power Apps, Power Automate, and Copilot-based bot solutions.

Resources

Keep in mind the saying "too much of a good thing can be bad" when managing your Power Platform environment. Power Platform enforces limits by placing utilization thresholds on key resources such as capacity, licensing, and site usage. To monitor your current capacity across Dataverse, Dynamics Apps, and Power Pages portals, follow these steps to check the Resources option:

1. **In the left navigation pane of your admin center, select Resources.**

   Additional options appear below Resources: Capacity, Catalogs, Dynamics 365 Apps, and Power Pages sites.

2. **Select the option for the type of resources that you want to access.**

   Your selection opens in the main window.

   Figure 2-8 shows an example of a Capacity Summary that displays current Dataverse use versus total Dataverse capacity available.

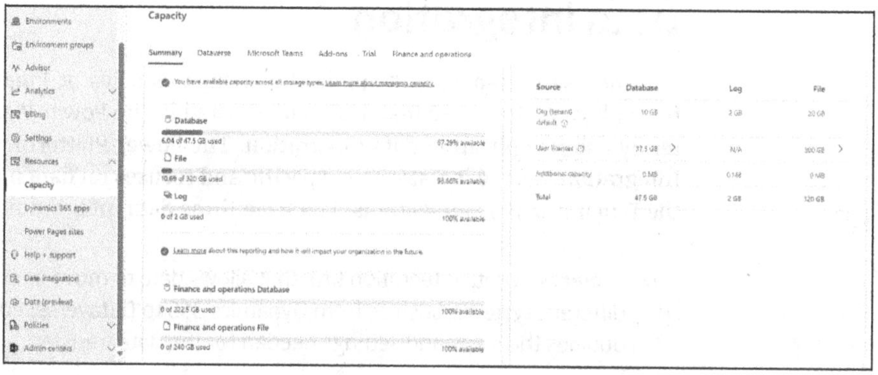

FIGURE 2-8: Managing resource capacity in the Power Platform admin center.

Help + Support

Sometimes, you simply can't figure out an issue by using one of the Power Platform applications. Microsoft has a built-in support center that admins can access, primarily offering self-help assistance. The Help + Support tool leverages Microsoft's documentation and technical notes. To access Help + Support, you must have at least one admin role in the Power Platform admin center, but the Global Admin or Power Platform Admin role gives you the most comprehensive access to Help + Support.

If you can't resolve your issues using the self-help resources available through Help + Support (which you can access by clicking the Help + Support option in the navigation pane), you can submit a support ticket by clicking Get Help + Support at the top-left of the interface (as shown in Figure 2-9). A form appears, asking you to provide details of your technical issue. Select the Known Issues tab to review common problems reported to the support team, as well as the Service Health tab, which displays the health status of your specific tenants.

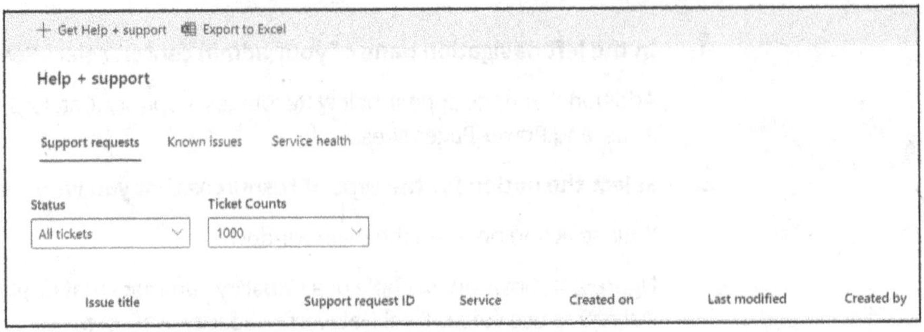

FIGURE 2-9: Getting help and support.

Data integration

You can use Dynamics 365 applications, such as Sales or Finance & Operations, through your Dataverse instance that's hosted in the Power Platform admin center by using application data integration. The Power Platform admin center Data Integration feature is Dataverse-specific and focuses on data management across the Dynamics 365 applications. You have three data integration options:

- **Projects:** A data integration task that allows data to move or sync between different systems, such as from Dynamics 365 to Dataverse. Power Platform outlines the steps and settings needed for the data transfer.
- **Connection Sets:** Provide the links between environments that handle how data moves between different systems, allowing you to manage connections. After you set up a connection, you don't have to configure that setting each time you use that connection.
- **Templates:** Premade setups for common data integration tasks, which give you a quick and easy way to start a project by using predefined settings and mappings. You can create templates as part of a project.

ON THE WEB

If you plan to integrate between Dynamics 365 applications, check out the documentation guides that Microsoft offers. Go to `http://learn.microsoft.com`, and enter **integrate data into Dataverse** in the search text box. These guides should pop up at the top of your results.

Data

In the Power Platform, gateways act as an essential component enabling secure data transfer between on-premises data sources and cloud services. Acting as bridges, gateways facilitate seamless encrypted data flow from local networks anywhere, from the computer under your desk or a corporate data center, to cloud-based applications. Having a gateway ensures that data remains protected during transmission.

There are two main types of gateways:

- **On-Premises Data Gateways (Personal):** Designed for individuals who need to connect data from their computer or an on-premises server to cloud services such as those available in Power Platform. Ideal for personal use, such as developing, testing, or running reports. But it's limited to single users, which means you can't share it with others. This mode is best suited for connecting to data sources during development or testing phases, not for broader organizational use.
- **On-Premises Data Gateway (Standard Mode):** Appropriate for more than just a single user — think organizational needs. This gateway type supports multiple users and various data sources, offering management, security, and scalability features. Also referred to as an *enterprise gateway,* Standard Mode On-Premises Data Gateways can provide secure and reliable connections to production environments, ensuring smooth data flow between on-premises systems and cloud services such as Power BI, Power Apps, and Power Automate.

REMEMBER

If you feel confused about what a virtual network gateway is, don't overthink it! When setting up a gateway, you choose whether the data source is on-premises or needs access through a virtual network. On-premises data gateways connect local data sources to cloud services, while virtual network data gateways securely access resources in an Azure virtual network without needing local installations.

Gateways are integral for various Power Platform services because data is the central resource among most if not all Power Platform applications. Power BI, Power Apps, and Power Automate all have a utility that allows them to connect gateways to the respective platforms. The gateways enable each application's services to access on-premises data for creating reports, custom applications, workflows, and integrations with cloud services. Figure 2-10 shows an example of two enterprise gateways created for integrations. You use the On-Premises Data Gateway connection for Power BI.

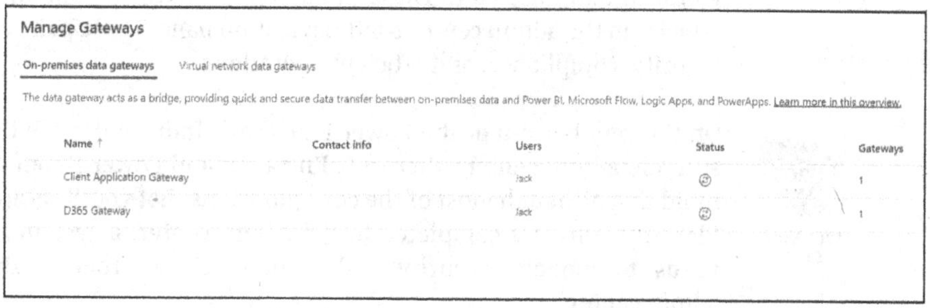

FIGURE 2-10: A couple of on-premises enterprise gateway connections.

WARNING

Setting up a gateway involves a lot more than just logging into the Power Platform admin center. You have to follow these steps:

1. **Download and install On-Premises Data Gateway software onto your Desktop.**

   Place the software on a suitable machine within the network (often the server that will be transporting data to and from the Power Platform instance). If you want to use your Desktop, save the download in a folder where you allow the installer to run on your computer.

2. **After the file downloads, double-click GatewayInstall.exe and let the application install in the selected environment.**

3. **Register your new data gateway by using the configuration wizard within the data gateway software.**

   After you finish the configuration, the connection appears in the admin center's Data panel. Now, you can create connections to on-premises data sources, which can then be managed between the native application and the admin center.

ON THE WEB

You can find detailed instructions from Microsoft on how to use the external data gateway software by going to `http://learn.microsoft.com` and entering **install on premises data gateway.** The results page provides you up-to-the-minute instructions.

Policies

Policies are meant to protect applications and the organizations that deploy them to targeted users. Within the Power Platform admin center (flip back to the section "Taking Control in the Power Platform Admin Center," earlier in this chapter, for the way to log into this center), you can manage a variety of policies to help secure your organization's Power Platform environment. Table 2-2 gives you an overview of the different types of policies that you can configure if you're a Power Platform administrator. These policy types appear as options when you select Policies in the admin center's left navigation pane. These policies help ensure data security, compliance, and efficient operations.

TECHNICAL STUFF

On the very bottom of the Power Platform admin center are links to the Microsoft 365 admin center, Microsoft Entra ID, and Power BI admin portal. Keep in mind that although most of the configurations that you'll complete for the Power Platform suite are completed in the admin center, a system administrator still needs to manage security and compliance controls in the Microsoft 365 admin center.

TABLE 2-2 Policy Types in the Power Platform Admin Center

Policy Type	What It Does
Data Policies	Manage and protect data within the Power Platform, including data loss prevention (DLP), such as data connector policies, that control data sharing and access. Because selecting Data Policies opens a list of 1,231 connectable applications (and growing), in the search bar on the right side of the Data Policies window, enter the name of the specific app that you want to connect.
Tenant Isolation	Allows a user to control settings and configurations at the tenant level, including tenant isolation, so that an organization can block external connections.
Customer Lockbox	Requires explicit approval for Microsoft support to access data during troubleshooting. You need specific Microsoft 365 or Office 365 subscriptions to access Customer Lockbox, and it works only on managed environments.
Enterprise Policies	Allows for managing environment use, resource allocation, and user access across the enterprise. These policies often relate to Azure resources and are applied to environments in the same region. If you use *customer-managed keys* (where the user controls the encryption keys to enhance data security), you need managed environments and specific Azure subscriptions. Managed environments provide advanced governance and security controls, ensuring that policies and resources are properly managed and compliant with organizational standards.
Billing Policies	Allows you to group one or more environments for billing to Azure if you also use Power Platform. Provides centralized cost and resource allocation.

Previewing the Maker Portal

Everyone has to start from somewhere, right? If you're a developer and have no administrative responsibilities, your starting point is the Power Apps Maker Portal. To access the Maker Portal, follow these steps:

1. **Log into your Power Platform admin center.**

   I give you the details for that process in the section "Taking Control in the Power Platform Admin Center," earlier in this chapter.

2. **Click the waffle icon at the top-left of the admin center.**

   All Microsoft applications to which you have a license appear.

3. **Enter "Power Apps" in the Search text box and click Search.**

   Power Apps will be the only application in the results list, (if you're licensed).

4. **Select Power Apps from the list of applications that appears.**

   Power Apps opens at the homepage, which is referred to as the Maker Portal.

TIP

You know you're accessing the Maker Portal if the URL of the page you're on starts with `http://make.powerapps.com`.

The Maker Portal is a web-based interface that allows users to create, manage, and share their applications within the Power Platform. It enables users to bring together assets developed across various Power Platform tools, such as Power BI and Power Automate, into a single solution. A key aspect of the Maker Portal is its focus on data, particularly through its integration with Dataverse. The Maker Portal is the only place you can access Dataverse, allowing developers to manage and manipulate data across different sources.

Figure 2-11 illustrates the Maker Portal interface. Figure 2-12 shows the Maker Portal navigation pane's More options, and Table 2-3 describes each feature that appears in that pane. (Some of the items listed in Table 2-3 are found under the Discover All button at the bottom of the More options, shown in Figure 2-12.) This section provides a menu of features that you can use in Chapters 3 through 9.

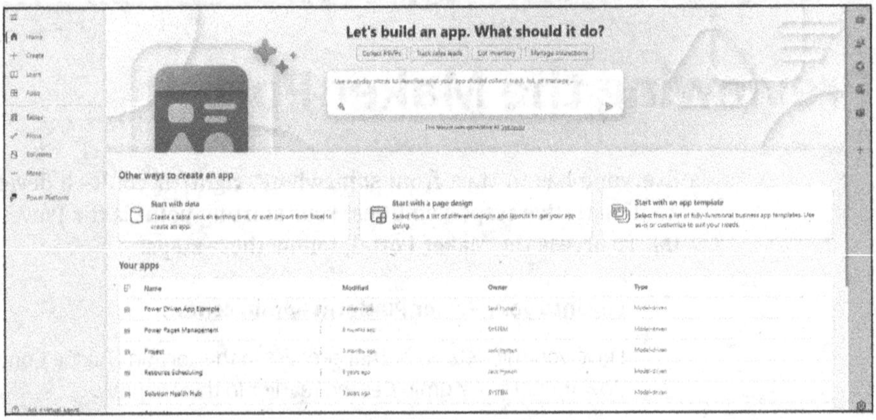

FIGURE 2-11: The Maker Portal interface.

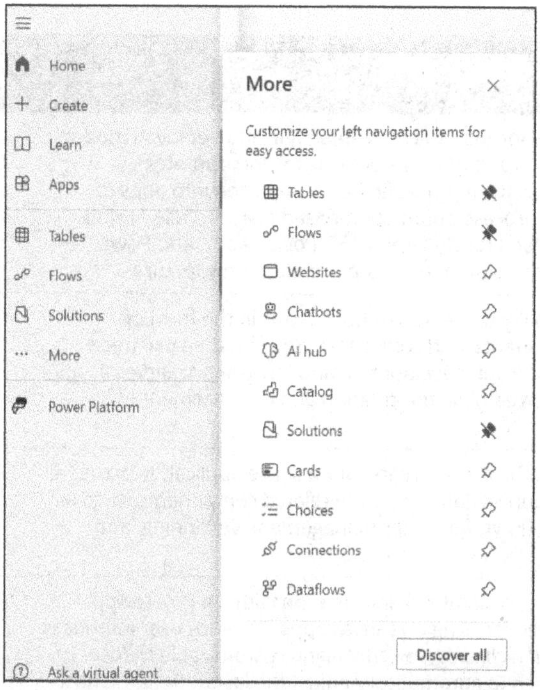

FIGURE 2-12: Navigating the features of the Power Apps Maker Portal.

TABLE 2-3 Power Apps Maker Portal Features

Feature	What It Does	Key Applications That Use It
Tables	Store and organize data by using Dataverse. Allow for structured data management and relationships for applications. Also allow developers to define fields, relationships, data types, and views for data modeling.	Dataverse
Flows	Automate workflows and processes by using conditional or trigger-based actions across all Power Platform applications, as well as third-party solutions.	Power Automate
Websites	External-facing portals that you can create by using Power Pages so that you can build and manage custom web portals integrated with Dataverse data.	Power Pages
Chatbots	Provide conversational interfaces for applications, enabling users to interact through natural language. A useful search tool to help a user find information quickly in a specific table or data source. Powered by the underlying Copilot AI infrastructure.	Power Virtual Agents (now part of Microsoft Copilot)

(continued)

TABLE 2-3 *(continued)*

Feature	What It Does	Key Applications That Use It
AI Hub	Provides a central location to create, manage, and deploy AI models by using AI Builder (part of Power Automate). Incorporates capabilities such as form processing and prediction into apps to support robotics process-automation-based tasks. To use AI Hub, you must be licensed for Dynamics 365, Power Apps, and Power Automate because most features are premium-only features.	AI Builder, Power Automate
Catalog	Offers you the ability to create pre-built assets in the form of templates, components, and connectors. You can then use these assets to accelerate app development and integration. Serves as a resource hub to streamline the creation and enhancement of applications.	Power Apps, Power Automate
Solutions	Bring together all the assets created for a single application across all Power Platform applications. Organize related components, such as apps, tables, and flows, for easier management, versioning, and deployment.	Power Apps, Dataverse
Cards	Display interactive, content-rich information within a Power App application, heavily focusing on canvas apps. Enhance user interfaces with *adaptive card technology*, a lightweight, customizable UI (user interface) approach to automatically adjust the layout to fit the hosting app or platform.	Power Apps
Choices	A way to globally define a set of predefined options for table columns, ensuring consistent and controlled data entry. Presented in the form of drop-down lists, ensuring data integrity. Can be configured within a Dataverse table, or done standalone and deployed across many applications that share the same environment. Choice values restrict user input to valid, pre-configured selections, preventing incorrect or inconsistent data entry.	Dataverse
Connections	Enables apps to interact with external data sources and services, facilitating integration and data access. Leveraged to trigger workflow actions when data movement occurs in an application, whether the action is Create, Delete, or Modify.	Power Apps, Power Automate
Dataflows	Allow for the extraction, transformation, and loading (ETL) of data from well over 50 third-party data sources into Dataverse.	Dataverse
Gateways	Provide secure bridges for data transfer between on-premises or virtual data sources and Power Platform. All Power Platform applications have some form of gateway utility.	Power BI, Power Apps, Power Automate
Retention Policies	Help with Power Platform governance requirements. This may include managing data lifecycle activities; defining rules for data storage, archiving, and deletion; and ensuring compliance and efficient data management.	Dataverse
Component Libraries	Allow developers to create, manage, and reuse user interface (UI) components across multiple apps, enforcing application and design consistency. Can be used across one or more environments.	Power Apps

Feature	What It Does	Key Applications That Use It
Wrap Projects	Enables makers to package Power Apps as mobile applications for Apple iOS and Google Android OS devices.	Power Apps
Publishers	Manage custom applications and components within solutions in the organization. Microsoft offers an array of publishers that you can use for application development. When starting an enterprise project, establish a new publisher for a project because you can manage custom applications and components within solutions across your organization.	Power Apps
Custom Connectors	Enable the integration of your own or third-party APIs and services within Power Platform, to increase flexibility with data functionality. Allows you to either display the data within Power Apps or distribute and automate data processes by using Power Automate.	Power Apps, Power Automate
AI Models	Created with AI Builder, which is powered by Microsoft Copilot. Add intelligence to applications by incorporating capabilities such as prediction, object detection, and language processing into an application. Example models include data and image extraction and predictive behaviors based on structured data sources.	AI Builder, Power Apps, Dataverse
AI Prompts	Guide users through tasks and provide suggestions based on insights found in structured data. Purpose-built from AI Models by using a combination of AI Builder and Microsoft Copilot Studio.	AI Builder, Power Apps

Addressing Security and Governance

Security and governance in Power Platform involve ensuring that all of your data, applications, and workflows are protected while maintaining control over how they are accessed and used. Protection occurs by using features such as role-based access control (RBAC), environment-level security, data loss prevention (DLP) policies, and compliance tools. Administrators can enforce governance policies to control who can create apps and flows, manage data sharing, and monitor activity across environments.

Microsoft's Power Platform addresses security and governance at both the platform and application level. You manage security controls at the environment level, but you can also configure them more locally at the application and table level, depending on what solution type you use. (I go over solution types in Chapter 4.)

REMEMBER

Managing applications goes beyond configuring security in the Power Platform admin center (which is shared with Dynamics 365). To fully implement comprehensive authentication and authorization, you must also apply advanced security and compliance measures within the Microsoft 365 admin center (as shown in

Figure 2-13). This includes configuring Security and Compliance options (which you can access by selecting in the right-hand navigation pane), to ensure full protection across the Power Platform and other Microsoft 365 services.

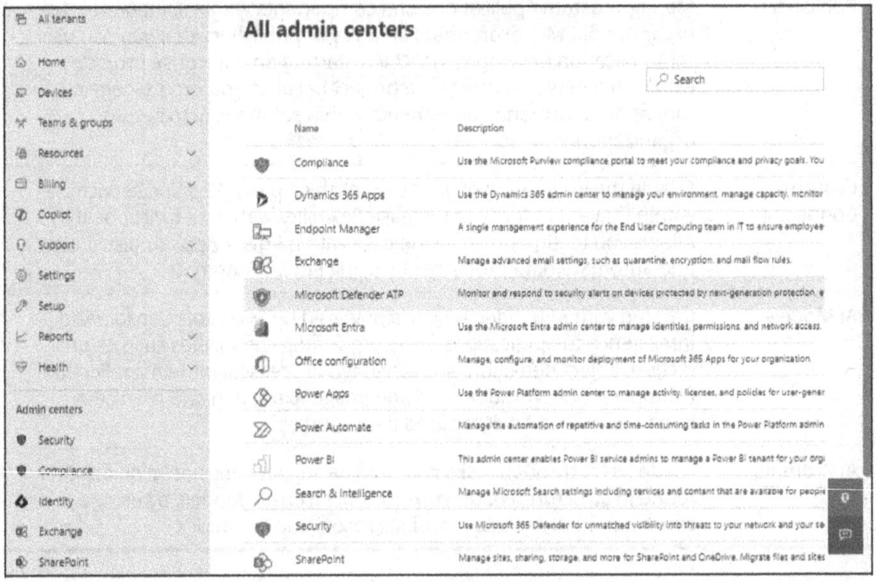

FIGURE 2-13: In the Microsoft 365 admin center, you can configure security controls.

Power Platform's architecture includes both a web frontend and backend cluster (which are distributed across multiple servers or regions). It also contains an infrastructure to support functionality for targeted application types, such as mobile-based solutions. The web frontend cluster manages authentication and directs interactions to the backend cluster, which handles system interaction and functionality. Such a design allows for scalability, as well as secure data, including backups and secondary cluster utilization for reliability.

If you purchase Power Platform premium capabilities, you gain access to premium infrastructure features that offer additional connectors, APIs, and data management features not available to those who use free access to Power Apps, Power Automate, and Power BI. For example, the mobile device management framework offered through the premium version of Power Platform ensures secure communication and data storage on Android, iOS, and Windows devices, using strong encryption and management tools such as Microsoft Intune.

Like security, governance in Power Platform is guided by Microsoft's global Online Services Terms and its enterprise privacy statements, all located in the Microsoft Trust Center (Microsoft's hub for Microsoft Office security settings). The platform applies strict security principles known as Security Development Lifecycle (SDL) to meet the necessary application lifecycle management standards. Key security standards that the SDL addresses include user authentication, data storage, and protection measures. The framework addresses concerns about data access, encryption, and auditing, as well.

Although you have many areas to tackle when addressing security and governance, the two most prevalent for the new citizen developer or budding professional are data policies and privacy settings, which I cover in the following sections.

ON THE WEB

Two websites that can give you the latest references on security and governance are

- **Power Platform Security and Governance Documentation:** Go to `https://learn.microsoft.com` and enter **Power Platform security and governance documentation** in the search box; this information should appear as a top link in the results.
- **Microsoft Trust Center:** `www.microsoft.com/trust-center`

Establishing data loss prevention policies

You need to establish data loss prevention (DLP) policies to safeguard organizational data by preventing unintentional exposure (such as sharing sensitive information with unauthorized apps or external services) and enhancing information security. These policies enforce rules regarding the use of data connectors within various environments, and you can apply them at both the environment and tenant levels, but not at the user level. You create such policies in the Power Platform admin center. (Flip back to the section "Taking Control in the Power Platform Admin Center," earlier in this chapter, for the details about the admin center.) DLP policies determine which data connectors are classified as business, non-business, or blocked. This classification controls how data can flow between different connectors, ensuring that sensitive information is shared only with those who need access to the data and no one else.

Connectors are classified into three groups:

- **Business connectors:** Designed to handle sensitive or business-critical data. Such connectors are isolated and can't share or exchange data with connectors from other groups (such as non-business connectors). This isolation helps maintain data security and compliance with organizational policies.
- **Non-business connectors:** Primarily meant for personal or less-sensitive data, such connectors are similar to business connectors, restricted from sharing data with connectors from different groups, maintaining a separation between business and personal data.

- **Blocked connectors:** Connectors that are restricted or disabled by policy enforcement (based on an organization or Microsoft-specific rules). You can't use these connectors at all when certain policies are enforced, typically for security or compliance reasons.

To implement DLP policies for Power Platform and your targeted application, follow these broad steps in the Power Platform admin center:

1. **Create a comprehensive policy that covers all environments except critical ones, such as production environments.**

   Make your policy broad and limit the available connectors to very targeted sources, such as Office 365 and other standard microservices, while blocking access to all other potential data sources.

2. **Establish more permissive DLP policies for shared user and team productivity environments.**

   For example, allow additional connectors, such as Azure services, based on your organization's needs.

TECHNICAL STUFF

For production environments, focus on just enough access for your applications. When planning your data loss prevention policies, work with your business units to tailor policies to their specific requirements and create tenant policies that include only the selected environments needed.

TIP

Although some might say that it's good to create many policies, I think that less is more. Minimize the number of policies per environment to avoid complexity among connectors. Centrally manage DLP policies at the tenant level and use environment policies primarily for categorizing custom connectors or addressing exceptions.

Managing DLP policies

You need data loss prevention (DLP) in Power Platform to protect organizational data from unauthorized exposure and misuse. To manage these data policies effectively (including creating, editing, or deleting policies), you need to have administrative permissions — either environment admin or Power Platform admin permissions. (I talk about the different types of permissions in Chapter 7.)

If you want to apply a policy across a tenant, you must have Microsoft Power Platform admin permissions or Microsoft 365 global admin permissions. On the other hand, if you need to focus on a single environment, you need only Power Platform admin environment rights. The following sections explain how to create, edit, and delete DLP policies within the Power Platform admin center (flip back to "Taking

Control in the Power Platform Admin Center," earlier in this chapter, for instructions on getting to this admin center).

Creating a data loss prevention policy

Creating DLP policies is the first step in protecting your mission-critical data. Know what data source you need to protect, and then classify it as business, non-business, or blocked before getting started. After you identify the data criticality, log into your Power Platform admin center and follow these steps to craft data policies:

1. **From the left navigation pane in the admin center, select Policies ⇨ Data Policies ⇨ New Policy.**
2. **In the Data Policies window that appears, enter a name for the policy and click Next.**

   The Assign Connectors page appears.
3. **From the Prebuilt Connectors window, click the appropriate button for the connector assignment that you want to make.**

   You can choose from the buttons Move to Business, Move to Non-Business, or Block.

   For example, you can move SharePoint and Salesforce connectors to the Business group and move Google Drive and Dropbox to Blocked.

   TIP

   Depending on the prebuilt connector you select, you may not be able to block some connectors. Other connectors may require you to select Move to Business to operate appropriately.

   The Assign Connectors page displays connector attributes, including

   - *Name:* Name of connector
   - *Blockable:* Whether the connector can be blocked
   - *Endpoint configuration:* Whether the endpoint requires configuration
   - *Class:* Whether it's a Standard or Premium connector
   - *Publisher:* Who's the publisher of the connector
   - *About:* The purpose of the connector
4. **When you finish reviewing the attributes, click Next.**
5. **In the screen that appears, click Add Custom Connector Pattern.**

   A Custom Connector pane appears on the right of the screen.

   A *custom connector pattern* in Power Platform enables integration with external services or APIs. Like your prebuilt connectors, you establish the custom pattern connection once and then assign it either Business, Non-Business, or Blocked status to support your DLP policy.

6. **Enter the custom connector pattern that you want to use.**

   You associate a custom connector pattern with a data group (Business, Non-Business, or Blocked), the host URL (the website URL where data patterns apply), and then the order or precedence for the data policy.

7. **After you enter your custom pattern settings, click Save on the Custom Connector pane, and then click Next.**

8. **In the screen that appears, define the Scope by selecting an option.**

   You can choose from the following options:

   - *Add all environments:* Adds the scope to all environments in the tenant.
   - *Add multiple environments:* Adds the scope to one or more environments, based on what you choose.
   - *Exclude certain environments:* Allows a user to initially select all environments, and then remove the environments that they don't want to include.

9. **Click Next, and then review the data policy configuration that you just created, which appears on the screen.**

10. **If you think the policy meets the necessary criteria, click Create Policy.**

    If you want to make changes, click the Back button.

Editing and deleting data policies

You can edit and delete policies in the admin center, as well as create them (as discussed in the preceding section). You can work with existing data policies in the Power Platform admin center Data Policies window (shown in Figure 2-14):

- **To modify a policy:** Select the policy, then click the Edit Policy button at the top of the window. You go through the same steps that you follow to create a policy (see the preceding section). The only difference is that you make modifications, instead of creating new configurations.
- **To delete a policy:** Select that policy in the Data Policies window, and then click the Delete Policy button. A prompt appears to confirm that you want to delete the policy. Click the Delete button, and Power Platform deletes that policy.

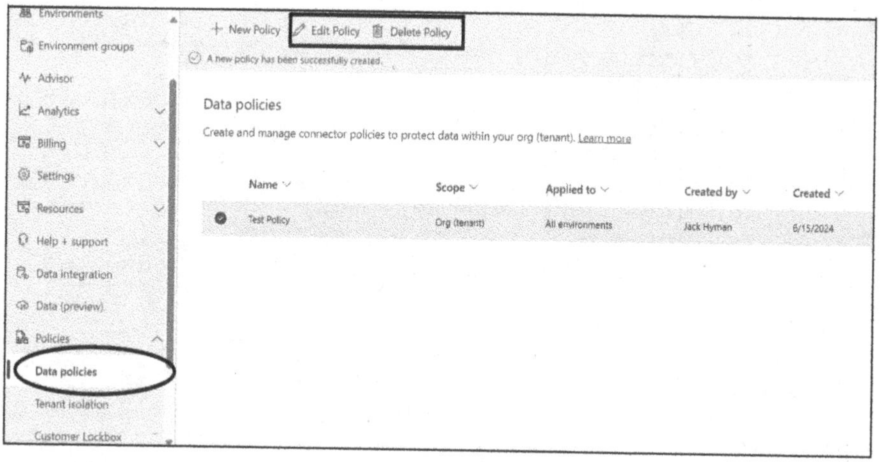

FIGURE 2-14: The Data Policies window allows you to create, modify, or delete data policies.

Privacy and security

With Microsoft Power Platform, you can manage privacy and security settings, especially as they relate to the Dataverse environment. You establish security settings to retain data integrity and ensure that data access complies with organizational policies. You can apply policies globally to an entire environment or specifically to the data table. Like most other software applications, you don't want to be too permissive. Instead, follow the *rules of least permissive access* — or just the right amount of access for that user and their organizational responsibility, nothing more.

To manage privacy and security settings, you need to be a system administrator or system customizer in a security role in Power Platform admin. To make modifications to the Power Platform admin center (which I explain how to get to in the section "Taking Control in the Power Platform Admin Center," earlier in this chapter), follow these steps:

1. **Select Environments in the left navigation pane.**
2. **In the Environments window that appears, select the environment whose security you want to change.**

   The window for that selected environment appears.
3. **In the specific Environment window, choose Settings ⇨ Product ⇨ Privacy + Security.**

   The Privacy + Security window opens (see Figure 2-15).
4. Make any changes that you want to in the Privacy + Security options.

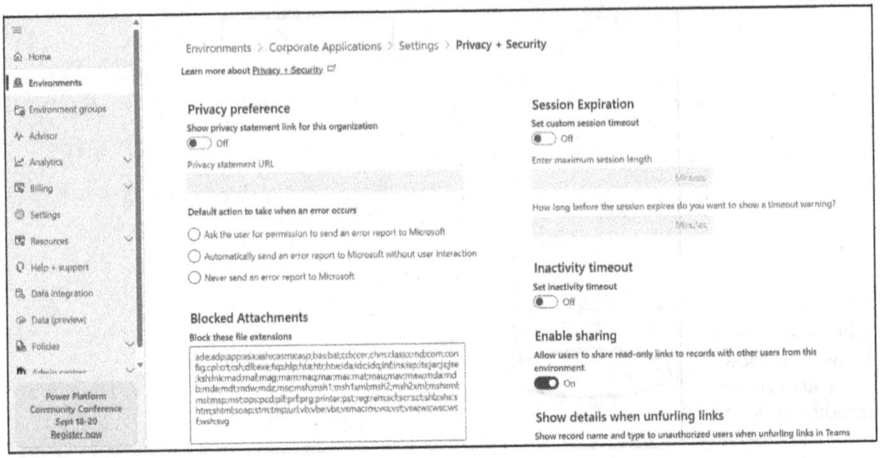

FIGURE 2-15: Accessing privacy and security settings.

The preferences you can change in this window include whether you want to

- Show the privacy statement
- Send error reports to Microsoft and selected third-party sources
- Block certain attachment types in an app
- Set an expiration timeout for a session (as well as how long to make it)
- Establish inactivity timeout rules
- Allow for read-only sharing
- Show details when unfurling links
- Manage IP-address-based cookies
- Block or allow Mime Types
- Apply content security policies for both model-driven and canvas-based apps

IN THIS CHAPTER

- » Understanding how Dataverse organizes datasets
- » Working with standard and custom tables in Dataverse
- » Using view types across Power Platform
- » Creating and editing model-driven app forms
- » Grasping the basics of Dataverse's security model
- » Evaluating ways to create business process flows

Chapter 3 Discovering the Dataverse

If you've been in the business world for a moment, you probably know the saying that data is the glue that holds together business decisions. Data transforms how you manage, secure, and utilize each application in the Power Platform, and Dataverse provides a data repository. Dataverse is at the heart of the Power Platform ecosystem, acting as the engine that pumps critical data to each application.

For example, for form entry in a canvas or model-driven app, Dataverse comes to the rescue. After you get the data into the Dataverse repository, you likely want to evaluate the data for trends and patterns, and the analytics outputs used by Power BI (which I talk about in Chapter 11) can access your Dataverse repository. When users add, change, or delete data in the Dataverse database, you may want to trigger a workflow, using Power Automate (discussed in Chapter 14), to notify one user or an entire department that the state of data has changed.

In this chapter, you can discover the key features of the Dataverse, as well as figure out how to craft a well-designed data platform that addresses role-based, row-level, and column-level security to maintain data integrity and compliance. And you can see how to use Dataverse as a tool for establishing business rules and automation across all your Power Platform applications.

Defining the Dataverse

Techies often struggle to pick out the storage capability of their dreams when deciding how to manage their data. Like every enterprise IT vendor, Microsoft has a laundry list of options. You can choose

- **Dataverse:** The native storage option for the Power Platform, designed to securely store data in tables with built-in business logic, security, and integration with Power Apps, Power Automate, and other Microsoft 365 services. Dataverse optimizes low-code solutions with relational data structures and supports real-time analytics.
- **Blob storage:** Binary Large Object (blob) storage; part of the Microsoft Azure Cloud. Cost-effective for storing unstructured data files, such as images, videos, and documents. While blob storage integrates with Dataverse for file storage, it lacks the relational data capabilities and metadata-driven architecture that Dataverse provides.
- **Azure SQL:** A relational database also available through the Microsoft Azure Cloud, is a fully managed relational database service designed for complex transactional systems. The enterprise-class database requires more setup and management than Dataverse.
- **Cosmos DB:** A non-relational database service that handles large volumes of unstructured or semi-structured data. It works best for scenarios that require flexibility and scale, such as real-time analytics. Unlike Dataverse, Cosmos DS doesn't allow for built-in data models.
- **Azure Data Lake:** Optimized for big data analytics, which means organizations that have millions (or even billions) of records. Can store vast amounts of raw data for large-scale processing and analysis. Although Azure Data Lake (and data lakes, in general) excels in handling structured and unstructured data for analytical workloads, it doesn't offer the transactional, relational storage, and business logic available in Dataverse.

If you want the best features from each platform, consider using Dataverse. The reasons are plentiful. Dataverse integrates the best features of all the storage methods listed within the Power Platform ecosystem:

- **Better than blob:** Dataverse leverages the same architectural principles as blob storage for file storage and retention, including storing unstructured data (such as images) and files as attachments to records so that it can manage both structured and unstructured content within a unified platform. Power Platform doesn't use blob storage as its primary storage class because of Dataverse's built-in security, access controls, and compliance features.
- **Handling relational data:** Dataverse securely stores data in structured tables, incorporating the relational data capabilities of Azure SQL. Azure SQL takes a long time to configure and is expensive to maintain, but Microsoft Dataverse supports transactional systems and low-code development at a much lower cost. With Dataverse, you can model relationships and perform advanced queries without needing deep database management expertise.
- **A simpler Cosmos:** Dataverse leverages the best of Cosmos DB's scalability and flexibility; however, it lacks the complexity of Cosmos DB's multi-model, globally distributed architecture, which emphasizes *low latency* (an only small delay in data responsiveness). Although Cosmos DB is typically used for distributed, non-relational data, Dataverse incorporates relational data capabilities with built-in business logic, security roles, and real-time analytics — features that Cosmos DB lacks entirely.
- **Analytics without a lake:** Dataverse incorporates elements of Azure Data Lake's advanced data processing and big data analytics capabilities through its integration with Power BI. Although Dataverse can't act as a data lake replacement, it facilitates advanced analytics, making it suitable for smaller, more agile datasets and moderately extensive analytic workloads at a fraction of the cost of using Azure Data Lake.

Dataverse, as a service, integrates features from various data infrastructures. However, Azure SQL is the core *relational database engine* (meaning it handles structured, relational data and supports advanced query operations). Without requiring coding knowledge, Microsoft Dataverse allows you to interact with your data by using a combination of T-SQL, OData, and REST API.

Through T-SQL, users can perform advanced querying on the underlying relational database for operations such as filtering, joining tables, and aggregations. With Dataverse, users typically don't know they're using T-SQL directly because Dataverse has simplified and designed the interfaces to allow no-code or low-code interaction. Furthermore, Dataverse leverages OData and the REST API to enable you to perform web-based querying, including CRUD (Create, Read, Update, Delete) operations and programmatic access, with little to no coding experience.

Microsoft designed Dataverse so that users can focus more on designing business applications, rather than worrying about the implications of coding for security and data management.

Of course, data within Dataverse is stored in tables. You can't escape from tables, the crux of the data universe for decades. Dataverse handles table management, including configuring rows (which it calls *records*) and columns (also called *fields* and *attributes*).

REMEMBER

Microsoft purpose-built Dataverse as a platform for Microsoft Power Platform, but you can also use it independently as a self-contained data store. It stores metadata and data in the cloud so that users can access and manage their data from anywhere that has an internet connection. Dataverse also provides access to robust security that uses role-based access control, ensuring data is securely stored and accessible only to authorized users. (You can read more about Dataverse security in the section "Security Foundations and Dataverse" later in this chapter.)

Before you start building your first table, ensure you have a Power Platform environment set up with Dataverse configured in it. Head to Chapter 2 if you need to see how to set up a Power Platform environment, including how to enable Dataverse.

Developers and non-developers alike need a common vocabulary when they discuss the business of data management. Table 3-1 provides the common terminology Microsoft uses when describing Dataverse.

TABLE 3-1 Dataverse Terminology

Term	What It Means
Table	A structured set of data that stores information, similar to a database table. Each table consists of *rows* (records) and *columns* (fields), where each row represents an individual record, and each column represents a data attribute (meaning a specific piece of information or characteristic about the record, such as name, age, or status) within the record.
Name	Method for defining your table. An example would be States for a table with information about U.S. states.
Column	Metadata associated with each record. Examples in a U.S. states table might include City or State.
Row	A specific record in a table that contains values for different columns. For example, a row could include TX (Texas) as a value in a State column.
Relationship	Describes a connection or link between one or more tables.

Term	What It Means
Keys	One or more columns that uniquely identify a row in a table.
Forms	Used by model-driven apps to view and edit row-level data. (See the section "Working with Model-Driven App Forms," later in this chapter, for details.)
Views	A customized display of data from a table; typically shows specific columns and records based on certain filters or sorting criteria.
Charts	A method to visualize table rows.
Dashboards	A customizable visualization of your data across one or more charts, with a focus on filtered data.
Business rules	Logic that's applied to one or more columns that impact row-level data.
Metadata	Properties and definitions of a table, such as its structure, relationships, and behaviors, which affect how apps and flows use the table, as well as how data is stored and managed in the table.
Commands	Customizable buttons that you can add to your model-driven app's command bar.

Tackling Tables in Dataverse

Like with your good ole traditional database, tables are the bread and butter of data storage in Dataverse. When you create an app, you either need to use a standard table in Dataverse, create a custom table, or point to another data source (referred to as a *virtual table*).

A table can contain business logic, a process flow, or a workflow (features built into Dataverse natively) to validate the data:

- **Business logic:** A type of rule often used to validate data across table columns while providing warning and error messages when rules are breached. A Canvas or model-driven app generally includes some business logic tied to Dataverse.
- **Business process flows and workflows:** Business process flows organize data so that it follows a specific order for data entry. Users are prompted to fill in the relevant fields for one section of the flow before they can advance to the next section of the app. Business process flows are exclusive to model-driven apps because these enterprise applications, unlike Canvas apps, have rigid data enforcement. When a user must follow the same steps to achieve an objective, business process flows and workflows help ensure consistency and reliability.

TIP

Sometimes, you might not have a table ready for prime time; or perhaps you need a bit of assistance creating the table so that you can optimize it for all apps in the Power Platform. You don't have to go at this alone thanks to *Copilot*, Microsoft's AI offering. I go over this process in the section "Creating tables by using Copilot," later in this chapter. But if you have a great data source ready to go, follow the approach I outline in the section "Configuring a standard Dataverse table," later in this chapter. It takes a bit of work to refine a table to your liking by using Copilot.

Selecting the right table type

A table defines the information that users can track as rows, which Dataverse calls *records*. Each row includes many columns (formerly *fields* in Dataverse-speak), such as Company Name, Location, Point of Contact, Email, and Phone. Within Dataverse, specifically when using Power Apps, users will encounter one of four table types:

- **Standard table:** The most common type of table; either prebuilt and comes with Power Platform environments or gets customized by a user, who inputs their own column structure.
- **Activity table:** A specific table that focuses on row-level data that are activity-based, such as a person associated with an email address, a company associated with a fax number, or a start/stop time associated with an event.
- **Virtual table:** When Dataverse connects to data from an external source, this data appears as a virtual table. The data doesn't reside in Dataverse; although it appears like a regular table, allowing you to interact with it, it remains stored externally.
- **Elastic table:** Elastic tables store very large datasets (exceeding tens of millions of rows). They're built for scalability and query performance. This optimization ensures fast read and write operations, efficient data retrieval, and handling large data volumes without performance degradation.

ON THE WEB

Each table type has its own security model that protects the data integrity and privacy of the user. You can combine business units, role-based security, row-based security, and column-based security across one or more tables in the same Dataverse instance. To find out more about Dataverse security, flip to the section "Security Foundations and Dataverse," later in this chapter; for even more detail, go to `https://learn.microsoft.com` and search for **Dataverse security** to access Microsoft's guide to Dataverse admin security.

Jumping into table basics

In Microsoft Dataverse, you create and edit tables using the Power Apps Maker Portal from the Table Settings Page. You don't need other tools; you do everything within the portal. By using the capabilities and options that Dataverse tables offer through the user-friendly interface of the Maker Portal, you can manage a table and its properties:

- **Table Properties:** Defines key characteristics, such as ownership, relationships, security, auditing, and behavior, which govern how data is stored, accessed, and managed within the table.
- **Schema:** Defines the table schema, which incorporates Columns, Relationships, and Keys.
- **Data Experiences:** Each table, when utilizing Dataverse with model-driven apps, is built around its own data experience, which allows for customizing Forms, Views, Charts, and Dashboards.
- **Customizations:** Create Business Rules tied to column data and commands. To see an example of all the Dataverse features you can manipulate, check out Figure 3-1.

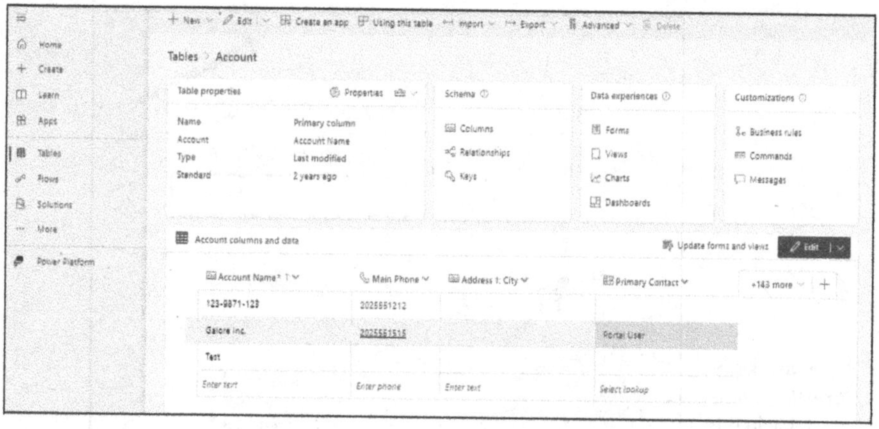

FIGURE 3-1: Power Apps Maker Portal Dataverse Table Settings pane.

Configuring a standard Dataverse table

You can find Dataverse access in the Power Apps Maker Portal. No application in Power Platform explicitly states that it uses Dataverse. But any time you see the reference to the table tab pointing to the Maker Portal, you're engaging with Dataverse. To create your first standard table in Dataverse, follow these steps:

1. **Go to `https://login.microsoft.com` and log in to your account by entering your username and password in the text boxes.**

2. **Navigate to `https://admin.powerplatform.microsoft.com`, and then enter your administrative credentials into the login screen.**

   The homepage of your environment Power Platform admin center opens.

3. **Click the waffle icon at the top-left of the admin center.**

   A menu appears, showing all of your Microsoft applications.

4. **Enter** Power Apps **in the Search text box and click Search.**

   If you're licensed, you see an icon for Power Apps.

5. **Select Power Apps from the menu that appears.**

   The Power Apps Maker Portal opens.

6. **Select the Tables tab in the Maker Portal left navigation pane.**

   A list of available Dataverse tables appears.

7. **Select New Table from the top of the window.**

   This option appears in Figure 3-2.

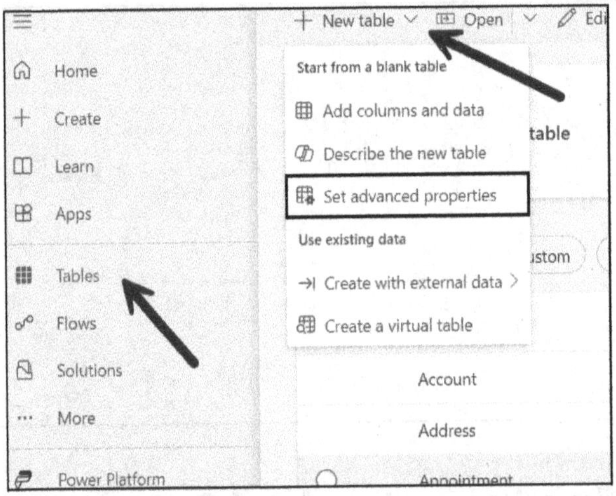

FIGURE 3-2: Creating a new table in the Power Apps Maker Portal.

8. **In the drop-down list that appears (see Figure 3-2), select Set Advanced Properties.**

   A New Table window opens.

9. **Define the table's Properties by entering values into the specific fields in the New Table window.**

   You can specify properties such as the Table Name, Primary Column Name, and Schema Name. This should include entering the name of the table that will be displayed in your app (as shown in Figure 3-3).

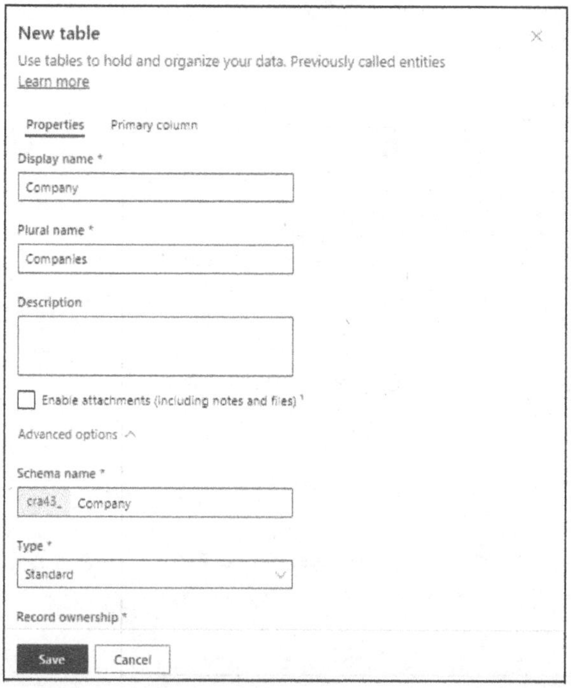

FIGURE 3-3: Configuring common table properties.

10. **Select Advanced Options at the bottom of the Edit Table pop-up window.**
11. **In the drop-down menu that appears, you'll be able to configure additional properties.**

    Options that you may want to configure in the fields in this tab include Schema Name, Type, Record Ownership, Primary Column, and Enable Attachments. (See Figure 3-4.)
12. **Click Save to create your table.**

    Your table opens in the Dataverse table designer, as shown in Figure 3-5.
13. **Add a column to your table by clicking the plus sign (+) button (labeled A in Figure 3-5).**

    The New Column panel appears (labeled B in Figure 3-5).
14. **Fill in the Display Name and Description text boxes.**

    Define the column name and then describe the purpose of the column.

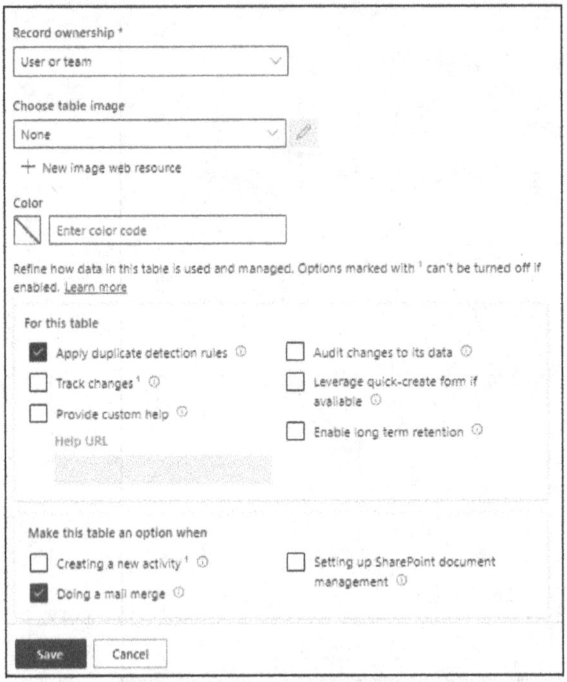

FIGURE 3-4: Advanced table configuration options.

15. **Select the appropriate options from the Data Type, Format, Behavior, and Required drop-down lists.**

    Making these selections helps define the type of data that you can store in each field, as well as specifying any relevant rules. For example, if you select Single Line of Text for the Data Type, and then choose E-Mail as the format, every entry must include an @ symbol with an e-mail extension.

16. **Select the Searchable check box if you want Dataverse and your Power Apps app to be able to search that column.**

    For now, just ignore the Advanced Options. I go into detail on the advanced options for columns in the section "Configuring a standard Dataverse table," later in this chapter.

17. **Click Save after you make all your selections.**
18. **Repeat Steps 13 through 17 as many times as you need to create all the columns that you want.**
19. **After you add all your columns, click Tables in the left navigation pane.**

    The main Tables window opens.

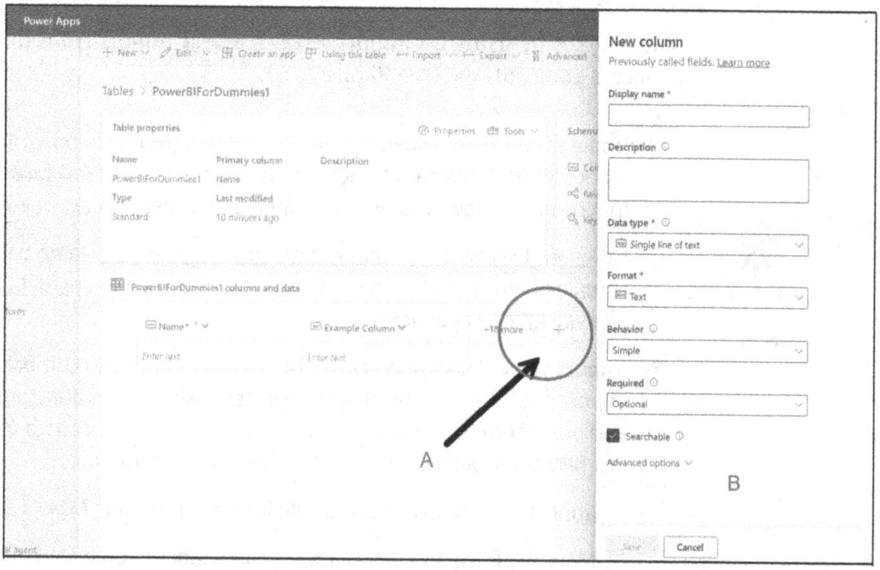

FIGURE 3-5: Adding a column to a table in Dataverse's table designer.

20. **Select your newly created table in the Tables window, and click Publish at the top of the window.**

    By publishing the table, you make the table available to all Power Platform applications, including Power Apps, Power BI, and Power Automate.

WARNING

When configuring a table, and especially columns, after you select the Save button, you can't go back and change some configurations, such as data type and format. Therefore, select the data type and configurations wisely.

Be sure to review advanced properties (which you can access by clicking Advanced Options in the New Column panel) when setting up a new table, especially those properties relating to field size limitations. Out of the box, Dataverse caps text field data entry to a mere 100 characters. Oftentimes, that's not enough. Also, if your form needs to input required data in a column (think of forms that have an asterisk next to the field to signify you have to complete that field), set the field to Business Required.

Creating tables by using external data sources

Sometimes, you have datasets already created in an application, such as SharePoint or Excel. Instead of having to recreate the table from scratch, you can import data sources by using an import wizard. Select Import from the top Tables menu to access your options (see Figure 3-6):

» **Import Data from Excel:** This option in the Import drop-down list is designed for quick and straightforward data import tasks — tasks based on a single document that contains a few columns and a limited number of rows. Think small datasets.

WARNING

However, Excel has limitations when dealing with very large datasets or complex data import scenarios because it lacks advanced data transformation and validation capabilities.

» **Import Data:** This option can handle more robust and comprehensive data import needs than importing from Excel, making it suitable for larger datasets and more complex data structures. And you can import data from more than just Microsoft-based data sources. This method supports

- Importing data from various file formats, including Excel, CSV, and XML
- Mapping from an array of relational database solutions hosted by cloud providers, including Microsoft Azure

The Import Data alternative offers a wizard that guides users through the process of mapping data columns to Dataverse fields. Using the wizard can minimize data errors and ensure data integrity in moving your table from one source to another. This process can involve data mapping, large-scale data imports, and integration with other systems.

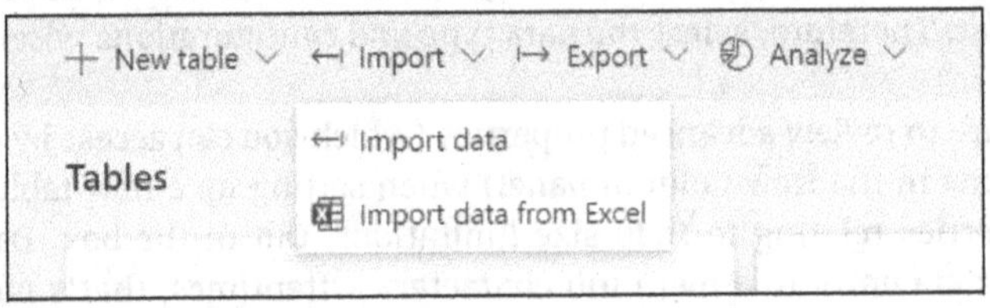

FIGURE 3-6: The Import menu in the Tables window.

To map an Excel spreadsheet by using the Import Data from Excel option, follow these steps:

1. **On the Tables page of the Maker Portal, click Import.**

   You can find out how to get to the Maker Portal in the preceding section.

2. **From the drop-down list that appears, choose Import Data.**

   The Choose Data Source window appears.

3. **Select Excel Workbook.**

   The Connection Settings window opens.

4. **Select the radio button for how you want to upload the file.**

   As you can see in Figure 3-7, you can select

   - *Link to File:* If you want to upload the file from your OneDrive account
   - *Upload File:* To upload the file from your computer desktop

   A pop-up window appears.

5. **Load your file.**

   A screen appears that confirms your selection.

6. **If a data connection isn't already established, establish your connection by using your Microsoft login credentials under the section Connection credentials.**

   After you upload the desired file, your connection should already be established because you're accessing the file from One Drive.

7. **After you log in and map your connection, click Next.**

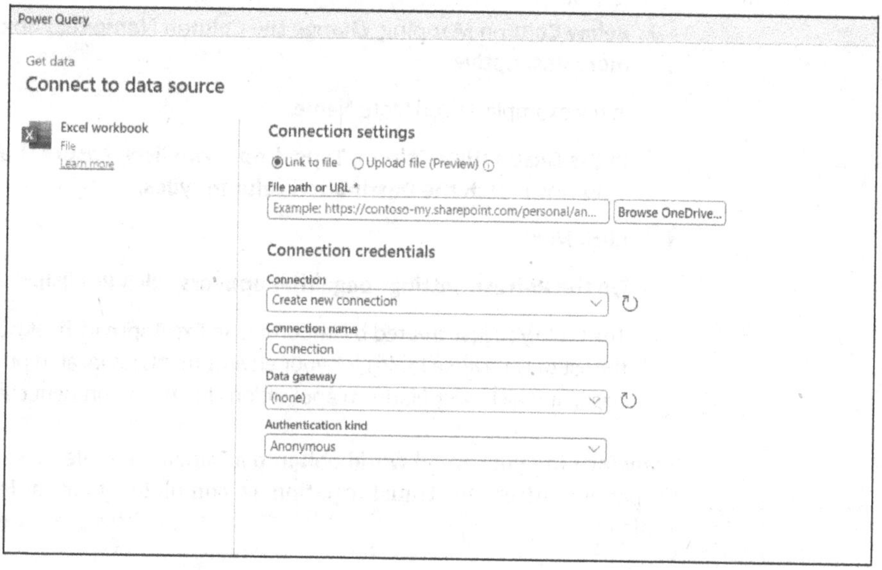

FIGURE 3-7: The Connection Settings window allows you to upload an Excel workbook into Dataverse.

8. **From the Power Query window, select the table that you want to import by using the Power Query Import Wizard, and then click Next.**

   In the Power Query Editor window that appears, you can make data transformations if you have issues with your data or the data type mapped to your application.

TIP

After you import data, you can't modify a data type. For example, you can't change a text field to a number field. So, make sure you select the accurate data types when you import your data.

9. **Modify any columns, including the Column Names. This includes data types and field values, when required.**
10. **After you finish editing your table, click Next.**

    The window to map your data fields appears, where you have one last opportunity to map the table to its destination.
11. **Select the Load to New Table radio button to create a new table.**

    The Map Tables window opens (see Figure 3-8).

    Alternatively, you can select Load to Existing Table (which allows you to map to a table that already exists). You can also select Do Not Load, which bypasses the entire loading and transformation process into Dataverse.
12. **Enter the table name in the Table Name text box.**

    I named my example 50 States.
13. **Below Column Mapping, change the Column Name text box to something more descriptive.**

    In my example, I used State Name.
14. **In the Destination Column Type drop-down lists, ensure that your Columns match the Destination column types.**
15. **Click Next.**
16. **On the Refresh Settings page that appears, click Publish.**

    The table you just created by importing an Excel spreadsheet now appears in the list of Dataverse tables for your environment. It's located on the Tables page, and all Power Platform applications in an environment can now use it.

Transforming your Excel workbook into a Dataverse table takes a few minutes, so be patient. After the transformation is complete, your table appears in your Table list.

WARNING

Data transformation isn't perfect. If you expect field types such as images, attachments, symbols, or managed metadata to carry over from systems such as SharePoint, guess again. Microsoft Dataverse doesn't support the mapping of these data types at time of publication.

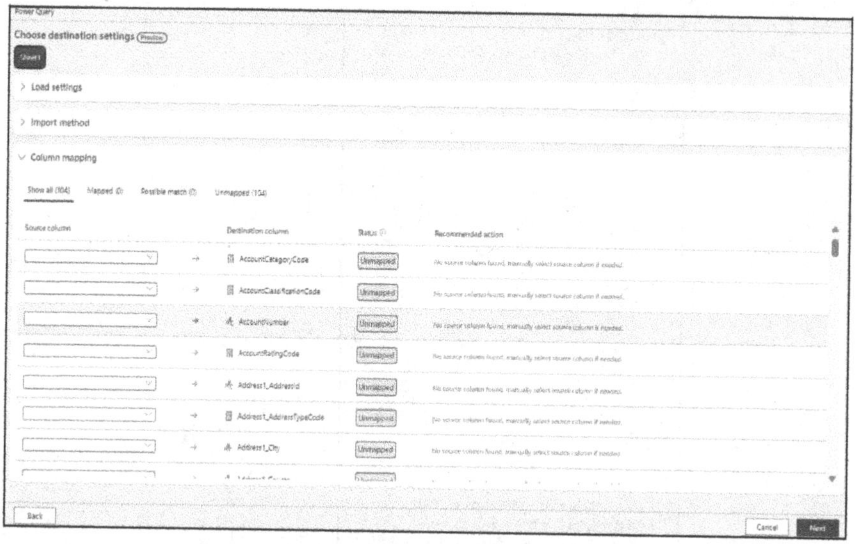

FIGURE 3-8: The Power Query Map Tables window.

Creating tables by using Copilot

If you don't know where to begin when it comes to creating tables, let Microsoft help guide your development efforts. You can simply provide some context to Microsoft Copilot, Microsoft's generative AI platform, which then uses your cues and its artificial intelligence capabilities to create your Dataverse table. Keep in mind that when you use Copilot, your initial output isn't perfect. You need to refine the logic in Copilot a bit, it almost certainly doesn't give you exactly what you want on the first try. Follow these steps to create a table with Copilot's help:

1. **Head to the Maker Portal home page.**
2. **Select the Let's Build an App. What Should It Do? option.**

   The Copilot editor opens in a separate window.
3. **In the text box, enter a description of the table that you want to make.**

   In my example (see Figure 3-9), I ask Copilot to map out cities, states, ZIP codes, the mayor of each city, its website, and the phone number to contact each city. Also, to ensure data integrity, I include a reference to the existing table 50 States, which I describe creating in the preceding section.
4. **Click Submit.**

   A few moments later, a prototype table appears, similar to the one in Figure 3-10.
5. **Repeat Steps 2 and 3, refining the terminology and description of what you want in your table.**
6. **After you're satisfied with your modifications, click Create.**

   Your new table now appears in the Dataverse Table listing.

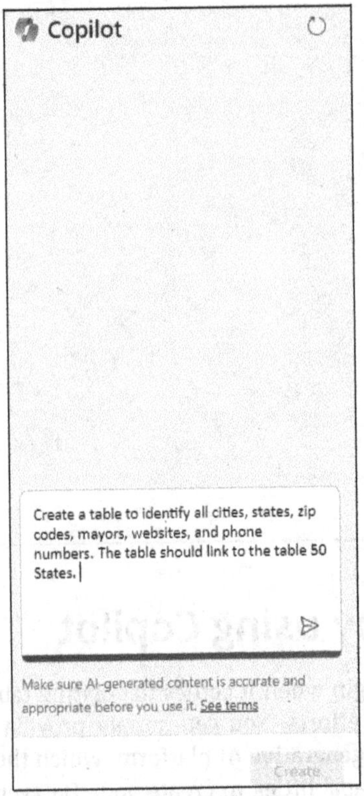
Copilot
Create a table to identify all cities, states, zip codes, mayors, websites, and phone numbers. The table should link to the table 50 States.
Make sure AI-generated content is accurate and appropriate before you use it. See terms

FIGURE 3-9: Asking Microsoft Copilot to create a new table.

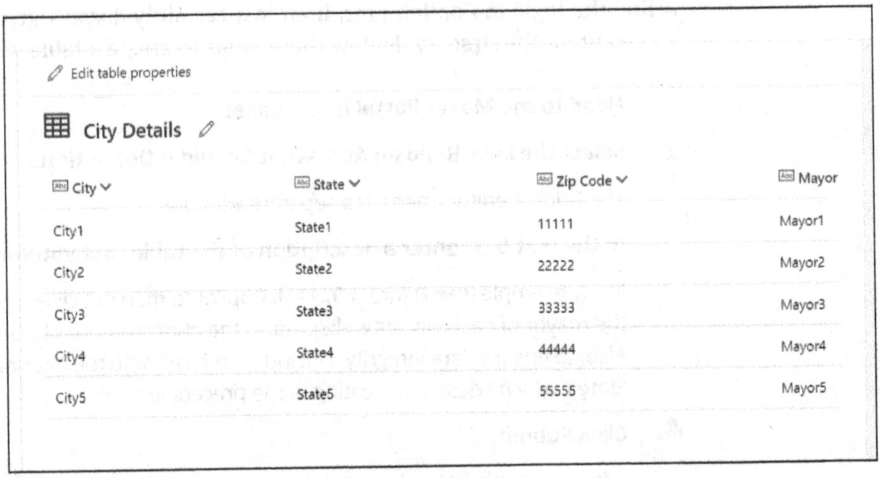
Edit table properties
City Details
City
State
Zip Code
Mayor
City1
State1
11111
Mayor1
City2
State2
22222
Mayor2
City3
State3
33333
Mayor3
City4
State4
44444
Mayor4
City5
State5
55555
Mayor5

FIGURE 3-10: A Dataverse table created by using Microsoft Copilot.

Working with virtual tables

Virtual tables, previously known as virtual entities in Microsoft Dataverse, represent data from external data sources, such as the big databases Microsoft Azure SQL Database, Oracle Database, or IBM DB2. A virtual table appears to have the data in Microsoft Dataverse, but those data are actually stored in the external data system.

REMEMBER

A virtual table enables users to interact with and utilize data within Dataverse applications, without needing any data storage in Dataverse itself. And that's important because Dataverse storage can get pricey if your dataset is exponentially large.

To create a virtual table in Dataverse, follow these steps:

1. **Select Tables in the left navigation pane of the Power Apps Maker Portal.**

   I show how to get to the Maker Portal in the section "Configuring a standard Dataverse table," earlier in this chapter.

2. **Select New Table from the Table window that appears.**
3. **In the drop-down list that opens (refer to Figure 3-2), select Create a Virtual Table.**

   The New Table from the External Data window appears.

4. **Select one or more external data sources from the data source list.**

   You can also create a new connection by pressing the New Connection button if the proposed data source you want doesn't appear in the list.

5. **Click Next to open the Connection screen.**
6. **Provide the connection details for the source of the data connection.**

   For example, if you select SharePoint as your external source, you point to that data source and provide the credentials to access the data. You do the same thing, regardless of the external data source you use.

   In my SharePoint example, you want to find a relevant SharePoint list.

7. **Click Next.**

   The prototype virtual table appears in the New Table from the External Data window's Configuration screen, as shown in Figure 3-11.

8. **After you confirm the connection between the two data sources, click Finish.**

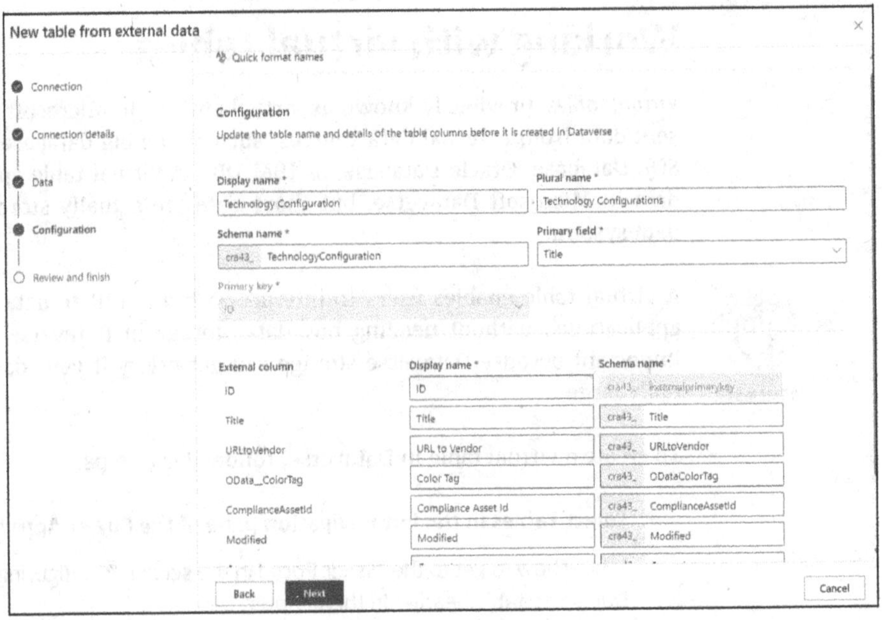

FIGURE 3-11: A SharePoint list virtual table Configuration in Dataverse.

Exporting data from Dataverse

A Dataverse table might be a goldmine of knowledge for an organization. When someone wants to analyze the data by using a tool besides Power BI (which I talk about in Part 3), they might ask for an exportable version of the Dataverse table. You can deliver on such a request by following these steps:

1. **In the Power Apps Maker Portal, select Tables from the left navigation pane.**

   For more detail about accessing the Maker Portal, refer to the section "Configuring a standard Dataverse table," earlier in this chapter.

2. **From the Tables window that appears, select the table from which you want to export data.**

   You can click one or more of the items in the list.

3. **From the top of the Tables window, choose Export ⇨ Export Data.**
4. **In the Export Data window, select the table from which you want to export data, and then press the Export Data button.**

   The export wizard processes your request.

5. **Download the exported data file (a CSV file) to your download destination of choice by clicking the download link.**

WARNING

Whether you import or export data, some of your table columns won't carry over in the way that you expect. For example, choice data doesn't carry over because the associated option set values don't get automatically translated or mapped because of the limited support for the data type. Instead, the data type transforms itself into a static text field. Images and files don't convey the same way system-generated data do.

Customizing a Dataverse Table

After you create your Dataverse table (flip back to the section "Tackling Tables in Dataverse," earlier in this chapter, to see your options), you can customize it. You probably want to add relevant columns to your table to support your data requirements. You have many data types to choose from, including a single line of text, currency, date and time, and lookup, to name a few fields.

To add a new column to a table, follow these steps:

1. **Click the plus sign (+) in the table's command bar.**

   Alternatively, from the toolbar, choose New ➪ Column.

   A New Column pop-up window appears, as shown in Figure 3-12.

2. **In the New Column pop-up window, enter attributes in the text boxes.**

   These text boxes include

   - *Display Name:* The name of the column.
   - *Description:* The purpose of the column

3. **Select the appropriate options from the drop-down lists.**

   Here are your options:

   - *Data Type:* Defines the kind of data that can be stored in a particular column
   - *Format:* Defines the way that each column's data is stored and appears, based on the Data Type you select. For example, the data type Date could have a Date format or Date and Time format.
   - *Behavior:* How specific columns, particularly those dealing with dates, times, and relationships, react to changes or events.
   - *Required:* A drop-down list where you can specify whether the column is required or not (Optional, Business Recommended, Business Required).
   - *Make Searchable:* Indicates that users can search the column in the table.

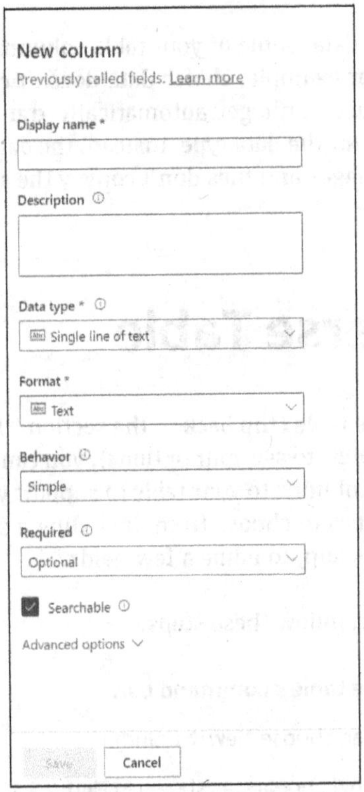

FIGURE 3-12: Creating a new column in your Dataverse table.

4. **Click Advanced Options at the bottom of the New Column pop-up window.**

   Additional attributes appear.

5. **Modify these attributes to refine your new column.**

   The configuration requirements (shown in Figure 3-13) include

   - *Schema Name:* The field's unique internal identifier for a given table.
   - *Maximum Character Amount:* The field size for the column.
   - *Input Editor:* Specifies how users input field values.
   - *Enable Column Security:* Restricts access to sensitive data fields.
   - *Enable Auditing:* Allows you to track changes made to the column.
   - *Enable in Global Dashboards:* Allows for the column to be made available in global dashboards.
   - *Make Sortable:* Allows the field to be sorted in views.

   Some features assume rigidity in data management, such as security and auditing. Enable these features only if you need them, such as for data compliance or tracking changes.

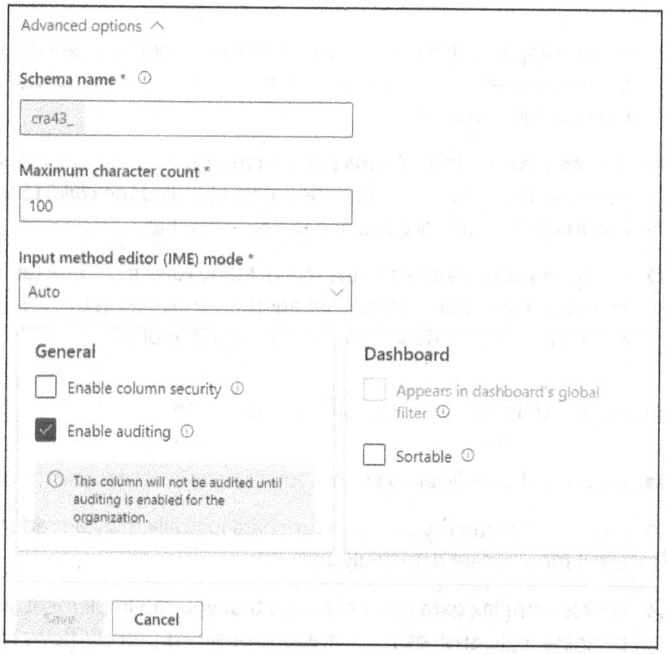

FIGURE 3-13: The New Column window's advanced options.

6. **After you enter all the necessary data in the form fields, click Save.**

   After you click Save, Dataverse saves your new table column, which appears in a list of all available columns that you can select, called a *table schema.*

Relationships and Dataverse tables

Tables in Dataverse don't have to work independently of one another; like your traditional database, they can include primary and secondary key relationships. Table relationships define how rows in one table can be associated with rows in another table. You may find yourself observing a one-to-one (1:1), one-to-many (1:N), or many-to-many (N:N) relationship. But you need to keep your data compartmentalized in its tables, following a practice called *data normalization,* which involves organizing data to reduce redundancy. Otherwise, you risk data inconsistency and inefficient storage.

Database tables also use *primary keys,* which are unique identifiers, to reference row-level data uniquely. In Dataverse, a relationship between two tables involves referencing primary keys.

Here are the three types of relationships that you can establish in Dataverse tables:

- **One-to-one relationships (1:1):** Each row in one table is linked to a single row in another table, ensuring a unique relationship between the rows. This relationship is highly restrictive and allows for only a single data value per table. You might implement a 1:1 relationship for data that doesn't contain multiple relationships.

- **One-to-many relationships (1:N):** In this type of relationship, you can associate many rows from the referencing (called the *child*) table with a single row from the referenced (called the *parent*) table.
- **Many-to-many relationships (N:N):** Many rows from one table can be associated with many rows from another. The rows in this relationship are called *peers*, hence they often reference one another.

You can use Dataverse relationships in tables to

- Organize data efficiently so that you can easily access and manage those data.
- Ensure data integrity and structure data logically to avoid redundancy and allow for accurate data analysis.
- Enable complex data interactions so that you can implement sophisticated business logic, such as when creating business process flows by using model-driven apps.
- Create user-friendly applications that provide a comprehensive view of related data across the system, not just in Power Apps but also when you use Power BI, Power Automate, and Power Pages.

Lookups and Dataverse

You can create lookup tables to ensure data is consistently presented and reusable across multiple tables. These tables store predefined values that you can use multiple times, not just once. The lookup appears as a drop-down list in other tables. For example, you may have a form that captures user demographic data, with a table called State presented as a lookup in the form. The main form then saves the selected value from the lookup table as data in the main table. Using lookups ensures consistency, reduces errors, and allows data to be easily reused across different tables.

Follow these steps to create a lookup column in a table:

1. **Open the table to which you want to add a lookup column.**

   To continue the address book example that I start in the section "Creating tables by using external data sources," earlier in this chapter, open the 50 States table.

2. **Click the plus sign (+) in the table's command bar.**

   Alternatively, from the toolbar, choose New ⇨ Column.

3. **In the New Column pop-up window that appears (refer to Figure 3-12), enter a Display Name and Description in the text boxes.**
4. **In the Data Type drop-down list, select Lookup.**
5. **In the Related Table drop-down list, select the table that you want to use as a lookup table.**

   I selected the 50 States table.

   For my lookup column to 50 States, I want to populate the repeatable field with a one-to-many relationship.

6. **Click Save when you finish making your setting selections.**
7. **Drag the new column from the Table Column pane onto the form page.**

   A repeatable lookup value appears on the form.

TIP

The value saved in the destination table must be stored in the lookup table's primary key column (generally, the Name column). In the example provided, the state abbreviations must be in the 50 States table's primary key column, named State, ensuring the correct data is linked and saved properly.

Venturing into Views

Views are customized presentations of structured data stored in tables. If a table has 100 columns, you may want to see only a subset of records, perhaps ten of the columns. Views allow you to quickly query those ten columns by using a filter and display the data in a user-friendly format. There are three types of views available within Dataverse:

- **System views:** Developed by the application developer, not by the end user. These are predefined views provided by Dataverse or a Dataverse developer that users can't delete but can customize. Examples include Active, Inactive, and Lookup views (the following section describes the different types of views).
- **Public views:** Created by either a developer or end user. Users who have appropriate permissions in an organization can access these views.
- **Personal views:** Private views, created with specific data points or visualizations that an individual wants to access, not the public.

Which type of app you have, model-driven or canvas, can affect how you use views in that app:

- **Model-driven apps:** In the case of model-driven apps (which I cover in Chapters 6 and 7), the view is a core feature, allowing the user to display and interact with their data within the app. A user can switch between different views to see subsets of data. Within each view, a user can additionally sort and filter based on pre-defined parameters configured by a developer.
- **Canvas apps:** A canvas app (discussed in Chapters 4 and 5) utilizes a view to query and display data in galleries or data tables. Because the app developer is responsible for building the canvas app interface, you have more flexibility in terms of layout and design of the the data presentation.

A Power Pages portal (check out Chapter 8) is like a model-driven app, except the data is delivered to the outside world as a public-facing website, not just internal data consumers. A Power Pages portal can display lists of records to users in a view format, based on columns of curated data, which in turn creates an interactive user experience through the Dataverse table and embedded Power BI reports.

Digging into model-driven view types

Views in a model-driven app define how data is organized and displayed from a specific table. A view specifies the columns that appear, their order, the sort order of the records, and any filters applied to restrict which records are shown. After a developer creates and publishes a custom view, users can select it from the View drop-down list to adjust their data display according to the predefined structure. Every navigation item that requires form entry generally starts with the user entering the view data, which acts as the equivalent of a launch pad to access and edit data.

Some public views exist by default for system tables and any custom table that you create. For example, the 50 States table (created from an imported Excel spreadsheet in the section "Creating tables by using external data sources," earlier in this chapter) is automatically generated when you create a table. After you create the view, you then need to update the user experience.

TECHNICAL STUFF

You can create custom public views for either *managed* (locked and packaged) or *unmanaged* (editable and untracked) solutions. (Check out Chapter 4 for a discussion of solutions.) However, you can't delete any system-defined views. If you want to delete public views in managed solutions, you must uninstall the solution to update the application properly.

Table 3-2 describes the model-driven app view types.

TABLE 3-2 Model-Driven App View Types

View Type	What It Does
Active	Displays records that are currently active. It typically includes records that are being actively used or managed, and excludes those records marked as inactive or archived.
Inactive	In contrast to the Active view, the Inactive view shows records that are no longer active in Dataverse; they're not deleted, they're just treated as archived data.
Advanced Find	Allows users to perform complex searches and queries by using various filters and conditions, much like an advanced search feature on the Internet. Developers can configure and customize the Advanced Find parameters, but users can also create their own queries directly without needing developer intervention.
Associated	Displays records that are related to a particular record. For example, this view might show all orders associated with a specific customer. Helps you understand and manage relationships between different data entities.
Lookup	Displays a list of records from the related table that are linked to the current record (see the section "Lookups and Dataverse, earlier in this chapter, for more info). For example, in the 50 States table, when selecting a city (a related table) in a form that tracks addresses, the view displays a list of cities associated with the selected state (the current record), so that the user can more easily choose the correct city.
Quick Find	Perform rapid searches across a table by entering keywords or search terms. Targets specific, pre-configured searchable fields, enabling users to locate relevant records quickly without sifting through the entire dataset. For example, in a table with fifty columns, the development may decide to only select five columns that are designated as searchable to optimize search performance and return results faster.

Creating or customizing a view

Developers can modify existing views when they create a table, or they can craft their own views. By customizing your view, you can create and present your data in a manner relevant to your organization and planned uses, instead of using the canned data fields provided by Microsoft.

To create or customize a view, follow these steps:

1. **Open the Power Apps Maker Portal.**

   You can find directions to this portal in the section "Configuring a standard Dataverse table," earlier in this chapter.

2. **In the left navigation pane of the Maker Portal, select Tables.**

   The Tables window appears.

3. **Click the table whose view you want to customize to open that table's details in the Table Settings page.**

4. **In the Data Experience pane of the Table Settings page, select the Views tab.**

   The list of existing views appears.

5. **Choose a view that you want to customize.**

   Either select an existing view (Figure 3-14, labeled A) or click New View to create a new view (Figure 3-14, labeled B).

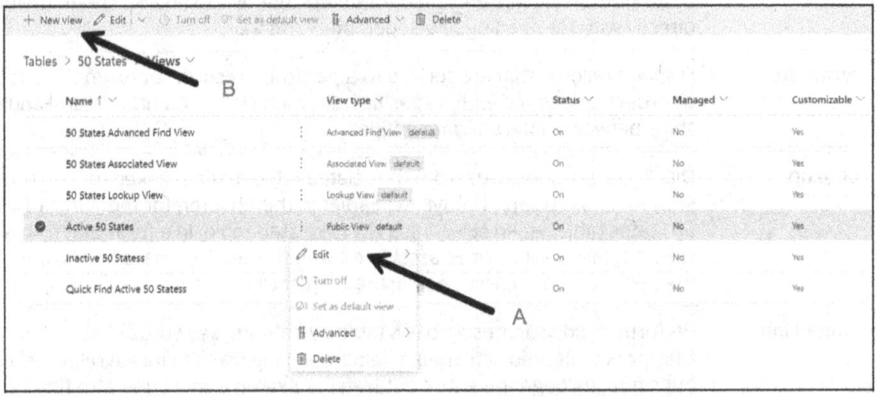

FIGURE 3-14: Choosing whether to create or edit views for a table.

   The View Designer opens, where you can add, remove, or reorder columns.

6. **Click + View Column to open a pop-up menu (as shown in Figure 3-15).**

7. **Select an option in this menu to include that column from the table in the view.**

   If you want to delete a column that appears in the view, select Remove from the drop-down menu.

   Repeat Steps 5 and 6 until you have all the columns you want (and none that you don't) in your view.

8. **To set the sorting order of a column, click one or more column headers, and then choose Sort Ascending or Sort Descending from the column.**

9. **Add filters to restrict the data displayed in the view. Click on the relevant field, and then choose the parameters by using the Filter By option.**

10. **After making all the changes you want, click Save and Publish.**

   The updated view now appears with all new customizations. Figure 3-16 shows a customized view of the 50 States table I create in the section "Creating tables by using external data sources," earlier in this chapter, with the table filtered by the Region value of South.

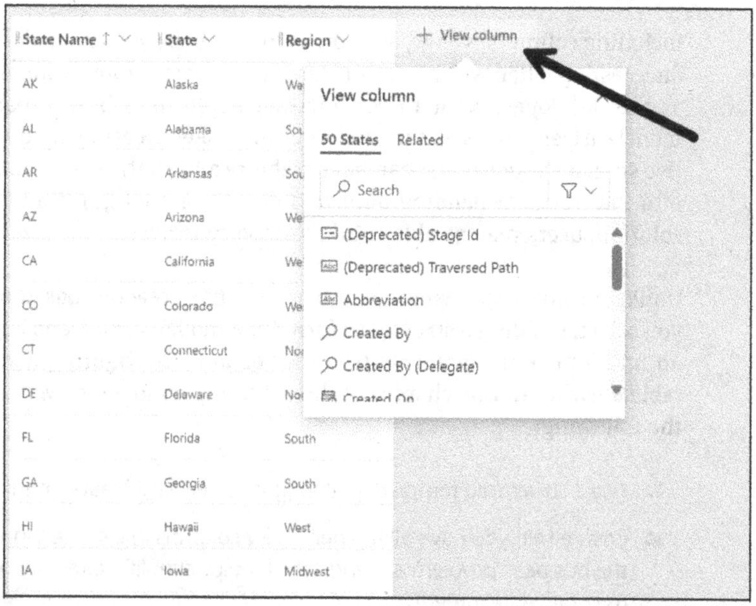

FIGURE 3-15: Adding new a column to a view.

TIP You need to edit all of the standard views to ensure your tables consistently present the data. For example, you can't just edit the Active view; you should also edit the Inactive view so that it mimics the View experience in Active view when presenting data to a user.

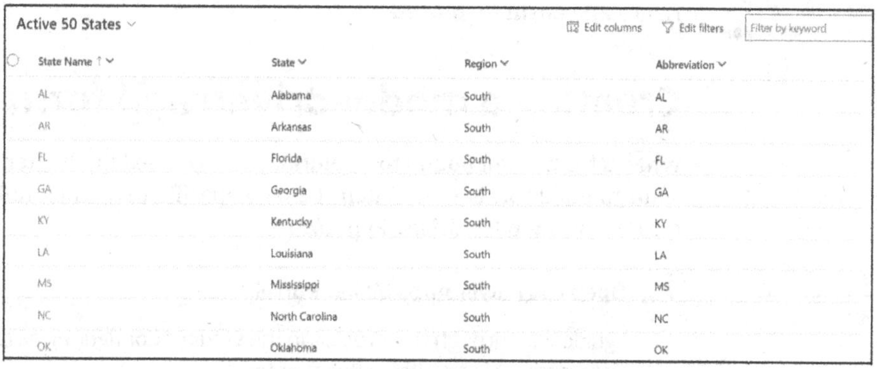

FIGURE 3-16: A customized view filtered by the Region value of South.

Working with Model-Driven App Forms

With model-driven apps, you must work within a highly structured interface experience because these apps focus on repeatability by using Dataverse columns to complete data entry. In an unmanaged solution, you can freely edit properties, including columns, views, and forms from tables; you can make changes and conduct testing whenever you want. After you have an application in production, you, as the developer, want to convert that application into a managed solution. A model-driven app as a managed solution makes creating or editing forms restrictive so that the developer can have stability and control over what data are entered into that form. Depending on how a developer configures a table for a managed solution, users may be able to add or modify forms.

Unlike a canvas app, where you have creative freedom based on the data source you select, building a structured form for a model-driven app begins with creating an initial table in Dataverse (see the section "Configuring a standard Dataverse table," earlier in this chapter). When creating a model-driven app form, consider the following:

- Use a structured template to configure views and create or edit forms.
- Ensure that you have all the necessary columns in a single table to address the business problem at hand, which helps simplify data relationships and maintain data integrity.
- Go into your design process knowing how you want to organize the data: Do you need to have the data across several tabs and sections, or do you want to make the form a single flowing page?

REMEMBER

The design of your forms reflects how many columns you have in your table. The number of columns in a table probably reflects the complexity of your form experience and business process.

Creating a model-driven app form

When a form is not bound to a solution, as discussed in Chapter 2, and you merely want to build forms that match the data specific to a table, follow these steps to create a new model-driven app form:

1. **Open the Power Apps Maker Portal.**

   I guide you through this process in the section "Configuring a standard Dataverse table," earlier in this chapter.

2. **Select Tables in the left navigation pane of the Maker Portal.**
3. **From the Tables window, select the table for which you want to create a new form.**
4. **In the Table Settings page that appears, click the Forms link below Data Experience.**

   A list of all pre-defined forms appears.

5. **Click New Forms and select the type of form you want to create from the drop-down list that appears.**

   In my example, I want to create a new *main form,* the primary form used to display and interact with the data of a table, by clicking New Form.

   REMEMBER

   Keep in mind that when you create a new main form, Maker Portal copies over the existing form, in essence duplicating it, and you have to modify it by adding additional fields.

6. **In the form designer that appears, change the name of the form that appears in the Properties pane.**

   You don't want to have two forms that have the same name.

7. **Add columns, sections, tabs, and other components to your form.**

   Use the drag-and-drop interface to arrange components between the Table Columns pane (labeled A in Figure 3-17) and the form designer (labeled B in Figure 3-17).

8. **Individually select each column or component on the model-driven app form and configure its properties by using the Properties pane (labeled C in Figure 3-17).**

9. **After you're satisfied with the form design, click Save and Publish.**

   You can now access your new main form in the Table form lists for the specific entity.

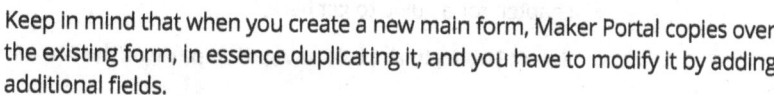

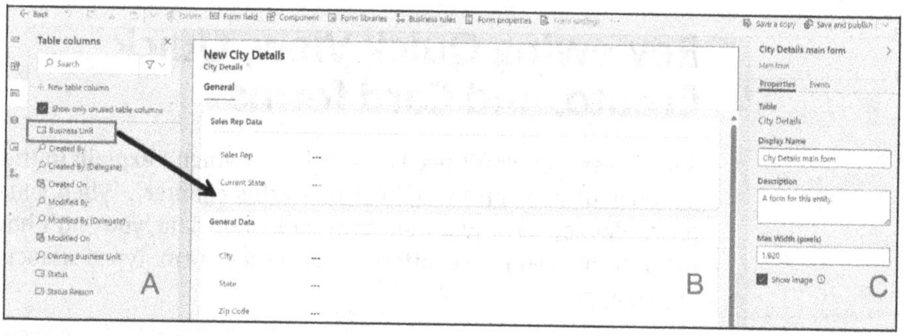

FIGURE 3-17: Creating a model-driven app form.

Editing a model-driven app form

With model-driven app editing, you can configure and manipulate only the data elements on a form; you can't craft a wildly unique user interface like you can with a canvas app. You can change elements in a model-driven app by using advanced programming techniques such as JavaScript, but that goes well beyond what I cover in this book. (If you want to dive into JavaScript, check out *JavaScript All-in-One For Dummies* by Chris Minnick [Wiley].)

To make basic changes to your model-driven app form, follow these steps:

1. **Open the Power Apps Maker Portal.**

   Check out the section "Configuring a standard Dataverse table," earlier in this chapter, for a guide to get here.

2. **Select Tables in the left navigation pane of the Maker Portal.**

   The Table window opens.

3. **Select the table that you want to edit.**

   The table opens in the app designer.

4. **Change your form by clicking the Forms button and selecting your main form from the Forms window that appears.**

   Your form of choice opens.

5. **Add, remove, or rearrange columns, sections, or tabs by interacting with them in the Table Column or Components pane.**

   You can also update properties for any component by selecting the specific column on the form and making property changes in the Properties pane.

6. **After you make all your changes, save your work by clicking Save and Publish.**

   The modified form has now been saved.

Reviewing Quick View, Quick Create, and Card forms

Sometimes, you don't need a main form (which I explain in the section "Creating a model-driven app form," earlier in this chapter). When you require only simplistic data entry or just want to enter lookup data, you don't have to start with the main form. Dataverse offers three other form types associated with model-driven apps:

- **Quick Create:** Provide a streamlined interface to quickly create new records. Users can input essential information without navigating away from their current context, improving efficiency and user experience. The Quick Create form is akin to a pop-up window, where users can rapidly add new entries without leaving the main page. (See Figure 3-18.)
- **Quick View:** Appears within the main form to display additional data from a related table referenced by a lookup column; essentially, a view within a view.

Check out Figure 3-19 for an example. Quick View forms enable users to see data from related records without leaving their current form.

- **Card:** Specifically designed for a compact, concise presentation of information. Data from Card forms are often gathered on a mobile or tablet-based device, as shown in Figure 3-20.

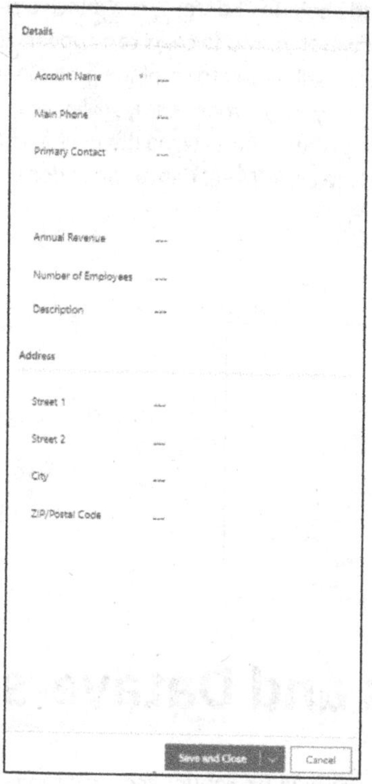

FIGURE 3-18: A Quick Create form for account information.

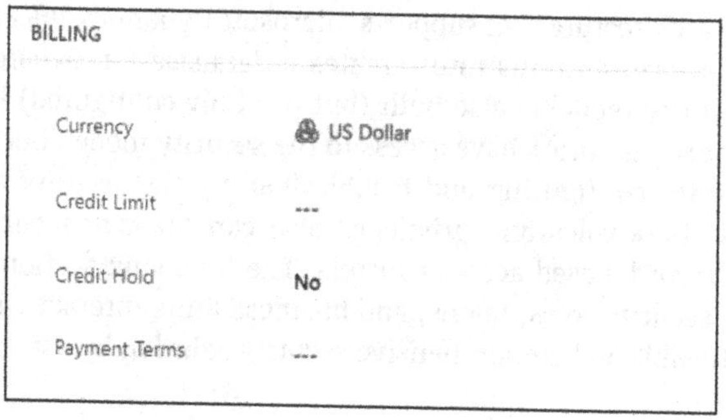

FIGURE 3-19: A Quick View form presenting billing information.

TECHNICAL STUFF

VISUALIZING DATA INSIDE DATAVERSE

Charts and dashboards in Microsoft Dataverse let you visualize business data graphically using Microsoft Graph, a charting technology embedded within Power Platform and Dynamics 365. Unlike Power BI (which I begin talking about in Chapter 9), a standalone application, Power Platform has the Microsoft Graph functionality built in.

Microsoft Graph, which you can read about in Chapter 7, can attach a chart to a specific table within a model-driven app. However, only one chart can appear alongside a grid at any given time. In contrast, dashboards allow you to combine multiple single-instance charts onto a single visualized pane, so you can more easily review and analyze your data comprehensively. You can design these charts using the built-in chart designer, which is accessible within model-driven apps. ***Note:*** Canvas apps don't have access to the chart designer.

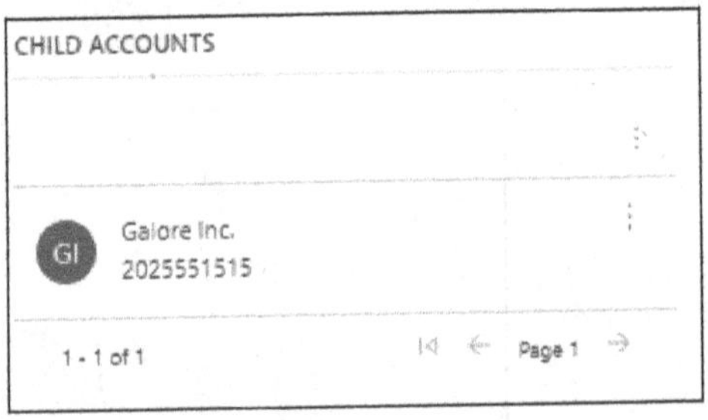

FIGURE 3-20: A Card displaying information on a child account.

Security Foundations and Dataverse

One of the key features of Dataverse is its robust security model that can adapt to various business scenarios. Dataverse uses the same security controls as the underlying architecture that supports Microsoft Dynamics 365 applications. When a Power Platform Administrator creates a database for Dynamics 365 or Dataverse, a security model is also built (but not fully configured) in the given environment. Administrators have access to the security model, but they're not solely responsible for configuring and troubleshooting the security access. Users who have appropriate roles and privileges also can manage security through role-based and record-based access controls. The following sections explain in more detail how security roles, teams, and business units interact with one another to provide a flexible and comprehensive security solution by using Dataverse.

ON THE WEB

I could write an entire book on how to secure Power Platform applications. To go beyond the high-level concepts described in this chapter, review Microsoft's tutorial found at `https://learn.microsoft.com`, and then enter **security concepts in Dataverse** into the Search text box. Check out the articles that appear in the search results for more security-related information.

Grouping privileges by roles

Dataverse uses a layered security model to control flexible access across organizational structures (see Table 3-3). Organizations must start at the top level, with the *environment* acting as the primary container in which you manage databases, apps, and resources, with access restricted at this level. Everyone may or may not have access to an environment. Within each environment, *business units* define security boundaries, segmenting users and data into manageable groups. Think of business units as big teams that you can break into smaller groupings. Each business unit can include a root unit and optional child units to compartmentalize further access based on the specific access needs. By segmenting data and users, business units ensure that information remains protected while allowing appropriate access to different parts of the organization.

The *role-based access credentials (RBAC)* are at the core of Dataverse security, where users and teams are assigned specific roles that contain privileges. In the Dataverse, usually someone such as the system administrator has complete system access. In contrast, others might be *system customizers,* meaning users who can change the system's configuration without complete administrative control. If that's still too much access, you can create a custom access credential to support a very specific access level for that user. Generally, your access level determines the scope of actions you can perform, such as limiting access to a user's records or extending access across an entire business unit.

Organizations streamline role assignments in the form of *teams* because users inherit the roles and privileges of their team. Similar to your traditional organization chart, a team can manage access based on their job function or user type, ensuring that only authorized personnel can perform specific actions on data within their business units.

Finally, if you want to get down to the nitty-gritty of security groups, Dataverse offers security based on record ownership and sharing, and column-level security:

» **Record ownership:** Determines who has access to a specific data record, and records can be shared between users or teams.

» **Column-level security:** Allows administrators to restrict access to particular fields within a table column. Such fine-grained security ensures that even users with access to a record cannot see information at the record level.

This combination of layered security — from the highest levels (the environment and business units) down to roles, teams, records, and columns — provides robust data protection to support just about any business use.

REMEMBER

An important concept in Dataverse security is that all privileges are cumulative, meaning the greatest level of access prevails, not the least permissive access. For instance, if you grant broad organization-level read access to contact records, you can't restrict access to individual records within that scope.

TABLE 3-3 **Dataverse Security Levels**

Level	Description
Environment	A top-level container where Dataverse databases and resources are created and managed.
Business Unit	Each environment has a root business unit; the default, top-level unit where all users and data initially reside. You can create additional child business units to further segment users and data, allowing for more granular control and organization-specific access management.
Teams	Groups of users within a business unit. Each business unit has a set of default teams, and you can create custom teams. Teams can be assigned security roles, and users within those teams inherit these roles.
Security Roles	Custom privileges define what actions users can perform. You can assign roles to either users or teams. Privileges within roles include creating, reading, writing, deleting, and so on.
Users	Individuals are assigned security roles directly or through team memberships to gain access to resources.
Privileges	Specific permissions within security roles, defining actions users can perform on different types of data. Examples include read access to contacts or write access to accounts.
Access Levels	Define the scope of privileges.
Record Ownership	Determines which business unit ownership level gets access to a record.
Column-Level Security	Allows for granular control over access to specific *fields* (columns) within a table, ensuring that sensitive data can be protected, even when users can access the entire record. Administrators manage this access by using Column-Level Security profiles, which define which users or teams can view or update the secured columns.

At a high level, Dataverse security is implemented through several layers:

- **User authentication:** Through *Microsoft Entra ID* (formerly Azure Active Directory, an identity and access management solution), which Power Platform administrators manage within *Microsoft Azure* (the cloud computing platform), ensuring secure access from the start of any Dataverse work.
- **Licensing:** The first real gatekeeper, determining who can access Power Apps components. You can't gain access to the functionality if you're not licensed for a specific Power Platform tool.
- **Security roles within specific environments:** Control the ability to create applications and flows, acting as the second gatekeeper. Users' access to apps is managed by administrative sharing applications directly with them or through Microsoft Entra groups, subject to Dataverse security role assignments.
- **Environments:** Serve yet another security boundary, tailoring security needs for organizational units or projects.

Advanced security settings in Dataverse environments, rather than those settings that don't rely on Dataverse as the data source, provide support for more granular access controls based on the control model described in Table 3-3. A Power Platform administrator can manage who can see and use apps, control access to data and services, and define permissions for flows and connectors — because all of these areas are tied to data. That said, only system administrators can manage these security settings in Dataverse.

Understanding the Dataverse/Power Platform security model

Microsoft constructed the security model within the Dataverse with a building-block approach:

- **Hierarchy:** Security includes business units, which form a hierarchy of users and teams, defining security boundaries and controlling permissions. Users and teams within the same unit have different access to records than those in other business units.

  Hierarchy security is based on a traditional management chain organization chart, like the one shown in Figure 3-21:

  - *Managers:* Each business unit or team has at least one manager. Managers can access their subordinates' data, perform tasks on their behalf, and view information that needs approval. Managers have full access to direct reports' data and read-only access to non-direct reports' data.

- *Users:* Below the manager; limited to only those features to which the administrator has granted them access.
- *Subordinate users:* If subordinate users exist below the user, the subordinates have even less permissive responsibilities.

» **Control:** Business units make reporting more controlled because you can filter reports based on security roles, which map to user access levels within different business units.

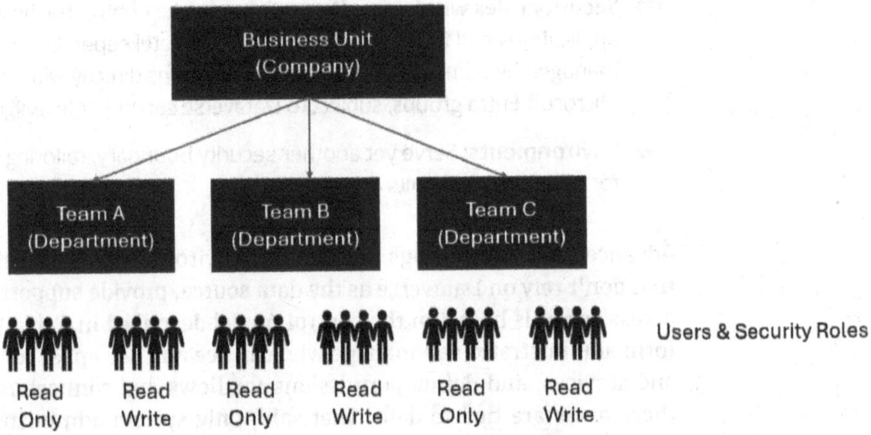

FIGURE 3-21: An example hierarchy-based security model in Dataverse.

REMEMBER

As security becomes more granular, focus on security roles, which define permissions by assigning privileges that specify what actions users can perform at different access levels. Although you typically assign security roles to individuals, teams can also act as a group of users working together within a business unit. In that case, you can also assign teams the same security roles, a setup that allows teams to support the use of an application or, at a minimum, perform specific functions within an application.

Going with the Business Process Flows

Consider using business process flows when you have a table that multiple parties need to access or if users must follow a specific process to consider an update complete. Explicitly designed for model-driven applications, *business process flows* are visual guides that lead users through a series of defined steps to help them complete a process and achieve a desired outcome.

Business process flows provide a structured and visual pathway to ensure users follow the correct procedures, minimizing the risk of human error. The flow clearly defines each step in the process, and each step can manage different scenarios by using various workflow states (similar to Power Automate, which you can read about in Chapter 14) such as conditions, actions, and branching logic. For example, a particular action can be triggered based on specific data or user input, guiding the process down one of several possible paths. The user may be required to enter only a subset of data, not the entire dataset, for the business process flow to consider the record complete. In essence, the workflow adapts dynamically to the situation while maintaining consistency in operations.

TIP

Business process flows can do more than just ensure procedural order. You can also use them to trigger workflows and automation across other Power Platform tools. For example, if you want to send a notification or update a record while a user progresses with their data entry in an application, a business process flow can aid with such routine tasks, ensuring accuracy and efficiency by automatically executing actions based on predefined conditions.

Creating a business process flow in Dataverse for a model-driven app involves following these steps:

1. **Go to Power Apps.**

   You can find the steps to do this in the section "Configuring a standard Dataverse table," earlier in this chapter.

2. **Sign in with your credentials.**
3. **Select the model-driven application that you want to utilize a business process flow for a business scenario or workflow.**
4. **Hover the mouse pointer over your selected application to open it in Edit mode.**
5. **In the Solution Explorer pane on the left, select Automation.**
6. **Click the Create Business Process button.**
7. **Fill in the basic information describing the business flow in the Create Business Process Flow window that appears.**

   This information includes the Display Name, Business Flow Name, and the table into which you want to incorporate a business process flow.

8. **After you fill out all fields, click Create.**
9. **In the Solution Explorer window, right-click the newly created process and select Edit in New Tab.**

   The Business Process Flow Editor window opens.

10. **Click Add, which appears at the top of the window, and then select Add Stage from the drop-down list that opens.**
11. **In the right pane, provide a name in the Display Name text box, select a category from the Category drop-down list, and select the Entity that you want the process flow to evaluate.**

    For example, you can select Qualify, Develop, or Propose as a Category. You can select any available Dataverse table as the entity.
12. **Click Apply.**

    The new step now appears on the Business Process Workflow Designer page.
13. **Specify the field that your new step relates to and the action required in the Data Step pane on the right of the screen.**
14. **Repeat Steps 9 through 13 for all stages and steps you want to add to your flow.**
15. **Set the conditions or branching logic associated with the flow by defining the criteria that must be met for each stage.**

    The example shown in Figure 3-22 has two stages:

    - *Qualify:* To move on to the second stage, the second data field in the Qualify stage can't be blank.
    - *Identify:* Requires a user to select the State Capital and Region before they can save the record and complete the process.

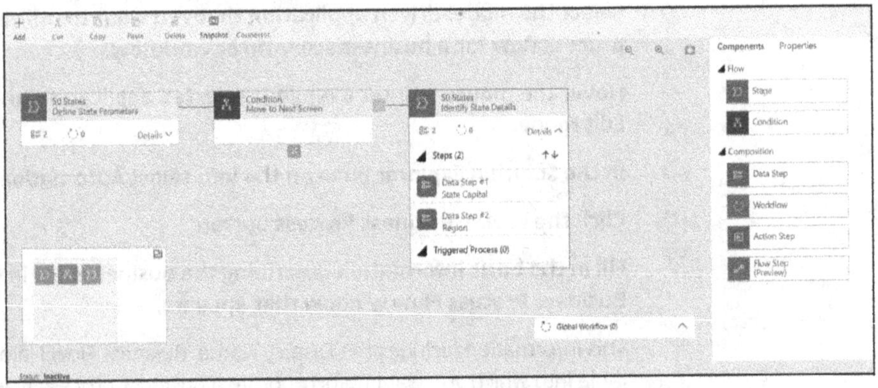

FIGURE 3-22: Data added to the 50 States table by using business process flows.

16. **After you complete your business process flow model, click the Validate button to validate that the model works as expected.**
17. **If the model is accurate, click Activate the Process Flow to enable it.**

18. **Click Save to publish the new business process flow.**

19. **Close the Business Process Flow Editor window.**

    Note: You don't have a button that takes you directly back to the model-driven app editor.

To make your business process flow visible to users in a model-driven app, follow these steps:

1. **In the Power Apps portal, select Solutions from the left navigation.**

   The Solutions pane opens.

2. **Choose the solution that contains your business process flow.**

3. **In the Processes section, confirm the business process flow is correctly configured.**

4. **After you verify the flow, click Publish All Customizations at the top of the pane.**

   This step applies the changes across the solution.

5. **Open your model-driven app to ensure that the business process flow is now visible and functioning for users.**

REMEMBER

Don't get confused between business rules in Microsoft Dataverse and business process flows:

- **Business rules:** Apply to specific fields in a form or table and help automate simple checks to ensure the data is correct and consistent. A business rule can automatically fill in field values, show or hide fields, and validate data based on certain conditions.
- **Business process flows:** Like step-by-step guides that help users follow a set procedure when entering data. These flows make sure users complete tasks in the correct order and according to the right conditions. A business process flow generally contains at least two or three steps that a user must complete in order to save a record.

2 Getting Your Power Apps Hat On

IN THIS PART . . .

Create canvas apps that allow developers to create their own user experiences.

Develop model-driven apps for enterprise and data-driven applications.

Build low-code websites to expose Dataverse assets, including apps and analytics.

IN THIS CHAPTER

» Recognizing the business value of Power Apps

» Creating canvas apps to create interactive, personal yet data-driven applications

» Crafting data-rich, highly structured applications by using model-driven apps

» Managing and deploying solutions for Power Apps apps

Chapter 4

Getting the Big Picture on Power Apps Development

You've probably heard stories where a citizen developer crafted a beautiful, one-of-a-kind application and successfully sold their masterpiece. Surely, they didn't just open the application and start cranking out the work. The developer had to go through a methodical process to deliver their end product. In the same way, you as a developer or analyst must consider what is most important to you, a customized look and feel or a design based on highly structured data outputs as you embark on Microsoft's low-code/no-code platform journey.

This chapter covers the planning and conceptualization of the apps you want to make using Microsoft's low-code/no-code application development solution within the Power Platform, called Power Apps. This chapter doesn't get into development just yet, instead, it addresses data and design realities. So, let's get the journey started down the Power Apps road.

Developing Applications by Using Power Apps

By using Microsoft Power Apps, a no-code/low-code application development solution, you can create custom, data-driven applications that are tailored to your business needs. Power Apps has a drag-and-drop interface and pre-built templates that you can use to quickly build functional apps based on one or more data sources. Power Apps also can integrate with other Microsoft products, such as Microsoft 365, Dynamics 365, SharePoint Online, or Azure, as well as numerous third-party applications or data platforms.

But that doesn't mean you can get away from code easily. Integrating JavaScript and other programming languages (such as C#, HTML, and CSS) with Power Apps allows for advanced customization and integration with external services and APIs. Using programming languages outside of the low-code environment allows a developer to deliver highly complex business logic, custom user interface (UI) elements, backend processing, and more sophisticated, responsive designs than what the core Power Apps development environment allows.

Some developers say that you can create a few different kinds of apps by using Power Apps. That's 100 percent correct! You can choose from three types of apps:

- **Canvas apps:** Offer a high degree of flexibility and customization to developers and users who require a customized user experience that can access one or more data sources. Ideal for specific tasks.
- **Model-driven apps:** Allow developers and users to focus on data and processes. Leveraging Microsoft Dataverse (which you can read about in Chapter 3), you get a more structured approach to app development. Model-driven apps focus on data quality and reporting, rather than the user experience, and generate user interfaces based on the underlying data model, making them suitable for complex business processes and scenarios. Model-driven apps are highly structured applications.
- **Portal apps and website experiences:** Bring together functionality from both canvas and model-driven apps. Websites built by using *Power Pages* (the Power Platform tool used to create the website or portal where these apps run) are often data-driven, not highly graphical or interactive. The main data source for the portal is Microsoft Dataverse. The portal and website experiences created with Power Pages heavily rely on Power BI (discussed in Part 3) for customizable and interactive reporting. To find out more about using Power Pages, see Chapter 8.

REMEMBER

When you combine the development tools offered in Power Apps with the capabilities embedded within Power Pages (covered in Chapter 8), you get a comprehensive platform that can address a wide range of business challenges. Before Microsoft Power Platform, developers formerly had to have extensive programming experience to create each of the components. Now, the time from planning to delivery is dramatically cut, and you can focus on how you want to use the data you have and what you want the user experience to be.

Reality check: Some coding required

Users can develop sophisticated applications by using the Microsoft Power Apps, but when push comes to shove, you do need to be able to enter some underlying code. Of course, you can drag and drop objects onto a canvas or connect a data source to an app without writing any code. But when you want to configure a behavior to work a certain way, you might require JavaScript to mimic the behavior. Or perhaps if you're using Power BI (which is an enterprise business intelligence solution) inside your application to display information a certain way, you need to use the Data Analysis Expressions language, known as DAX, to calculate and present a complex formula.

REMEMBER

Power Apps — and, for that matter, Power Platform — doesn't eliminate the need for coding. Creating certain app behaviors requires some coding sophistication, especially when integrating with other services or scaling applications. You need to have basic knowledge of the functional expression language called Power Fx when you work with Power Apps. Power Fx works a bit differently than your traditional C# language. When building model-driven apps, you also need to know JavaScript to control aesthetic behaviors.

WARNING

The freemium version of Power Apps that comes included in a Microsoft 365 subscription has some limitations. It doesn't, for example, allow you to use premium data connectors and provides limited data storage. This free version of Power Apps limits you to using only connectors associated with other core Microsoft productivity and not much else. If you want the full advertised benefits of using Power Apps, you need to fork over some cash for the Premium version of Power Apps.

Despite requiring development when your application has complex needs, the low-code/no-code platform Microsoft Power Apps remains the best product in the market because it has the most data integration options. You don't have to write pages of code. Instead, you write snippets to essentially connect the dots between the application components.

Inevitably, all the platforms on the market, including Microsoft Power Apps, require some level of custom coding when you try to build features that support scalability and flexibility while also maintaining security and compliance. Make sure that the upfront development investment costs will be offset by long-term cost savings, operational efficiencies, and productivity gains, after all the integrations come together to support your business requirements.

Connecting Power Apps with data sources

Unless you create a canvas app that you want to act as a simple calculator (which doesn't require a data source to store the data), you need to connect the app to one or more data sources for it to work. You do this by adding *connectors* to bridge the gap between your app and the data that brings it to life. Each connector provides access to a single data source.

Connectors allow you to tap into an array of both online and on-premises data sources. Power Apps — and really, the entire Power Platform suite — includes hundreds of data connectors. Figure 4-1 shows a list of connector options that includes SharePoint, SQL Server, Salesforce, and (of course) Dynamics 365.

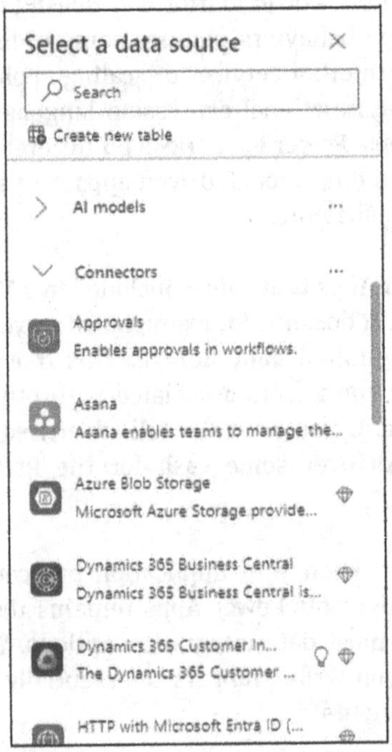

FIGURE 4-1: Some connector options in a canvas app.

You can also start building your app by using the Power Apps Start with Data interface, which allows you to select from five options:

- Create with SharePoint list
- Create with Excel or .CSV file
- Start with a blank table
- Select an existing table
- Select external data

If you don't have a data source and don't know what it should include, you can use the integrated Copilot capabilities by clicking the Start with Copilot button, shown in Figure 4-2. Clicking this button accesses Microsoft's generative AI capability to develop Dataverse tables and canvas-based apps.

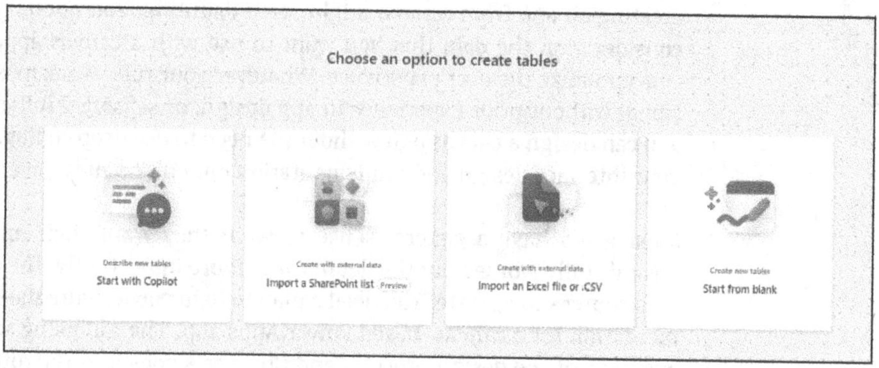

FIGURE 4-2: Select a Microsoft data source or use Copilot to create a new data source.

REMEMBER

Model-driven apps rely on Dataverse exclusively. I discuss Dataverse in Chapter 3. When you need to reference connectors, work with a canvas app, as described in this chapter and Chapter 5.

Connecting data to actions

Connectors do much more than merely present data within your app; they also provide an *action conduit*, meaning a way to invoke a trigger inside your app. Table 4-1 describes the types of connectors available within Power Apps.

TABLE 4-1 Power Apps Connector Types

Category	What It Does
Data connectors	Facilitate data retrieval, manipulation, and storage. Example connectors include SQL Server, Dataverse, Excel, and SharePoint.
Actions connectors	Allow for the execution of tasks, operations, and activities. Example connectors include Microsoft 365 Outlook for e-mails, X for social media tweets, and Dynamics 365 for records creation.
Hybrid connectors	Combine capabilities of both data and action connectors. Examples include the use of Azure Blob Storage, Google Drive, Dropbox, and OneDrive, which all allow for both data and action-oriented connectivity.

Designing a Canvas App

If you're new to creating canvas-based apps through Power Apps, the process of creating an app from scratch might seem daunting. You not only need to take into consideration the data that you want to use with a canvas app, you also have to conceptualize the user experience. Whatever your role — business user, IT professional without prior experience in app design, or seasoned full-stack developer — you can design a canvas app without the need to use deep coding. But you may find your interface design and implementation options a smidge overwhelming.

Most users have a general sense of what they want their app to do, but they haven't fully worked out the details and, more importantly, the way they want the data sources to operate. You need a plan to help you execute the design and implementation for a canvas-based Power Apps app. The following sections provide an overview of the design process, and Chapter 5 goes into the nitty gritty details of designing the app.

Identifying a business need

Planning is the most critical phase of developing a canvas-based app because in this phase, you create a framework for your entire application development project. During the planning stage, you need to identify

- The problem the app aims to solve
- Who will use the app
- What do you want the app to do

Like writing the main idea for a paragraph in a school essay, articulate in one or two sentences what the problem is and how the app can help solve the issue. In other words, a well-defined problem statement guides the design process, preventing *scope creep* (adding too many bells and whistles) and ensuring the app remains practical (rather than being overcomplicated).

Planning your canvas app involves

- **Exploring the app theme:** From a business perspective, the overall purpose and goals of the app.
- **Knowing business processes:** You need comprehensive knowledge and data about the processes that you aim to address with your app.
- **Identifying your data source:** You can find this data housed in existing databases, external services, or cloud storage solutions.
- **Anticipating automation:** When you know what you need and what you're working with, you can then assess the level of automation appropriate for your app.
- **Conceptualizing the user experience:** Know how your data sources work and how the data will flow through the app, from input to output, including data entry and the results that you expect to see when querying.

For an example where Microsoft essentially builds the app for you without requiring much effort on your part, look at a SharePoint List. Follow these steps to create an app from a SharePoint List:

1. **Open a SharePoint List and click Integrate.**
2. **In the menu that opens, make a selection.**

   You have three options: Power Apps, Power Automate, and Power BI. For example, if someone in your organization creates a SharePoint List and then decides they want to make it an app, they can make that change here.
3. **Select Create an App.**

   A three-page canvas app is created — without an ounce of coding from you.

The app's flow is simple: (a) display the data in list format, (b) add data, (c) review the data details, and (d) edit the data.

Each page within the app incorporates other actions by using a combination of icon and navigation components, such as Back, Forward, Delete, and Refresh buttons in the navigation bar. You can see an app produced from a SharePoint List in Figure 4-3, depicting an activity tracker. The app captures relevant travel data for an employee, including trip purpose, travel data (to/from), dates of travel, length of travel, and accommodations required. All data from the activity tracker is saved to the SharePoint List as your data source.

TIP

You might wonder, "Why do I even need Power Apps if I can create a fully built Power Apps app by using SharePoint?" Well, the answer is simple — data sources and added complexity:

- **Data:** A SharePoint List is just one type of data source from which you can create an app.
- **Complexity:** The app created using SharePoint is fairly simplistic. Most organizations require far more customization for their data entry needs than a fill-in-the-blank Web-form-based experience (which is what you get when you use the built-in Power App integration.

Connecting to necessary data

In the example I use in the preceding section, the main ingredient of the app, the data source, was a SharePoint List. For the most part, Power Apps applications have to use external information stored in a data source. Beyond the SharePoint List, you might find relevant data in sources such as Excel, OneDrive, or using the connectors to establish connections between relational databases or enterprise applications. (You can read about connectors in the section "Connecting Power Apps to data," earlier in this chapter.)

Using a connector to create one or more connections allows for the interaction of reading and writing data in Microsoft Power Apps applications because Power Apps can present the tables from one or more applications, in one of two ways in a canvas app:

- Through a gallery, in which you can display a collection of data
- In a form for read-and-write capabilities to a data source

TECHNICAL STUFF

A special kind of data source is exclusively available to canvas apps called *a* collection. A *collection* is a data structure that's local to an app instance because the data is temporarily stored in a table and not backed by a connection to a service. Information is exclusively stored in the app, which means users can't share that information among devices.

Designing the canvas app interface

If you plan on creating a canvas app, you need to know the type of user interface (UI) you want to use. Have an idea of not only data but also the controls — specifically, the branding capabilities — available for an app. Controls include text boxes, buttons, drop-down lists, galleries, and grids to name a few examples. Furthermore, you can place objects, such as images and icons, and personalization, such as color schematics, onto the canvas. For each item placed on the canvas, you have to put logic behind the object — hence the low-code part of working in Power Apps.

Before you can customize and place an object on the interface, you need to configure the control properties. Follow these steps:

1. **From the Components pane, select the component or control that you want to configure.**

   For example, select a button, text box, or gallery.

2. **In the Properties pane that appears, modify attributes, as necessary.**

   Figure 4-3 shows a gallery's Properties pane. You can modify attributes such as Size, Color, Font, and Text Alignment to match your app's design requirements for object types such as icons, images, and controls.

3. **Select the Advanced option to open the Advanced pane.**

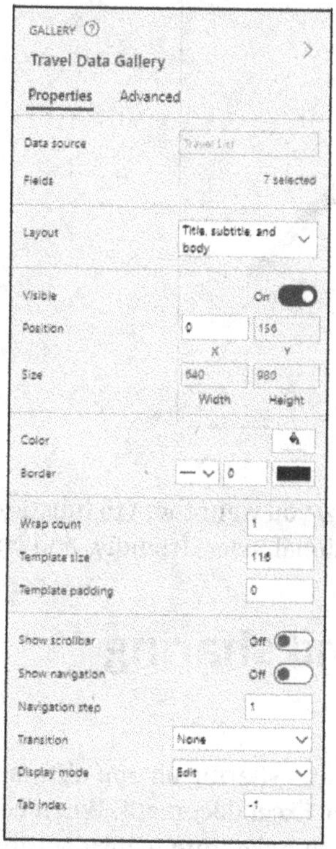

FIGURE 4-3: Configuring a canvas app's gallery properties.

4. **Add code to support the behavior properties.**

   For example, the `OnSelect` action for buttons determines what happens when the button is clicked.

   Examples of code snippets put in the `OnSelect` property include `Navigate()`, `Back()`, and `Launch()`. As seen in Figure 4-4, I've adjusted the Advanced pane for the gallery with the code for `Navigate()` in the `OnSelect` field.

TIP

Using Power Fx formulas in the Formula bar can help you dynamically adjust properties based on the interaction requirements or data changes. One such example involves applying the property of `Visible` to a control, to show or hide a control based on specific conditions.

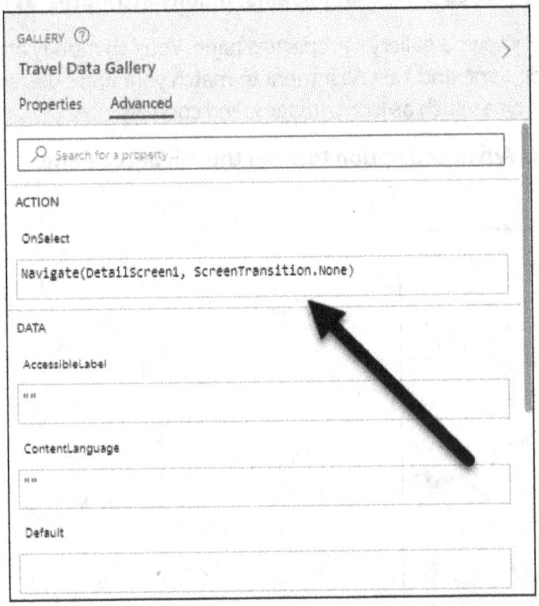

FIGURE 4-4: Configuring Advanced properties to support an action associated with a button.

REMEMBER

Mastering the use of controls and how you want them to function ensures that you can design a canvas app that's functional, user-friendly, and visually appealing.

Saving your work and sharing your canvas app

The process of saving your changes and sharing an app differs significantly from saving and sharing a typical Word or Excel document. When collaborating with a team on app creation, you need to take into consideration issues such as managing version control, data access, and permissions. As part of your planning and design process, carefully consider how you plan to save and share the app, particularly when you have multiple developers involved. If each developer works on the app in their own environment and then attempts to merge their work, you likely run into differences in configuration and data settings.

When you save your changes to a canvas app, the changes are initially published only for you, the app developer, or you and those who have Edit permissions. If you are not assigned the necessary permissions as the Editor of the app, you don't see the changes instantaneously. In that case, to fully see your app changes, select Publish in the toolbar.

When you save your changes to a canvas app, the changes are initially published only for you, the app developer, or you and those who have Edit permissions. If you don't have the requisite permissions — meaning you lack the necessary rights to publish the app or access all features in the environment — you don't see the changes immediately. For example, if you're a contributor to the design and development of an app, but you're not the person who initially configured the app environment, you may not have those publishing rights. If AutoSave is enabled, it applies to saving changes that you make to the app while you're developing it; but that doesn't mean that others can automatically see those changes unless you publish them.

You can make saving a manual or automatic process. You have the following save options available within Power Apps:

- **Save button:** To save manually, select the Save button. Selecting this button applies any unsaved changes.
- **Save drop-down list:** Open this list to choose from the following options:
  - *Save with Version Notes:* Add some historical context to changes by selecting this option and entering a description so that you can add notes about what has changed in this version.
  - *Save As:* If you want to make an exact copy of the app, click Save As. You can change the name of the app to something different from the original app.
  - *Download a Copy:* Export your current application to your Desktop so that, if you want to create a new app in another Power App environment, you can then import the app later.
- **Publish button:** When you're ready to publish the app for the world to see, select the Publish button to the right of the Save button.

If you set up AutoSave, Power Apps stores your changes every two minutes. You may not want to use AutoSave in a few situations, such as when changes require approval, you have to test your changes in a production environment before saving, or you want to have a clear path to follow if you want to retrace versions of the app. To enable AutoSave, follow these steps:

1. **From the Canvas Apps toolbar, select Settings.**

   The Settings window appears.

2. **Click the General tab to open it.**
3. **Turn the AutoSave option on or off by moving the switch.**

REMEMBER

Even though you have an app saved automatically, the app isn't published to all users until you click Publish.

Creating an app history

Each time you save a new version of the application, Power Apps then creates an entry in the history. This allows you to track changes over time.

If you want to add some historical context to changes, you can also open the drop-down list by selecting the Disk icon in the toolbar and then selecting Save with Version Notes. An Add Version Notes window appears, where you can add notes about what changes you made in the current app version. If you select the Download a Copy option, you can import and export your app to other Power Apps instances.

WARNING

Don't use AutoSave in Power Apps when you need to control the release of changes so that you don't accidentally deploy untested updates to end users. Also, avoid the use of AutoSave if someone needs to review or approve changes because you can inadvertently bypass a formal validation process.

Reviewing app versions

You can review your app history and the changes among app versions by going to the App Details from the Maker Portal Homepage. To access app details, follow these steps:

1. **Locate your app on the homepage of Maker Portal under the apps list, and then select the three ellipses next to the app name.**

   A drop-down menu opens.

2. **Select Details from the drop-down list.**

   The Details Window opens.

3. **Select the Versions tab (shown in Figure 4-5).**

   A list of app versions appears. The latest version of the app appears at the top of the list and hasn't been published yet. This version is accessible only to those who have Edit Access. On the other hand, all users can access the Live version, as displayed in the Published column.

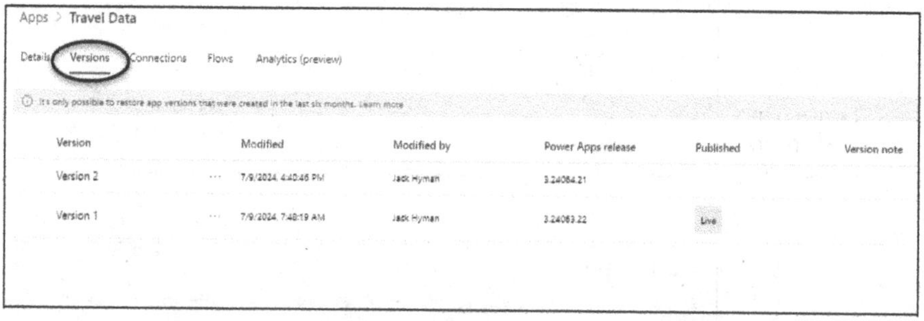

FIGURE 4-5: An application's save history in the Versions tab.

TIP

End users can't view your changes until you save your work and explicitly publish the app. If you don't publish the latest version of your app, no one can see that version — they still can only access the version you most recently published.

Sharing and distributing your canvas app

To share and distribute your canvas-based app, you need to know the users who will be accessing the app by using Power Apps. You effectively have two options when saving an app:

» **Share your application with targeted users.** From the Makers Portal homepage, click the ellipsis next to the app and select Share ⇨ Share from the pop-up menu that opens (as shown in Figure 4-6).

  The Share pop-up window appears (see Figure 4-7):

  - Enter the group (or specific user) that you want to add in the Enter a Name, Email Address, or Everyone text box.
  - Personalize the invitation to the app by entering your message in the Email Message text box.
  - If you want to make a user a co-owner, select the Co-Owner check box, which means that you give the user Edit access.
  - Select the level of data permission the group or user gets for the app.

  After you fill out all the items on the form, click Share to share your app with the groups and users you specified.

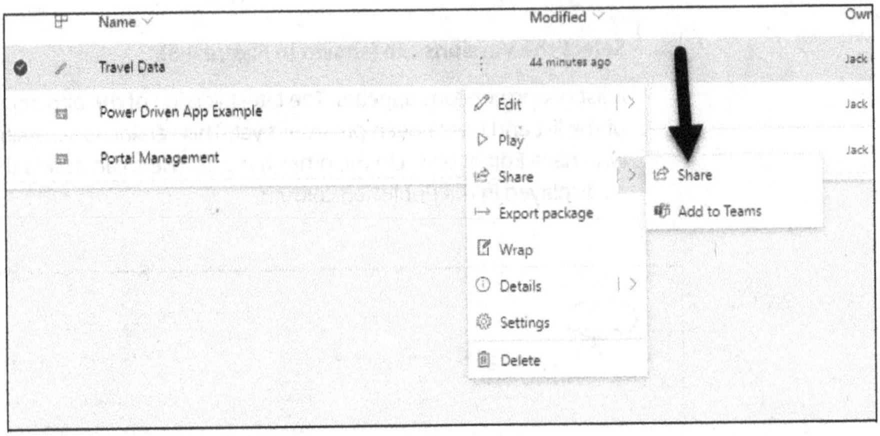

FIGURE 4-6: The menu to share an application.

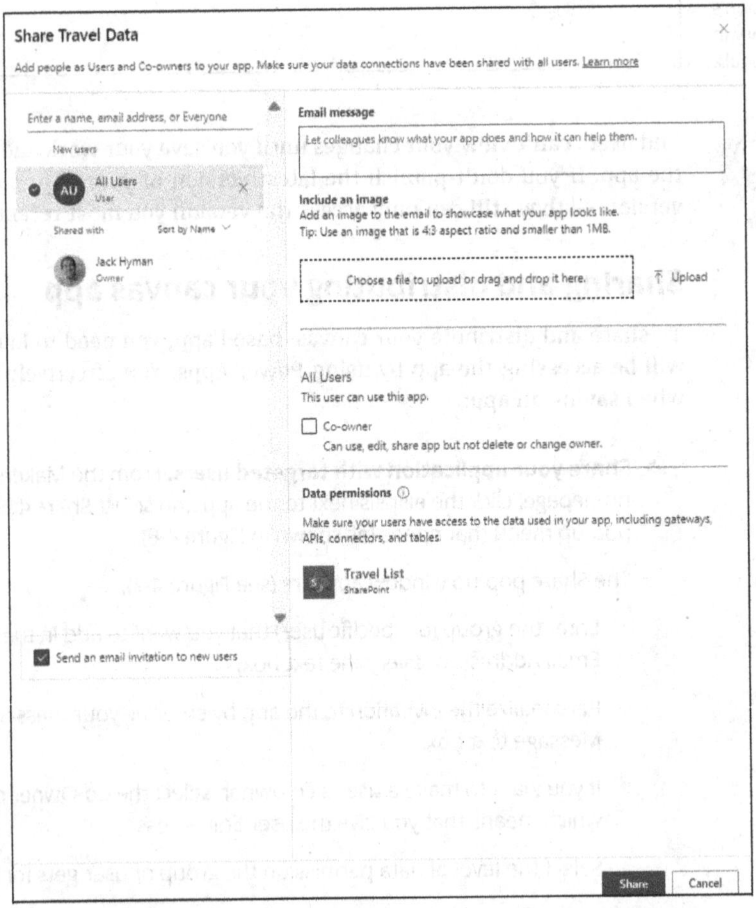

FIGURE 4-7: Selecting which users gain access to a canvas app.

- **Distribute the apps through Microsoft Teams.** Publish your app directly to your organization's Microsoft Teams tenant (making it available across all teams and channels) or to a specific team or channel (limiting it to a single site or group within Teams). This option gives you some flexibility in app distribution, ensuring the right teams or the entire organization can access the app.

Putting Together a Model-Driven App

Model-driven app design, unlike that for canvas apps (which you can read about in the section "Designing a Canvas App," earlier in this chapter), standardizes user experiences and squarely focuses on data. With an emphasis on data, model-driven apps allow developers to quickly create forms, views, charts, and dashboards from tables. Each table may have one or more relationships between each other, which is referred to as a 1:1, 1:M, or M:M relationship:

- **1:1 (one-to-one):** Each record in one table corresponds to a single record entry in another table.
- **1:M (one-to-many):** A single record in one table can be associated with one or more records in another table, but each of those records relates to only one record in the first table. For example, the one state of Virginia can be associated with many cities, including Arlington, Alexandria, and Fairfax.
- **M:M (many-to-many):** Many records in one table can be related to many records in another table, and vice versa. You typically manage an M:M relationship by using a junction table, which holds foreign keys from both related tables, such as a Books and Authors scenario, where an author can write many books, and each book may have many authors.

With canvas apps, a single form is typically based on one data source (or table), although you can manually integrate data from multiple tables. In contrast, model-driven apps support forms that can display and interact with data from multiple related tables, making it easier to handle complex relationships between data. For example, each drop-down menu (also referred to as a *lookup*) pulls data from a single table. A model-driven app form could have many lookups, which means the main form incorporates as many tables as there are lookups.

REMEMBER

You must be consistent and uniform when designing your model-driven apps based on the data in your tables. Unlike a canvas app, where the user interface starts blank and you can paint it in an unlimited number of ways, a model-driven app's user interface is somewhat limited by the components available in the drag-and-drop app designer. Each component is typically tied to a field or relationship within your data tables.

Unlike canvas apps, model-driven apps are suitable for situations that must follow a logical order of progression when capturing data. For instance, managing intricate processes, such as sales pipeline management, employee onboarding, personnel records, performance management, training and certification, and benefits management all tie together by using a common set of variables — specifically, an employee's name and ID. Each form within the model-driven app needs to capture a very specific set of data, following a logical progression.

Your classic sales lead capture provides a great example:

> **Step 1:** Your first form might involve identifying your customer and their general attributes.
>
> **Step 2:** Figures out what the customer wants to acquire (the *lead*).
>
> **Step 3:** Captures the data related to closing the deal.
>
> **Step 4:** May relate to customer maintenance and general notes.

So the lead has four progressive steps, and you could make each one of them a separate form (or tab) in a model-driven app. The data is highly structured. In comparison, a canvas app requires many screens to set up that kind of data collection structure. You have to independently design each screen. But the design of the model-driven app makes data collection systematic.

With model-driven apps, all roads lead back to Dataverse. (Flip to Chapter 3 for a rundown of Dataverse.) Without a robust data model, a model-driven app has essentially no functionality. The data model defines the structure and relationship across all features, including complex processes, workflows, and interactions among data elements.

Benefits of model-driven apps

Model-driven apps offer several benefits compared to canvas apps. A model-driven app offers a predefined user interface; as the developer, you simply determine where to place the components within the app's framework. This structured approach has notable advantages, including a faster build process because model-driven apps feature-rich, component-focused low-code/no-code components that the developer sets up on the form after they configure the data model and relationships. If you get your model right, you can build a model-driven app much more easily than you can a canvas-based design. But canvas app development does give you complete control over the app layout.

REMEMBER

If you're looking for guaranteed accessibility and compliance, then your best bet is to go with a model-driven application. Model-driven apps ensure a consistent user interface across various devices. The application is automatically accessible and responsive for virtually any device a user might have (well, maybe not that smartwatch — but certainly a desktop, laptop, smartphone, or tablet). Because you can create a uniform user experience, you have to build the app only once, and regardless of the device used, the user has the same experience.

Furthermore, migrating apps between development, test, and production environments is streamlined by using *solutions*, ways to package all Power App components, (which I talk about in the section "Managing and Deploying Solutions," later in this chapter), enhancing the efficiency and manageability of the development process. These features make model-driven apps a powerful choice if you want efficient, consistent, and scalable application development.

Defining the model-driven app lifecycle

Model-driven apps are a bit easier to create than canvas apps (because you don't need to bother with an interface), but don't take the build process lightly. The data model drives all facets of the process, from requirements elicitation to deployment. As with canvas apps, you have to consider a defined lifecycle when you develop a model-driven application. First, you model and identify your data and processes, and then you can build and deploy the app. Until you complete the due diligence for data and process evaluation, you can't really go to market with a model-driven app.

Consider your data model the foundational asset to building your app; it contains the core business logic and processes. During the requirements and data modeling phase, you define the data structure to ensure Dataverse has the ability to efficiently store, retrieve, and manipulate essential information. You need to create entities, fields, and relationships that reflect the business requirements and processes that you and the business determine are necessary as part of the data collection. Without proper data modeling, your app will likely lack stability and capacity to operate adequately.

Here are the basic steps of the model-driven app lifecycle:

1. **Define your business processes.**

   Data modeling ultimately drives business processes. Without the data, you can't build the interfaces, workflows, rules, and automation that guide how the model driven app captures, stores, and retrieves the data. For example, if you intend to use Power Automate within your model-driven app, you plan for it during this phase because most business processes that you might automate rely on data elements to trigger their corresponding workflow activity. Furthermore, if you need to make your application highly secure, you must identify which forms and views require data integrity enforcement in this phase.

2. **Compose the app.**

   After you define the data and process components, you can compose the app by bringing together the visual and functional elements. Visual elements include the form fields placed on the form, images stored as objects, and dashboards generated from the data sources. Processes are then put in place to help the user enter data based on conditional events or triggers.

3. **Configure security roles.**

   Data security ensures that only certain users have access to specific forms, views, and reports in a model-driven app.

   First, configure security in Microsoft Entra (see Chapter 7 for more about Entra and permissions), where you can properly establish users and groups. Then comes the hard part: creating the security profiles for your application. Follow these general steps:

   a. *Create these profiles within Microsoft Dynamics 365.*

      Flip to Chapters 6 and 7 for a broader discussion of Dynamics 365 usage within model-driven apps.

   b. *After you establish the security profiles, assign users to each profile.*

      You need to assign users for both your Dataverse data source and your application (which I discuss in further detail in Chapter 7).

   Only after you configure all security capabilities can you then assign roles and responsibilities properly at the interface level of an application.

4. **Share the app.**

   Sharing a model-driven app is virtually identical to sharing a canvas app, at least when it comes to sharing the app in Teams. If you want to distribute the app to specific end users or groups, select Share ➪ Share from the Maker Portal. In the Share page that appears, explicitly call out the users or groups that you want to gain access to the application and based on what security role.

   Microsoft offers three model-driven app user groups automatically: Basic Users, System Customizers, and System Administrators. You can assign the user to one of these roles or to your own self-created user group.

WARNING

To use model-driven apps, a user needs to be licensed to use Power Apps. If the user can't access Dataverse, they simply can't use the app. Each user, or user within a group, must also be explicitly tied to a user role (which is a way to enforce license management).

Knowing model-driven app terminology

You need to understand some big concepts to really see how model-driven apps work. If you talk to any developer about model-driven apps, the discussion often focuses on data rather than user interface (UI) concepts. Although some of the data-related concepts in Table 4-2 spill over into canvas apps, others are exclusive to model-driven apps because they specifically relate to *data modeling* (meaning how data is structured in the app).

TABLE 4-2 Key Model-Driven App Concepts

Concept	What It Means
Business process flows	Provide a means to guide users through a defined set of steps when entering data into forms. Ensure that users follow the same steps each time they interact with a particular business process, helping to maintain consistency and efficiency in data entry and workflow operations.
Business rules	Allow for the automation of business logic within a model-driven app. Apply logic directly within forms and data to ensure consistency.
Charts	Created using tables from Microsoft Dataverse, which can leverage data connections, including Microsoft Graph (which is available for every Dataverse entity, but not Power BI directly). Provide visual representations of data, typically using one to three variables that you can embed in forms and dashboards. Chart formats include bar, line, pie, and more.
Dashboards	Aggregate multiple views, charts, and other visual elements into a single interface.
Embedded Power BI	Integrate interactive reports and dashboards directly into Power Apps applications. Use Embedded Power BI rather than Dataverse charts and dashboards, if you need advanced features that go beyond what Dataverse charting features offer.
Relationships	Connect tables based on one or more common columns. Helps define how data in one table relates to data in another. Enable data integrity, as well as complex queries and data analysis by establishing links between different data entities.
Site maps	Define how users navigate and access different parts of the app. The site map determines the availability and organization of tables, forms, views, and other components, ensuring that users can efficiently access the appropriate areas of the app.
Solutions	Package all the components of a model-driven app together for distribution. Might include tables, forms, views, and business logic. Used for deploying, managing, and distributing apps and customizations across different environments.
Tables	Tables in Microsoft Dataverse serve as primary data storage, similar to database tables available through Azure SQL or Access. They store data in rows and columns, representing specific entities, and provide the foundation for app functionality by enabling efficient data organization, access, manipulation, and presentation through forms, views, and business processes.
Views	Predefined reports displaying sets of data from tables in a structured, tabular format. These reports allow users to view specific subsets of data based on predefined criteria or filters, making it easier to focus on relevant information within a larger dataset.

Collectively, each component of a model-driven app is an essential element of the final application, much like individual puzzle pieces that fit together seamlessly. Each of the elements listed in Table 4-2 contribute to a specific aspect of the app's functionality and user experience.

Managing and Deploying Solutions

You need to manage and deploy *solutions*, your bundling of all components within an app package, including the views, forms, reports, security, and tables (literally everything), for both canvas and model-driven apps by creating different versions of the app to ensure the consistency, reliability, and scalability of applications while the apps mature through the development lifecycle. A solution allows you to compile all the parts of an application and package them reliably so that you can repurpose the application in multiple hosting environments without having to recreate the wheel, so to speak.

To package a solution for deployment by bundling together components such as forms, views, entities, charts, and workflow, follow these steps:

1. **In the Maker Portal, choose Solutions ⇨ New Solution.**

   The New Solutions window appears on the right-hand side of the portal.
2. **Enter the Solution Name and a friendly Display Name in the appropriate text boxes.**
3. **Select the *publisher* (how all components follow a specific naming convention) that you want to use to build out the solution from the Publisher drop-down list.**

   For example, if you set your publisher to "PPFD", each item will have a naming convention that starts with PPFD_<name of field> or PPFD_<name of table>.
4. **(Optional) If you need to create a new publisher, select the New Publisher button.**
5. **In the pan that appears, fill in the Display Name, Name, Description, and Prefix text boxes.**

   The *Prefix* refers to the consistent naming convention for the publisher.

   You can see how every control in your app will appear.
6. **Click Save.**

   After you create the new publisher, select the publisher you created from the Publisher drop-down list.
7. **Enter the version of the app based on the Solutions page.**

8. **After you fill out all the fields, click Create.**

   You can begin adding each component to your app.

Managed and unmanaged solutions

As a pre requisite for both canvas and model-driven app development, be aware of the difference between a managed solution and an unmanaged solution.

To see whether your application is managed or unmanaged, in the Maker Portal, the directory containing your apps allows you to select Unmanaged, Managed, or All to see the selected type of apps in the table. Figure 4-8 shows a table of unmanaged apps.

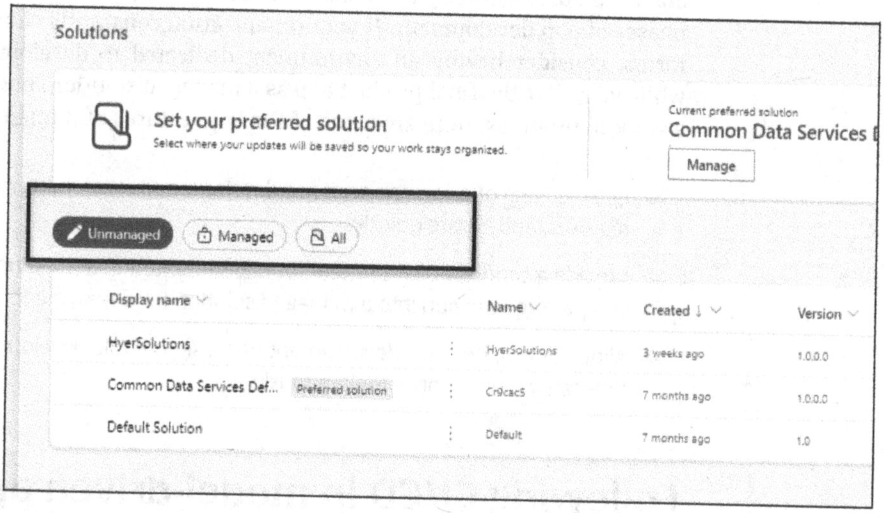

FIGURE 4-8: A table of unmanaged apps.

REMEMBER

Use an unmanaged solution only if you want to leverage a source control system, enabling version tracking and rollback capabilities. After you complete development and testing, only then convert the unmanaged solution into a managed solution for production deployment.

Managing a managed solution

Managed solutions are packaged and locked versions of application components that developers use primarily to distribute applications to end users and customers. A managed solution ensures that users can't modify the components within the package, maintaining the app's integrity and consistency, as well as preventing unauthorized changes.

TIP

If you intend to distribute the application that you build to a platform such as the Microsoft Marketplace, convert your work product to a managed solution so that no one can tinker with the code base except the originating developers and designers.

Managed solutions work best in production environments in which you must have app stability because managed solutions ensure the app deploys only the intended functionality and configurations, reducing the risk of errors and inconsistencies.

Letting things go with unmanaged solutions

Unmanaged solutions are editable, customizable app packages that incorporate all the components that you create within a Power Apps app. The unmanaged solution offers more flexibility than managed solutions (see the preceding section), and developers typically use these solutions during the development and testing phases of app development. If your organization constantly changes features and forms, consider having an environment dedicated to development and testing while you offer the final product app as a managed solution, not intertwined with a work in progress. Here are some of the key features of unmanaged solutions:

- » Allow editing of all components, so developers can make changes, test new features, and iterate quickly.
- » Provide a sandbox environment for experimentation and refinement before you package the app into a managed solution for deployment.
- » Allow for collaborative development because multiple developers can work on different components simultaneously.

Following CI/CD in model-driven apps

To efficiently and reliably develop apps across the Power Apps platform, you must implement practices that support continuous integration (CI) and continuous deployment (CD), also referred to as CI/CD:

- » **CI:** Involves regularly integrating developers' changes into a shared repository, such as GitHub or Azure DevOps, where automated builds and tests by developers can quickly lead to identifying and fixing issues.
- » **CD:** Takes the CI process one step further by automatically deploying tested changes to production environments, ensuring that you apply updates consistently across stages in the application lifecycle. (See the section "Defining the model-driven app lifecycle," earlier in this chapter.)

When you use pipelines within Power Platform, you streamline the process of deploying solutions and configurations to different environments. A pipeline helps automate the transfer of components, such as *connections* (links to external data sources), *connection references* (preconfigured links to specific external services that apps rely on), and *environment variables* (settings that differ between environments, such as URLs or credentials). These components are bundled into a purpose-built package, called a *pipeline*, ensuring that those components are properly configured and deployed in the target environment, such as development, testing, or production.

ON THE WEB

Some developers create a single application and let it run its course. However, enterprise customers can't afford to take the risk of building an application and leaving it unattended. An app is a dynamic asset that requires ongoing attention and maintenance. If you're building business applications, consider application lifecycle management (ALM). To get Microsoft's perspective on ALM and how to implement the full lifecycle for Power Platform, explore their best practices and tools at `http://learn.microsoft.com/power-platform/alm`.

IN THIS CHAPTER

» Determining what you want your canvas app to do

» Designing a basic canvas app

» Configuring the screens and controls of a canvas app

» Integrating navigation into a canvas app

» Building a sample app

Chapter 5

Personalizing and Creating Canvas Apps in Power Apps

The blank canvas is always intimidating for the artist. Although the artist's ideas can run wild, eventually, that artist pulls together their concept and designs a beautiful work of art. That same mentality applies to creating canvas-based apps in Power Apps. Each canvas page provides you with a blank slate that you can craft by using controls and data components. When you, as the developer, have all the controls and components in place, you then have to logically use the low-code tools available to you. In this chapter, you can explore how to design and build a simple canvas app from start to finish.

Building the Canvas App Foundation

Canvas apps are one of two core app options available to users of Microsoft Power Apps. (The other option is model-driven apps, which you can read about in Chapters 6 and 7.) By using Power Apps, developers can create custom applications through a drag-and-drop interface without the need for extensive coding knowledge. You complete Power Apps app configurations primarily by modifying control properties and using formulas to business processing logic. Power Apps has its own low-code programming language called *Power Fx.*

Power Fx is specifically designed to help you create custom applications through a formula-based approach. You don't need to create hundreds of pages of code just to make a single function operate. Similar to Microsoft Excel, Power Fx uses an expression language to define logic, manipulate data, and control app behavior. You can use operations such as mathematical calculations, text manipulation, data filtering, and conditional logic. You likely have to apply some aspect of Power Fx to each control and component that you use in your app, whether to call out how you want the app to display data or how to derive a calculation if the user selects a button.

TECHNICAL STUFF

Don't get Power Fx confused with Data Analysis Expressions (DAX), a programming language used for data modeling and analytics. By using DAX, you can create calculated columns, measures, and custom aggregations within data models through *Power BI* (which is Microsoft's enterprise business intelligence solution; I talk more about Power BI in Chapter 9). You use Power Fx to define Powers Apps app behavior, manipulate data, and control the user interface through formulas.

ON THE WEB

To access a list of all Power Fx functions, go to `http://learn.microsoft.com` and enter **Power Fx formulas** in the Search text box.

Starting your canvas journey

Microsoft has more than a few URLs that can help you along your Microsoft Power Platform journey. For Power Apps, Microsoft has a couple of specific addresses (shown in Table 5-1) that offer users access to app creation, management, and administration tools. To access the tools, you must first log in to Power Platform.

The Power Studio offers a pretty complex interface full of features. Figure 5-1 shows the Power Studio interface, which includes all of the following features (numbered from 1 to 11 in the figure):

- **Toolbar (1):** Presents a different set of commands based on the control that you select within the canvas app design area.

TABLE 5-1 Key Microsoft Power Apps Web Pages

Web Page	URL	Purpose
Maker Portal (also known as Power App Studio)	`http://make.powerapps.com`	Manage all aspects of canvas and model-driven apps, as well as solutions. Additionally, create Dataverse (formerly Common Data Service) tables and AI components.
Power Apps Canvas App Creation Portal	`http://create.powerapps.com`	An older version of the Power App Studio, focused on canvas app development, with limited functionality to edit and build your specific applications. By early 2025, Microsoft is moving away from this version of the Studio experience and merging it with the Maker Portal.

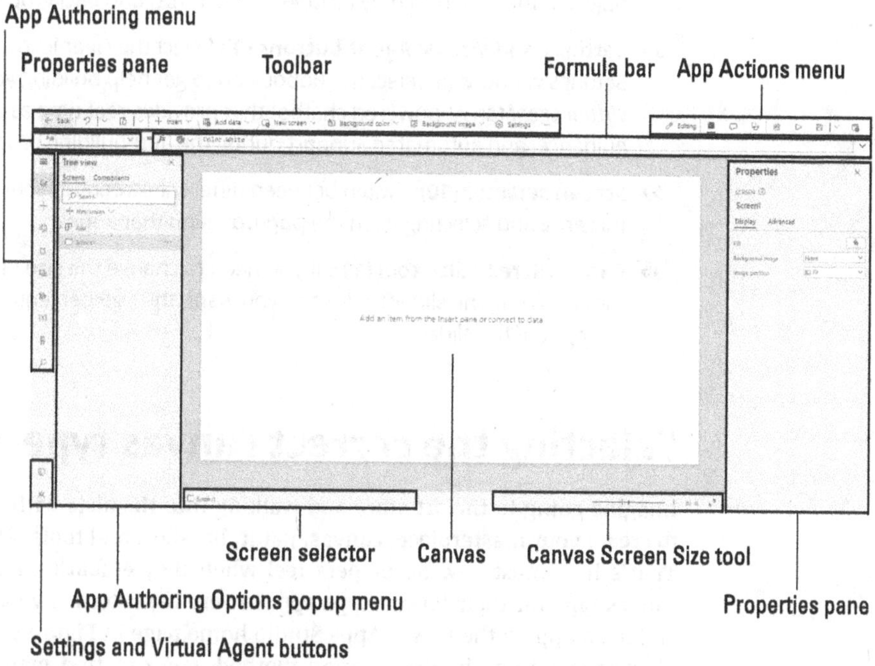

FIGURE 5-1: All the parts of the Power Studio interface.

- **App Actions menu (2):** Rename, share, run the app checker on, add comments to, preview, save, or publish your app.
- **Properties pane (3):** A list of properties that you can adjust for the selected object control.
- **Formula bar (4):** Where you compose or edit a formula for the selected property, applying one or more functions.
- **App Authoring menu (5):** Click the *hamburger menu* (the three horizontal lines that expand the left pane) to open the navigation panel. From this panel,

you can access various options, such as switching between different data sources, navigating to screens, and inserting new elements (such as controls, media, and data connections) into your app.

- **App Authoring Options pop-up window (6):** Allows you to apply relevant options to the components and structure of an app. (Figure 5-1 shows the options pane open in Tree View, which is a hierarchical structure of your screens, controls, data sources, components, and media included within an app.)
- **Canvas (7):** Where you place all the objects that you want to include in a canvas app, creating the user interface (UI) structure.
- **Screen pane (8):** Allows you to apply specific preferences for the selected object in the UI, which may include colors, fonts, and backgrounds.
- **Settings and Virtual Agent buttons (9):** Select the Gear icon to open the App Settings window; or select the Robot icon to get help building your app from a *virtual agent* (an AI-powered chatbot that provides real-time assistance, guidance, and automated support during the app-building process).
- **Screen selector (10):** Switch between different screens in your app by clicking this area and selecting from the pop-up menu that appears.
- **Canvas Screen Size tool (11):** If you need to change the size of the canvas, click and drag the slider to the size you want; the size percentage appears to the right of the slide.

Selecting the correct canvas type

Imagine going to the art store and walking into the aisle with all the ingredients to create your masterpiece: canvas, paint, brushes, and tools. Where do you start? That's how most new developers feel when they embark on selecting the right canvas type for their Power Apps app. In very basic terms, you have four ways to create an app on the Power Apps Studio home page in Figure 5-2. When you dig a bit deeper into each app-creation method, you can find many more options to consider for each approach:

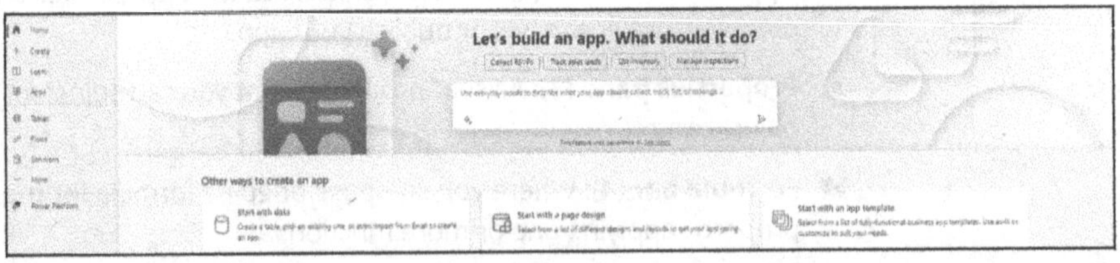

FIGURE 5-2: Start to create a canvas app on the Power Apps Studio home page.

» **Start with Data:** When you click this option, the Select an Option to Continue window appears (see Figure 5-3), offering a variety of data source-based options:

- Create with a SharePoint List
- Create with Excel or .CSV file
- Start with a Blank Table
- Select an Existing Table (which comes from Dataverse)
- Select External Data Source

These options all focus on data-driven solutions, mostly powered by using Microsoft data sources, such as Excel, SharePoint, and Dataverse. But you can integrate with other sources if you select the external data option.

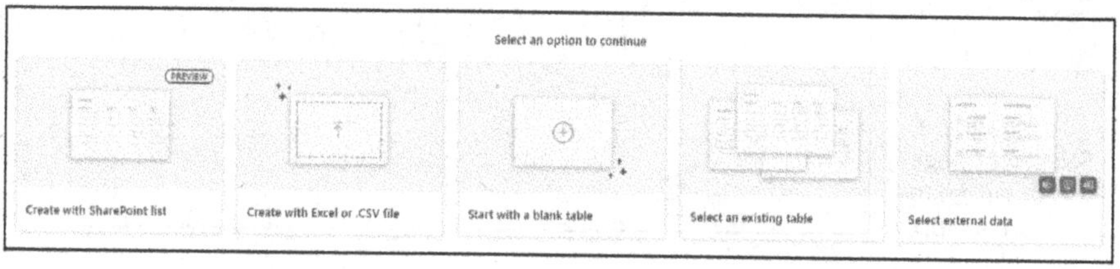

FIGURE 5-3: Options to create a canvas app when you start with data.

» **Start with a Page Design:** When you select this option, the Select a Page Design to Start Your App window opens, as shown in Figure 5-4. Some of these options are canvas-based, while others are model-driven. (Flip to Chapters 6 and 7 for discussion of creating model-driven apps.) The canvas-based options here are

- Gallery Connected to Table
- Gallery Connected to External Data
- Blank Canvas
- An Image or Figma File
- Split-Screen
- Sidebar
- Header, Main Section, Footer

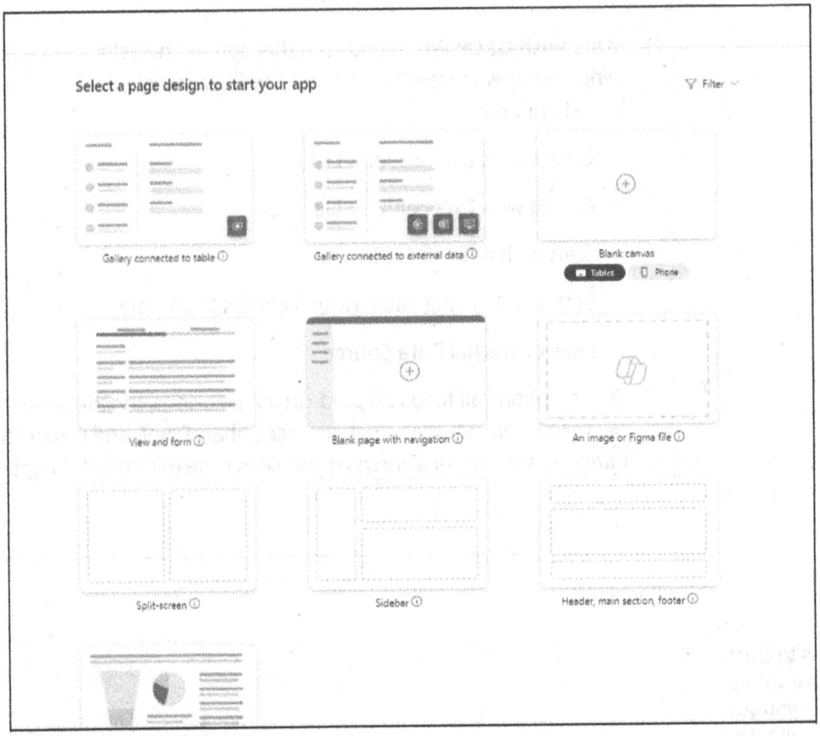

FIGURE 5-4: Selecting a page design to start an app.

- **Start with an App Template:** When you select this option, the window that appears offers to connect you to a Microsoft-based data source. Alternatively, you can use one of the pre-built solutions available. Options include Invoice Management, Onboarding, Expense Management, and Budget Tracker. Figure 5-5 shows some examples of what options you may find.

REMEMBER

- **Let's Build an App. What Should It Do?:** Use the Microsoft Copilot interface (which utilizes the large textbox at the top of the Power Apps Studio home page) through the Let's Build an App. What Should It Do? feature (refer to Figure 5-2). This section of the homepage allows you to enter a prompt to describe what you want to include in your app and Dataverse table. After you submit your prompt by clicking the Paper Airplane icon, Microsoft Copilot generates a three-page canvas app, along with a single Dataverse table. After Copilot generates the app, you can fully customize the canvas user experience, adding enhancements to suit your needs.

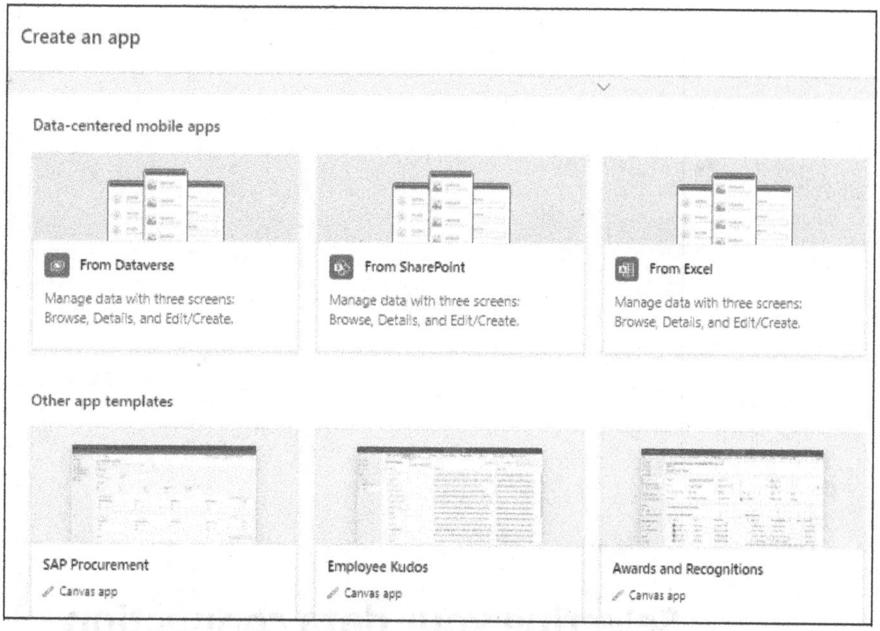

FIGURE 5-5: Start with an app template.

Touring the canvas apps toolbar

The canvas app toolbar, which appears at the top of the Power Studio interface (refer to Figure 5-1), comes jam-packed with every major feature you might need to craft the user experience that you want. The toolbar feature that folks use most often is the Insert drop-down list because it contains all the controls that you can add to a canvas app. Table 5-2 goes over each major toolbar feature, and Figure 5-6 shows an example of the canvas app toolbar, with the Insert drop-down list open.

TABLE 5-2 **Canvas Apps Toolbar Menus**

Menu	What It Does
Insert	Choose from all the controls and components that you can add to a canvas.
Add Data	Add data sources to your canvas app.
New Screen	Select the interface design that you want to use for your app.
Theme	Configure a specific color scheme for your app.
Background Color	Make the canvas a specific color — any color — by clicking the Background Color button and then picking the preferred color from the available palettes.
Background Image	Add a graphic to the background of your app (maybe for branding purposes).

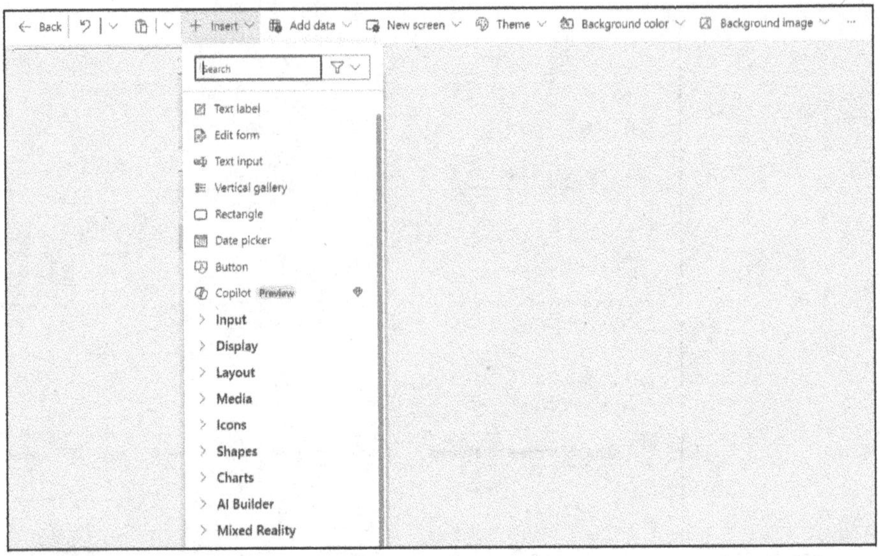

FIGURE 5-6: The canvas apps toolbar, displaying the Insert drop-down list.

Selecting your data connection

To select your canvas app's data source, either create a new canvas app or add a data source to the app you already created. (Check out the section "Selecting the correct canvas type," earlier in this chapter for details about your app creation options.) You don't have to use a Microsoft product as your data source; you can connect to virtually any source as long as the chosen data source has a way to pass the data, usually through an application programming interface (API), a set of rules and protocols that allow one or more applications to communicate and exchange data with each other.

Adding data sources to a blank canvas app

If you want to start with a blank canvas app, and then make your data connection, follow these steps:

1. **In Power Apps Studio, choose Start with a Page Design ⇨ Blank Canvas.**

   The Data window appears in the App Authoring menu.

2. **Select Add Data.**

   The Add Data drop-down list opens (see Figure 5-7).

3. **Select Connectors in the Add Data drop-down list.**

   A list of available connections (see Figure 5-8) opens.

4. **Select the connection that you want to use from the list by double clicking it in the list.**

   That connection now appears in the Data pane in your app.

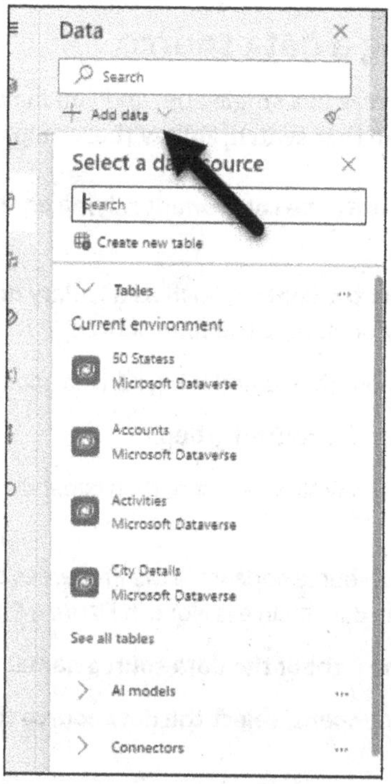

FIGURE 5-7: Adding data from the Add Data drop-down list.

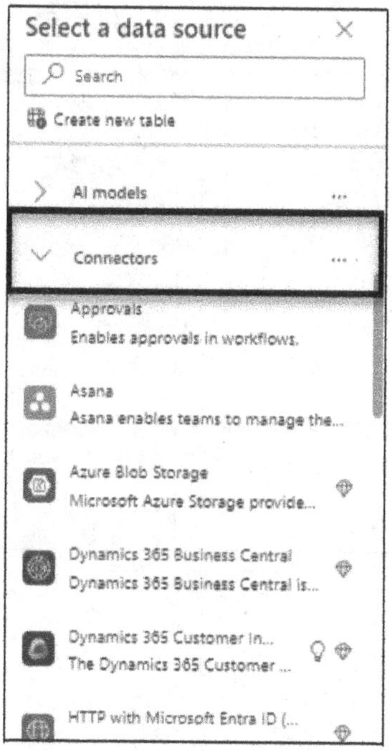

FIGURE 5-8: Select a connector from the Connectors menu.

Identifying or changing a data source

You may have multiple data sources in a single app, and you may need to swap one connection for another. To make that switch, follow these steps:

1. **In the app design view, identify the component relying on the data that you plan to add or modify.**
2. **From the Insert pane, select the control, such as a gallery or grid, for which you want to identify or change the data source.**

   I talk about the controls for both canvas and model-driven apps in Chapter 4.
3. **Click to expand the appropriate control group.**

   For my example, I add a gallery by clicking Insert, then expanding the Layout drop-down list.

   The name of the current data source appears in the Properties pane on the right side of the window. (The data source is None in Figure 5-9.)
4. **Click the down arrow to the right of the data source name.**
5. **From the pop-up menu that opens, select the data source that you want to use for this app.**

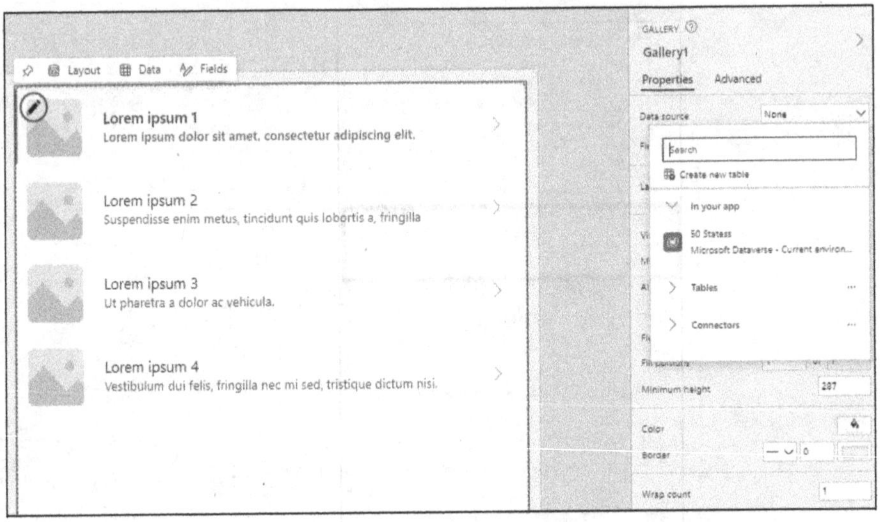

FIGURE 5-9: Changing a data source in the Properties pane.

Establishing the required screens

Before you start cranking out your app design, plan out each of your required screens. Figure out what controls and components you want the app to include on each screen. Microsoft offers pre-built canvas layouts, which you can find in the Power Studio toolbar by selecting New Screen (see Figure 5-10). In the New Screen pop-up menu, you can select from 20-plus designs.

Depending on the app layout that you choose, the screen options vary. For example, if you want to build a mobile phone app, select the appropriate template in the Start with a Page Design window; then only mobile device layout options appear (as shown in Figure 5-11). On the other hand, if you select one of the canvas or model-driven app templates specifically meant for a desktop or tablet app, you open layout options for your device of choice, not just mobile screen sizes.

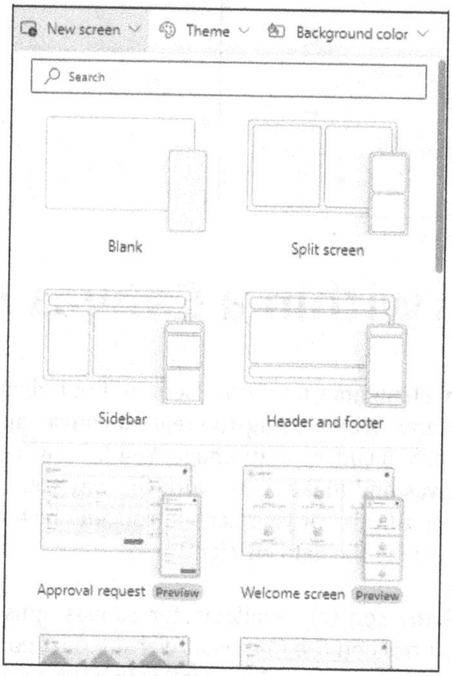

FIGURE 5-10: Desktop, tablet, and mobile screen layout options.

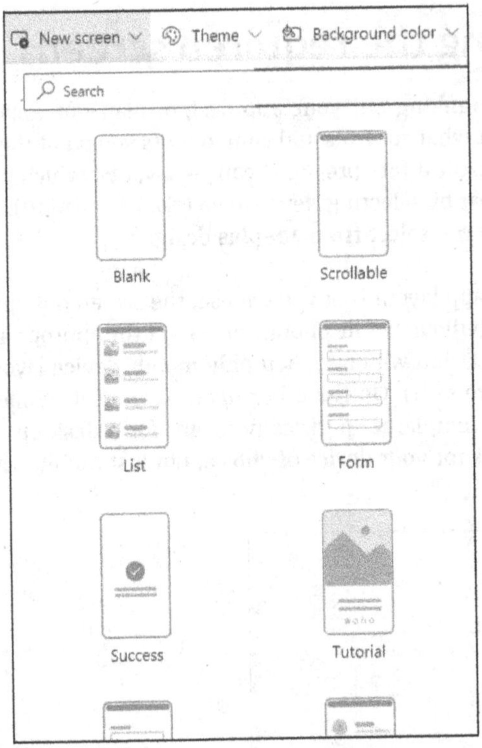

FIGURE 5-11: Mobile-specific layout options.

Controlling Basics within a Canvas App

Controls are interactive elements that allow users to input, display, and manipulate data within their app. When trying to create a canvas app, controls might include a label, a text box, a slider, or an image. You face the challenge of how to place them on the canvas and make them work the way you want them to with your data. Depending on the size of your screen, consider how many controls you use and how you can display the data efficiently.

ON THE WEB

Look for a list of all the controls available for canvas apps and the relevant properties for those controls on the Microsoft website: just go to `http://learn.microsoft.com` and enter **controls and properties in canvas apps** into the Search text box. The first article that appears should have all the info you could want on these controls.

Adding and selecting a control

To create a user experience, you need to add user controls to your canvas app. Follow these steps to add and select controls in Power Studio:

1. **From the Power Studio home screen, click the Pencil icon to the right of your app's name in the list of apps found at the bottom of the page.**

   Your app opens in the canvas.

2. **In the App Authoring menu, click the Insert tab.**

   The Insert tab looks like a plus sign (+), as shown in Figure 5-12.

3. **Choose the type of control that you want to add from the Insert pop-up menu that appears.**

   For example, you can select Button, Text Input, or Text Label.

   That control appears on your canvas.

4. **Move the control to the appropriate location.**

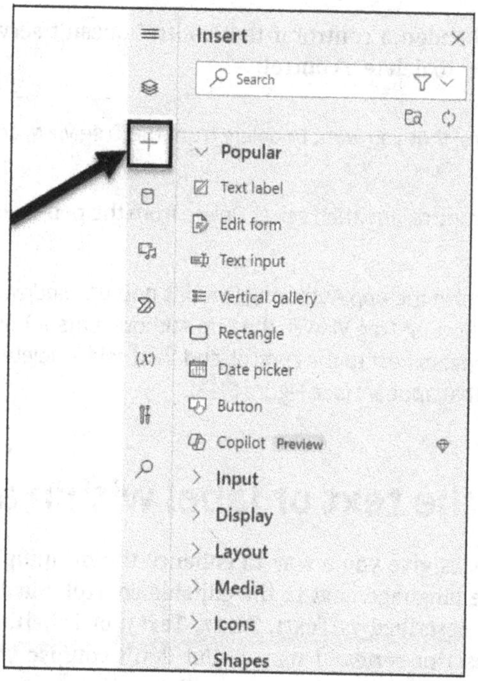

FIGURE 5-12: The canvas app authoring menu's Insert tab options.

Renaming a control

Put some thought into naming your controls. Not everything should be the out-of-the-box option. For example, if you have 100 labels, and each is called Label1, Label2, Label3, and so on, how in the world can you remember which does what?

Make your control's names descriptive. You can rename a control by following these steps:

1. **From the canvas area, select the control that you want to rename.**

   That control's Properties pane appears on the right of the window.

2. **At the top of the Properties pane, click the control's Name field.**
3. **Enter the name that you want to give the control in the Name field within the display tab of the Properties pane, and then press Enter.**

   The control now has a new name. Each control must have its own unique name.

Deleting a control

You may need to abandon a control if that control doesn't serve a purpose. You have options on how to delete a control:

- Select the control that you want to delete from the Tree view, and then press Delete.
- Right-click the control, and then select Delete from the pop-up menu that appears.
- Go to the control in the App Authoring Options pop-up window (which you can get to by selecting Tree View in the App Authoring menu), select the ellipses that appears next to the control, and then select Delete from the pop-up menu that appears (see Figure 5-13).

Changing the text or label within a control

Labels and text boxes give you a way to enhance the meaning of a data field by putting descriptive language next to the editable control. Maybe you don't want each control to be described as Text1, Text2, Text3; or Label1, Label2, Label3; or some other nondescript series of names. But don't confuse your label with the actual name of the control (see the section "Renaming a control," earlier in this chapter). This section deals with changing the text that describes the control. If you want to make your labeling conventions meaningful, follow these steps to customize the labeling schema for both text and label objects that you drag onto the canvas:

1. **On the canvas or in the Tree view of the Options pane, select the control whose text or label you want to change.**

   The Properties pane for that control appears on the right of the window.

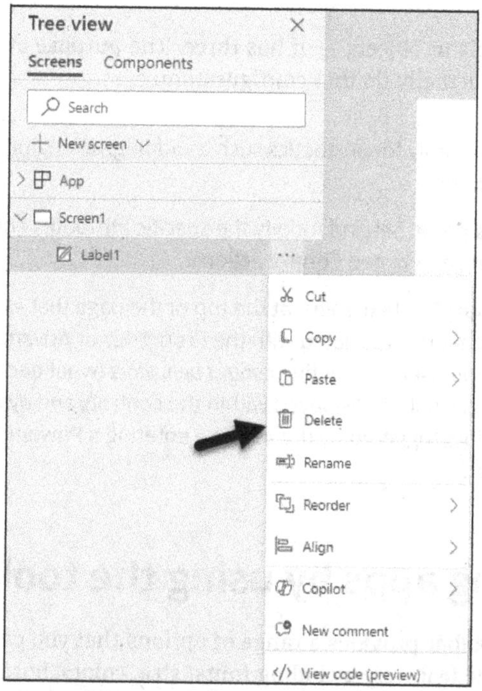

FIGURE 5-13: Deleting a control that you no longer want.

2. **Click the Text field for the property that you want to change.**

   Alternatively, you can click the Default property to set the initial value of text input fields.

3. **Enter the new text or label in the Text field.**
4. **Press Enter.**

   Alternatively, you can simply click outside the Properties pane to confirm your changes.

   Adding the text in the Text field applies the changes to the label or text box.

Managing Screens and Controls

After you place all the controls on your canvas that you want (see the section "Controlling Basics within a Canvas App," earlier in this chapter), you need to configure each control and object so that it displays data and responds to input in the way that you want it to. Power Apps doesn't have just one place where you can configure all controls or objects — it has three. The purpose of the configuration dictates where you actually do that configuration:

- **The toolbar:** Primarily for aesthetics such as adding, arranging, and styling controls in your app.
- **The Properties pane:** Set and modify the specific attributes and settings of a control, including associated Control actions.
- **The Formula bar:** The text editor at the top of the page that allows you to modify configurations associated with the Properties or Advanced pane for a particular control. Users can define *control behaviors* (what each control does), *data bindings* (how data is displayed within the control), and *dynamic properties* (specific behaviors triggered by the user) by entering a Power FX formula into the Formula bar.

Configuring apps by using the toolbar

The Power Apps toolbar provides a range of options that you can use to configure your app's aesthetic features, including fonts, size, colors, borders, and justification for a given control. You can also update these attributes in the Properties tab (see the following section) and Formula bar (discussed in the section "Applying changes with the formula bar," later in this chapter). But you're probably already familiar with the design of the toolbar, which is akin to what you see in applications such as Microsoft Word and Excel.

TIP

Design features apply to more than just text. You can also modify the canvas by applying a global color scheme by using the theme capability as well as apply a different background color besides white. If you want to integrate a background image, you can by using one of several menus found as part of the toolbar.

The right side of the toolbar also allows you to Share, Check, Comment, Play, Save, and Publish a canvas app.

Configuring apps through the Properties and Advanced panes

When you configure controls by using the Properties pane, you can customize each control's attributes and settings, both aesthetically and functionally. The Properties pane provides a detailed interface where you can modify various aspects of a control, such as the fonts, size, and alignment (similar to the toolbar, which I talk about in the preceding section). However, you can see the real richness of the Properties pane when you make changes to a control, such as name, position, data source bindings, and appearance settings. Use the Properties pane to set static properties such as text values, default selections, and visibility, as well as more dynamic attributes such as conditional and data-driven formatting behaviors.

For example, you can

- Set the Text property of a label to display specific information.
- Bind a drop-down list to a data source by configuring its Items property.
- Adjust the Visible property of a button to show or hide it based on certain conditions.

The Properties tab (see Figure 5-14) has comprehensive options that let you fine-tune your app's functionality and appearance. You can do some action-based control tuning by using features in the Advanced tab (shown in Figure 5-15).

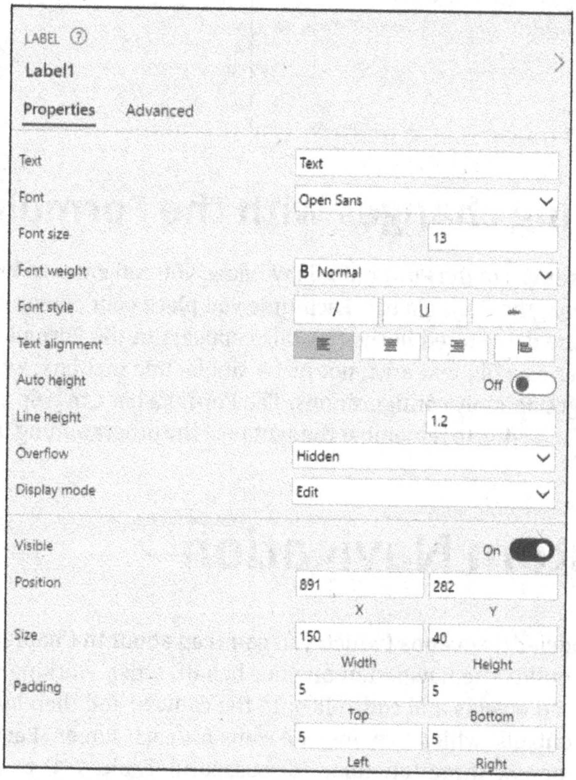

FIGURE 5-14: Formatting a label in the Properties pane.

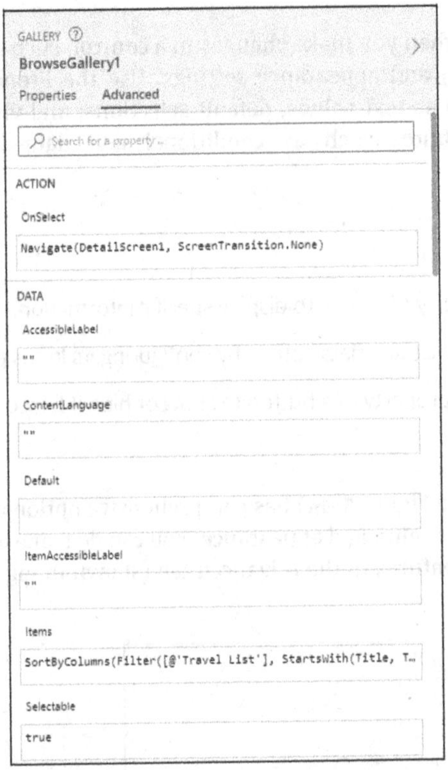

FIGURE 5-15: Configuring a gallery in the Advanced pane.

Applying changes with the Formula bar

Above the canvas in the Power Studio window, you can enter code and formulas in a long text box, the Formula bar. Each time you place your cursor in an Advanced tab property, the data stored in the field also appears in the Formula bar. Think of the Formula bar as a big text area, not just a single-line text box, where you can make code changes or apply configurations. The Formula bar can help you visualize snippets without having to remember the syntax of the programming language Power Fx.

Building Custom Navigation

Unlike model-driven apps (which you can read about in Chapters 6 and 7), where Microsoft builds the navigation on your behalf, when working with canvas apps, you must add objects and controls onto the canvas, and then build the navigation by using controls, which may include icons for each screen. Each object or control then uses one of three functions (discussed in Table 5-3) to go back and forth between screens. You can add code for each option in the Properties pane's Advanced tab.

TABLE 5-3 Navigation Functions, Purposes, and Examples

Function	Purpose	Usage	Example
Navigate()	Switch from one screen to another within an app; use if you want to create smooth transitions and optional animations.	Navigate(*Screen Name, ScreenTransition*)	Navigate(HomePage, ScreenTransition. Fade)
Back()	Allows users to return to the previous screen in the app's navigation history. Remembers only the last screen in the flow, a common navigation pattern that most applications offer.	Back(*ScreenName*)	Back(HomePage)
Launch()	Integrate external data resources with your canvas app; open a web address (URL) in the device's default web browser or launch another app if you can't include the code in the canvas app.	Launch (*Parameter1, Parameter2*)	Launch ("`http://www.dummies.com`")

Creating a Three-Screen To Do Lists App

The following sections show you how to create a three-screen canvas app in Power Apps with which the user can make a To Do list. To create this app, you need a data source already created in SharePoint, Dataverse, or Excel that contains fields Task, Start Date, End Date, Task Owner, Finished, and Notes. (I show you how to create a Dataverse data source in Chapter 3.) Each screen that you can create in the following sections serves a distinct purpose: browsing tasks, viewing task details, and editing or creating tasks.

Setting up the To Do Lists app

To create a To Do Lists app, you first need to select the appropriate app type and establish the name of your app based on the template you choose. Just follow these steps:

1. **Open Power Apps by going to the Maker Portal.**
2. **On the home page of the Maker Portal, choose Power Apps ⇨ Start with a Page Design ⇨ Blank Canvas.**

   The Canvas Type window appears.
3. **Select the Phone option, and then click the New option.**

   The New option looks like a circled plus sign (see Figure 5-16).
4. **In the Tree View Options pop-up window, select App.**

   The Properties pane appears on the right side of the window.

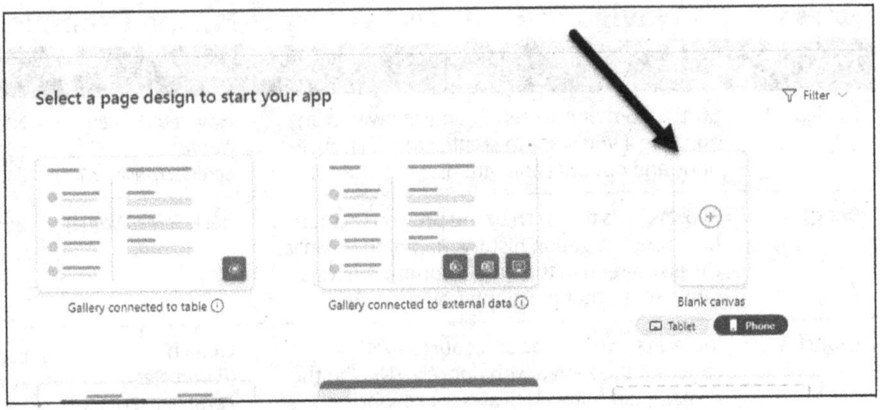

FIGURE 5-16: Adding a blank canvas to your app.

5. **In the Properties pane, click in the App Name text box and enter** To Do List **as the name that you want to use.**

   Figure 5-17 shows this name changed to To Do List.

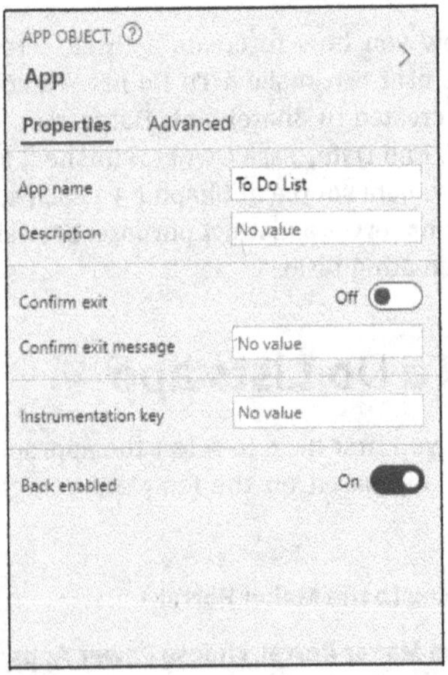

FIGURE 5-17: Changing your app's name in the Properties pane.

6. **In the Tree View Options pop-up window, click the New Screens button twice to add two additional screens.**

   When selecting the screen type for additional canvas pages, select Blank.

7. **Rename each screen by repeating Step 5.**

   Name one screen BrowseScreen, the second screen DetailScreen, and the third EditScreen.

Creating a Browse screen

If you have a data source that you plan to use (I talk about data sources in Chapters 2 and 3), in the app's Browse screen, you just need to add a variety of components that allow a user to browse the data in the To Do Lists app's data source. Components include the gallery control, a field, and a few icons.

The Browse screen allows a user to see the list of all To Do tasks in a summary format, as well as search for specific tasks. The following sections walk you through creating the Browse screen.

Step 1: Add a gallery to the canvas

You need to add a gallery control to the canvas so that you can present all of the records available in the system. To add and configure the gallery control, follow these steps:

1. **Select Insert in the App Authoring menu.**
2. **In the Insert Options pop-up window that appears, drag and drop a gallery to the canvas (as shown in Figure 5-18).**

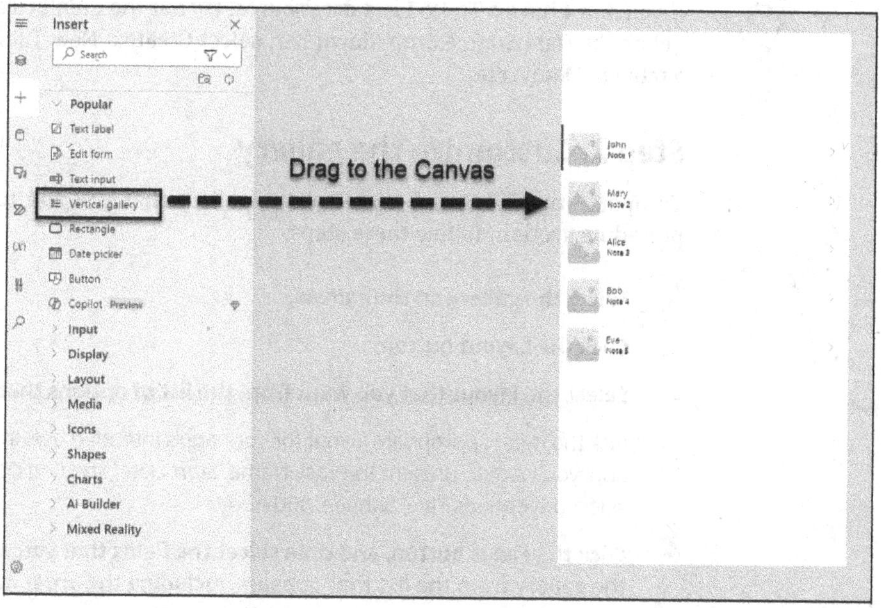

FIGURE 5-18: Drag a gallery onto your canvas.

Select the gallery that best suits your desired layout. In my example, I change the layout by selecting the Layout Button.

The Properties pane appears to the right of the canvas.

3. **Select your self-created data source.**

   My data source is called To Do Lists (see Figure 5-19).

   I explain how to create a data source in Chapter 3.

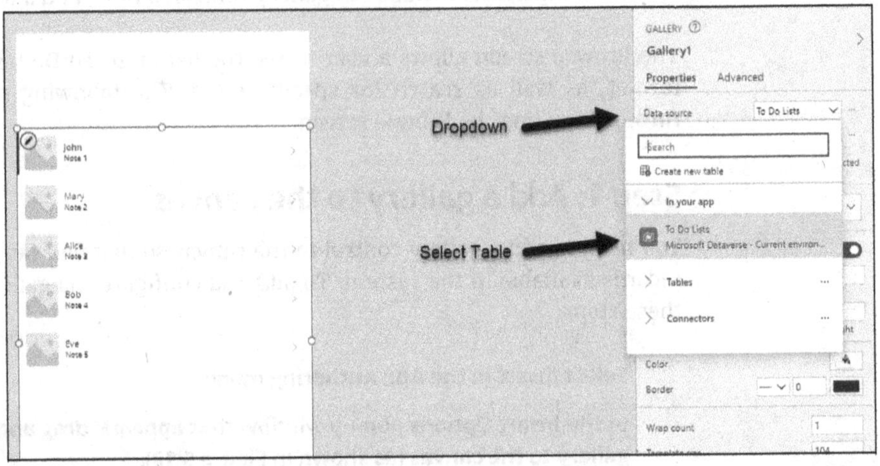

FIGURE 5-19: Select the data source that you want to connect to your gallery.

TIP

If you don't have a To Do Lists data source, try out the Copilot Table Creation tool. Below the Data Source drop-down list, select Create a New Table. Copilot creates a table in Dataverse.

Step 2: Customize the gallery

To update the fields and layout of the gallery that you add to your app in the preceding section, follow these steps:

1. **Select the gallery on the canvas.**
2. **Click the Layout button.**
3. **Select the layout that you want from the list of options that appears.**

   Pick the most appropriate layout for your app's intended use. In this To Do List app, you want to present the Task Name, Start Date, and End Date. Therefore, select the options Title, Subtitle, and Body.

4. **Click the Fields button, and then select the fields that you want to put in the gallery from the list that appears, including the order of those fields.**

   Admittedly, this process isn't intuitive, but after you get the hang of working with canvas apps, you can easily order your app's fields however you desire. In my example, I make the first field, Body 1, the End Date; Subtitle 2 the Start Date; and Title 2 the Task field.

5. **Customize the layout by selecting the first gallery area only, and then selecting each item in that block.**

   Examples of customization include making labels bold or changing text color in the Properties pane.

   The gallery can incorporate labels, too, which you can drag from the Insert pane and then modify in the Properties tab. You may also want the task to appear in bold, for example, so that it has a distinctive look and feel.

6. **Change the Task object.**

   Follow these steps:

   a. *Highlight the Task text in Formula bar.*

   b. *On the main toolbar, select Bold and a larger font size (for example, 18 rather than 12).*

      In my example, I chose the settings Arial 18 Semibold.

   c. *In the Properties pane, change the color of the background to something dark and the color of the text to white.*

      This contrast makes the Task stand out in the vertical gallery and on the canvas.

7. **On the toolbar, select Insert, and then drag a label from the pop-up menu to the first gallery area block.**

8. **Place the field where you want it to appear in the first gallery area block.**

   Move the existing data objects around to make the fields look aesthetically pleasing.

9. **Change the name of the label to** Start:.

   The section "Renaming a control," earlier in this chapter, goes over how you can change a label's name.

10. **Repeat Steps 7 through 9, naming this second label** End:.

11. **Add a border to the vertical gallery control.**

    Just follow these steps:

    a. *On the canvas, select the gallery.*

    b. *In the Properties pane that appears on the right of the window, select the Border option.*

       A color palette opens.

    c. *From the Properties pane, pick a Border Size greater than 1 and a color that will make the gallery stand out.*

12. **Click Advanced to the right of Properties to open the Advanced pane.**

13. **In the OnSelect field, enter** Navigate(DetailScreen, ScreenTransition.None) **so that a user can navigate to the Detail screen.**

Figure 5-20 shows the custom gallery layout for my example Browse screen.

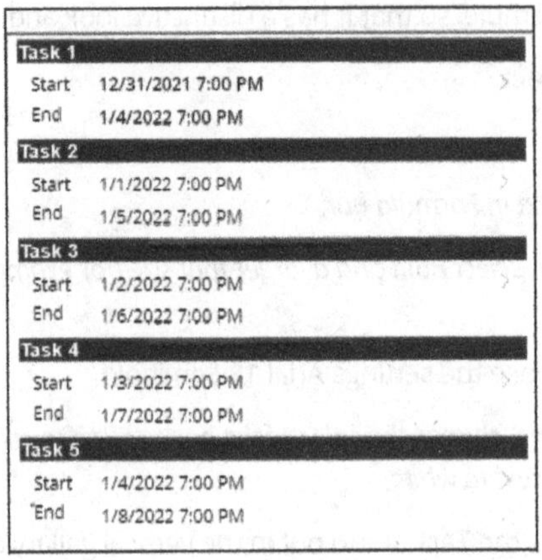

FIGURE 5-20: My customized To Do Lists gallery's Browse screen.

Step 3: Add a Search capability

If you want users to be able to search the To Do Lists in its entirety, you need to add two objects to the canvas: a label and a text box. For all the renaming steps in the following list, flip back to the section "Renaming a control," earlier in this chapter, for the procedure. To create the search experience, follow these steps:

1. **Click the Insert option in the App Authoring menu.**

   The Insert Options pop-up window appears.

2. **Drag and drop the Label option to the canvas.**

3. **Stretch the label by selecting and dragging one of the corners to fill the entire width of the canvas.**

4. **Change the Label name Label1 to** Search.

5. **Rename the label** SearchLbl **in the Properties pane.**

   Making this change allows you to explicitly call for the label later on, instead of using the generic name.

6. **Drag and drop the Text Box item from the Insert Options pop-up window to the canvas.**

   Place your new text box next to the Search label.

7. **In the Properties tab, erase the Text Input in the Text Box field.**

   Make sure the Text Box field is blank.

8. **In the Properties tab, rename the search box** txtSearch.
9. **Select the gallery on the canvas.**
10. **In the Properties pane that appears on the right of the window, select Advanced to open the Advanced tab.**
11. **Enter a code snippet in the Items field.**

    Here's the code snippet for my control:

    ```
    Search('To Do Lists',txtSearch.Text,Task)
    ```

    Now, whenever someone uses your To Do Lists app to search for particular tasks, the results filter only entries that contain words that the user enters in the Search text box.

Step 4: Put Reload, Sort, and Add navigation on the Browse screen

You can get a bit creative with how you set up your Browse screen navigation. You can

- Add labels to the header to describe each screen.
- Place buttons at the top of the app to help guide the user from screen to screen.
- Use icons only, and then apply *Alt Tags,* metadata that offer descriptions of an app's content to help those who have visual challenges.

As the developer, you decide what navigation options to offer, but if you're designing the app for an enterprise user, you need to incorporate all of these components and their associated attributes because, otherwise, a user can't effectively navigate, making the application unusable.

In this section, I show you how to give all the icons functionality to support navigation actions, including Refresh, Sort, and Create. In addition, I also demonstrate how to add a label to describe the app on the Browse screen, which also acts as the home page. Follow these steps:

1. **From the Insert pane, drag a label to the top of the canvas.**
2. **Stretch the label to cover the entire canvas from left to right.**
3. **Select the label, and then modify the color in the Properties tab.**

4. **In the Properties tab, rename the label by clicking the Text textbox and entering "To Do Lists."**

   Figure 5-21 shows the path that you take when you follow Steps 1 through 4.

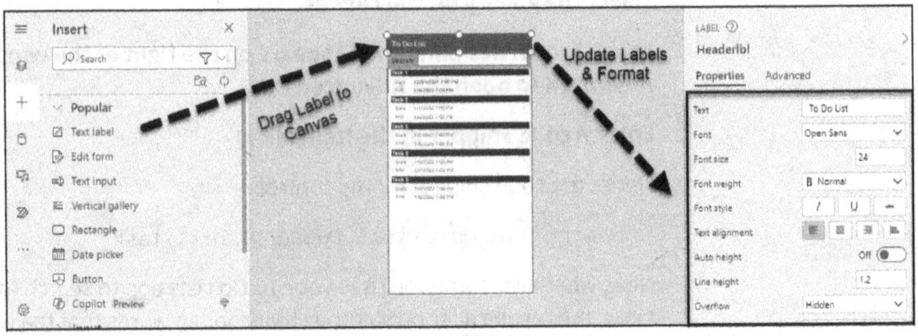

FIGURE 5-21: Adding a label and updating the text and format in the label.

5. **Click Insert in the App Authoring menu.**
6. **From the Insert Options pop-up menu that appears, drag and drop a Button control onto the canvas.**

   The Properties pane for that button appears on the right of the screen.

7. **Click the Advanced tab of the Properties pane, and enter the appropriate command from Table 5-3 to make this button active.**
8. **Repeat Steps 5 through 7 for two more buttons.**

   You want to create buttons for Reload (an arrow making a circle), Sort (two arrows pointing up and down), and Add (a plus sign).

9. **Place the buttons flush at the top of the label.**
10. **Select one of the buttons on the canvas.**
11. **In the Properties pane that appears for that button, change the Color option by clicking the color palette button, and then selecting the color desired.**

    Figure 5-22 shows making this change for the Add button.

12. **Select Advanced to the right of Properties to open the Advanced pane for the icon.**

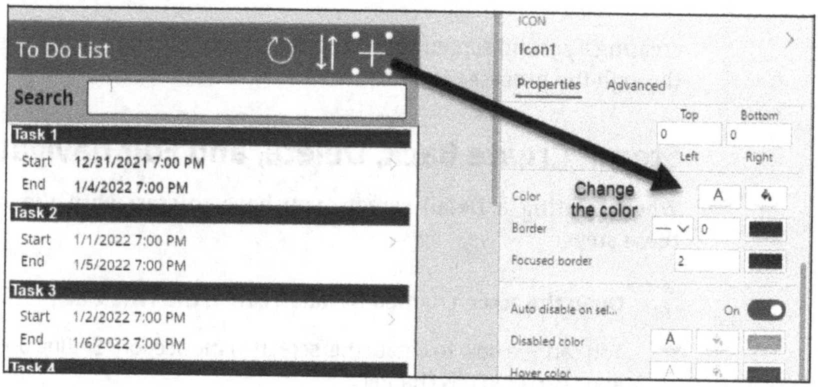

FIGURE 5-22: Customizing navigation icons at the top of the label.

13. **Enter the code snippet for the appropriate navigation action in the OnSelect field.**

    Each navigation icon needs to handle a specific action:

    - *Refresh:* `Refresh('To Do Lists')`
    - *Sort:* `UpdateContext({SortDescending1: !SortDescending1})`
    - *Create:* `NewForm(EditForm1);Navigate(EditScreen, ScreenTransition.None)`

14. **Repeat Steps 10 through 13 for each of the buttons.**
15. **On the canvas, select the gallery, and then click Advanced in the Properties pane.**

    The Advanced pane for that gallery opens.

16. **Update the OnSelect text box by entering the appropriate code snippet.**

    The code snippet I used for this app is

    ```
    Navigate(DetailScreen, ScreenTransition.None)
    ```

After you complete the preceding steps, someone using your app can refresh to see the latest data, sort the data into descending order, and open the Create a New Record screen. (See the section "Adding a Create/Edit Screen," later in this chapter, for how to put this screen together.) Also, you can view the Detail screen for a given task (which I show you how to make in the following section) when you select an item in the gallery.

Adding a Detail screen

You give the To Do Lists app user a snapshot of tasks with the screen that you can put together in the section "Creating a Browse screen," earlier in this chapter. But you can let a user view the specific details for a task in a read-only format by creating a second screen called the Detail screen. The following sections guide you through the process.

Step 1: Create Back, Delete, and Edit navigation

When creating a Detail screen, you have to start with the navigation. Follow these steps:

1. **Open the screen named DetailScreen in the Tree view.**

   You can see how to create this screen in the section "Setting up the To Do Lists app," earlier in this chapter.

2. **Add a label to the screen.**

   I go over how to add a label to the Browse screen in the section "Step 3: Add a Search capability," earlier in this chapter; the process is similar for the Detail screen.

3. **Insert a Back button in the header by selecting the appropriate icon.**
4. **Select the Back button place on the header.**
5. **In the Advanced tab of the Properties pane that appears on the right of the window, enter the text** Navigate(BrowseScreen) **in the OnSelect text box.**

   Alternatively, you can use `Back()` instead, which takes the user back to the previous screen, the original Browse screen.

6. **Insert a Delete button by adding another icon to the header.**
7. **In the Delete button's Properties pane, set the OnSelect property on the Advanced tab.**

   Enter this code snippet:

   ```
   Remove(
       [@'To Do Lists'],
       Gallery1.Selected
   ); Back(ScreenTransition.Fade)
   ```

   Clicking this button now deletes the current record from the dataset.

8. **In the Insert pane, drag the Edit icon to the header, and then select that button on the canvas.**
9. **Set the OnSelect value in the Advanced tab of the Properties pane.**

   Enter the following code snippet:

   ```
   EditForm(EditForm1);Navigate(EditScreen,
     ScreenTransition.None)
   ```

REMEMBER

Keep in mind that you haven't added anything to the Create/Edit screen yet, so this function can operate only after you follow the instructions in the section "Provide an Edit/Create screen," later in this chapter.

Step 2: Display a selected task

To display the data in read-only mode on the Details screen, follow these steps:

1. **Click Insert in the App Authoring menu.**
2. **From the Insert Options pop-up menu that appears, drag and drop a Display Form onto the canvas.**
3. **Select the new Display Form in the canvas.**

   The Display Form's Properties pane appears on the right of the window.
4. **From the Data Source drop-down list in the Properties pane, select the same data source that you use in the Browse screen.**

   You can see how to input a data source for the Browse screen in the section "Creating a Browse screen," earlier in this chapter. In my example, I use the To Do Lists data source.
5. **Modify the Items property by entering a code snippet in the text box.**

   Enter the code snippet `Gallery1.Selected`.

   When you first move a Display Form from the App Authoring menu to the canvas in Step 2, it gets placed in a random location on the canvas, so you probably want to organize your controls based on your desired design.
6. **Click the Fields button on the Display form.**

   Figure 5-23 shows the Fields pop-up menu that appears.

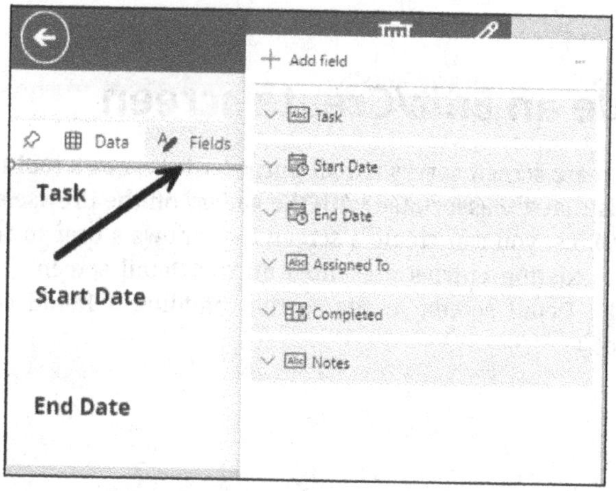

FIGURE 5-23: The Fields button pop-up menu.

7. **Organize the fields as desired by dragging them up or down in the Field pop-up menu.**
8. **After you have all fields organized as you see fit, click Display Form.**

   The updates appear in the Details screen.

After you follow the preceding steps, a user can access an individual record with all its details displayed on the Detail screen. A user can also edit and delete a record by using the buttons you created in the navigation on the right side of the header by clicking one of the buttons you created. Finally, the user can then go back to the Browse screen, which acts as the home page, to review all tasks by clicking the back arrow. You can see my example Detail screen in Figure 5-24.

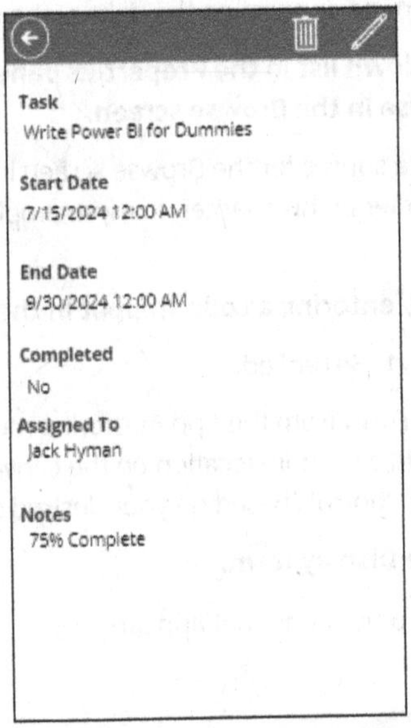

FIGURE 5-24: A Detail screen from my To Do Lists app.

Provide an Edit/Create screen

The Edit/Create screen serves a dual purpose: It acts as a tool to both create and edit records that are associated with the gallery on the Browse screen. In the following sections, you can create a screen that allows a user to add a new entry or modify the existing entries presented on the Detail screen. (See the details on creating the Detail screen in the section "Adding a Detail screen," earlier in this chapter.)

Step 1: Add a form to the Edit/Create screen

To create your Edit/Create screen, you first need to add an Edit Form control to the canvas so that a user can either Add or Edit the data in the To Do Lists app. Follow these steps:

1. **Open the screen named EditScreen in Tree view.**

   The section "Setting up the To Do Lists app," earlier in this chapter, shows you how to create this screen.

2. **Select Insert in the App Authoring menu.**

   The Insert Options pop-up menu appears.

3. **Drag and drop the Edit Form control from the Insert tab to the canvas.**
4. **In the Data Source property on the Properties pane, select the same data source that you use in the other screens.**

   Each screen in my example uses the To Do Lists data source.

5. **Enter a code snippet in the Item property under the Advanced tab of the Properties pane.**

   Set the Item property to `Gallery1.Selected`.

Step 2: Create Save and Cancel navigation

Unlike the Detail screen (see the section "Adding a Detail screen," earlier in this chapter), the Create/Edit screen incorporates

- **Cancel button:** Takes a user back to the previous screen, either to the Browse or Detail screen (whichever screen you were last on). Depending on the previous page that you decide to go to, the `OnSelect` action varies.

  If a user decides they don't want to save the record, either when they Create or Edit a record, they can click the Cancel button to exit the interface without saving.

- **Save button:** Saves the newly created or edited record to the dataset.

Follow these to create navigation for your Create/Edit screen:

1. **Add a label to the Create/Edit screen.**

   The section "Step 3: Add a Search capability," earlier in this chapter shows you the process for adding a label to a screen.

2. **Click Insert in the App Authoring menu.**

3. **From the Insert Options pop-up menu that appears, drag and drop the Cancel badge on to the canvas.**

   The Cancel badge acts as a button.

4. **In the Properties pane on the right of the window, change the color of the icon to White by updating the color property.**
5. **In the OnSelect field on the Advanced tab of the Properties pane, enter the appropriate code snippet.**

   Use the following code snippet:

   ```
   ResetForm(EditForm1); Back()
   ```

6. **In the Insert Options menu, drag and drop the Save icon to the canvas.**
7. **In the Save button's Properties pane, select the Disk icon, and then change the color of the icon to White in the Advanced tab.**
8. **Select the Save icon again and enter the appropriate code snippet in the Advanced tab of the Properties pane's OnSelect field.**

   Use the following code snippet:

   ```
   SubmitForm(EditForm1); Navigate(BrowseScreen)
   ```

Your final Create/Edit Screen should look similar to Figure 5-25.

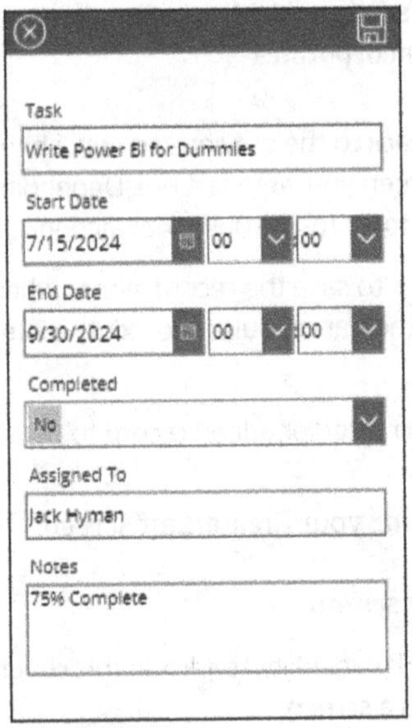

FIGURE 5-25: The final Create/Edit screen.

Reviewing the final product

After you design and configure each of the three screens in your To Do Lists app (which I cover in the preceding sections), follow these steps to finish things up:

1. **Click the App Checker button in the toolbar.**

   Power Apps checks to see whether the application has any errors.

2. **If the App Checker shows Red or provides corrective action feedback, correct the error by following the instructions.**

3. **After making corrections, follow Steps 1 and 2 again.**

4. **After you no longer have errors, save the app by selecting Save on the toolbar, and then select Publish.**

   REMEMBER

   As the app designer, you can see all the changes, but until you publish the app, users don't see those changes reflected in their version of the app.

Figure 5-26 shows the three screens of the final product that you create.

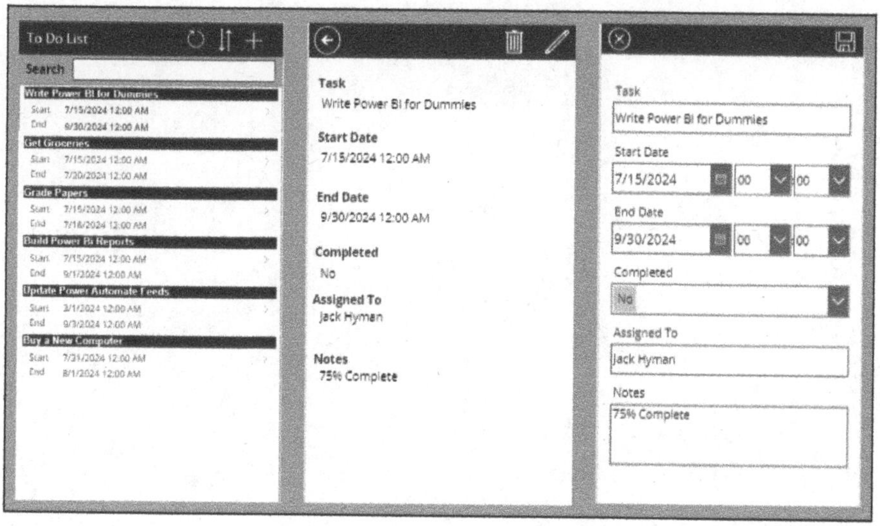

FIGURE 5-26: The finished three pages of the To Do Lists canvas app.

TIP

If you want to render your app in a device simulator so that you can see how it will behave when accessed through different devices or operating systems, select one of the options to the right of the canvas, and then select Play. Your app starts to operate as if you're using the selected option and allows you to begin using all available capabilities. You can choose from Desktop, Mobile, and Tablet devices, notably Apple, Motorola, and Samsung device simulators.

IN THIS CHAPTER

» Knowing when model-driven apps are the way to go

» Working with the key components to build a model-driven app

» Setting up your app's interface by using forms

» Designing views to help the user search the app's data

Chapter 6 Building Data Solutions with Model-Driven Apps

Microsoft Power Apps simplifies interface design for model-driven applications (apps) so that you can focus instead on the data these apps handle. Instead of spending time creating screens (as you do with canvas apps; flip back to Chapter 5), your venture into data modeling ensures that every piece of data stored in your Dataverse tables has value. This chapter shows how to plan and build a basic model-driven app, focusing on using Dataverse forms, views, and basic application security.

Exploring Model-Driven Apps from a High-Level

Model-driven apps are entirely *component-focused*, meaning the user has limited control over the app's layout. The components selected by the user determine the app's structure, but instead of manually placing each component on a canvas,

Microsoft defines the application's layout based on a standardized look and feel. The App Designer selects components — including forms, views, charts, and dashboards — from its Dataverse tables. A typical user might choose a form for data entry and editing, along with views to display records created from that data. In model-driven apps, you don't have drag-and-drop control over layout like you do in canvas apps (see Chapter 5 for the canvas app route); instead, Power Apps automatically organizes the model-driven app components to ensure a What You See Is What You Get (WYSIWYG) experience. So the layout you see during the model-driven app-building process closely mirrors, and often exactly matches, what the end user experiences, resulting in a consistent and responsive app.

Dipping into design

Some users say that when working with model-driven apps, which are entirely based on Dataverse tables, you don't actually design anything; you're simply configuring. Other users might claim that you're designing the application and its user experience because you must also plan out more than just the interface (as represented by the form pages); you also establish the data and automation processes. The truth is, when you create a Dataverse table, you're already planning the data output for your forms and views in the app. Everything is interconnected, from creating the table to defining the column relationships and entity types. These underlying responsibilities that you complete in Dataverse impact how the data appears in the app and how users interact with it.

Here's how these terms apply to model-driven apps:

- **Pages:** Incorporate the navigation points in your app or the screens that the user interacts with.
- **Data:** Includes all Dataverse tables that are specifically part of your app (meaning all the tables that you include and configure within the app, which I talk about in Chapter 3), as well as any other tables within the Dataverse environment. Your Dataverse environment can contain many tables and automation capabilities accessible not to just one particular model-driven app, but others, even if those other apps aren't using that functionality.
- **Automation:** Represents any application business process. Specifically, a *business process flow* within a model-driven app is a series of steps that guide users or the system through specific tasks. A combination of triggers and actions often kicks off such a process. *Triggers* are events that initiate the automation, such as creating a new record in a Dataverse table, while the *action* is the task performed as a result of the trigger, such as sending an e-mail or updating one or more records.

REMEMBER

Power Platform builds model-driven apps exclusively by using Dataverse tables. That doesn't mean that Dataverse must be your only data solution. You can use virtual tables from third-party sources as long as you include them with Dataverse. Chapter 3 can show you more about how Power Platform works with Microsoft Dataverse.

Starting with pages in model-driven apps

To add a new page to a model-driven app, select Add Page from the App Designer. You can choose from five-page types:

- **Dataverse Table:** To create a form and view, select Dataverse Table. For example, if you have a table named Customers, choosing that table automatically generates a page for you. So you get a form that allows users to perform actions such as adding new records and updating existing rows of data. This also creates a view to display the data in a structured, tabular format.
- **Dashboards:** Combine multiple components, such as charts, views, and reports. The data for the Dashboards may come from one or more Dataverse tables. A Dashboard page allows users to interact with real-time data through visual representations such as graphs, summaries, and lists, making monitoring key metrics and performance easier than relying on model-driven app views and the data entry screens.
- **Navigation Link:** Direct users to an external URL without creating a separate app screen. After you select this page type, you enter a website URL, such as `www.dummies.com`, and the website's title. After you click Add, a link appears in the navigation that points to the external website. When a user clicks that link in the app navigation, a new browser window opens to that page.
- **Web Resource Page:** Embed external files or third-party resources directly into your application. Examples of web resources include PDFs, Word documents, HTML files, JavaScript, or other custom web elements typically added to a solution. A web resource page lets you incorporate content that you can't directly store in a Dataverse table.
- **Custom:** Embed a custom user interface directly into your model-driven app, such as a calculator or other custom functionality created by using canvas app features. This approach gives you the design flexibility of a canvas app without building a full custom app — you simply integrate a single custom page within the model-driven environment.

You can add pages to the model-driven app by clicking the New button (which looks like a plus sign) and then selecting the page type desired, as shown in Figure 6-1.

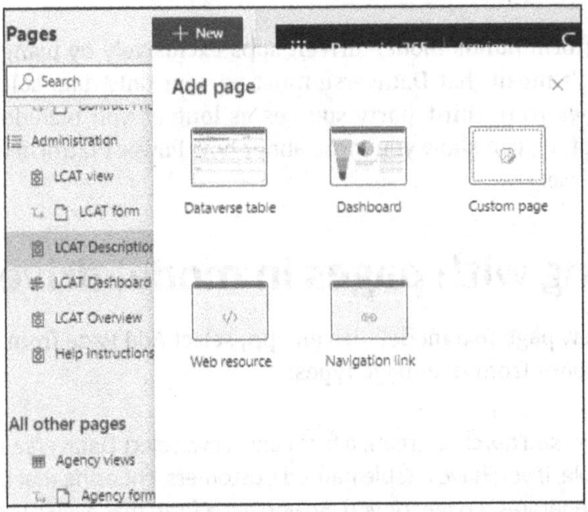

FIGURE 6-1: Adding new page types to an app.

Automating business processes in model-driven apps

In model-driven apps, business rules and process flows serve distinct yet complementary purposes:

- **Business rules:** Enforce logic and automation directly within forms, allowing you to define conditions, apply validations, and automate actions (such as hiding or showing fields, setting default values, or locking fields) without writing code. You then use rules at the form level to ensure that users follow predefined logic when interacting with data.
- **Business process flows:** Guide users through structured stages to complete tasks in a specific order. Each page within the flow may incorporate one or more Dataverse tabs. Business process flows are useful for processes such as lead qualification or sales approvals, which incorporate multiple steps to gather data from the user.

REMEMBER

Whereas model-driven apps allow for business rules and process flows, canvas apps (discussed in Chapter 5) can implement business rules only by integrating them with Power Automate (which you can read about in Chapters 14 and 15) to enable automation.

Following business rules

Business rules enforce business logic for each Dataverse column to ensure data integrity and consistency. You can apply business rules to individual forms and views of a Dataverse table, and those rules include conditional logic to set field values, enable or disable fields, show or hide fields, and validate data. Logic is executed on the client or server side (within the forms within the Dataverse back-end). You can set up these rules by using a drag-and-drop interface from the Power Apps Maker Portal.

To create a business rule, navigate to the Tables section of the Maker Portal, select the desired table, and click the Business Rules tab. You can design rules by dragging conditions and actions onto a flowchart-style canvas.

Going with the business process flows

Business process flows guide users through a series of stages and steps in a specific sequence, ensuring consistent execution of business procedures. A familiar example happens at a doctor's office: First, they might ask you for your personal information (the primary stage), followed by your medical insurance and clinical history (secondary and tertiary stages). Each of these steps represents a different stage in the flow.

Flows might span multiple Dataverse tables, meaning that different stages involve various types of records. For instance, your personal information could be stored in a Patient table, while your insurance details and medical history are in separate tables called Insurance and Medical Profile.

Business process flows offer a visual representation of the process at the top of a model-driven app form so that users can easily see their progress and understand the required next steps. By customizing the business process flow stage, you can tailor each step to different user roles. Furthermore, you can ensure that the flow steps are relevant to the user's responsibilities and incorporate automation within each step.

Figure 6-2 shows a business process flow for qualifying a sales lead.

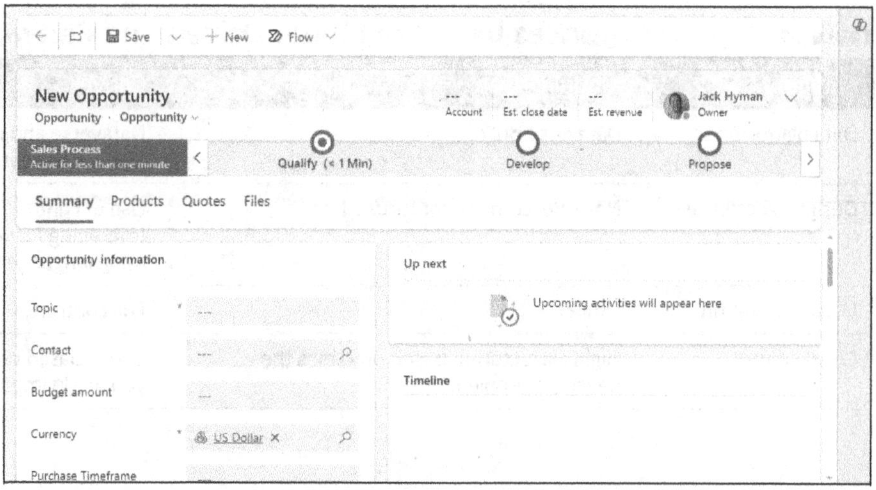

FIGURE 6-2: A business process flow for a new opportunity.

Knowing when to use the model-driven approach

When should you create a model-driven app versus a canvas app (which I cover in Chapter 5)? Unlike a canvas app, where the designer has complete control of the app layout, with a model-driven app, the components that you add to the app largely determine the interface. Using model-driven apps has some advantages:

- **Rapid development:** When the developer gets the data model and relationships correct, you can rapidly develop the forms because you don't get bogged down in coding.
- **Consistency:** The developer builds model-driven apps by using a uniform interface structure across all device types. This structure ensures all users can access the interfaces, including those with disabilities. This structure is also responsive, meaning the user experience remains consistent and optimized, regardless of the device used.
- **Efficiency:** By using a *solution* — a compilation of all the assets that comprise a model-driven app (discussed in Chapter 4) — you can efficiently migrate your app and ensure consistency across development, test, and production environments. You can't necessarily achieve the same efficiency by using a canvas app because you have to customize canvas apps more manually; they don't inherently follow the structured data model or standardized environment deployment processes that model-driven apps do.

Table 6-1 breaks down the difference between a model-driven app and a canvas app (see Chapter 5), which may help you decide which approach best suits your development and business requirements.

TABLE 6-1 Differences between Model-Driven and Canvas Apps

Category	Model-Driven	Canvas
Data platforms	Dataverse only	Dataverse and connectors to 100 + other data sources
Design experience	No-code, component focused	Use of controls on the canvas, leveraging Power Fx programming language functions
UI customization	Limited	Full control
Consistency	Highly structured; based on tables the developer implements	Varies based on how deliberate you are in implementing controls

Category	Model-Driven	Canvas
Migration	Simple; uses Dataverse and the solution package to go from environment to environment (for example, from development to production)	Varies based on the data type utilized; it can be complex
Speed to create	Depends on the number of forms and views; can be rapid	Relative to the complexity of the interface design, but always much slower than model-driven apps
Responsiveness and accessibility	Automatic	Developer must implement Alt Tags to support accessibility
Navigation	Automatically built based on relationships and configurability of Dataverse tables	Designer must implement navigation; requires significant code configuration to operate

Identifying minimum requirements for a model-driven app

In the same way that you can't drive a car if it doesn't have an engine, windows, or seatbelt, you can't build a model-driven app without establishing at least one environment for development (where you code), testing (where you validate your application before going live), and production (a live environment). This series of environments is referred to as *application lifecycle management* (ALM) conditions. (ALM is also covered in Chapter 4.) As a developer, you need to have the following in place for your model-driven app:

- A Microsoft Power Apps license.
- Dataverse storage capacity (at least 1GB).

REMEMBER

Access to Dataverse storage capacity depends on your licensing for Power Apps and Dynamics 365. If you're using the free version of Power Apps with Microsoft 365, you don't get Dataverse capacity and need to upgrade to a Premium Power Apps license to use Dataverse. However, if you're using Dynamics 365, Dataverse comes included by default as part of your Dynamics 365 subscription, so you don't need a separate Power Apps Premium license.

- An active Power Platform environment and admin access.
- Privileges for you, the developer, either as a system administrator or system customizer, to adjust the environment's security roles:
  - *System administrator:* Has full access to manage all data, settings, and users within the system.
  - *System customizer:* Can modify the system's components and features without getting full access to operational data.

» A minimum of a single Dataverse table that contains at least one column. Each Dataverse table includes a view to display records and a form to enter data.

» Create a site map to add the tables, forms, views, and dashboards for solution compilation.

Using Core Components to Build a Model-Driven App

To build a model-driven app, you first create a Dataverse table. The table acts as the foundation for storing your app's data. In the table, you define columns (sometimes known as *fields*) to hold specific data types, such as text, numbers, dates, or options. When you give the table at least one column, you can begin configuring key components such as

» **Forms:** For data entry

» **Views:** To display data in a list or grid format

» **Charts:** For data visualization

» **Dashboards:** To give an overview of key metrics

These components are automatically rendered as pages within your model-driven app, providing a user-friendly interface to view and interact with data.

In the Data Experiences section of your Dataverse table (like my To Do List table shown in Figure 6-3), you can click Forms, Views, Charts, or Dashboards to open the App Designer interface, where you can create each component to later integrate into the app. To build the framework of the app, though, you can most easily do the development in the Dataverse entity that you create. You can add columns to a table in two ways:

» **In Dataverse:** Add a new column in your Dataverse table by clicking the plus sign (+) to the right of the table in Dataverse (see Figure 6-3). Clicking this button opens the New Column pop-up window, as shown in Figure 6-4.

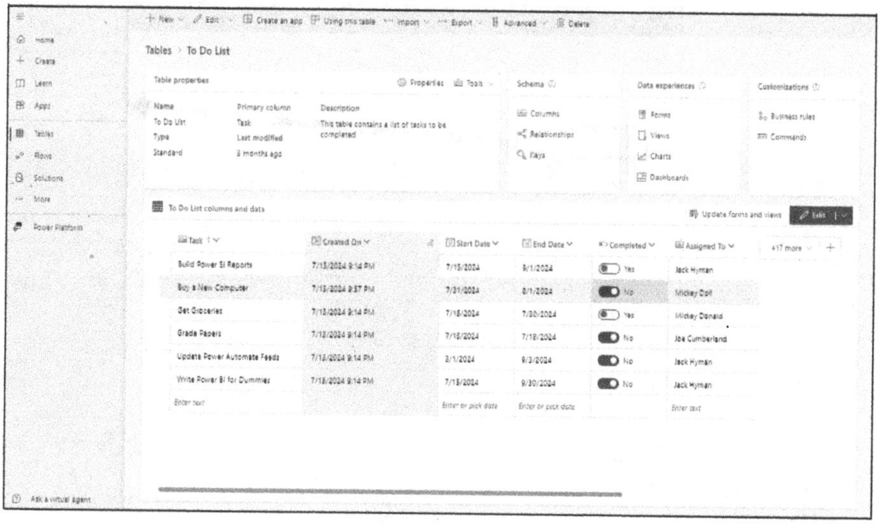

FIGURE 6-3: My To Do List table in Dataverse.

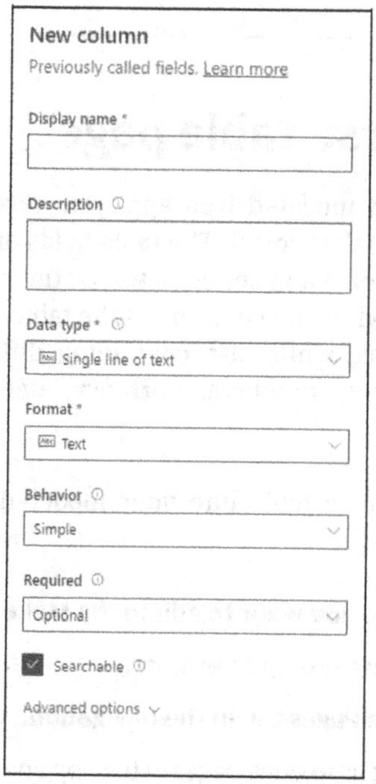

FIGURE 6-4: Dataverse's New Column pop-up window.

» **In your model-driven app:** After you create a form and add it to your app, you can create a new column from within your model-driven app by selecting New Table Column in the left navigation pane and filling out the New Column pop-up window that opens (see Figure 6-5).

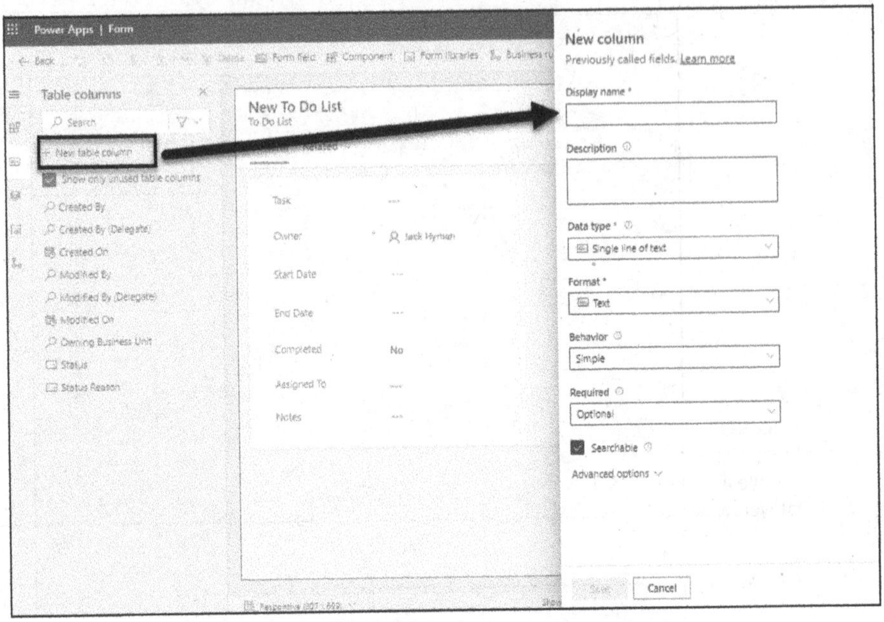

FIGURE 6-5: Adding a table column directly from your model-driven app.

Creating a Dataverse table page

To create a Dataverse table for a model-driven app, you must first define the structure in the Table tab of the Maker Portal. The table holds and organizes your app's data. It also builds a basic form and set of views for the model-driven app. To utilize a form or view, you need to add columns to the table. A Dataverse table consists of one or more columns, while also containing different data types. Example data types include text, numbers, currency, dates, lookups, and choice options.

To create and integrate a Dataverse table into your model-driven app, follow these steps:

1. **Open the Power App app that you want to edit in the Maker Portal.**
2. **Select the pencil icon to access the App Designer.**
3. **In the App Designer, click the Pages tab in the navigation.**

   A new window opens, showing all existing pages in the app and a New button.
4. **Click the New button.**
5. **To create a new Dataverse Table page, click Dataverse Table from the options.**

   If you want to add a different type of page, you can also select one of the other options described in the section "Starting with pages in model-driven apps," earlier in this chapter.

In the Dataverse Table Page selection window that appears, you can select an existing table (which you do in this step list), or you can create a new table (as I describe in Chapter 3).

6. **Select the check box next to the table you want to use from the list of Dataverse tables.**

7. **(Optional) If you want the table to appear in the app's navigation, select the check box above the Add button.**

8. **Click Add to add the table to the navigation.**

   The form and view for that table now appear in the app's navigation.

You can modify the View and Form layouts directly from the model-driven app's App Designer. Users can also access the specific form directly from the navigation.

In my example, I added the Company table to the model-driven app navigation, and Power Apps automatically renamed it Companies. This addition to the navigation includes both a view and a form:

- **View:** Provides a read-only display of selected columns from your Dataverse table. In Figure 6-6, you can see the Companies view I created. Note that A represents the App Designer, and B shows how the navigation will appear to users. All active company listings appear in this view.
- **Form:** Used for data entry, allowing users to input or update data. Figure 6-7 shows my Companies form, which users can interact with to add or modify data.

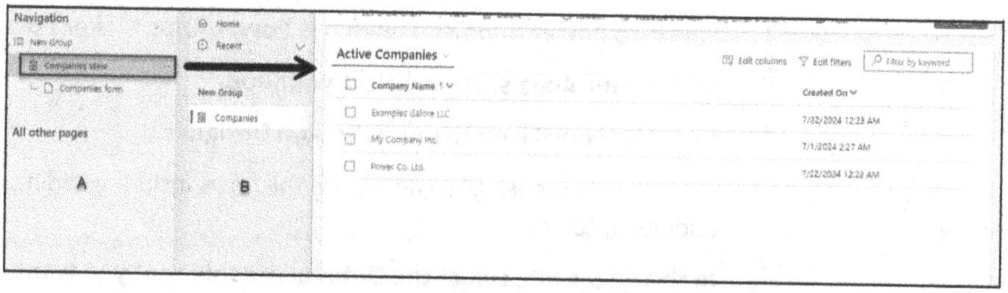

FIGURE 6-6: The Companies view navigation and listings.

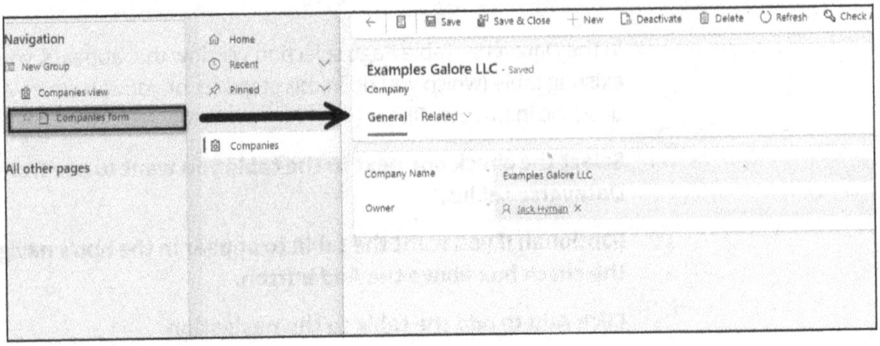

FIGURE 6-7: The Companies form available to users.

Modifying a Dataverse table and its form elements

You can add form fields from a Dataverse table to your model-driven app on the fly, from within your app, by using the App Designer (which allows you to customize the form). You can make changes to a form, including

- Add new columns to the form.
- Remove columns from the form.
- Add columns to the table, and then add them to the form.
- Remove or add *tabs* (sections of a form that organize fields) from the form.

Hiding a table column

To hide a column in a Dataverse table, follow these steps:

1. **Sign into Power Apps and open the Power Apps Maker Portal.**
2. **In the Your Apps section, select your app.**
3. **Click the Pencil icon to open the App Designer.**

   In the App Designer, you can modify the form, including hiding or adding additional columns.
4. **In the Pages tab, select the Dataverse table that you want to edit.**
5. **Select the specific Form associated with the Dataverse table that you want to modify.**
6. **In the Form Designer that opens, select the column that you want to hide.**

   The column must already appear on the Form Designer. You can't hide the field from the Table Columns pane.

7. **From the Column Properties pane that appears on the right of the screen, click the Hide check box.**

   The field is then hidden from the form.

Making a hidden column reappear

TIP

To unhide a column, follow these steps:

1. **In the Table Columns pane, uncheck the Show Only Unused Table Columns box (see Figure 6-8).**

   The column then appears in the list on the Table Columns pane.

2. **Double-click the column to add it back to the form, effectively undoing its previous removal.**
3. **Click Save and then click Publish to apply your changes.**

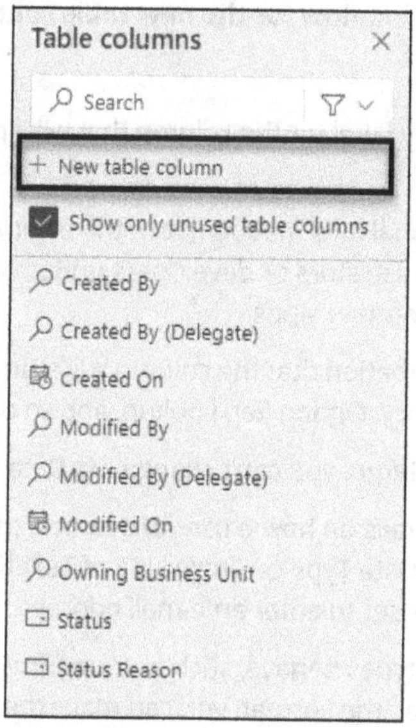

FIGURE 6-8: Hiding (and unhiding) used table columns.

Adding a column from the app

If you need to add a new table column from the app, follow these steps:

1. **Select New Table Column in the Table Columns pane (refer to Figure 6-8).**

   A pop-up window like the one in Figure 6-9 opens.

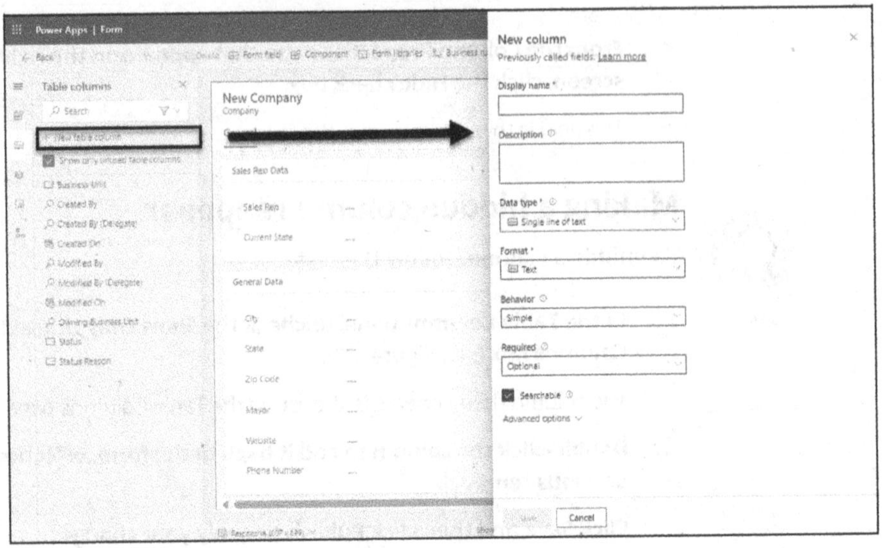

FIGURE 6-9: Adding a new table column to a form.

2. **Fill in the fields in the pop-up window for the new table column.**

   These fields include

   - *Display Name:* A user-friendly label for the column that will appear in forms, views, and dashboards.
   - *Description:* Provides additional information about the column's purpose or intended use, helping administrators or developers understand its role in the system, particularly in complex apps.
   - *Data Type:* Defines the information that the column will store, such as Text, Number, Date/Time, Currency, Option Set, Lookup, and so on.

     WARNING

     After you put data in the column, you can't change the Data Type format.
   - *Format:* Provides further details on how a user can format the data entered into a field. For example, a Data Type of Single Line of Text that has the Format of Email forces the user to enter an e-mail address.
   - *Behavior:* How certain data types behave, such as Date/Time or a Text field. For example, if you select Text as the Format, you can make the Behavior either Simple (plain data entry) or Calculated (determined by a Power Fx formula).
   - *Required:* Whether the column must have a value for each record. You can set Required as Optional (the user can leave the field blank), Business Required (the user must enter a value), or Recommended (the user doesn't have to enter a value, but they're strongly encouraged to fill in the field).
   - *Searchable:* The system indexes the data for future searching if you check the Searchable box.

The example in Figure 6-9 shows adding a table column named E-mail Address, with the Data Type of Single Line of Text and a Format of Email to ensure that users enter only valid e-mail addresses.

3. **Click Save.**

   The pop-up window closes, and the field appears in the Table Columns pane.

4. **Drag the new column from the Table Columns pane to the Form Page pane.**

   You can place the column anywhere on the form.

5. **Click Save, and then click Publish.**

   Your new table column now appears in the model-driven app's Form Designer.

TIP

Deleting an item from a form is as simple as highlighting the field and clicking Delete in the toolbar that appears at the top of the apps Form Designer. The field goes back into the Table Columns pane.

Getting creative with page components

You can get only so creative with a model-driven app because you're limited by what the available page components allow you to accomplish. However, to make your model-driven app more user-friendly and avoid overcrowding a single form, you can divide the data entry process into tabs, which break the form into multiple sections or pages.

Tabs provide a way to organize data entry logically and improve usability. In addition, model-driven apps allow you to break forms into structured sections, with each tab supporting up to four sections. These sections help organize and display related data in a clear, manageable way.

Here's a breakdown of the parts of the App Designer in a model-driven app (see Figure 6-10):

- **Components pane (labeled A in Figure 6-10):** Contains various form controls that you can drag and drop from the Components pane onto the Forms pane to customize the form's layout. You can add columns, sections, tabs, and more.
- **Tabs (labeled B in Figure 6-10):** Divide a single form into smaller, organized sections, making it easier for users to navigate different parts of the form. You can add tabs from the Components pane.

» **Form pane (labeled C in Figure 6-10):** Where you build the form by adding components from the Components pane to the Form Designer. Include sections to help break up the table columns into logical groupings on a given tab, making the form more straightforward to use and understand.

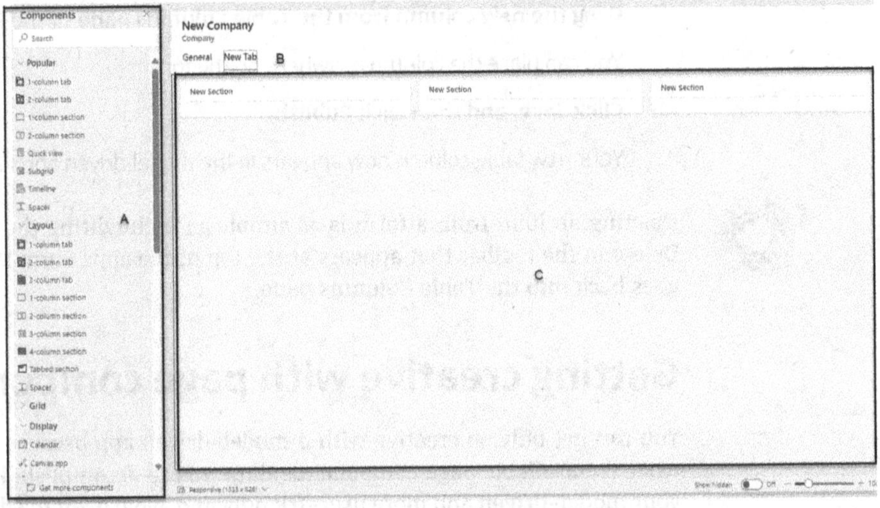

FIGURE 6-10: The parts of the model-driven app Form Designer window.

Getting a better look with Tree view

Although you might think that you can easily manage a model-driven app because the layout is all data-driven, don't underestimate the complexity of how many components you can place on a form. You create a hierarchy among components, from the header of a page to the footer. You can use the Tree View pane to quickly identify each form's properties, including columns, sections, tabs, and components. To work with Tree view, follow these steps:

1. **Open the Tree View pane by clicking the Pencil icon to the right of the form's name.**
2. **Click the Tree View tab that appears on the left.**
3. **Drill down in the Tree View pane to find the specific form component.**

   You can expand or collapse a *node* (the arrow next to each main section) by clicking it, which either displays or hides the elements within that node.

4. **Select a component in the Tree View pane.**

   That component becomes highlighted in the Form Designer (in Figure 6-11, I've selected the Sales Rep column), and the Properties pane on the right side of the window displays all the relevant properties for the selected column object.

TIP

If you need to hide a component, you can switch it from Show to Hide, and vice versa, from the toolbar on top of the page in Tree view. You can also delete components from the same toolbar.

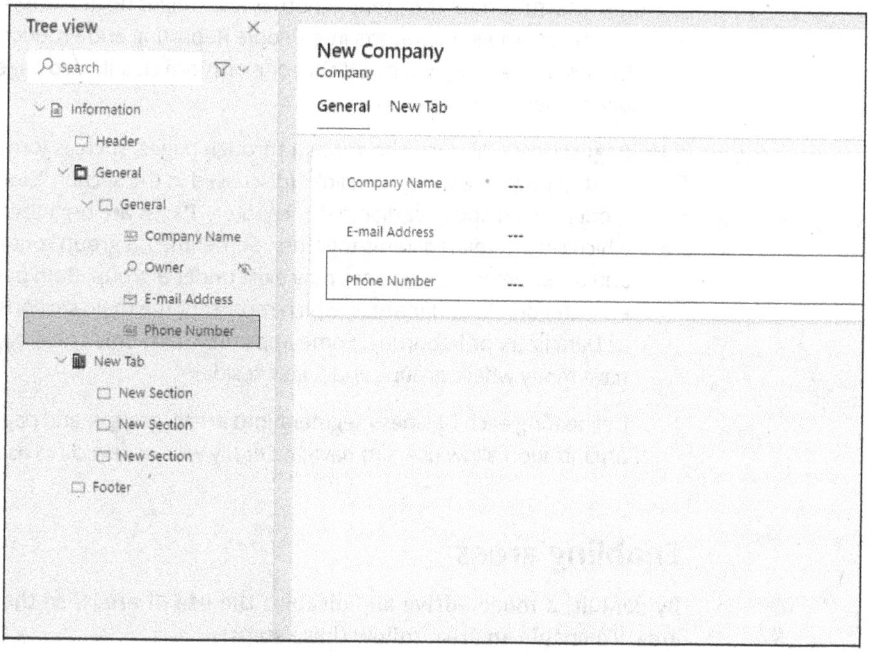

FIGURE 6-11: Looking at a model-driven app in Tree view.

Creating a page structure that supports navigation

Everything in a model-driven app is highly structured, including each page, the form created on each page, and navigation. You, as the application developer, can segment form pages and views into only one of three components:

» **Areas:** If your app has several key functions, you can organize it into different areas. You might break these areas down into major parts of the app's navigation, such as Data Entry, Reporting, or Administration. In a model-driven app, these areas appear in the lower-left corner of the navigation pane, so users can easily switch between different app capabilities.

If you don't want your end user to have access to an Administration part of your app's navigation, you can limit them to only having access to Data Entry and Reporting based on role-based access (discussed in Chapter 7).

- **Groups:** If your app has related functionality, you can organize all forms and data views into groups, which act as subcategories within an area. This structure helps users quickly navigate between different sections and related tasks.

  For example, an app may offer a user an area called Data Entry that includes two groups: People Forms and Product Forms. Each group would have one or more forms under the group. Another area might be dedicated to Reporting, which separates the reports into People Reporting and Product Reporting. Under each group, you might find one or more Dashboard pages or embedded Power BI reports.

- **Pages:** Users interact with content through pages, such as forms, dashboards, custom pages, or navigation links (discussed in the section "Starting with pages in model-driven apps," earlier in this chapter). Pages are organized within groups, which cluster related items together. Sometimes, a group contains a single page, and other times, many pages may exist under a group. Both pages and groups are categorized under areas, which represent the main sections of the app, such as Data Entry or Reporting. Some apps may have only one area, while others may have many where groups and pages reside.

  Delineating each business segment into areas, groups, and pages helps an organization allow users to navigate easily with as few clicks as possible.

Enabling areas

By default, a model-drive app disables the use of areas, so the app has only one area. To enable an area, follow these steps:

1. **In the App Designer, select Settings.**
2. **In the Settings window that appears, select the Navigation tab.**

   The Navigation tab has several check boxes that you can enable or disable.
3. **Select the Enable Areas check box.**
4. **Click the X.**

Adding a new area

To add an area in a model-driven app, you need to work within the app's *sitemap*, which organizes the app's navigation by dividing it into areas, groups, and pages. Some apps have more than one area, while a more simplistic app can actually have only one area. To add an area so that you can break up an app into more defined topics, follow these steps:

1. **On the left navigation pane of the App Designer, select Pages.**

   The Pages pane opens.

2. **From the Areas drop-down list at the top of the page, choose New Area.**

   On the right side of the window, the new area's Properties pane opens.

3. **Modify the properties to identify the area.**

   The properties you must fill out include the Title and ID.

4. **Click Save.**

5. **Repeat Steps 2 through 4 to create as many areas as you need to segment the app appropriately.**

6. **After you add all the areas you want, click Save, and then click Publish.**

   The new areas now appear on the left side of the app interface.

Creating a group

When dealing with creating groups, you have one of two scenarios to consider: The first is if you've never added a page before; the other is when a page exists, and you just want to break your pages up into more granular units:

» **If you've never added a page before:** Start by adding a page (explained in Chapter 6). When you add a page, it automatically gets assigned to the default group (because you have only one group initially). To modify the group name, select the topmost option in the navigation pane, and in the Properties pane (located on the right side of the window), update the Title and ID details.

» **If you already have a page:** You should see at least one group listed in the navigation pane on the left side of the window. To create an additional group, select the *ellipsis* (three dots) next to the existing group's name. From the pop-up menu that appears, choose New Group. Enter the Name and ID of the new group in the Properties pane that opens.

Having Fun With Forms

Apps are only as good as the data they allow in and out. If the app's interface doesn't allow the user to find or enter information, the app is worthless. The gateway to supporting all interface activity is a *form*, which is the primary method to collect and manage your app's data. You can create a fairly simplistic or complex form in a model-driven app. If your form includes a lot of components, you probably have more data complexity, which means you need to carefully manage the form's layout and logic to ensure usability and performance. For example, you may need to break a single form into multiple pages to maintain a user-friendly experience.

WARNING

When you, as an application designer, set out to develop an app, create the app's solution as *unmanaged* (meaning it can be edited and modified later) so that users can continue to add new forms and components. After you convert the solution to *managed* (meaning it's locked and no longer editable), Power Apps puts the app in production and restricts changes. In a managed app, you can't create new forms or edit existing forms for tables. Therefore, if you and the app's users require ongoing development, it's crucial to implement Application Lifecycle Management (ALM), as described earlier in this chapter and in Chapter 4.

The four out-of-the-box form types that you can use in a model-driven app are

- **Main form:** Where you can create the main user interface; for detailed data entry and management.
- **Quick Create:** Allows for quick — fast and minimal — data entry. Consider this form type if you have just a few fields that don't need to occupy an entire screen.
- **Quick View:** Read-only and used to display related data without editing. If you need to compare and contrast data and don't need data entry, this option offers a streamlined way to visualize and analyze information without complex input requirements.
- **Card form:** A small, compact form that you might have embedded in a main form to display key details or provide a quick overview of related data from another Dataverse table or a summary of associated data.

The four form types in model-driven apps share a common purpose of facilitating data interaction, whether data entry or data modification. You can customize all forms, but regardless of which form you customize, you want to organize and present data in ways that suit different tasks. All four form types provide flexibility in how users interact within the app.

Getting started with form layouts

Some forms might be simplistic, requiring a user to fill out only a few fields for before clicking the Save button. However, an enterprise-level model-driven app likely requires more complex data collection than a simple single form that has a few fields on one page. Enterprise model-driven apps often contain many (possibly in the tens to hundreds of) forms. Before designing your app, plan out the form layout carefully by considering the following:

- **Number of tabs:** You want each tab to contain a distinct dataset type. Think of tabs like the different sections of a filing cabinet, where each tab represents a separate folder containing related information. In the same way that each folder organizes specific documents within a larger system, each tab in your model-driven app organizes related data into manageable sections.
- **Number of columns and sections per tab:** The first rule of application design is to minimize scrolling. Another rule is to group similar data together on a form by using the sections component for a given form. If you have a large amount of data to display on a single page, use tabs to organize related topics into separate areas.

  For example, in a job application, place Contact Information in one tab, Former Employers on the second tab, and Education in the third tab. Within each tab, if you need to capture yes/no or short-answer data, you can use multiple columns by adjusting the layout to split the fields into two or more columns, making the form more concise and easier to navigate.
- **What components to integrate:** You can use various components, such as grids, images, custom forms, or cards, available from the Components pane. Or you may want to include lookups and choice fields that you create in the Table Column pane. (You can read about creating lookups in the section "Adding a grid and a lookup field to a tab," later in this chapter.)

To design an effective form, follow these general steps:

1. **Identify the columns that you need based on the data entry and display requirements.**
2. **Determine how to organize your components within those columns.**

   Decide whether to use grids, images, lookups, or custom forms to either display the data or allow for user input.

For more details on selecting and configuring columns that are part of a form, see Chapter 3, where I delve into how to choose the right columns and components for your Dataverse data entry needs.

Creating a main form

When you create a table in Dataverse, you get a head start because Power Apps creates a main form automatically. But, of course, it's not like your work is done just because Power Apps created the form. You have to configure and populate each form with the components that you plan to use to complete data entry. To create and format the main form, follow these steps:

1. **Log in to access the PowerApps Maker Portal.**
2. **On the left-hand side, select the Tables tab, and choose the table you want to work with.**
3. **In the Tables window that opens, click the name of the table for which you want to create or edit a form.**

   The Table window appears for the table you selected.

   In my example, I click the Company table.
4. **In the Data Experiences column of the Company table window, select Forms (see Figure 6-12).**

   The Company Forms window opens.

FIGURE 6-12: The Company Table window with the Data Experiences column highlighted.

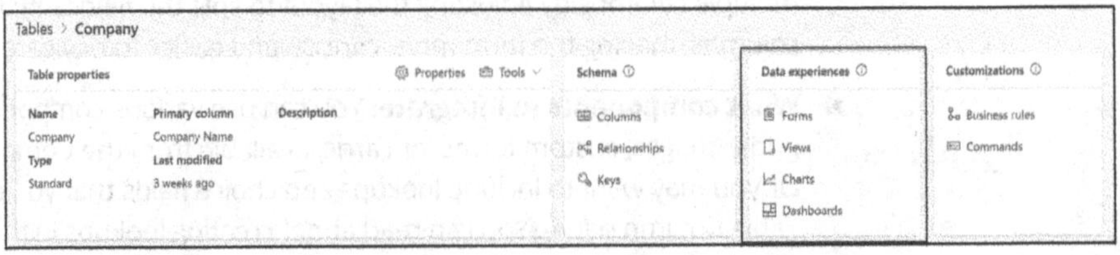

5. **Click the three vertical dots to the left of the Form Type.**

   TIP

   Every default form created by Power Apps is named Information. You can leave it as is or modify the table name.
6. **From the pop-up menu that appears, choose Edit ⇨ Edit.**

   Figure 6-13 shows this menu.

   The main form for your table appears, where you can apply the appropriate tabs to the form.

Adding tabs to your form

To create tabs, follow these steps:

1. **In the Components pane on the left of the Main Form window, drag and drop the 1-Column Tab into the main form.**
2. **Select the tab to open its Properties pane.**

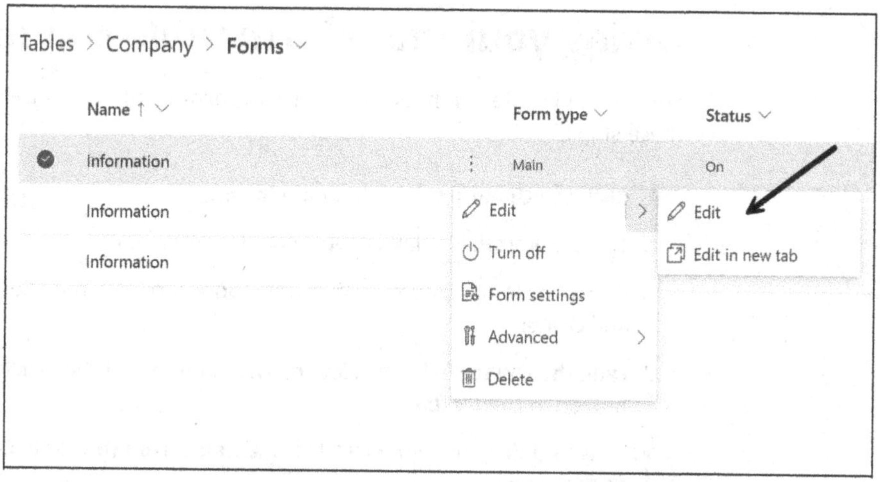

FIGURE 6-13: Opening the Edit window for a form.

3. **Change the tab's name in the Label field.**

   For my example, I'm changing the name to Locations.

4. **From the Components pane, drag and drop the 2-Column Tab to the form.**
5. **Repeat Steps 2 and 3 for the new tab.**

   I changed the tab name to Contracts in my example. Figure 6-14 shows how the form incorporates the two tabs, Locations and Contracts.

6. **Click the default Related tab and select Hide in the toolbar.**

   The Related tab in a model-driven app form shows data from other tables that are connected to the current record (which this record doesn't have).

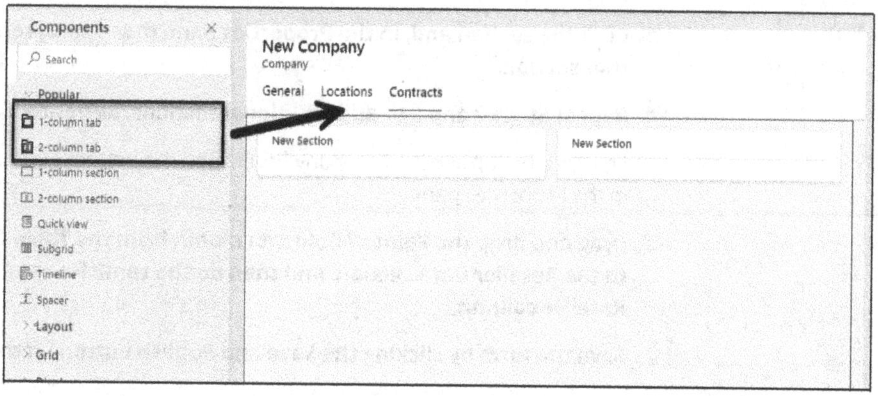

FIGURE 6-14: A form that has added tabs.

Giving your main form table columns

You can add table columns to your main form in the Form Designer. Just follow these steps:

1. **Click the General tab in the main form.**

   The General tab is a default tab created for every form.

   For this example, assume two columns appear on the form: Company and Owner.

2. **Hide the Owner field by selecting the column and then clicking the Hide button in the toolbar.**

3. **Drag and drop the E-mail and Phone fields from the Table Column pane to the form.**

4. **In the Table Column pane, select New Table Column.**

   The New Table Column pane appears on the right.

5. **Create a new column called Point of Contact with the Data Type of Single Line of Text.**

   You can see how to create a column in the section "Adding a column from the app," earlier in this chapter.

6. **Repeat Step 5 to add another column called Reseller that uses the data type option Yes/No.**

   Both table columns appear on the Table Columns pane.

7. **From the Components pane on the left side of the window, drag and drop a 1-Column Section onto the General tab.**

8. **Click the section and, in the Properties pane that opens, rename that section.**

9. **Repeat Steps 7 and 8 to add additional sections, as desired.**

   I named the top section Company Profile and the bottom section Reseller Data in the Properties pane.

10. **Drag and drop the Point of Contact column from the Table Column pane to the Reseller Data section, and then do the same for the Reseller column.**

11. **Save the form by clicking the Save and Publish button on the toolbar.**

Adding a grid and a lookup field to a tab

In this section, I show you how to add a grid and a lookup field to a tab. You can use the Locations tab that you can create in the section "Adding tabs to your form," earlier in this chapter. And to follow these steps, you need to create additional tables (including one named States, which I show you how to make in Chapter 3). You need to have additional tables pre-populated before you can use each component. After you create those tables, you can integrate the data into the form. Follow these steps to set up a grid and lookup drop-down list on the Location tab:

1. **Go to the Locations tab by clicking it from the Form Designer.**
2. **Create a new table column by clicking the New Table Column button in the Table Column pane.**
3. **In the Column Name text box that appears, enter** Company HQ.
4. **From the Data Type drop-down list, select Lookup ⇨ Lookup.**
5. **Select the States table in the Related Table drop-down list.**
6. **Click Save.**

   Users can now select the state's name for the Company HQ from a predefined list.

7. **Drag and drop the newly created Lookup column from the Table Columns pane to the Locations tab, then position it in the Form Designer.**
8. **Repeat Steps 2 through 7 to add additional table columns from the Table Columns pane.**

   You can also add components from the Components pane.

   In Figure 6-15, I'm adding an editable grid to the form (under the Locations tab).

   ON THE WEB

   Configuring some components, such as the editable grid, can get pretty complex. An editable grid is particularly useful for bulk updates or when you need quick, efficient data entry across multiple records. To get the skinny on how to configure the editable grid component, go to `http://learn.microsoft.com` and enter **editable grid control** in the Search text box. The results can give you a better idea of how to use editable grids.

9. **Select Save and Publish.**

   All users can now access the updated main form with its new lookup column.

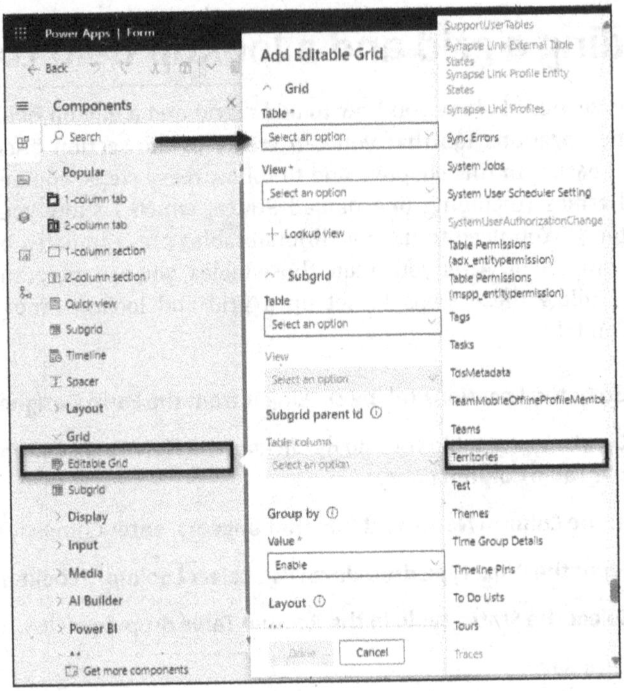

FIGURE 6-15: Creating an editable grid.

Veering into Views

You want to give your model-driven app users a means to query the records stored in Dataverse tables they've entered using a form. Based on a defined query, you can present records in a read-only format through a view. Unlike a form (discussed in the section "Having Fun with Forms," earlier in this chapter), a *view* is a snapshot of a Dataverse table's dataset. With a view, you configure the columns you want to display, along with specific filters limiting which records appear on the model-driven app page. A view may consist of:

- A minimum of one column
- A default sort order (if it contains multiple columns)
- Filters to restrict a record set based on a finite condition

The developer decides each of these characteristics based on the user type, such as a sales and marketing professional who has a public view or all end users who have access to a system view. (You can get the scoop on role-based access principles in Chapter 7.) Keep in mind that an app designer creates public and system views, but a user, if they get permission from the System Administrator, can also create personal data views.

Assigning views based on roles and responsibilities

Not all users see the same data. Everyone can access views if you set the view as Public; you can also limit access to views to just a single person by enforcing Personal views. Views depend on your security roles and responsibilities, which I discuss in greater depth in Chapter 7. The three types of views include

- **Personal view:** The data that the user creates, assuming the user has access to create and share the dataset within the app.
- **System view:** A predefined view available to all users based on their security roles. These views aren't tied to an individual model-driven app, but are instead linked to Dataverse tables and can be used across multiple apps that access the same data. Only system administrators or customizers, roles associated with Dataverse, can modify the system views.
- **Public view:** A general-purpose view that all app users can access. Users can apply custom filters to column data in their application instance, but they can't save changes to the public view unless they have permission to create personal views.

Understanding public views

The easiest way to create a new view or modify an existing view is to start from your Dataverse table because each table, by default, comes with six pre-built views, as shown in Figure 6-16.

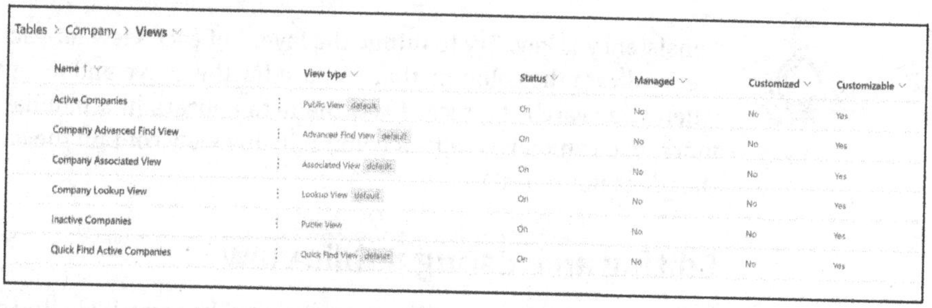

Tables > Company > Views
Name
View type
Status
Managed
Customized
Customizable
Active Companies
Public View default
Company Advanced Find View
Advanced Find View default
Company Associated View
Associated View default
Company Lookup View
Lookup View default
Inactive Companies
Public View
Quick Find Active Companies
Quick Find View default
On
No
Yes

FIGURE 6-16: The available view types for a Dataverse table.

Table 6-2 describes each view type available for a Dataverse table.

REMEMBER

A user can toggle a record between Deactivate and Activate to make a record Active or Inactive if they have the appropriate permissions. The ability to make a record Active or Inactive also impacts all the other public views because an Inactive record appears only if you filter a record set to be inclusive of inactive data.

TABLE 6-2 Public View Types

View Type	What It Shows
Active	A public view displays all records marked as Active. Records are considered *active* once they're saved. Until a user *deactivates* a record (marking it as inactive), that record remains in the Active status and appears in the public view.
Inactive	An Inactive view displays all records that a user has deactivated. These records are typically archived and no longer actively seen by a user; but you can keep them for reference or historical purposes.
Quick Find	Search across multiple columns pre-defined by the system administrator. The view then displays the results in a list format, showing only those records in which the data in the specified columns match the search parameter.
Advanced Find	Create custom queries that have specific filters, enabling users to search for data across multiple tables. Displays the matching records based on the filters applied in the query.
Associated	Displays all related records from another table linked to a specific record.
Lookup	Displays key data from a record when you search for and select it. Typically shows one or two key columns of data, providing a concise view of the record.

Creating or editing a view

A user can either modify any of the existing public views available or create their personal view for a given entity. To create or edit an existing table, go to Tables in the Makers Portal. You should then select the table that you want to either create or edit a view for under the Data Experience section.

The following sections show you how to modify an existing view, as well as create a new public view.

TIP

Consistency is key. Try to mimic the layout of each view for each table. For example, replicate the columns that you use for the active and inactive options so that when you search the record set, the data appears in a familiar format. Furthermore, you can make the first column in any view contain the *unique value* (a value that does not repeat).

Editing an existing public view

Follow these steps to modify an existing public view, including adding Sort By and Filter conditions:

1. **From the Dataverse Table list, select the table that you want to use.**

   In my example, I select the table Company.

2. **In the table, click Views in the Data Experiences section.**

   A list of available views created by Power Apps appears.

3. **Click the link for the view that you want to modify.**

   I selected Active Company.

   A default interface appears.

   You can adjust this default interface, for example, by including additional columns or removing unnecessary columns.

4. **Select the + View Column button to the right of the Public View.**
5. **Double-click each column you want to add from the View list.**
6. **Repeat Steps 4 and 5 for each column that you want to add to the Active View.**

   In my example, I added the columns Company HQ, E-mail Address, Phone Number, Reseller, and Point of Contact.

   Alternatively, you can drag and drop the fields from the Table Column pane onto the View pane. The columns appear from left to right in the order you added them.

7. **(Optional) To delete unwanted columns in the Active View, click the column and select Remove from the drop-down list that appears.**

   In my example, I removed the Created By column.

8. **Rearrange the columns so that they appear in a particular order by dragging and dropping the column's header.**

   For this example, I moved Point of Contact from the last column to the third column, between Company HQ and E-mail Address.

9. **(Optional) To add multiple sort options beyond the first column, in the Properties pane for the selected view, click Then Sort By.**

   The first column in the example (see Figure 6-17) is Company Name. I sorted by Company HQ and then added a secondary sort parameter.

10. **If you want to add a filter parameter as well, click Edit Filter in the section Filter By.**
11. **In the Edit Filter window that appears, add each condition that you want to filter by.**

    The filter parameters that you can choose from include Contains, Status, or Equals.

    I created a Filter By condition that equals Company Name Contains, shown in Figure 6-17.

12. **To save the view in Dataverse, click Save and Publish.**

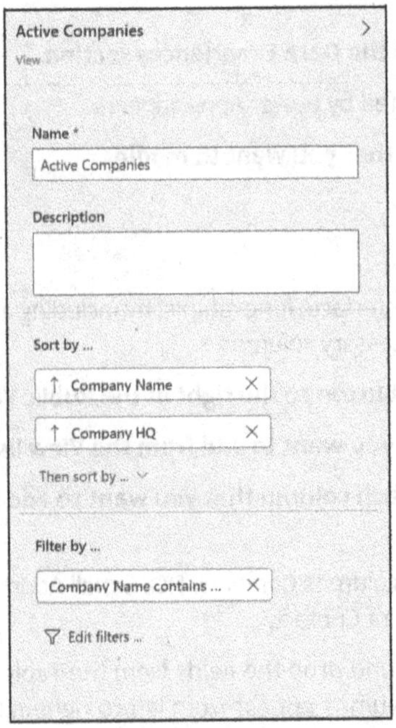

FIGURE 6-17: Creating a Sort By and Filter By condition for a view.

The updated Active Company view (see Figure 6-18) incorporates all the values that I added, as well as the Sort By and Filter By conditions shown in Figure 6-17. The view updates in the app only when you republish the app by clicking the Save and Publish button found in the toolbar.

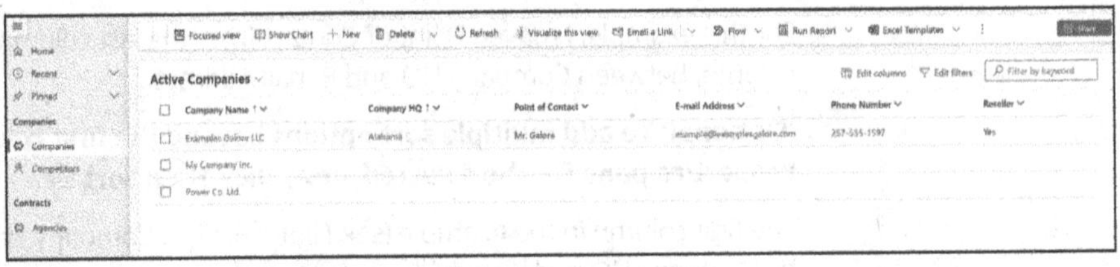

FIGURE 6-18: A customized active view in a model-driven app.

Creating a new view

To create a brand-new view in your model-driven app, start at your Dataverse table of choice. In the example, go back to the Companies table that was created under Views. Instead of accessing an existing view, you can create a new view by following these steps:

1. **Click the New View button at the top of the View pane.**
2. **In the New View window that opens, add the Name and Description of the proposed view in the appropriate text boxes.**

   I add the Name as Company HQ View and provide a description of the proposed view.
3. **Click Create.**

   The primary column — in my example, Company Name — appears as the only column listed in the view.
4. **Add an additional column to the Company HQ View.**

   You can either

   - Drag the columns from the Table Columns pane, or
   - Click the + View Column button on the right of the last column in the View.

   I added the column Company HQ.

   Two columns now appear in your new view.
5. **Click the Save and Publish button in the toolbar to save your new view.**

   You can now use the view that you just created as an Active view throughout the model-driven app.

IN THIS CHAPTER

» Integrating charts and dashboards into a model-driven app

» Building business process flow automation

» Securing data that your model-driven app captures and presents

Chapter 7

Extending a Model-Driven App

To gain the most benefit from the data you collect using your model-driven apps, you usually want to find a way to use that data to tell a story. For example, if you're running a business, you may want to convey that story by using visualizations based on the data stored in Dataverse and integrating charts and dashboards into your model-driven apps.

Most developers immediately assume they should jump to Power BI for data visualization and Power Automate for workflow management to handle activities related to automating data analytic outputs or business process flows, but as you see in this chapter, you also can manage these activities through Dataverse, which happens to work exclusively with model-driven apps.

In this chapter, I also show how to create and assign security roles that specify which users can access the data you capture and present through your model-driven apps.

Charting and Dashboarding

When you plan your model-driven app, consider what the user expects the output to be in the fully-built app. You can use *tabular reports* (which are simple, row-based data displays) in Dataverse to quickly access record-level data. However, many users don't necessarily need that level of detail; they want a snapshot of their data to quickly understand what their data means, similar to telling a story.

For visual insights, a user can use either the Dataverse chart or dashboard capabilities, which are available in the Dataverse Table Settings. A developer can then make the visualization available (and even interactive) in a model-driven app. Alternately, if you want to allow users to access sophisticated reporting and distribution, you can enable embedded Power BI reporting within a solution.

REMEMBER

If you stick with chart and dashboard functionality in Dataverse, you don't need a secondary Power BI license. However, every user of the apps you create must be licensed as a Power Apps user. Check the Microsoft 365 admin center or Power Platform admin center to make sure that all users who plan to use your app have the appropriate Power Apps premium license.

In Dataverse, *charts* are visual representations that display data from one or more columns in a single Dataverse table. For example, you can have a table named Company that contains several columns. A chart can analyze the data from the Company table and its columns, but it can't directly analyze data from other tables, such as Customer or Products, unless those tables have a defined relationship in Dataverse.

So, say that a user wants to determine a table's distribution of specific values. A single chart can *aggregate the responses* (meaning summarize or group the data) and present that visually. You can design your chart to present such data by using one or more visualization types, including columns, bars, areas, stacks, lines, bubbles, or pie charts.

With model-driven apps, developers can also use the *grid control* (a tabular layout displaying rows of data from a Dataverse table) by configuring the view to display the data in a grid format. A grid control can

- **Present data in either a read-only or editable format:** Grids can display data as *read-only* (for viewing only) or *editable* (allowing users to update records directly). Read-only grids are generally used for final reports; editable grids enable users to update their data without leaving the interface or going to each record individually.
- **Allow filtering and drill-down operations that affect only visualization:** Modify the visible data without affecting the record. A user can narrow the view of the dataset based on a filter, which can enhance data exploration.
- **Present multiple table points across a single table, rather than summarize one column:** Instead of combining the data from one column, grids can

show multiple data points (for example, Sales, Cost, Profit) side by side, providing a more comprehensive view of all data relevant to a record.

- **Compare values between two table columns:** Similar to presenting multiple tables, you can also compare values by using a grid to spot differences or trends. Features such as conditional formatting can further highlight critical insights.

TECHNICAL STUFF

You can import external visualizations into a model-driven app to help further explain a chart, integrating web resources in the form of HTML files or images, such as JPEG, PNG, GIF, into a custom visualization. To see how to programmatically incorporate web resources, go to `https://learn.microsoft.com/en-us/power-apps/developer/model-driven-apps/web-resources`.

Crafting visualizations from Dataverse

Your model-driven app can contain charts and dashboards:

- **Chart:** A single snapshot of data from a table. You can have any number of charts associated with a table, and each chart stands on its own.
- **Dashboard:** Brings together charts for a single table in one window so you can review all data in a visual format on a single page.

To create a chart, follow these steps:

1. **Access the Power Apps Maker Portal by going to `http://make.powerapps.com`.**
2. **In the Solutions pane on the left, click Tables.**

   The Tables window appears.
3. **From the Tables window, select the table from which you want to create a chart.**

   The Tables Settings page for your selected table opens.
4. **From the Data Experiences pane, click Charts.**
5. **Select the New Chart button in the command bar (as shown in Figure 7-1).**

   Alternatively, from the list of charts that appears on the right, you can select any existing chart (that you have access to).
6. **In the New Chart window that appears, enter a name for the chart in the Enter a Chart Name Here text box.**

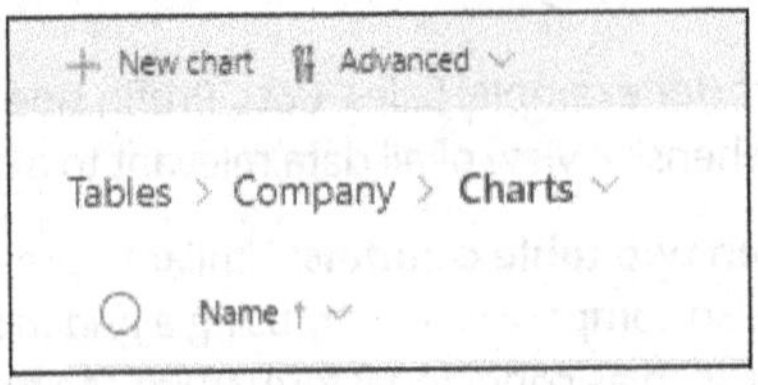

FIGURE 7-1: The New Chart button and Charts drop-down list.

7. **Select the type of chart that you want to display from the Chart Type drop-down list.**

   The basis of your chart is the View Data selection, which means the chart will base the output on the selected view from the table that you select in the drop-down list.

   In my example, the chart will analyze the Active City Details view from the Company table (see Figure 7-2).

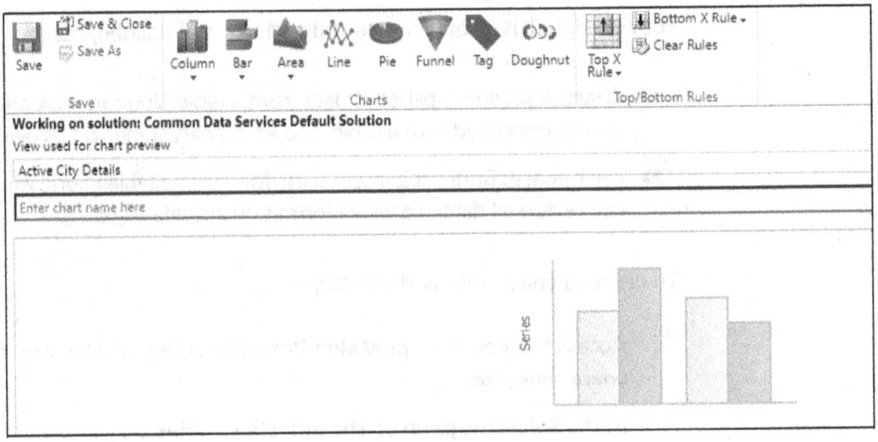

FIGURE 7-2: The New Chart window, where you can select the type of chart to create.

8. **Select the data that you want to appear in the chart.**

   Figure 7-3 shows the Chart Configuration window, where you can specify the data you want to use.

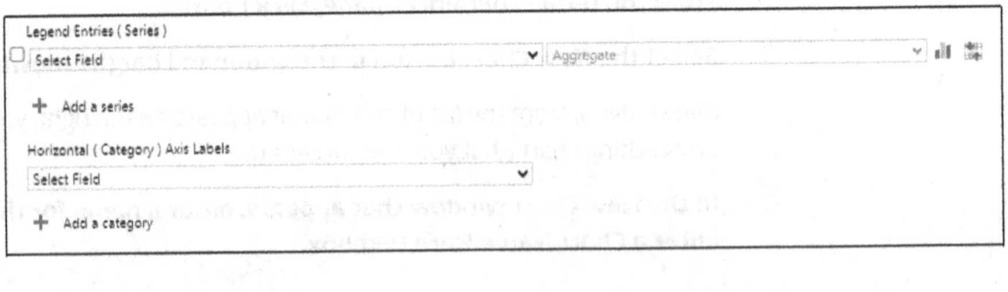

FIGURE 7-3: The Chart Configuration window.

9. **In the Legend Entries (Series) section of the Chart Configuration window, select the data you want to graph from the Select Fields drop-down list.**

10. **Configure the series data to specify how you want to itemize that data.**

    The summarization options typically include Average, Count, Max, Min, and Sum; but they vary depending on the field type. Numeric fields offer all options. But text fields generally provide only the Count option, and date fields may offer Min and Max.

    In my example, I selected the State data and the itemization option of Count:All.

11. **In the Horizontal (Category) Axis Labels section, select from the Select Field drop-down list a field that categorizes your data.**

    If you want to *summarize* (count) data, select the same field that you selected in Step 9.

    In my example, I selected State. I want to use the chart in Figure 7-4 to determine the number of Sales Reps associated with a State by summarizing the instances of a specific state.

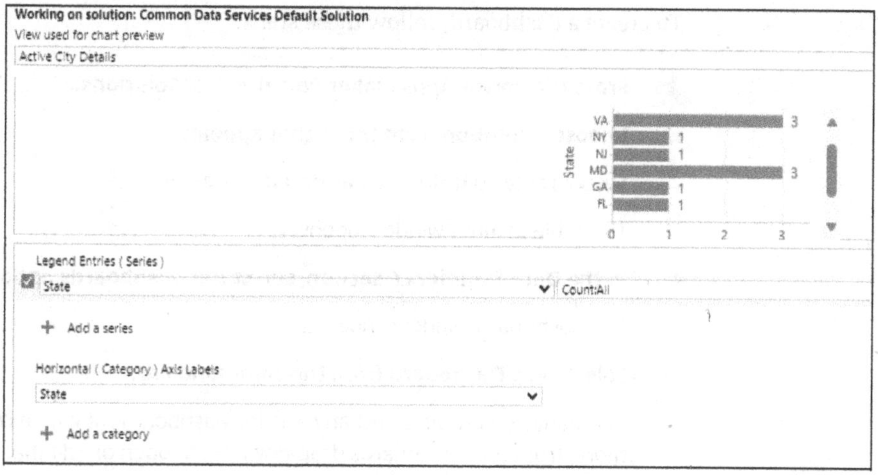

FIGURE 7-4: A preview of a chart created from a Dataverse table.

12. **(Optional) Add a description for your chart in the Description field.**

    A description helps other users understand the purpose of the chart.

13. **After you're satisfied with your chart, select Save and Close to close the Chart Designer window and return to your list of charts.**

    The chart is saved to the table's Dataverse Table Settings.

TIP

By default, the name of the chart in the Charts tab is the comparison of the two columns evaluated. You can change the name of the chart to make it more descriptive by editing the Chart properties.

Telling a story by using dashboards

A single chart provides only one piece of the story about your data. Using the Company table example from the preceding section, imagine you want to view the number of active employees per state, the number of cities in which employees work per state, and the total number of current employees assigned to a territory. Each of these data points tells a unique story about the employment structure for a potential company within the Company Dataverse table.

To convey this information, a developer might create several charts, each highlighting various aspects of the company's status. When these charts are brought together on a single page, they collectively tell a broader story, such as the distribution of sales representatives across various data points. This collection of visualizations on a single page is called a *dashboard.*

To create a dashboard, follow these steps:

1. **From the Power Apps Maker Portal, select Solutions.**
2. **Choose a solution from those that appear.**
3. **Select Tables within the solution that opens.**

   The Table Settings window opens.
4. **In the Data Experience section, select the Dashboards option.**

   The Dashboard window appears.
5. **Select New Dashboard from the command bar.**

   Alternatively, you can select any existing dashboards (if you've created one or more) from the Dashboards drop-down list to open or edit that dashboard.
6. **In the pop-up menu that appears, select your preferred Dashboard Type format.**

   You have four options (see Figure 7-5):

   - 4-Column Overview
   - 3-Column Overview (Varied Width)
   - 3-Column Overview
   - 2-Column Overview

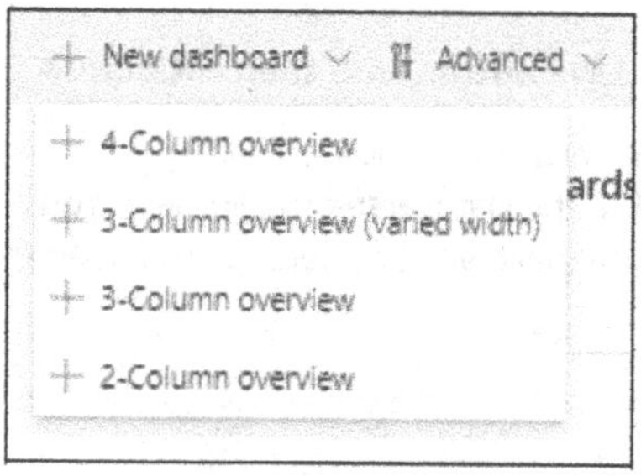

FIGURE 7-5: Selecting the Dashboard layout.

I selected the 3-Column Overview (Varied Width) layout option for my example.

A template appears in which you can complete the configuration of your dashboard.

7. **In the Name text box, enter a name for your dashboard.**
8. **Select the method by which you want to filter the data from the Filter By drop-down list.**

   The Filter Entity option should already have the table selected that you specified in Step 2.
9. **In the Time Frame drop-down list, select the data that you want to present based on what period of time.**
10. **Select which view to derive the data from in the Entity View drop-down list.**
11. **In the Visual Filters section, select the charts associated with the entity.**

    Depending on the layout you use, the number of charts varies.

    My example includes two additional charts besides the State-by-State chart I created in the preceding section.
12. **Click the Chart icon in the toolbar.**
13. **Select a chart from the list that appears.**
14. **Repeat Steps 12 and 13 for the two remaining charts.**

    Three charts appear side by side, one in each Visual Filter panel, as shown in Figure 7-6.
15. **Add a stream to your dashboard by clicking the Stream button.**

    In the context of a Dataverse dashboard, a *stream* refers to the continuous flow of data or updates from a Dataverse table. Unlike a static chart, a stream allows a user to monitor and visualize. In other words, when your dataset updates, the view associated with that dataset also updates without a manual refresh.

16. **Before exiting, click the Save button, and then click Close.**

Dataverse saves the dashboard and associated configurations with the specific tables you select in Step 6 to the Dataverse environment. You can now make it available to users by associating it with any solution that uses the relevant Dataverse table.

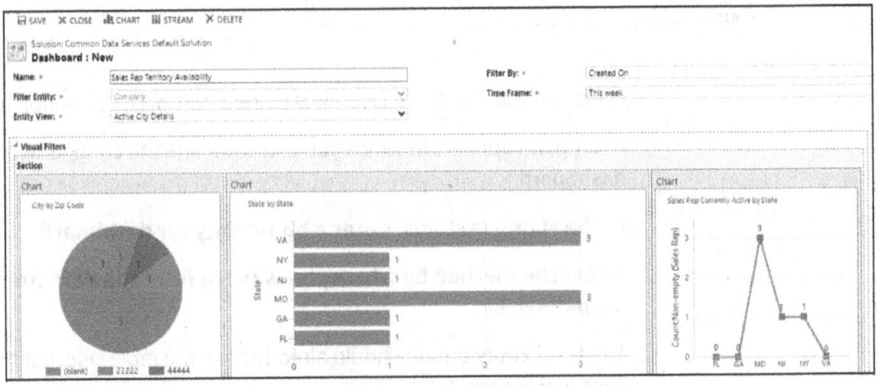

FIGURE 7-6: Creating a 3-Column Overview (Variable Width) dashboard.

Embedding a dashboard into a model-driven app

After you create a dashboard (see the preceding section) or any other Dataverse component, you must manually associate the component with a solution in Dataverse. Dataverse doesn't automatically link these components to your model-driven app, so it's your responsibility to add them.

Solutions in Dataverse allow you to bundle various components, such as tables, dashboards, forms, and workflows, used to build apps. Solutions make managing, versioning, and deploying across environments easier.

WARNING

You can't embed something that doesn't exist, so ensure that you've created all dashboards and reports that you want to associate with your app before attempting to embed them.

To embed a component, such as a Dataverse dashboard or report, in a model-driven app, follow these steps:

1. **Log into `http://make.powerapps.com` to access the Power Apps Maker Portal.**
2. **Select Solutions from the left navigation pane.**

   You need to integrate your dashboards and embedded reports as part of a solution.

   The Solutions list opens. This list displays all the solutions available in your environment, including *managed* (pre-built and non-editable) and *unmanaged* (editable for development).
3. **Select the solution that you intend to use from the Solutions list.**

   After you select a solution, you can then see all the components associated with a solution.
4. **From the Dashboard toolbar, choose New ⇨ Dashboard, and then select the format that you want to create from the Dashboard pop-up menu that appears.**

   Figure 7-7 shows you the Dashboard pop-up menu. If you're embedding a dashboard, choose the same configuration that you chose for your Dataverse-based dashboard (which you can see how to create in the preceding section).
5. **After you format your dashboard (modify fonts, font alignment, and any other formatting), click Save.**

   The updated dashboard or report appears in the Components list.

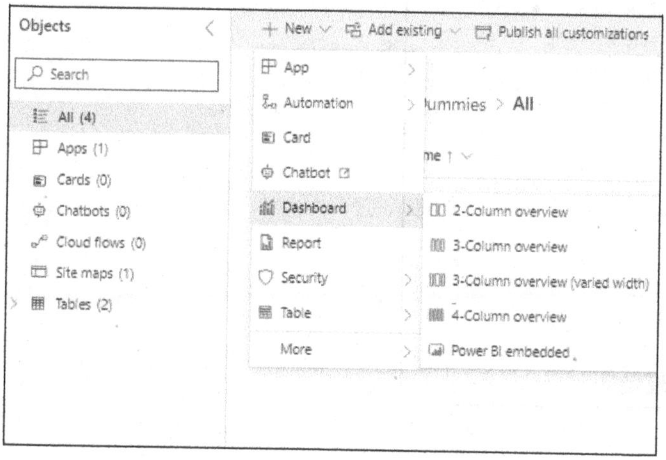

FIGURE 7-7: Creating a new Dataverse dashboard.

Embedding Power BI reports and dashboards

Sometimes, when adding components from outside Dataverse, you may have to complete a few extra steps to integrate those assets fully into your app. One of the most common integrations, particularly for complex reports or dashboards, involves embedding Power BI content. You can embed a single Power BI report or dashboard, following a process similar to the one you use to embed Dataverse dashboards and reports (discussed in the preceding section), with a few additional steps.

To embed a Power BI report into a model-driven app, follow these steps:

1. **Select the Power BI Embedded option in the Dashboards menu.**

   The New Power BI Embedded pop-up window opens (see Figure 7-8).

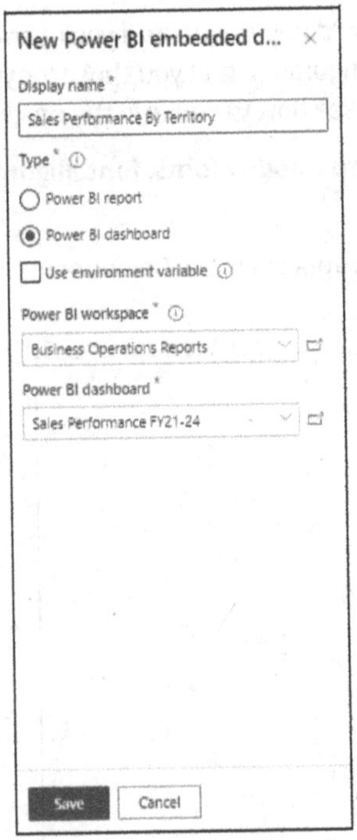

FIGURE 7-8: The New Power BI embedded dashboard pop-up window.

2. **In the Display Name text box, type in a name that reflects the purpose of the Power BI embedded asset.**
3. **In the Type section, select the radio button for Power BI Report or Power BI Dashboard.**

   Power Apps doesn't automatically assume a default type, so you choose between embedding a Report or Dashboard. Either of these components reflect real-time data from the Power BI service.
4. **(Optional) If you want to dynamically link Power BI content by using environment-specific settings, select the Use Environment Variable check box.**
5. **In the Power BI Workspace drop-down list, select the Power BI workspace that contains the dashboard you want to embed.**
6. **Select the report or dashboard that you intend to embed into the app from the Power BI Dashboard drop-down list.**
7. **Click Save.**

   The updated dashboard or report appears, displaying your newly embedded content within the Components list of your solution.

REMEMBER

After you save and publish, an embedded dashboard or report may take a few minutes to appear active in an app, so don't panic if you don't immediately see it.

Integrating embedded components into a model-driven app

Even after you add your component to the solution (see the preceding sections), you haven't yet added it to the app navigation. Follow these steps to fully integrate your dashboard:

1. **Open the Power Apps Maker Portal at `http://make.powerapps.com`.**
2. **In the Solutions area, choose the solution containing your model-driven app and components.**

   The solution contains your model-driven app and the embedded components.
3. **Click the app's name in the Solution that appears.**

   The App Designer is open.

4. **In the App Designer, click Pages.**
5. **In the Pages section at the top of the App Designer, click Add Page.**
6. **From the list that appears, select the Dashboards page type.**

   The Select a Dashboard pop-up window opens (see Figure 7-9).
7. **Select the type of dashboard you're looking for from the All Dashboards drop-down list.**
8. **From the list that appears in the Select a Dashboard window, select the dashboard that you want to add to the page.**

   You can also use the Search box to locate your dashboard.

   After you select the dashboard, it appears in the model-driven app.
9. **Customize the remaining properties from the Properties pane.**
10. **Click Save, and then click Publish to apply the changes to the app.**

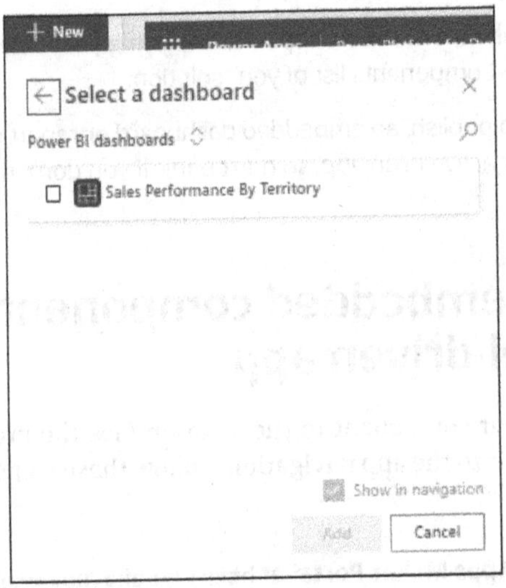

FIGURE 7-9: Selecting a dashboard.

In the example shown in Figure 7-10, I selected the Power BI embedded dashboard, which you can see in the navigation, which gives the user a more interactive and dynamic experience. The chart formats seen in Figure 7-10 aren't available in your traditional Dataverse charting and Dashboarding experience, hence the integration with Power BI. Figure 7-11 shows a new dashboard that has been integrated by using Dataverse chart data, which illustrates a more streamlined format based on a single table.

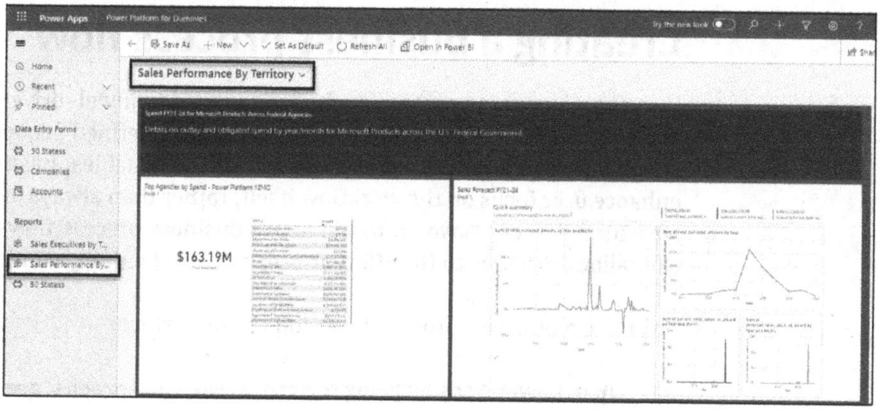

FIGURE 7-10: Example Embedded Power BI Dashboard.

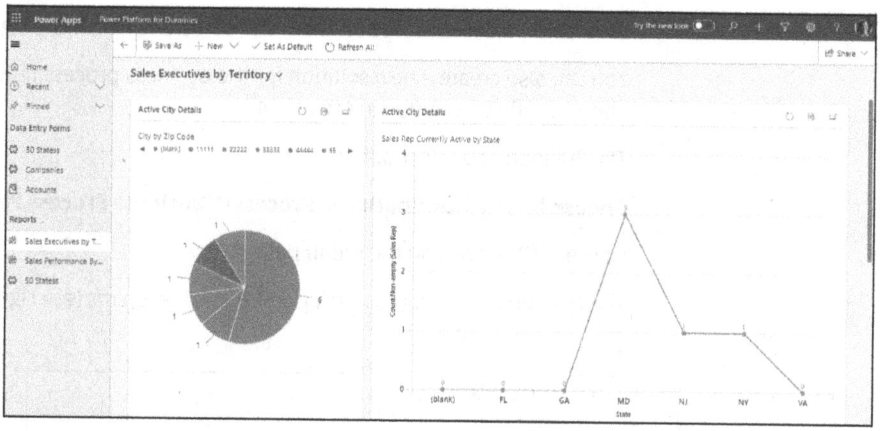

FIGURE 7-11: Example Dashboard created using Charts from Dataverse.

Building Out Business Process Flows

Organizations may want to collect data that leads to a decision or outcome. Business process flows ensure data consistency and standardize steps for customer interactions, such as handling service requests uniformly or requiring invoice approval before order submission that lead to such events. These steps provide a guided user experience tailored to different security roles, streamlining processes, and reducing the need for extensive training by allowing the process to guide users through tasks based on stages.

Business process flows define the stages and steps that appear at the top of each page of a model-driven app, with each step representing a column for data entry on a form. A business process flow makes sure that the user performs the required steps before that user can advance to the next stage, a process known as *stage-gating*.

Creating a business process flow

Creating a business process flow in PowerApps for model-driven apps streamlines complex workflows by guiding users through a defined sequence of stages and actions. By linking rows from up to five different tables, business process flows enhance user focus on the workflow itself, rather than always focusing on the data structure. You can have up to ten active business process flows per table, so you can tailor processes to fit different user roles and varying conditions.

To create a business process flow, follow these steps:

1. **Open Power Apps by going to `http://make.powerapps.com`.**
2. **Select Solutions from the Solution bar on the left.**
3. **Choose an existing solution from the solutions list in the right pane.**

   You can also create a new solution for the business process flow. You can read about creating a solution in Chapter 4.

   The Solution you select opens.
4. **Choose New ⇨ Automation ⇨ Process ⇨ Business Process Flow.**

   Figure 7-12 shows you the menu path.

   The New Business Process Flow pop-up window opens (see Figure 7-13).

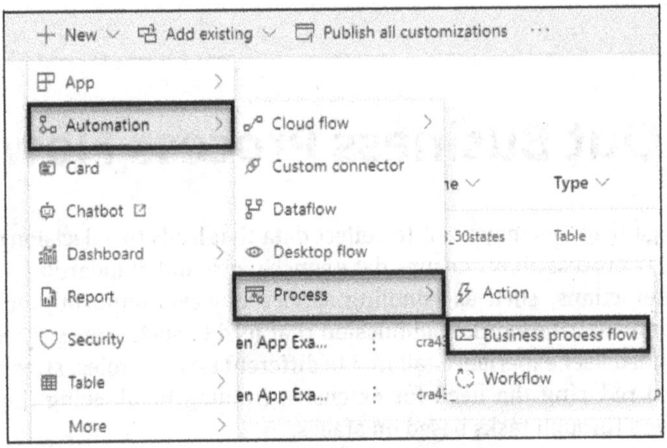

FIGURE 7-12: The menu path to create a new business process flow.

5. **Type a name into the Display Name text box.**

   After you enter the Display Name of your flow (for example, "Trigger an Email"), the system generates the logical name in the Name field (something like cr043_triggeranemail). The name combines the Publisher Name (discussed in Chapters 2 and 4) and the Display Name.

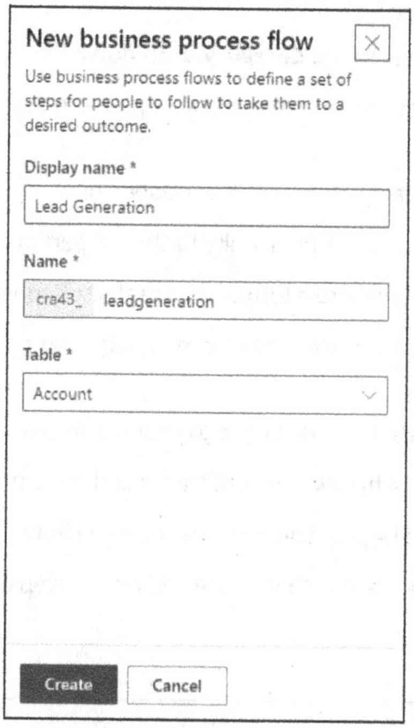

FIGURE 7-13: The New Business Process Flow pop-up window.

6. **Select the table you want the flow to use from the Table drop-down list.**

   In my example, I selected the Account table from the Table list.

7. **Click Create.**

   The new business process flow has a single stage and now appears listed in your selected solution.

Configuring stages

After you create a new business flow (see the preceding section), you can add stages to that flow. To progress from one business stage to another, follow these steps:

1. **Drag a component from the Components tab onto the plus sign (+) in the Designer canvas.**

   Figure 7-14 has five existing stages already.

   A new stage opens.

2. **Type the stage's name into the Display Name text box in the Properties pane.**

3. **Select a stage category from the Category drop-down list.**

   Select the stage that best represents the action or phase in your mapping process:

   - *Qualify:* Evaluate or qualify a lead, case, or opportunity.
   - *Develop:* Develop the case or opportunity further as part of the intake process.
   - *Propose:* When transitioning to a formal proposal or offering a solution.
   - *Close:* The final stage of a process (for example, case completion or sales closure).
   - *Custom:* When the stage listed is unique to your organization's specific process.

   The example in Figure 7-14 has two custom stages and three pre-built stages.

4. **Click Apply to save the stage to the business process flow.**

   You follow this same process, whether you're adding one step or many in your business process flow.

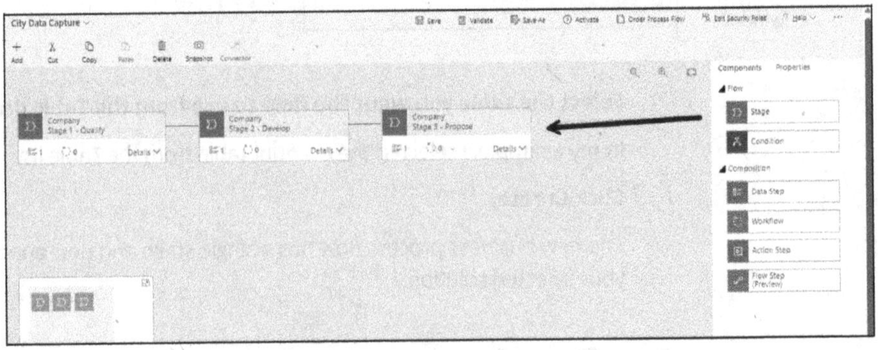

FIGURE 7-14: Adding a stage to the Business Process Flow Designer by pressing the plus sign (+).

Configuring steps

After you add a new stage (see the preceding section), you need to configure the steps that the user has to perform in order to proceed to the next stage. To configure the steps, follow these instructions:

1. **Open the stage that you want to configure by double-clicking the stage.**
2. **Select Details in the lower-right corner of the stage.**
3. **Drag the Composition step that you want from the Components pane to the stage.**

   In Figure 7-15, you drag and drop from A to B.

Your options include

- *Data Step:* Requires the user to input or review data, such as a specific column name.
- *Workflow:* Automates business logic and processes that run in the background. You can base the flow on a business process flow or business logic found in the model-driven app.
- *Action Step:* Triggers specific actions within the app, such as sending an e-mail based on a defined condition.
- *Flow Step:* Allows you to integrate the app with Microsoft Power Automate to run predefined flows.

Availability of these options may vary based on the configuration or updates made to the system. Each option requires a specific configuration depending on the business scenario for that stage.

In the example in Figure 7-15, each gate requires two Data Steps, meaning the user must fill out two fields before proceeding to the next stage.

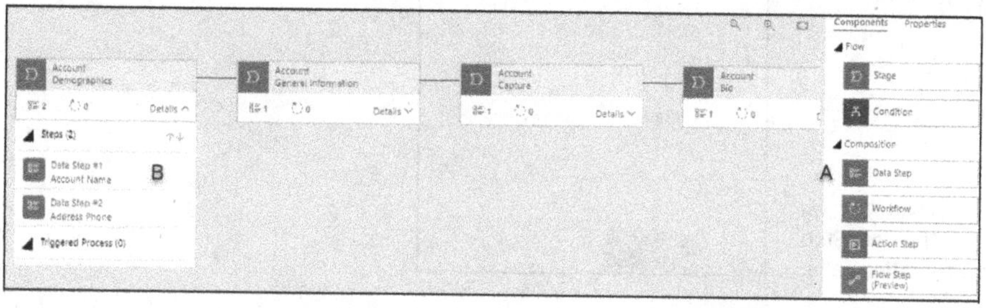

FIGURE 7-15: Available steps that can be incorporated into a stage.

4. **Repeat Step 3 until you have all the steps that you want in this stage.**
5. **Double-click to select the step within the stage that you want to configure.**
6. **In the Properties pane for the particular step, enter a display name in the Step Name text box.**

   Figure 7-16 shows the Properties pane for the data step Account Name.
7. **(Optional) Select the appropriate column from the Data Field drop-down list if users need to enter data to complete the step.**
8. **(Optional) Select the Required check box if the user must enter something in the column to complete the step.**

   The Sequence drop-down list determines the order in which users must complete steps within a stage.

9. **Click Apply.**

   The step is now committed to the stage.

10. **Repeat Steps 1 through 9 as many times as necessary to fill in all steps across all stages of the business process flow.**

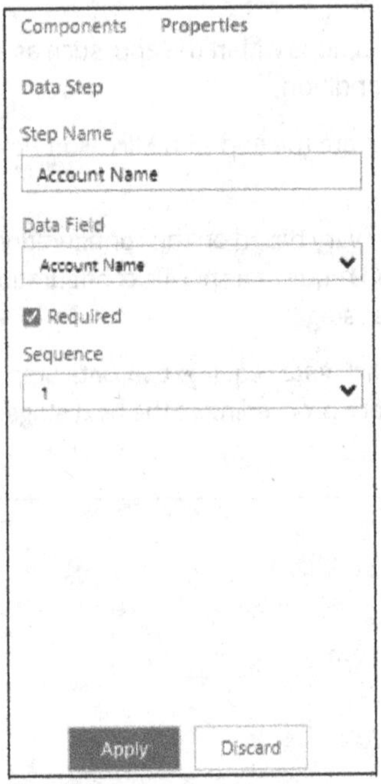

FIGURE 7-16: The Data Step Properties pane.

WARNING

Be careful when configuring steps. If you have multiple options, remember that if you use a two-option Boolean column (for example, Yes/No) and set the column to Required, users must select Yes to proceed. If you use a Choice column, the user can select either Yes or No and still proceed (so choose wisely).

Applying branching conditions

You can use a *branching condition*, which is a conditional step when you expect the user to follow specific steps, format a step a certain way, or perhaps when you want to ensure the user enters all data into the form before proceeding to the next step in the business process flow. For all purposes, branching conditions act as your roadblocks to get to the next stage in the business process flow. To add a branching condition, follow these steps:

1. **In the Business Process Flow Designer window, drag and drop the Condition option in the Flow section of the Components tab to a plus sign (+) between two stages in the flow.**

   TIP

   The plus signs (+) may not always be visible in a business process flow view within the Designer. They do, however, typically appear when you hover between stages, indicating where you can add conditions.

2. **In the Properties pane of the Business Process Flow Designer window, set the properties for your branching condition.**

   The properties you set include the *field* (what data will the condition evaluate), *operators* (if the condition is equal to, contains, less than, and so on), and the *value* (what's being measured).

   In Figure 7-17, I applied two conditions. Both require data to exist in the fields before a user can move to the next stage.

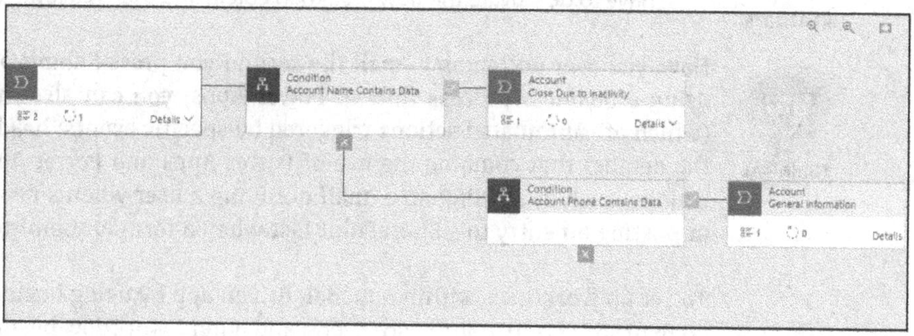

FIGURE 7-17: A business process flow that has branching conditions.

3. **Click Apply in the Properties pane when you're done setting up your branch.**

   The branching condition now takes effect, indicating an either-or state exists for the flow to continue.

4. **Repeat Steps 1 through 3 for each branch you want to add.**

Finishing up your business process flow

After you add all the elements to your business process flow (see the preceding sections), follow these steps to validate and activate the flow:

1. **Click the Validate button in the Business Process Flow Designer's toolbar.**

   The validation action checks for errors or inconsistencies in your flow, including missing required steps or improperly configured stage, step, or branching conditions.

2. **Review the error messages that appear in the Validation pane.**

   Errors typically relate to missing required fields, incorrect conditions, or incomplete stages.

3. **Click an error message.**

   The Designer takes you directly to the part of the flow that requires attention.

4. **Correct the issue by adjusting the properties of the relevant components.**

   For example, you may need to ensure that all required fields are present or that all steps are properly connected.

5. **Repeat Steps 3 and 4 until you resolve all of your errors.**

6. **When your flow is error-free, click Activate.**

   Activation makes the business process flow available to users. However, if you want to make specific changes (such as adding new stages or conditions), you have to deactivate the flow first, then edit it, and then reactivate it.

REMEMBER

TECHNICAL STUFF

Have you ever gotten an e-mail the second you press Submit on a web form? By using a business process flow in Power Apps, you can also integrate *workflows* (which are automated actions triggered by specific events; head to Chapter 14 for the details) that combine the use of Power Apps and Power Automate to trigger actions, such as sending an e-mail notifying a user when a new record is created or posting an entry to a SharePoint List when a form is submitted.

To set up workflows within a model-driven app by using business process flows, go to `http://learn.microsoft.com` and enter "workflow business process flow" into the Search text box, then press Enter. Click the link to the article that appears on the results page.

Controlling Security in Model-Driven Apps

To allow the user to access model-driven apps, the administrator has to assign all users a predefined security role. Therefore, the administrator must license each user for Power Apps Premium. (I talk about licensing in Chapter 2.) With role-based security, the administrator associates a particular security role with privileges that define what a user who has that role can do when they access a table by using an app. In other words, one user in a certain security role can write data to an app, but another user with a different security role can only view the data. Another user's security role allows them to write, delete, and read the records.

By default, a Dataverse table has two roles assigned. Both roles can fully update the configuration of a system. Here are the differences:

- **System Administrator:** Has access to all records in the system
- **System Customizer:** Can modify only the records that they create themselves

As a developer, you need to create a new security profile if you need more than these two roles (which is often the case).

REMEMBER

Sharing a model-driven app is completely different from sharing a canvas app (which you can read about in Chapters 4 and 5). Model-driven app sharing depends on how the administrator assigns the Microsoft Dataverse data table privileges in the app. If the administrator hasn't defined security roles for the app, reach out to a Power Platform administrator (such as those who manage the license assignment for your Power Apps) to assign the appropriate roles.

Creating a security role

To create a security role for a model-driven app, follow these steps:

1. **Sign in to the Power Platform admin center.**
2. **From the Environments tab, select the environment that hosts your model-driven app.**

   The selected Environment details page opens.
3. **Select Settings in the Environment Details pane.**
4. **In the Settings menu that opens, choose Users + Permissions ⇨ Security Roles.**

   Figure 7-18 shows some of the security roles available. Often many security roles are based on what applications you have in the environment.
5. **Select New Role in the command bar.**
6. **In the Create Roles window, enter a role name in the Roles Name text box.**
7. **Select a business unit from the Business Unit drop-down list.**

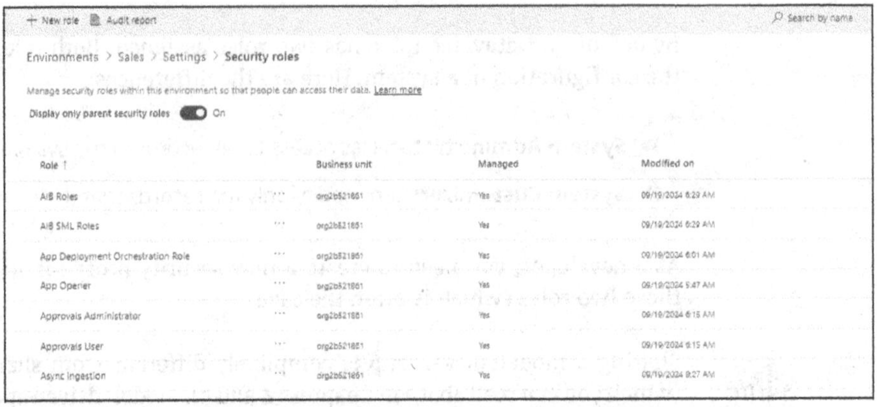

FIGURE 7-18: Examples of security roles.

8. **Apply privileges to a user or team, depending on the business requirement.**

   TECHNICAL STUFF

   If you want team members to inherit the role's privileges when they're assigned to a team, accept the default Member's Privilege Inheritance setting, the Direct User Access Level. Otherwise, select Team Privileges. Furthermore, if you anticipate a user will need the new role in order to run model-driven apps, accept the Default On setting for Include App Opener Privileges for Running Model-Driven Apps for either the Direct or Team privileges you set.

9. **Click Save in the New Role window.**

   Your new role is now saved and added to the environment.

10. **In the Search bar at the top-right corner of the Security Roles window, enter the name for a table for which you want to give a user permissions and click Search.**

11. **Click the table name to open the table's permission settings.**

    In my example, I selected the Company table to configure the security roles and permissions.

12. **Configure the table based on the requirements for the users who will access one or more tables in the environment.**

    The requirements define the level of access that different users need to have for the data in that table. For example:

    - *In the Read permission settings:* Select the Organization option to create a Read-Only role for all users in the organization. The setting listed allows all organization users to view data without making changes, providing read-only access across the entire system.

* *To create a user role that allows reading, creating, and updating records:* Set the permission for Read, Write, and Create access to Business Unit. This setting restricts those users from accessing or modifying records outside their unit.
* *To add the ability to delete a record:* Select the Delete option in the Delete permission settings and select the Business Unit option for the other permissions.

13. **After assigning all the permissions you want to a role, click Save.**

    The new security role, Sales End User, has been created.

ON THE WEB

For a rundown of the full scope of permission assignments and how to assign roles, go to `http://learn.microsoft.com` and enter **Security Roles and Privileges** in the Search text box, then press enter. Click the link to the article that appears in the list of results that opens.

You can assign users more than just organization-level permissions (such as the role created in the preceding steps). You can click the Manage Role button to open a pop-up menu of other permission options (see Figure 7-19). Table 7-1 explains what each security role allows.

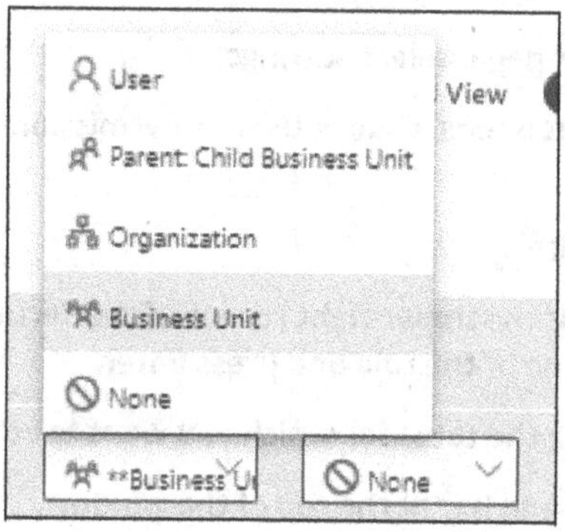

FIGURE 7-19: Security Role options.

Editing a security role

If you, as the developer, want to update an already-in-use role, follow these steps:

1. **Go to the Power Platform admin center.**

   You can access the admin center from `http://admin.powerplatform.microsoft.com`.

TABLE 7-1 Security Roles in Power Platform

Role	Description
User	Based on permissions administrators assign, users can access only records they own and objects shared with them or the team. Most users get User-level access because it limits their access, ensuring data security and proper access control.
Parent: Child Business Unit	Users can access records in their business unit and all subordinate units only. These roles are usually granted to administrators and managers who need access across one or more business units.
Organization	Users with this level of access can view all records across the organization, regardless of their access in the business unit hierarchy. To protect data security, restrict this level of access to those who truly need it. Typically, only administrators and managers are assigned this role.
Business Unit	Users can access only the records associated with their business unit. This role is typically assigned to managers, but an individual user can also be granted access if all members need team-wide, bilateral access.
None	No access is granted.

2. **Select the environment that hosts your model-driven app from the Environments list.**

   The Environments dashboard opens.

3. **In Environment Settings page, select Settings.**
4. **In the Settings pane that opens, choose Users + Permissions ⇨ Security Roles.**

   The Security Roles interface opens.

5. **In the Search text box at the upper-right corner of the Security Roles interface, enter the name of the role and press Enter.**
6. **In the list of roles, select the table for which you want to edit the role.**
7. **Select Edit in the command bar at the top of the window.**

   The Security Role editor appears.

8. **In the Search text box (labeled A in Figure 7-20), enter the name of the table that you want to modify.**
9. **Select the table in the Table Permission pane (labeled B in Figure 7-20).**

   The table permissions grid appears.

10. **Use the matrix (labeled C in Figure 7-20) to modify the permissions to meet the updated requirements.**

    For example, you can adjust Create, Read, and Write permissions.

11. **Click Save + Close at the top of the window (labeled D in Figure 7-20).**

    Pressing Save + Close saves your changes, and the Security Roles window closes.

In the example in Figure 7-20, a user has more than Read Only permission; I gave them Create, Read, and Write permissions.

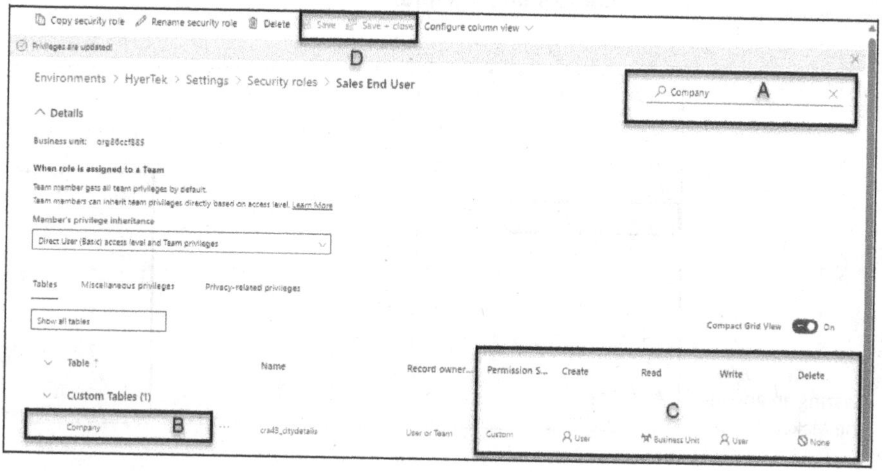

FIGURE 7-20: Editing a security role to include additional permissions.

Sharing an app

For users to access a model-driven app, they have to meet two key requirements. They must be

- » A licensed Power Apps user.
- » Assigned a security role. This assignment happens when an administrator shares the app with the user.

The security role manages permissions for the Power Apps app itself and related services, such as the Dataverse table associated with the Power App. This role ensures users have the necessary entitlements and permissions across these platforms, providing a secure and integrated user experience.

To assign a security role to a user and share an app with them, follow these steps:

1. **Open the Power Apps Maker Portal by going to `http://make.powerapps.com`.**

2. **Select Apps in the left navigation pane.**

   The Apps option is labeled A in Figure 7-21.

   Locate the app you want to share in the app list that appears.

3. **Click the ellipses (. . .) to the left of the app's name.**

   A drop-down list opens (labeled B).

4. **Choose Share ⇨ Share.**

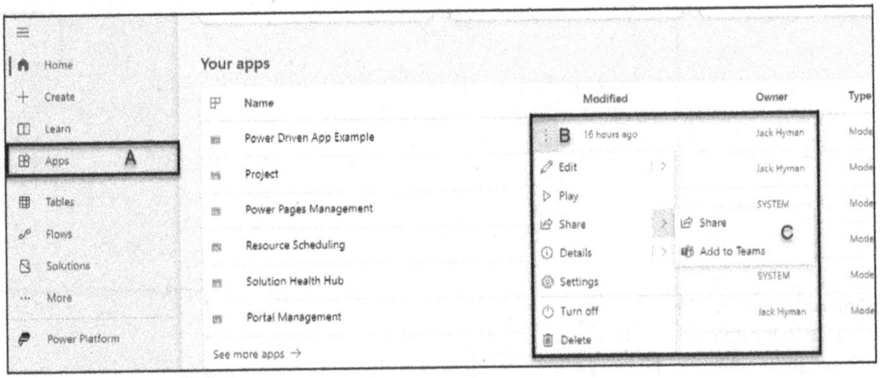

FIGURE 7-21: Sharing an app in the Maker Portal.

5. **In the Share App screen that opens, select the app in the App navigation pane on the left of the screen.**

   Figure 7-22 shows the Power Driven App Example selected (labeled A).

6. **In the Security Role pop-up menu on the right side of the screen (labeled B in Figure 7-22), select the role you want to edit.**

   In Figure 7-22, I've selected Sales End User (labeled C).

7. **In the Users section, select a licensed user associated with a specific environment.**

   In my example, I select the Help Desk user.

   The Assign Security window opens.

8. **In the Dataverse menu, select the security role you want to assign this user.**

   By default, the role selected is System Administrator.

9. **Uncheck the System Administrator and Sales End User check boxes.**

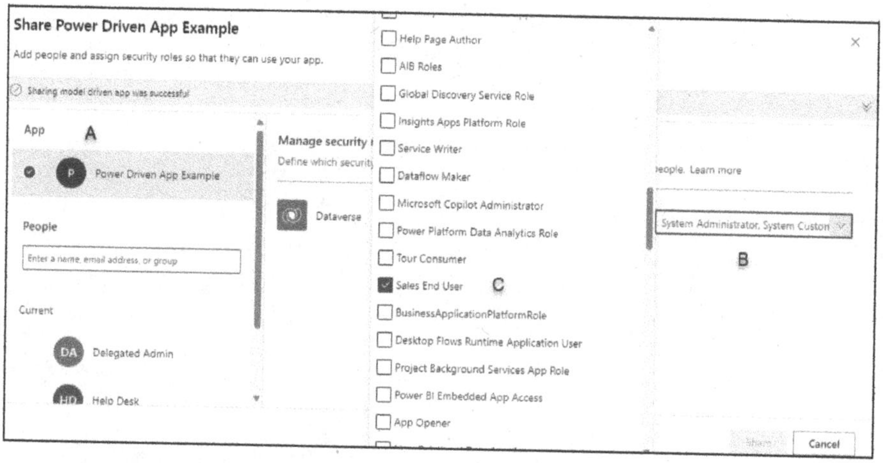

FIGURE 7-22: Configuring a security role for a model-driven app.

10. **Repeat Steps 7 through 9 for each user that you want to edit.**
11. **Click Share after you assign all the roles you want to assign.**

    The user or users that you assigned a security role can now access the shared model-driven app.

ON THE WEB

If you're the system administrator, you can assign a user based on not just an individual role, but also a Business Unit, Teams, or a Microsoft Entra Group. You can find Microsoft's take on these advanced Dataverse security considerations if you go to `http://learn.microsoft.com` and enter **Security in Microsoft Dataverse** in the Search text box, then press Enter. A link to the article appears on the results page.

IN THIS CHAPTER

- **Understanding how Power Pages integrates with Power Platform**
- **Getting to know the tools and components available in Power Pages**
- **Integrating lists, forms, and Power BI visualizations into a Power Pages site**
- **Exploring the extensibility features of Power Pages**

Chapter 8

Building Sites with Power Pages

Low-code technologies have drastically changed how organizations deliver public-facing websites, especially sites that have a great deal of data. Since the early 2000s, SharePoint has been Microsoft's go-to robust tool for internal content management and team collaboration. Although SharePoint used to allow users to create public-facing websites, its primary focus deals with collaboration within organizations through Microsoft 365 tools. In 2019, Microsoft updated their product direction, introducing the Power Apps Portal, which they rebranded as Power Pages.

Power Pages allows you to create public-facing websites that connect with Microsoft's Dataverse (covered in Chapter 3) so that users external to your business can interact with data securely. You can use Power Pages to design and launch websites, even if you have only limited technical knowledge. This chapter shows how to create sites with Power Pages, from setup to designing your first website.

Knowing What Power Pages Can Do

When organizations use websites to publish items such as lightweight applications or detailed analytics reports, they often find that the standard content management system (CMS) solutions — tools such as WordPress, Drupal, and DotNetNuke — simply don't cut it. You can use these tools to embed apps and reports into a website. (When you *embed* something into a site, it means incorporating external content such as applications, reports, or multimedia into its structure, allowing users to interact with them directly on the page.) But embedding items limits what you can do with them. For one thing, you can't take full advantage of the capabilities provided by Power Platform.

So, more organizations are turning to Power Pages for their websites. They need a platform that can handle data securely while also integrating data analytics and lightweight applications built by using Microsoft Power Platform. Power Pages enables you to integrate items sourced from Dataverse into your website. *Integrating* means presenting the raw data in an organized, attractive format on a page. By integrating items such as tables from Dataverse or reports from Power BI, you can create interactive, data-driven experiences for your users. What's more, you can integrate Dataverse items without much coding experience.

REMEMBER

Power Pages enables low-code/no-code users to integrate Dataverse outputs, such as detailed analytics reports, into their organization's website. Incorporating these items allows entire interaction with the data, enabling users to filter, sort, and drill down into reports directly on the webpage. In contrast, embedding items means simply placing them into the website as static content, limiting functionality and user interaction. When deciding whether to develop a standalone application or build a Power Pages site, consider the reasons in favor of Power Pages listed in Table 8-1.

TABLE 8-1 Key Reasons to Use Power Pages

Reason	Description
Low-code development	You need minimal coding experience to develop, deploy, and manage the website.
Integration with other Microsoft technologies	Fully integrates with all Power Platform applications, including Power BI, Power Apps, Power Automate, and Dataverse; also includes strong support for all Microsoft 365 applications.
Data-driven apps	Apply *contextual data models* (a way to organize data around specific business processes efficiently) and define relationships between entities while ensuring robust security and compliance throughout your application.

Reason	Description
Customization and extensibility	Power Pages can support JavaScript, HTML, CSS, and other advanced languages.
Scalability	Hosted on Microsoft's global infrastructure, giving the site worldwide reach.
Security and compliance	Provide personalized user experiences based on role-based credentialing. Fully supports SSL encryption.

Your organization might benefit from Power Pages if you want to

- Integrate analytics, form-based solutions, and business process automation into your website.
- Leverage Power Pages for personalized user experiences through role-based authentication and authorization integration. Power Pages allows users outside an organization to sign into a website, maintaining an identity ranging from super administrator to contributor, or even viewing the site anonymously. Your organizations can benefit from Power Pages' role-based authentication by providing secure, personalized access, ensuring appropriate content visibility based on a user's role.

REMEMBER

All other apps in the Power Platform suite besides Power Pages require a user to have at least one role and responsibility. (You can read about roles in Chapter 7.)

TECHNICAL STUFF

INTEGRATING POWER PAGES WITH DATAVERSE

Power Pages is a component of Power Platform and works in conjunction with Dataverse, which acts as the underlying data storage and management layer. Power Pages can use Dataverse's features, such as centralized administration, metadata management, security, and auditing. Essentially, Power Pages is a tool for building external-facing websites, and it integrates with Dataverse to store and manage data securely.

If you also need multilingual support, which may involve using forms, views, and business logic for process automation (features commonly found in Dynamics 365 or model-driven apps), Power Pages can provide similar functionality. Power Pages allows you to create dynamic, multilingual websites that integrate with Dataverse (where all your site content is securely stored). You can edit and manage the content from a Power Pages site by using various tools, including the user-friendly Power Pages Design Studio, the legacy Power Apps interface for more advanced configurations, or professional website and application development tools such as Visual Studio Code.

Provisioning a Power Pages website

You must *provision* (meaning set up and configure). Power Pages websites in a Power Platform environment can be accessed through the Power Platform admin center. (See Chapter 2 for an intro to the admin center.) Every Power Pages website must include a Dataverse database. When it comes to design, after you deploy a Power Pages site, you gain access to a set of customizable templates from Microsoft that target specific business scenarios.

When provisioning your site, enter the name, default address, and language that you want to present your website in (you can set up your website with multilingual support, as mentioned in the sidebar "Integrating Power Pages with Dataverse").

TIP

A Power Pages site always starts as a *trial offering* (meaning a temporary, limited-use version for testing and evaluation) that you can later convert to a *production site* (meaning fully operational that costs money to operate).

To provision your Power Pages site, follow these steps:

1. **From the Welcome to Power Pages start page (see Figure 8-1), click Get Started.**

   You can access this page at `http://make.powerpages.microsoft.com`.

   The setup wizard appears.

FIGURE 8-1: The Power Pages start page.

2. **In the Environment drop-down list on the right side of the screen, select the environment for which you want to configure your Power Pages site.**
3. **Click Get Started.**

   The next page of the setup process opens.

4. **In the Organization Type option, choose the type of organization for which you want to design your website.**

   In my example, I choose Other, which means this will be intended as a generic website.

5. **Select Next.**

   The template selection page opens.

6. **Provide basic information on the site, including its name and proposed Power Pages website address (URL), as shown in Figure 8-2.**

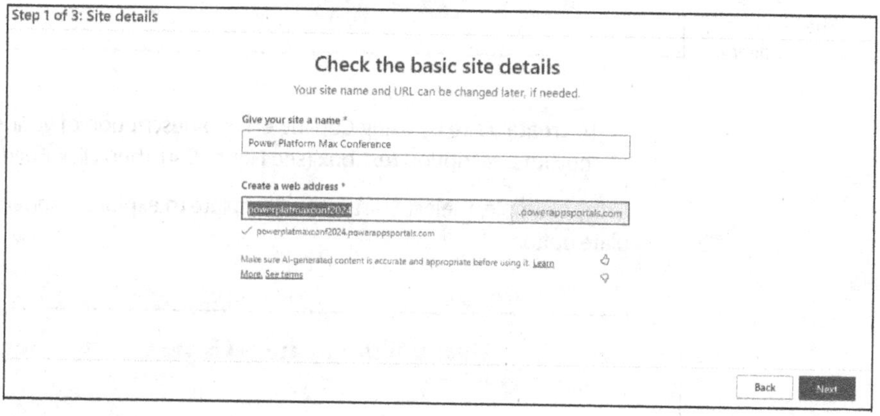

FIGURE 8-2: The basic Site Setup screen.

7. **Select Browse Templates to choose a template for your site.**

   Templates offer options. Site templates let you quickly set up a standard site that includes predefined structures, or you can use Copilot (Microsoft's AI assistant) to create your template by generating personalized content and design elements based on your input.

   - *Common templates:* Power Pages offers templated sites based on common scenarios and industries.
   - *Template ideas from the Template Gallery:* Review prebuilt template ideas. (Figure 8-3 shows the Template Gallery.)
   - *Copilot template creations:* Have Copilot build you a template framework appropriate for your business.

TIP

When you use Copilot, because you tell the system what the site must include, it does its best to generate an appropriate site structure and design (though don't expect perfect results).

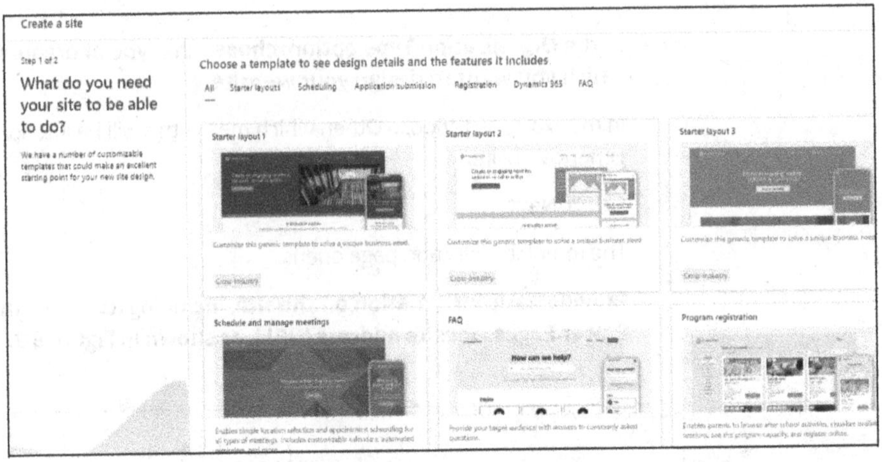

FIGURE 8-3: The Template Gallery.

To create a site by using Copilot, enter a description of your site concept in the Site Description text box (see Figure 8-4), then click Build My Site.

In my example, I select Start with a Template to explore standard-use template options.

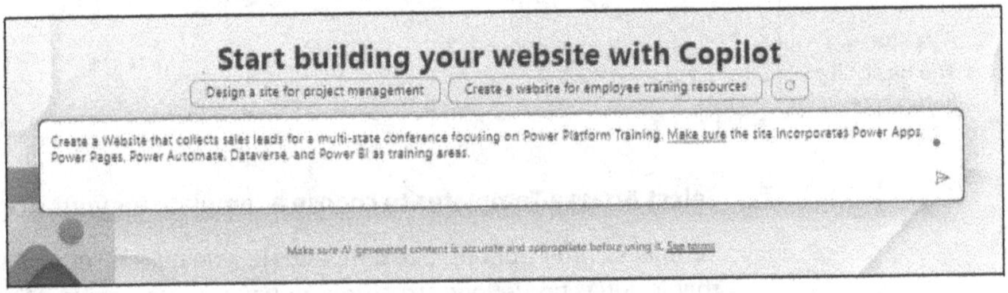

FIGURE 8-4: Telling Copilot what you want in your Power Pages site template.

The Choose a Template window opens, displaying predefined template concepts, as shown in Figure 8-5.

8. **Select one of the Starter layouts or Blank Page option.**

   The various template options appear.

   If you want to use Dynamics 365 to create your new site, you can choose specific templates based on the app that you want to use such as Sales, Project Operations, and Field Service. Keep in mind that you have to install the Dynamics 365 apps at the time you set up your environment, including Dataverse (discussed in Chapters 2 and 3).

   I selected Starter Layout 2 in my example.

9. **On the bottom of the page, click the Choose This Template button.**

   The Site Details window opens, as shown in Figure 8-6.

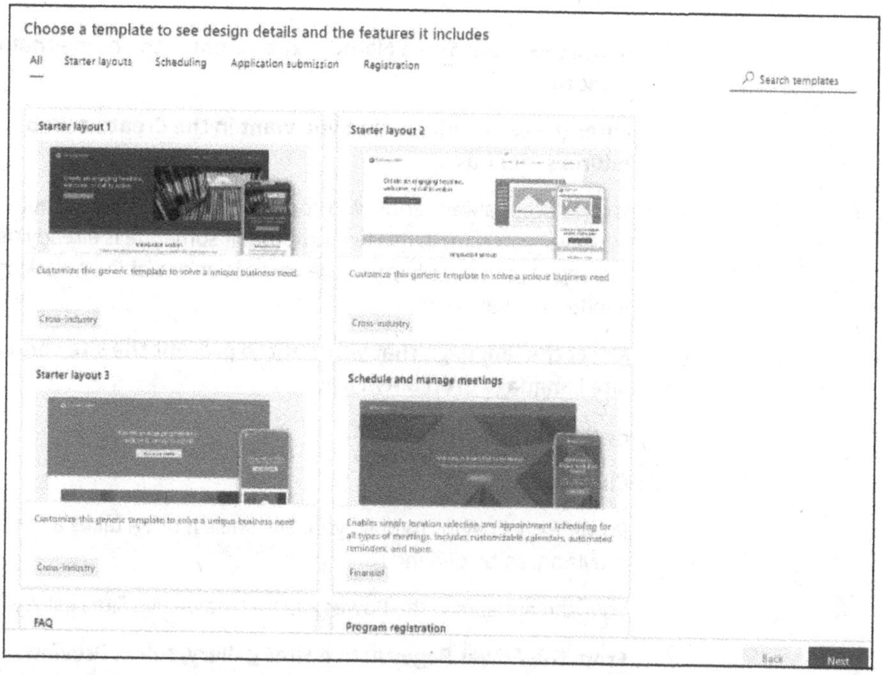

FIGURE 8-5: You can choose from many site design templates.

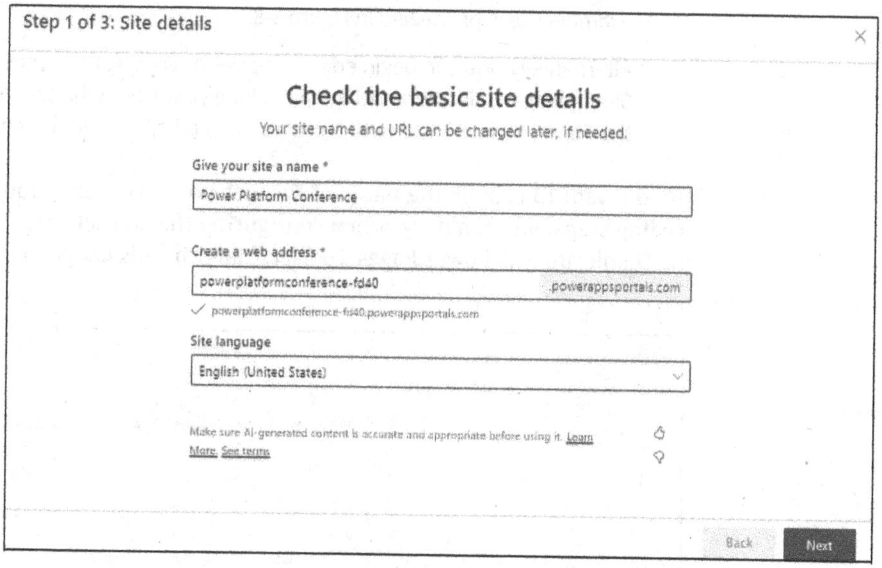

FIGURE 8-6: Specifying your website name, web address, and language.

10. **In the Give Your Site a Name text box, enter the name that you want to use.**

11. **Enter the web address that you want in the Create a Web Address text box.**

    Your address always ends with `.powerappsportals.com`, but you can put whatever you want in this text box. (But if someone is already using that text, a message appears, telling you the name is unavailable and asking you to pick another relevant name).

12. **Select the language that you want to present the site content in from the Site Language drop-down list.**

    By default, English is chosen.

13. **Click Done.**

    Power Pages begins to build your site shell. It often takes a few minutes to fully provision, so be patient.

    Your site appears in the Power Pages Portal Active Sites gallery (Figure 8-7).

14. **From the Power Pages Active Sites gallery, select Preview.**

    The Preview Site page appears, where you can review the design of the site. My example site is previewed in Figure 8-8.

    Alternatively, you can begin editing the site by clicking the Pencil icon in the Sites gallery. I talk about diving into editing your site in the section "Navigating the Pages, Styling, Data, Setup, and Security tabs," later in this chapter.

If you want to change the name of the website or URL that you enter in the preceding steps, you can do so when configuring the site settings (which I talk about in "Exploring the Power Pages Toolset," later in this chapter).

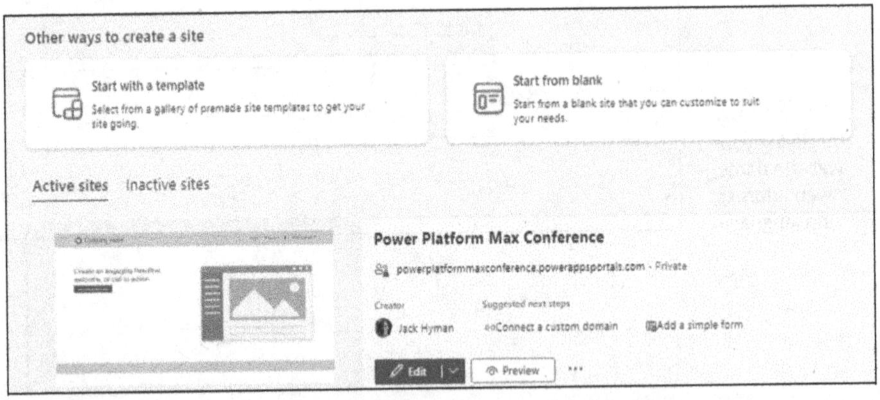

FIGURE 8-7: The Power Pages Active Sites gallery.

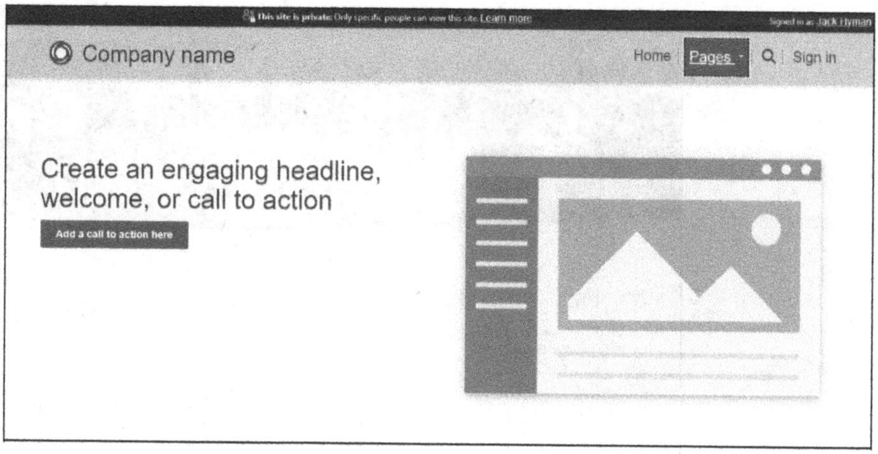

FIGURE 8-8: Getting a preview of a Power Pages site layout.

Using Dynamics 365 templates

Dynamics 365 is a suite of business applications heavily used within Power Platform, particularly in Power Pages. Specifically, Power Pages allows users to create and deploy web portals that extend Dynamics 365's functionality to external audiences, such as customers, partners, or vendors. Each app has at least one application-specific template within the Power Pages template gallery, which you can access during the portal creation. In the Power Pages Template Gallery, you can find templates for each significant Dynamics 365 domain, including

- **Customer Experience:** Allow customers to resolve issues with core features such as case management, knowledge base access, and community forums. When integrated into a Power Pages portal, these features help reduce workloads and improve user satisfaction.
- **Service:** Facilitate real-time work-order management, scheduling, and resource tracking for field technicians.
- **Supply Chain:** Use the Order Portal templates to support the order lifecycle management process. Such templates can streamline vendor collaboration, inventory management, and logistics tracking.
- **Finance:** Securely present financial data, invoice tracking activities, and reporting to improve financial transparency and streamline payment and expense management processes.

Additional template examples include Self-Service Portals, Field Service, Community Sites, Sales, and Orders Portals.

Figure 8-9 shows the Partner Portal template, which provides Dynamics 365 Sales Enterprise functionality, along with standard CMS capabilities.

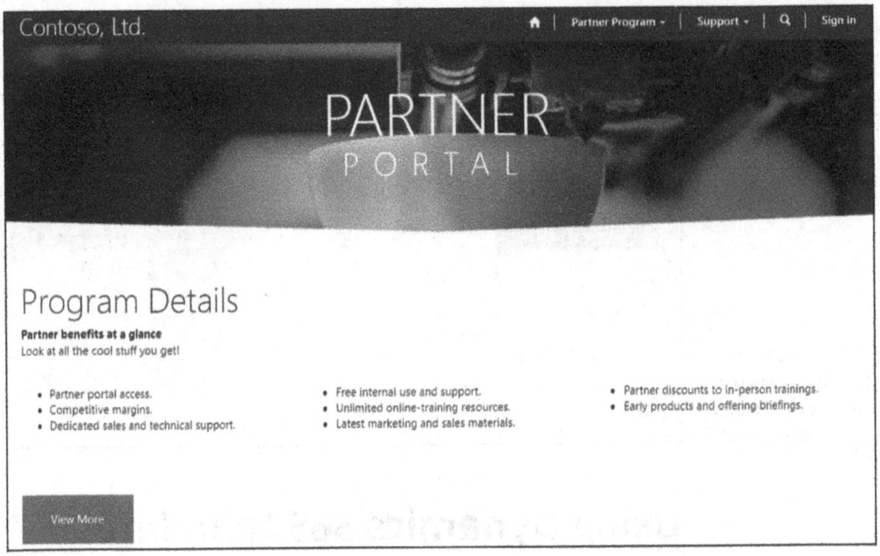

FIGURE 8-9: A Dynamics 365 sales Power Pages template.

You can't access the full range of tables available for a Power Pages site if you don't own the Dynamics 365 module. Still, you get the essential capabilities for basic portal functionality, including managing users, web content, and limited data management. For the Partner Portal template displayed in Figure 8-9, for example, if you own the Dynamics 365 module, you can access features not shown in the figure. These additional features enable managing partner profiles, viewing shared opportunities, and collaborating on sales or service-related activities by using the Dynamics 365 Customer Services tables.

REMEMBER

Rather than spending weeks building all these website components, as a web developer, you just need to customize the content on the site by using pre-built components available to you in Power Pages. Components that are easy to integrate include Power Apps forms, Power BI visualizations (such as charts and dashboards), or Power Automate workflows. Best yet, you can get target access to all of these items based on your role (configured by the Power Platform developer and administrator). For example, a visitor may only see reports, but a contributor may be able to enter data.

Creating a Dynamics 365 website follows the steps in the section "Provisioning a Power Pages website," earlier in this chapter.

Exploring the Power Pages Toolset

Regardless of what content management platform you use, you have to store your website content somewhere, including references to the structure, layout, and functionality within the site. When you use Power Pages, you store all data, including page functionality in Dataverse. But you don't need to make all your edits in Dataverse tables. When working with Power Pages, many developers ask two questions:

- » How do I add and manage the content with Power Pages Design Studio?
- » How can I integrate business data into the site from other Power Platform applications such as Power Apps and Power BI?

The following sections go over Power Pages toolset to help guide you on your website development journey.

Power Pages Design Studio

Power Pages Design Studio is the primary tool that you use to create and customize Power Pages websites. In Design Studio, you can create a simple web page and add Power Platform components (such as forms, reports, and dashboards) to the portal templates by using a drag-and-drop environment very similar to the environments in Power Apps (discussed in Chapters 4 and 6), Power BI (flip to Chapter 12), and Power Automate (see Chapter 14).

Before you start using Power Pages Design Studio, you need to provision a site (see the section "Provisioning a Power Page website," earlier in this chapter). After you provision the site and Power Pages builds your site's template structure, follow these steps:

1. **Go to `http://make.powerpages.microsoft.com` and sign into your account.**

   The Power Pages Design Studio home page opens, where editing begins.

2. **In the Power Pages Design Studio, select your Power Pages site from the Active Sites gallery.**

   The Site Overview page opens.

3. **Select the Edit Site button, which appears on the right side of the Site Overview page.**

   Your site opens in the Design Studio's editing mode.

4. **(Optional) If you want to access the site code, click Edit to open a drop-down list and select Edit Site Code.**

   The code editor opens, allowing you to make advanced customizations.

Navigating the Pages, Styling, Data, Setup, and Security Tabs

The left side of the Design Studio houses a series of tabs (see Figure 8-10) that break down into key areas: Pages, Styling, Data, Setup, and Security. Each area supports different aspects of creating and managing your Power Pages portal:

- **Pages:** Allows you to create, edit, and organize web pages for your site, similar to what you experience when using a standard document editor such as Microsoft Word. Besides acting as a standard editor, this tab also allows you to add new content pages, manage existing pages, and adjust layouts or navigation elements, making it the primary hub for website structure and content management.
- **Styling:** When it comes to the style of your pages — or, for that matter, the site — you head over to the Styling tab, where you can customize the visual appearance of your site, such as changing themes, colors, fonts, and other design elements across the entire site or for specific sections. The Styling tab helps you ensure your portal aligns with a common brand and creates a cohesive user experience.
- **Data:** Developers can connect to the data that powers your site, allowing you to manage and integrate tables from a multitude of data sources, including Dataverse or Dynamics 365.
- **Set Up:** Configure core settings for your portal, such as site metadata, URLs, language settings, and other operational configurations. Think of this as the cockpit for all generic site settings, including how your site behaves and integrates with external services or modules.
- **Security:** Crucial for configuring user access, authentication, and role-based permissions. A developer can define who can view, edit, or contribute to different sections of your site based on user or group assignments.

REMEMBER

Each tab provides the essential tools so that a developer can create and personalize the site's content or structure.

Pages tab

In the Pages tab, you can add new pages to your website, as well as create the navigation structure for the site. Each template comes with, at a minimum, a home page; you add the rest of the pages and select the layouts for those other pages.

FIGURE 8-10: The Design Studio tabs.

Setting up your navigation

Before you start creating web pages, you need to build the navigation by following these steps:

1. **Select the Pages tab to navigate to the home page.**
2. **Select the *ellipsis* (three dots) to the right of the home page (see Figure 8-11).**

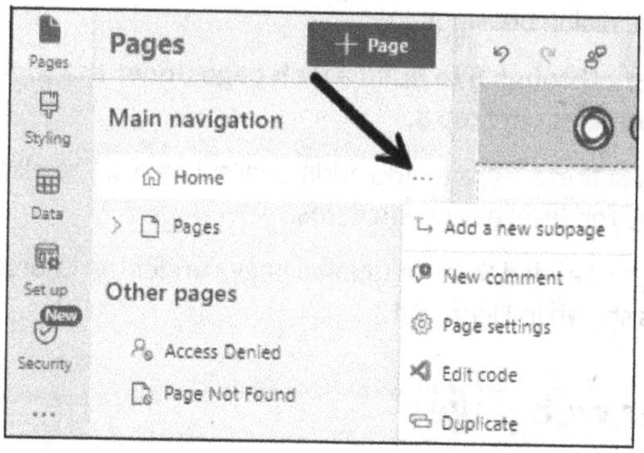

FIGURE 8-11: Click the ellipsis to access additional page options.

3. **Select Add a New Subpage from the pop-up menu that appears.**

   Determine how many subpages you need based on your site's navigation structure and the content that you plan to place under each menu or submenu. Although you do get other chances to add subpages to your site (a website is an ever-changing platform), planning the site hierarchy in advance helps ensure smooth navigation and logical flow from the start.

4. **Enter a name in the Page Name text box.**

   The name you enter appears in the site's navigation unless you customize it later.

5. **Pick the desired layout template from the Layout Templates drop-down menu.**

   You can choose the structure of the page, such as a single-column or two-column layout, or other available configurations. The layout not only determines how blocks of content appear on the page, but also influences the user experience by controlling how information flows and is presented. Additionally, the layout defines the placement of key elements — such as the header, footer, and navigation menus — to ensure a cohesive design that adapts to different screen sizes and devices.

6. **Click Add.**
7. **Repeat Steps 2 through 6 for each main section that you want to create in the navigation.**

   These sections appear as top-level items in the navigation bar. If needed, you can also create subpages beneath each top-level navigation item by following the same steps.

   For my example, I added four top-level navigation sections named About the Conference, Courses, Products, and Travel Logistics (see Figure 8-12).

8. **In the Pages tab, click the ellipsis next to one of the sections that you built.**
9. **Select Add a New Subpage from the pop-up menu that opens.**

   The Add Page dialog box appears.

10. **Follow Steps 2 through 6 to build a web page under the top-level navigation that you select in Step 8.**

    You can repeat these steps to add additional subpages. The ellipsis appears next to all the top-level navigation items.

    In my example, I added three additional pages under the Courses top navigation item, as shown in Figure 8-12.

Editing your web pages

After you set up a page, if you want to change the name of the page or the URL, or limit who has access to the page, follow these steps:

1. **Click the ellipsis next to the page that you want to edit and select Page Settings from the pop-up menu that appears.**

   The Page Settings pop-up window opens.

2. **In the Page Details pane, change the Page Name by editing the text field.**

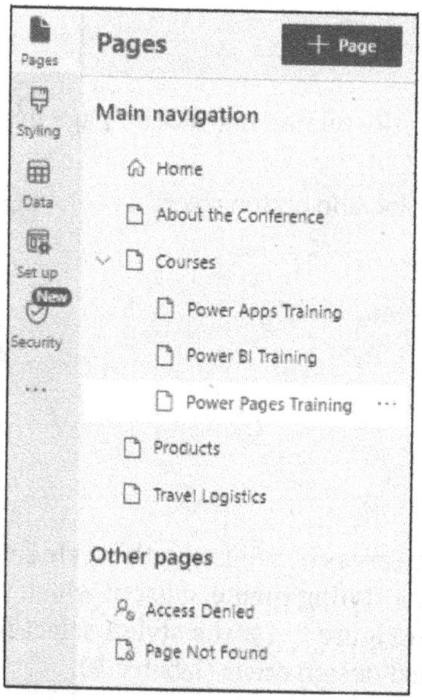

FIGURE 8-12: Adding navigation and pages to a Power Pages site.

3. **Change the editable part of the URL by updating the Partial URL field in the text box.**
4. **Click the Permissions tab (shown in Figure 8-13).**

   The radio button Anyone Can See This Page is selected by default.
5. **(Optional) Select the I Want to Choose Who Can See This Page radio button, and from the drop-down list, select who you want to have this ability.**

   You can choose Administrators Only, Authenticated Users, or both.
6. **After you have the settings the way you want them, click OK.**

   Your changes are saved, and the Page Settings window closes.

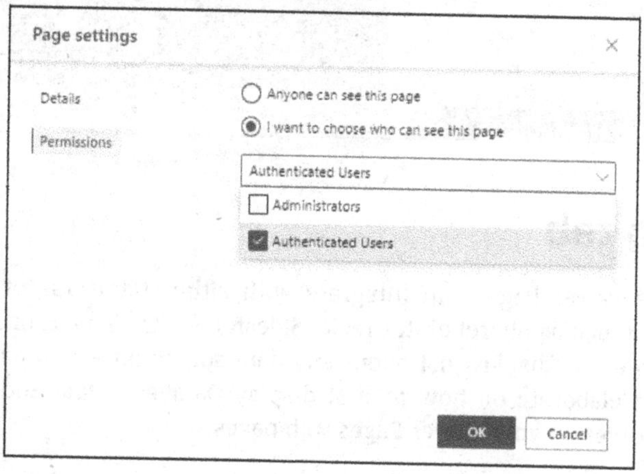

FIGURE 8-13: The Page Settings pop-up window's Permissions pane.

Styling tab

The Styling tab covers all aesthetic-related matters on page design, including

- Color palette, background color, and button colors
- Fonts
- Headers and footers
- Titles and sections
- Margins and spacing
- Link style and hover effects

You can customize each of these areas by adjusting the style settings. If you don't want to customize, you can use a styling theme, a list of which you can find on the left side of the Styling pane. In Figure 8-14, the style I select in the Styling pane (labeled A) changes the specified design areas (labeled B).

TIP

The Styling tools in Power Pages are almost identical to the tools that you can use when editing a document in Microsoft Word — from typing in the document editor to highlighting text, selecting fonts, and resizing text.

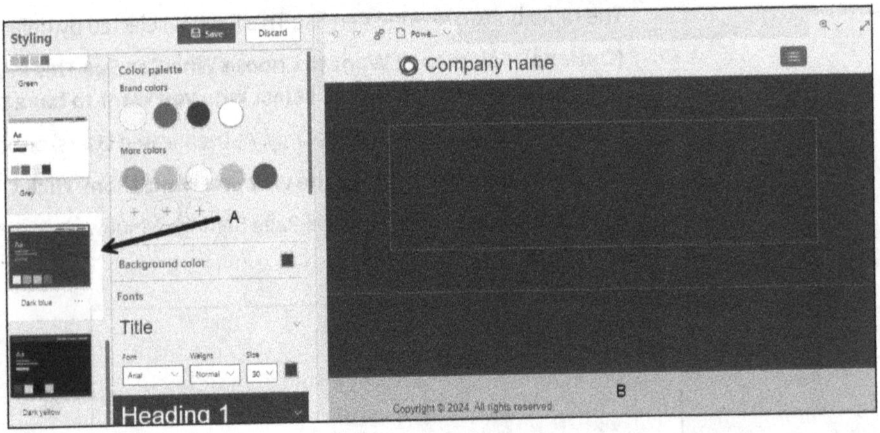

FIGURE 8-14: Selecting options in the Styling tab and seeing the changes in the Design pane.

Data tab

Because Power Pages can integrate with either Dataverse or third-party data sources (such as SharePoint, Oracle, Salesforce, SQL Server, or Microsoft Fabric), you can easily display just about any data source on a web page. The following sections elaborate on how to first display Dataverse data and then third-party data sources on your Power Pages web pages.

Displaying Dataverse data

From the Dataverse tab, you can create a new Dataverse table within Power Pages or import a Dataverse table from a shared environment (which you can read more about in Chapter 3). By using Dataverse, web developers can ensure data consistency, security, and accessibility across different applications. Unlike using third-party data sources, Dataverse tables guarantee that your data is stored in a structured and relational format, which you can easily link to forms, views, and lists on a Power Pages site.

To implement Dataverse for a Power Pages site, follow these steps:

1. **Click the Data tab in the left navigation pane.**

   This tab is labeled A in Figure 8-15.

   The Dataverse pane appears.

2. **Click the Table button on the upper left side (labeled B in Figure 8-15).**

   Alternatively, if you want to use an existing Dataverse table, simply go to the Tables pane in the Dataverse window and select one of the tables that appears in the Existing Tables list on the left side of the screen.

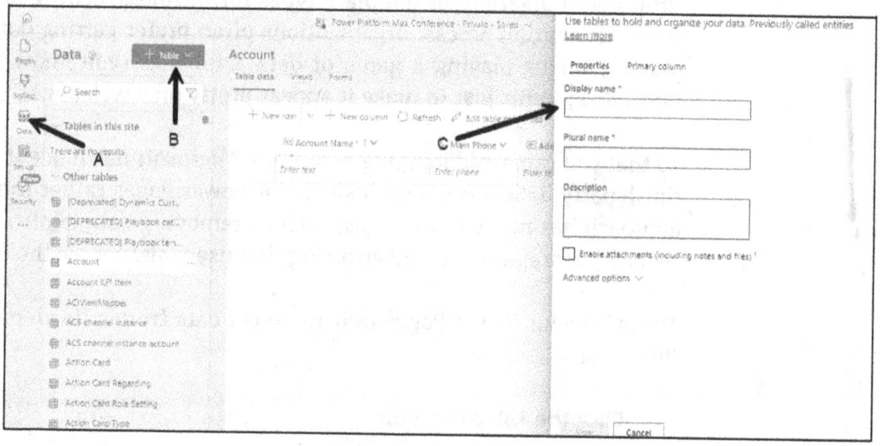

FIGURE 8-15: Adding a table in the Data tab.

3. **In the Tables pane that appears, click the New Table button.**

   The Create Table pop-up window opens.

4. **In the Properties pane, enter a name in the Display Name text box (labeled C in Figure 8-15).**

5. **In the Plural Name text box, enter the plural form of the table's name.**

6. **Enter a brief description in the Description text box of the tables purpose.**
7. **(Optional) Select the Enable Attachments (Including Notes and Files) check box if you want the table to support file attachments such as Word documents or PDF files.**
8. **Click Save at the bottom of the pop-up window.**

   Your new table is saved in Dataverse.
9. **Add the columns that you want to include in the table.**

   To add columns, follow the steps outlined in Chapter 3, which explains how to define column names, data types, and required fields.
10. **After you finish configuring the table, click Finish.**

    The table now becomes available in the Power Pages portal so that Pages can consume the data on relevant web pages.

Accessing third-party data sources

Sometimes, you just can't use Dataverse as your primary data source. Instead, your Power Pages portal may require that you access and integrate data from external systems, such as databases or cloud-based applications. Power Pages comes with a variety of template types for business-centric activities. For real-time information access, organizations often prefer getting data from the actual system, versus playing a game of data acrobatics (you know, shuffling data to multiple systems just to make it appear pretty on a web page).

So that you can avoid juggling your data, Microsoft has made it possible to access third-party data sources exclusively for Power Pages rather than Dataverse. This approach has many advantages, such as removing data duplication in Dataverse, reducing storage costs, and ensuring that users always see the latest information.

To set up your Power Pages website to get data from a third-party source, follow these steps:

1. **Click the Table button.**
2. **Click the Data tab in the left navigation pane.**

   The Tables view appears.
3. **Click the Table button at the top of the screen.**

4. **In the Tables view that opens, click the New Table from External Data button.**

   The New Table from External Data window appears.

5. **Select the external data connection that you want to use from the drop-down list.**

   Available connections include options such as SharePoint or SQL Server.

6. **Click Add Connection to the right of the external data source.**

   The Add Connection window appears.

7. **In the Add Connection window, click Open Connection.**

   The Connection Settings panel opens.

8. **Select the connection method that you want to use**

   Here are your options:

   - *Connect Directly (Cloud Service):* Choose this option if you're connecting to a cloud-based option, such as a SharePoint site.
   - *Connect Using an On-Premises Data Gateway:* Choose this option if you're connecting to a SharePoint site hosted on-premises (on a server), which requires an on-premises data gateway.

9. **Click Create Connection.**

   A prompt appears for authentication.

10. **Follow the prompts to authenticate by entering your credentials for the SharePoint site.**

    The system notifies you when the connection has been validated.

11. **After the connection is validated, click Next.**

    The Data Source Selection window opens.

12. **Select the targeted data source from the drop-down list.**

    After you select the data source, a Data Preview window opens.

13. **Configure the data source by selecting the necessary fields or columns that you want to map to Dataverse.**

14. **Click Next in the data mapping window.**

    The system imports the data source into Dataverse as a virtual table, an external connection to a live data source.

TECHNICAL STUFF

Virtual tables in Dataverse provide real-time access to external data sources, such as SharePoint, without storing the data in Dataverse, allowing Dataverse to reference and interact with the SharePoint data as if it were native, including maintaining referential integrity and relationships.

15. **Review the data mapping and field settings.**

    If anything needs to be changed, make the necessary adjustments to the data mapping and fields settings at this time.

16. **Click Finish.**

    The data source now appears in Power Pages as a Dataverse table. The user can use the data to create forms, tables, or other content as they see fit.

Set Up tab

To set up a website, you need to know more than just how to create content. If your site has data and security requirements, you must configure those requirements under certain conditions. Microsoft provides tools so that a non-developer can monitor the health and reliability of a site while they build it.

TIP

If you want to add a custom domain, configure IP restrictions, or configure a content delivery network (CDN), select the Set up tab in the left navigation pane, and then select Open Admin Center at the bottom of the pane that appears.

Here are the features you can access from the Set Up tab:

- **General:** Addresses key system attributes and operational capabilities:
  - *Site Details:* Offers a meter that indicates the reliability of the current security configuration. You can use this information to evaluate and improve your site's security settings. In the case of the site created in Figure 8-16, I've successfully configured 5 out of the 7 security measures that the system checks. This meter also displays the key site preferences, including areas that need attention to ensure optimal security.
  - *Go-Live Checklist:* Helps ensure that you design your site with all the bits it needs, not just in terms of content, but also infrastructure. The checklist includes seven criteria, as shown in Figure 8-17.
- **Mobile:** This menu item has only one option under it, Progressive Web Application, which focuses on mobile adaptability of your Power Pages site. If you want to create an experience explicitly for a mobile device, in Power Pages, you can create custom packages that include a targeted start page, custom splash page, custom offline page, and mobile-specific web certificates.

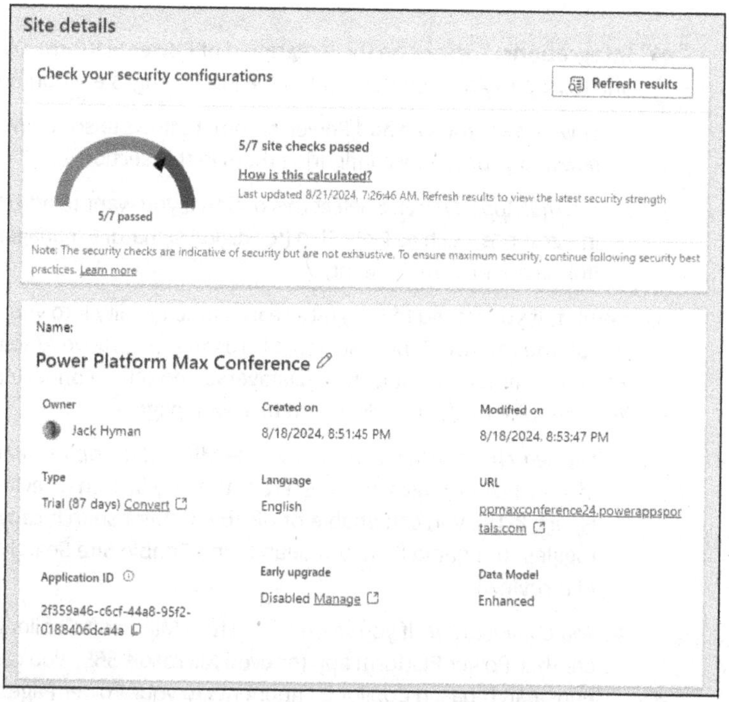

FIGURE 8-16: The Site Details statistics, focusing on general site performance.

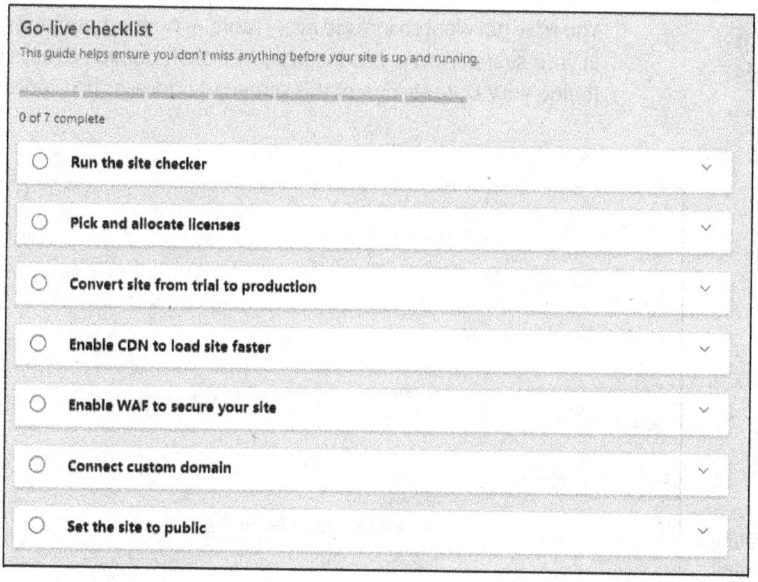

FIGURE 8-17: The Go-Live Checklist window.

» **Integrations:** Focuses on the integration of Power Platform, Dynamics 365, and third-party data sources within the Power Pages environment:
  - *Cloud Flows:* You can add Power Automate flows (also referred to as *cloud flows*) to your site by configuring them in this section.
  - *External Apps (Preview):* Select this option if you want to add third-party integrations, such as DocuSign (for digital signature management) or Stripe (for payment management).

» **Copilot:** If you intend to integrate search functionality into your Power Pages portal, you can use Copilot Search, Microsoft's generative AI solution, to query and retrieve search results from Dataverse and other connected data sources. You can have the results displayed on a web page.
  - *Site Search (Preview):* You can include Microsoft Copilot search capabilities in your Power Pages website. From the Site Search (Preview) screen (see Figure 8-18), you can enable or disable Copilot search capabilities, with the toggles for Enable Keyword Search and Enable Site Search with Generative AI (Preview).
  - *Add Copilot to Site:* If you've built a custom Microsoft Copilot integration for another Power Platform app (or even Microsoft 365), you can add those non-search-based Copilot components to your Power Pages site by configuring them in this screen (shown in Figure 8-19).

TIP

You may not want to include every table — or, for that matter, every column — in your search results produced by Microsoft Copilot. If that's the case, use the Refine Your Data section of this screen to address such concerns.

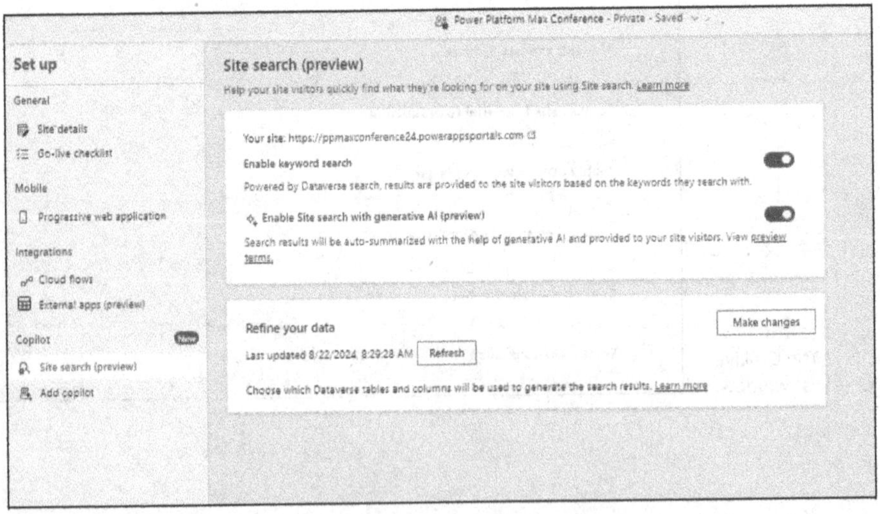

FIGURE 8-18: Integrating search-oriented Microsoft Copilot capabilities in your Power Pages website.

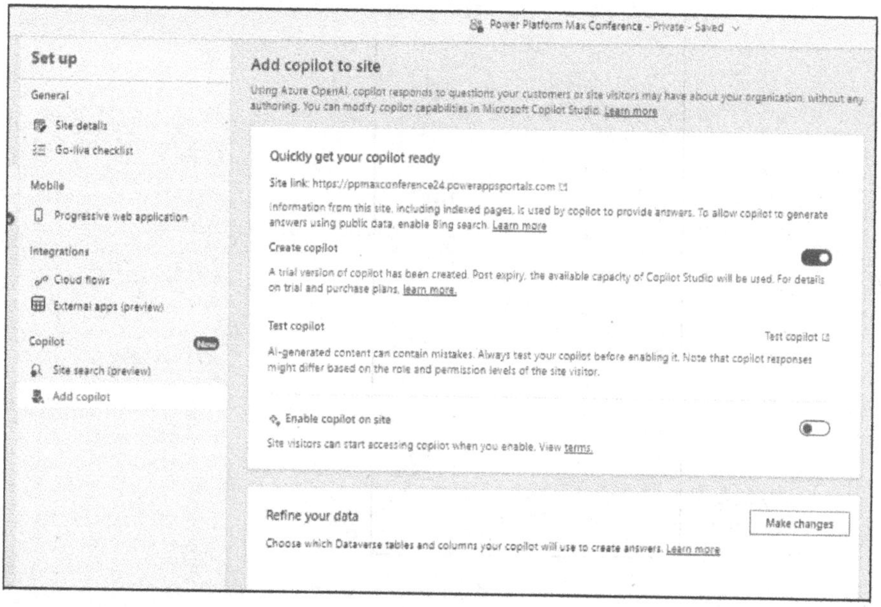

FIGURE 8-19: Adding custom Copilot components to Power Pages.

Security tab

In the Design Studio's Security tab, you can monitor, protect, and manage a variety of content types in Power Pages. Most, if not all, of the security ties to the Dataverse permissions that you configure with your Power Pages Site Settings (see the section "Pages tab," earlier in this chapter) because security relates to page, table, and application permissions. Figure 8-20 shows the Security tab menu, and Table 8-2 briefly describes each option.

Power Pages Management app

Sometimes, you need to go a bit more under the hood to configure your Power Pages website. If you need to go beyond basic configuration management that the Power Pages navigation tabs offer, click the ellipsis that appears below the Security tab. For example, in the menu that opens, you can create automated workflows by selecting Flow from the toolbar and then selecting the Create a Flow option, which takes you to Power Automate (you can read about Power Automate in Chapters 14 and 15) and the Power Pages Management app. You have hundreds of configurations available.

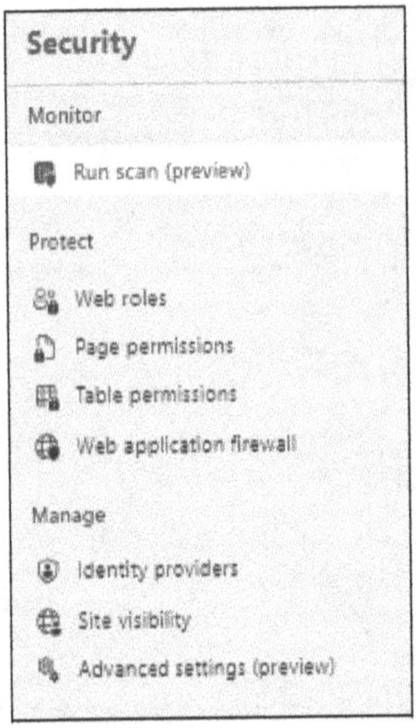

FIGURE 8-20: The Security tab menu.

TABLE 8-2 Security Tab Options

Security Option	What It Does
Run Scan	Checks the website for common issues and vulnerabilities, providing recommendations to improve the site's security.
Web Roles	Defines roles that developers and administrators can assign to users or groups of users. Web roles control access to specific site areas, or the ability to perform certain actions within the site.
Page Permissions	Controls access to specific pages on the website, ensuring that only authorized users can view or interact with certain content.
Table Permissions	Controls access to data stored in Dataverse tables, defining who can read, write, create, or delete records.
Web Application Firewall	Protects your site from web-based attacks and other vulnerabilities by filtering and monitoring traffic.
Identity Providers	Indicates which authenticated users can access your site. A provider such as Microsoft Entra (formerly Azure Active Directory) manage and verify user identities, allowing users to log in by using their credentials from various platforms or systems.
Site Visibility	Controls who can view the websites. Visibility options include *Public* (accessible to all) or *Restricted* (limited to authenticated users or specific roles, applied to the entire site or individual items and/or pages).
Advanced Settings	Opens the Advanced Settings window, where you can configure advanced features related to data storage, encryption, security settings, and other administrative functions for Microsoft Power Pages.

The Power Pages Management app can help you efficiently manage and configure the sites that your organization creates within the Power Pages platform by automating and streamlining common tasks. Figure 8-21 shows the interface of the Power Pages Management app.

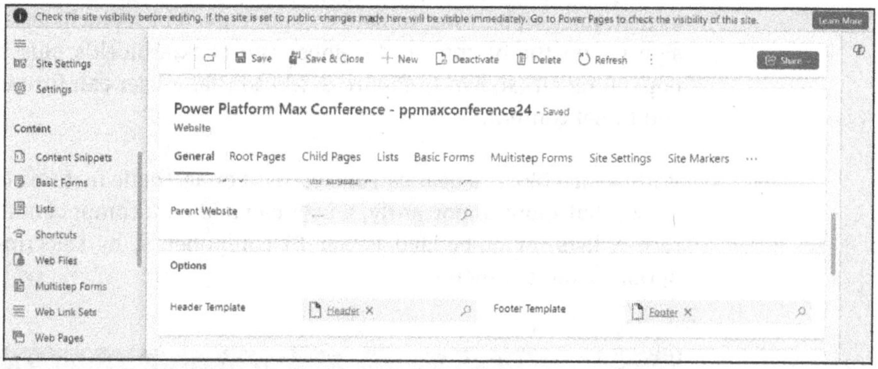

FIGURE 8-21: The Power Pages Management app.

This app helps streamline the development and maintenance process, allowing you to perform administrative tasks from one location, including overseeing the portal's content, structure, security, and user experience.

ON THE WEB

If you want to explore some of the 50-plus configuration options (and counting) that the Power Pages Management app offers to help you structure, enhance content, or secure your website beyond the basic tabs, head over to `http://learn.microsoft.com`, and enter **portal management app** in the Search box, then press Enter. A link to the article should appear in the search results.

Integrating Functionality into Power Pages

If you structure a data source to integrate it into a page, you can most certainly give it a home in Power Pages. From the Data tab within Power Pages Design Studio (flip back to the section "Data tab," earlier in this chapter) or the Power Pages Management app (see the preceding section), you can easily create, manage, and visualize business data for your site by using data, forms, and links as site components. Any time you insert a list or form, Power Pages renders the object and incorporates the components within the page layout by using data from Dataverse. The list and form *definition* (the way the data is displayed from Dataverse, including the layout from viewing and editing records) may include interactivity. You can make it read-only, limiting access to certain users. You may also want to give all users full access (called *write privileges*). The following sections explain how to integrate lists and forms into your Power Pages web pages.

Integrating lists into a Power Pages site

When you open a web page in Power Pages Design Studio, the pages appear broken into blocks. Each of the blocks on a page consists of distinct sections of the page, including headers, footers, body content, or widgets, which are organized to control layout and structure of the page. These blocks typically contain elements such as text, images, buttons, or data components. A block includes a frame with a plus sign (+) on the bottom. A developer can click a block's plus sign (+) to open a pop-up menu (shown in Figure 8-22) so that a user can format the block or add additional content.

Within each block, a user can add content or aesthetic features by customizing the layout; but more importantly, a user can add data components, such as galleries, forms, lists, or embedded Power BI components, by selecting the appropriate options from the menu.

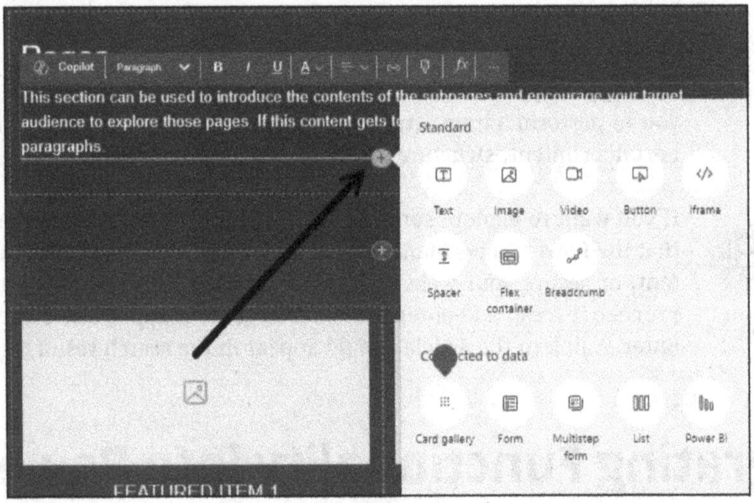

FIGURE 8-22: Integrating Components to a Power Pages web page.

When you select List Data in Power Pages, you pull a specific set of records from a Dataverse table, called a *Dataverse view.* For example, in Figure 8-23, I'm pulling data from the Accounts table by using the view Accounts I Follow. After you integrate the data, the list from the Accounts table appears on your web page, as shown in Figure 8-24, displaying the records as part of the page.

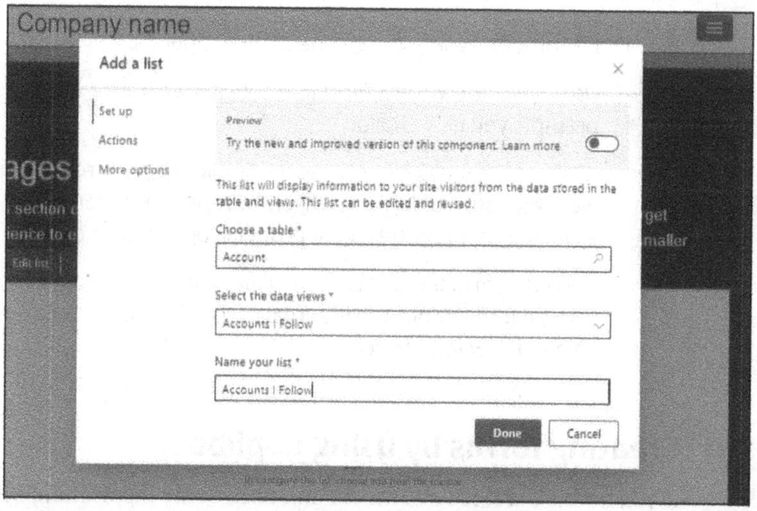

FIGURE 8-23: The Add a List pop-up window.

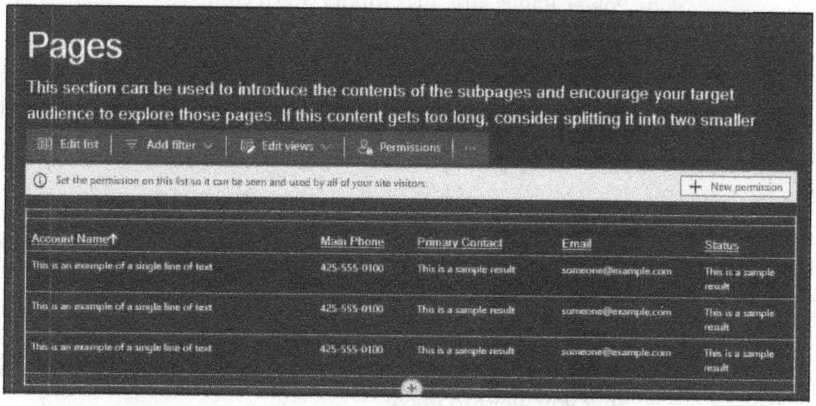

FIGURE 8-24: An example Dataverse list presented on a Power Pages site.

Incorporating forms into a Power Pages site

You can generate forms in Power Pages in a few different ways, such as with the use of Microsoft Copilot or pre-built assets made available by Microsoft, or you can also create your own from existing Dataverse tables. Similar to adding a list (see the preceding section), follow these steps to add a form:

1. **Click the plus sign (+) at the bottom of the block where you want to add the form.**

   The content options menu opens.

2. **Click the Form button.**

   The Form Designer appears.

3. In the Form Designer, choose one of three options:
   - *Use Copilot:* Describe a form to create it. Generate a form based on prompts you give Copilot.
   - *Choose from prebuilt forms created by Microsoft:* Microsoft does all the hard work for you, crafting forms likely to support mission critical needs, including user registration or product support data capture.
   - *Select a form that you've created in the past or Add a Form:* Either you can select a form you've already created that's stored in Dataverse, or you can create a new form based on a Dataverse table.

Creating forms by using Copilot

If you haven't created a form yet and need some inspiration, Microsoft's generative AI platform, Copilot, can guide you through the process by creating a form for your Power Pages site. Just follow these steps:

1. **Click the Form button.**

   The Describe a Form to Create It text box appears upon clicking the Form button.
2. **Enter what you want to accomplish with your form.**

   You can see the form entry window in Figure 8-25.
3. **Click the Submit button (which looks like an airplane) to submit your text description.**

   A sample form appears on the right.
4. **In the Do You Want to Make Any Changes text box, enter the changes that you want to make.**

   For example, if you ask Copilot to include a Product Name field, the first time around, it likely creates that field as a text box; you can ask Copilot to make the Product Name field a drop-down list.
5. **Click the Submit button again to see the changes in the form.**
6. **Repeat Steps 4 and 5 until you have the elements that you want incorporated in your form in the preview on the right of the window.**
7. **(Optional) Move the fields around by clicking the appropriate buttons on the left side of the window.**

   Figure 8-26, for example, shows Move the Email Address Field Up and Remove the Quantity Field.
8. **After you have your form just the way you want it, click OK.**

   The form is now saved to Dataverse and available for your Power Pages site.

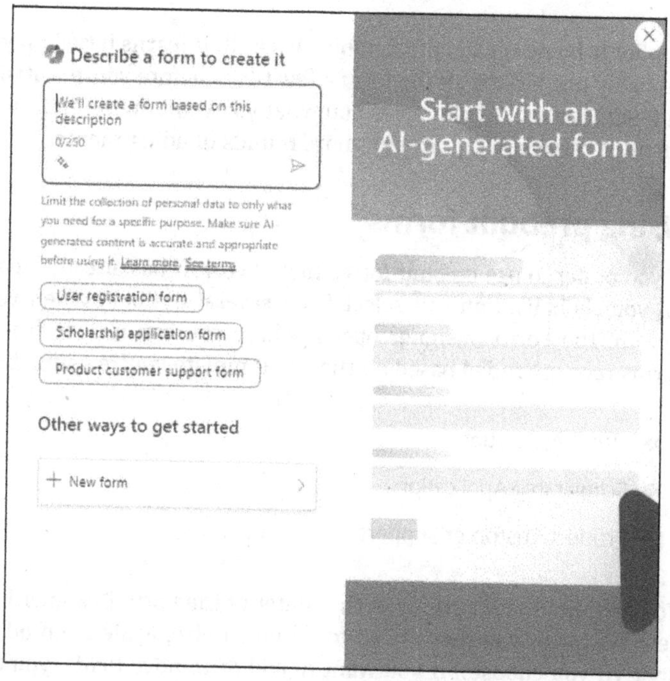

FIGURE 8-25: The Describe a Form to Create It in text box form generator.

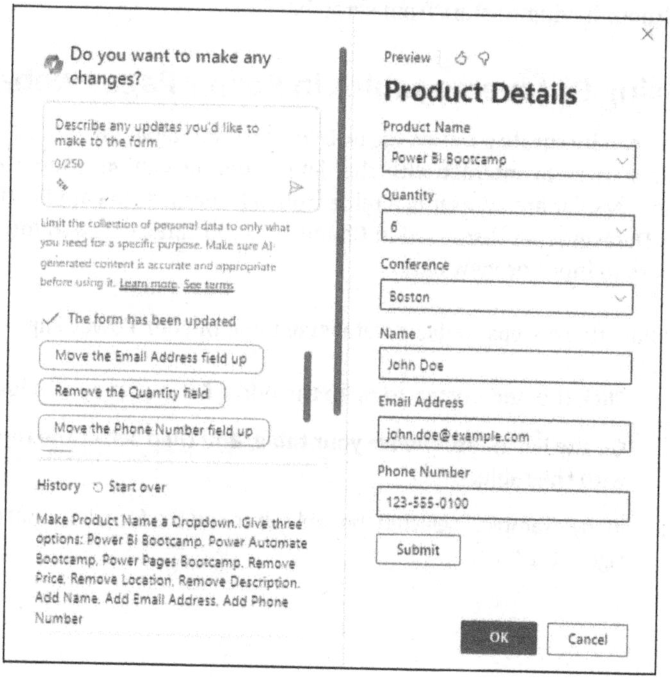

FIGURE 8-26: Preview and tweak the form that you create by using Copilot.

WARNING

Copilot is by no means predictable. After all, it learns based on your requests. You probably need to tweak the form a few times before you're satisfied with the output. Sometimes, Copilot gives you what you want on the first or second try; other times, you have to go through more rounds of adjustments.

Using prebuilt forms

If you prefer to use prebuilt forms that Microsoft has already created (and designed on your behalf), you can select from several options. When you click the Form button, the Form Designer opens, where you can choose from a few pre-built forms recommended based on the site template you're using. Examples include

- User Registration
- Scholarship Application
- Product Customer Support

You can find these options in the center of the Form Designer interface. After you select a form, you don't need to do much else, aside from adjusting the form's style (if you choose). If you want to add or remove fields, you can easily do that, too. Microsoft provides a prebuilt structure so that you can focus on customization without having to start from scratch.

Using Dataverse tables in Power Pages websites

You can integrate a Dataverse or Dynamics 365 table into your Power Pages site to allow users to interact with the data. Whether you've created a table directly in Dataverse or are accessing a table from a Dynamics 365 application (which is built on Dataverse, as discussed in Chapter 3), you can easily add forms to your site for users to input or view data.

Follow these steps to use a Dataverse table in your Power Pages website:

1. **Click the Add button to open the Add a Form pop-up window.**
2. **On the Form tab, choose your table, and then select the form associated with the table.**

   In my example, I selected the table User and the form Information (see Figure 8-27).

3. **Select the Data tab and choose whether you want to allow a user to create new records, update existing records, or have access to the data as read-only.**
4. **Click the On Submit tab and enter a message that appears to the user when they click the form's Submit button.**

   For example, if the form creates a new record, you may want to tell the user "Thank you for submitting a new entry."
5. **(Optional) If you want a CAPTCHA with your form, check one or both boxes in the CAPTCHA tab.**

   A *CAPTCHA* is a kind of challenge-response test to confirm whether a user is actually a human.
6. **(Optional) If you want to allow users to submit attachments as part of the form, click the Attachments tab, and switch the Yes/No toggle to Yes.**

   If you select Yes, a user can save files to a record.
7. **(Optional) Click the AI Form Fill tab and set the Yes/No toggle to Yes if you want AI to help users fill out the form.**

   Selecting Yes enables Microsoft Copilot on your form, assisting the user with their data entry.

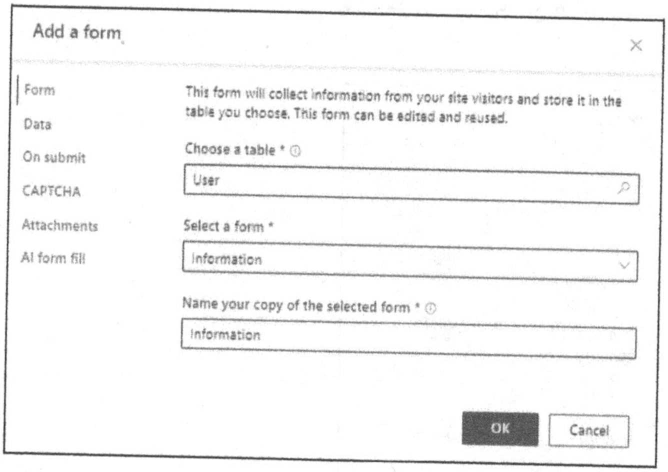

FIGURE 8-27: The Add a Form interface for Dataverse in Power Pages.

Incorporating Power BI into a Power Pages site

Power BI can give your site a magic touch if you want to present an image by using a report or a dashboard to text-based content. To use a Power BI-based data visualization in your Power Pages site, first enable Power BI by following these steps:

1. **In the Power Platform admin center, click the Gear icon at the upper-right corner of the window.**
2. **In the Settings menu that appears, click Admin Center.**

   The Admin Center Settings window opens.
3. **Choose Resources ⇨ Power Pages Sites.**

   A list of all active Power Pages Sites appears.
4. **In the Sites list, click the name of the site for which you want to enable Power BI Services.**

   The configuration for the specific site opens.
5. **In the Services pane on the right of the screen, click the Power BI Visualization, Power BI Embedded Services, and SharePoint Integration toggles to set them to Yes.**

   Figure 8-28 shows this Services pane.

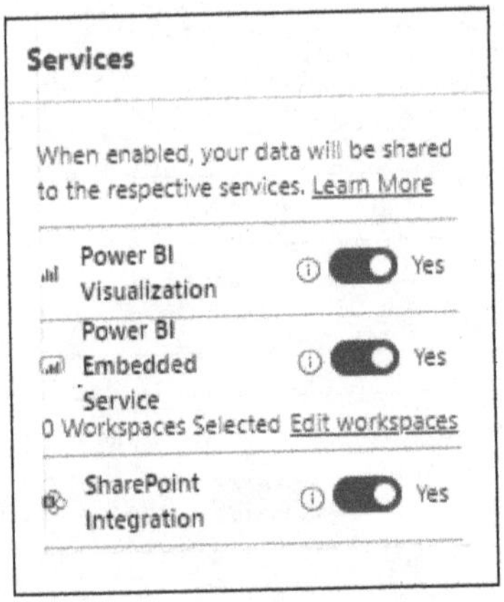

FIGURE 8-28: The Services pane of Power Pages Management.

6. **Return to your Power Pages site and add a Power BI component within a block.**

7. **Click the Edit Power BI button that appears in the upper left corner of the block where you added the Power BI component.**

   This action opens a pop-up window (see Figure 8-29) where you need to configure several parameters for your Power BI visualization.

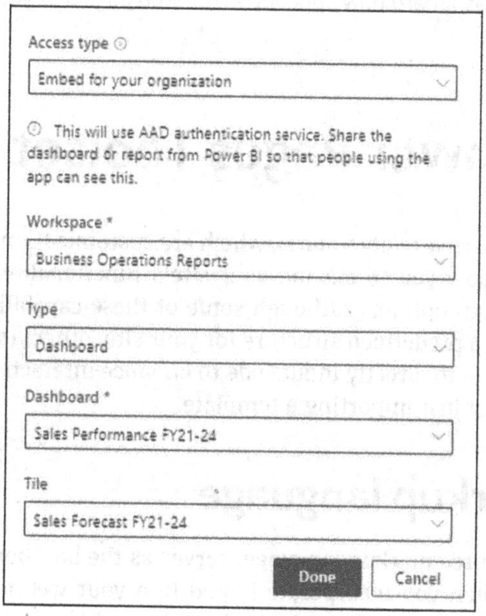

FIGURE 8-29: Configuring a Power BI visualization.

8. **Choose an option from the Access Type drop-down list.**

   You can choose either embed the Power BI visual for a specific customer (limited access), Embed for Your Organization (all users internal to your domain), or publish to the Web (accessible to all users).

9. **From the Workspace drop-down list, select the Power BI Workspace from which you can access your report or dashboard.**

   Refer to Chapters 12 and 13 regarding reports, dashboards, and workspaces.

   REMEMBER

   In order to embed a Power BI Report or Dashboard, you must already have content created and stored in Power BI Services — specifically, an accessible workspace (not a personal workspace) — which requires a premium license.

10. **Select whether you want to embed a Report or Dashboard from the Type drop-down list.**

    In my example, I selected Dashboard.

    Based on the Type you select in Step 10, a drop-down list appears for you to select the specific item that you want to embed on the page.

11. **Select the item to embed.**

In my example (refer to Figure 8-29), I placed on the page a dashboard saved in the workspace Business Operation Reports as Sales Performance FY21-24.

12. **After you're satisfied with all your selected options, click Done.**

The Power BI Dashboard now appears on the web page that you specified to embed in Step 6.

Extending the Power Pages Toolset

Power Pages offers *extensibility features*, which are customization and development capabilities that allow you to expand your site's functionality beyond standard templates and design options. Although some of these capabilities (such as web templates) provide a predefined structure for your site, others (such as Liquid and JavaScript) allow you to directly input code to enhance interactivity and data presentation, instead of just importing a template.

Liquid markup language

Liquid, an open-source markup language, serves as the backbone of Power Pages web templates. When you incorporate Liquid into your web templates, you can create interactive features such as customized views, filtered data lists, and conditional displays, all based on user input or role-based access. For example

- Show each user a personalized dashboard by retrieving and displaying their relevant data from Dataverse.
- Create forms that update dynamically based on user choices.

You can use Liquid to integrate dynamic content, and also reduce the need for excessive custom code, like other Power Platform tools.

ON THE WEB

To find out how to code by using Liquid, Microsoft provides information on its site, at `http://learn.microsoft.com`. Just enter **Liquid** in the Search box, and then press Enter. The results page offers links to articles on using Liquid.

Web templates

Web templates in Power Pages are HTML-based page structures that define a page's layout and design within the portal. The template uses a combination of standard HTML and the Liquid markup language (see the preceding section) to dynamically pull data from Dataverse so that you can display both static and dynamic content. Here are some of the key features of web templates:

- **Reusable:** Can offer a consistent design across multiple pages.
- **Highly customizable:** You can build one from scratch to meet specific design or functional requirements.
- **Integrated with Dataverse:** Supports enabling dynamic content generation so that developers have control over page layouts.

ON THE WEB

Find out how to build repeatable Web templates by heading over to `http://learn.microsoft.com`, entering **Web Templates** in the Search box, and pressing Enter. A link to Microsoft's article about these templates should appear in the search results that open.

JavaScript and CSS

Power Pages allows you to customize your site by using JavaScript and Cascading Style Sheets (CSS):

- **JavaScript:** You can use JavaScript in webpages, templates, forms, and lists to add dynamic behaviors such as user input validation, calling external web services, and accessing Dataverse functions, as well as interactive features such as auto-filling fields or showing custom error messages. Although JavaScript often works through reusable code snippets, it does require a certain level of coding knowledge.
- **CSS:** Styles HTML elements, instead of functioning as a markup language such as HTML or XML, so you can use CSS to control the visual presentation of a Power Pages site. Although you can do some basic styling in the Design Studio's Styling workspace (See the section "Styling tab," earlier in this chapter), you can further refine your site's appearance and behavior by using CSS to enhance the user experience with relevant fonts, colors, spacing, and other design elements. You can also use CSS to implement specific design features without relying on JavaScript, such as hiding elements or adjusting the layout.

Using code editors

Power Pages offers a lightweight version of Microsoft's Visual Studio (its integrated development environment, or IDE) called Visual Studio Code for the Web that you can access within the Power Pages Design Studio. By using Visual Studio

Code for the Web, you can directly edit HTML source code. Having access to this code editor can help you create complex layouts and do extensive customization of your Power Pages website, beyond the standard templates provided by Microsoft. To work with Visual Studio in Power Pages, click the Edit Code button in the command bar. The code editor window appears, where you can access the full capabilities of this code editor.

ON THE WEB

If you want to figure out the nuts and bolts of using Visual Studio Code for the Web, access documentation, or download a copy of the software to your desktop, head to `http://code.visualstudio.com`. Enter **Visual Studio Code for the Web** in the Search box and press Enter to access a list of articles about this code editor.

3

Telling the Data Story with Power BI

IN THIS PART . . .

Explore how to prepare and cleanse data in Power BI.

Learn the data visualization options available in Power BI Desktop.

Discover how to create reports and dashboards using Power BI Desktop and Power BI Services.

Expand your knowledge on how to complete basic administrative functions with Power BI Services.

IN THIS CHAPTER

» Understanding your options for business intelligence tooling

» Familiarizing yourself with Power BI terminology

» Understanding the licensing options available from Microsoft

Chapter 9

Power BI Foundations

Picking out the correct version of Power BI might be like visiting the world's biggest candy store: You can choose from many alternatives with subtle nuances. The choice boils down to wants, needs, scale, and, of course, money. Some versions are free (well, sort of), and other versions can be expensive. And, of course, the most obvious difference is that some versions are desktop- or server-based, whereas others offer online-only capabilities.

If you visit the Microsoft website on any given day and search for products, you notice quite a few versions of Power BI exist. However, the Pricing page and the Products page don't necessarily match. (Thanks for the help, Microsoft!) It isn't clear whether "Free is free" or whether products are inclusive within specific Power BI versions. This chapter clears up any confusion you may have so that, moving forward, you know which product you should use.

Before moving forward with purchasing and licensing information, this chapter explores the basic capabilities of Power BI and reviews some terminology.

Looking Under the Power BI Hood

Power BI is a conglomeration of many products that together create an enterprise business intelligence and data analytics platform. If you've ever used Excel, you'd be familiar with functionality such as Power Query, Power Pivot, Power View, and

Power Map. Combined with Power BI-specific features such as Power Q&A built for Power Platform, the final product you will come to know about is either Power BI Desktop or Power BI Services. Both of these products allow users to organize, collect, manage, and analyze big datasets. *Big data* is a concept where the business and data analyst will evaluate extremely large datasets, which may reveal patterns and trends relating to human behaviors and interactions not easily identifiable without the use of specific tools. A typical big data collection is often expressed in millions of records. Unlike a tool such as Microsoft Excel, Power BI can evaluate many data sources and millions of records simultaneously. The sources don't need to be structured using a spreadsheet, either. They can include unstructured and semi-structured data.

REMEMBER

Structured data is organized in a predefined format, such as with Dataverse tables, with clear rows and columns, making it easy to search and analyze. *Semi-structured data* lacks a fixed schema; this type of data uses markers and tabs. XML and JSON are two examples of semi-structured data. *Unstructured data* has no defined format, such as the data contained in your typical Microsoft Word document, Adobe Acrobat PDF, or photo formatted in a JPG or PNG format.

After pulling these many data sources together and processing them, Power BI can help you come up with visually compelling outputs in the form of charts, graphics, reports, dashboards, and KPIs (Key Performance Indicators) to help you better understand data such as satisfaction, customer insights, growth rates, and efficiency targets, as shown in Figure 9-1.

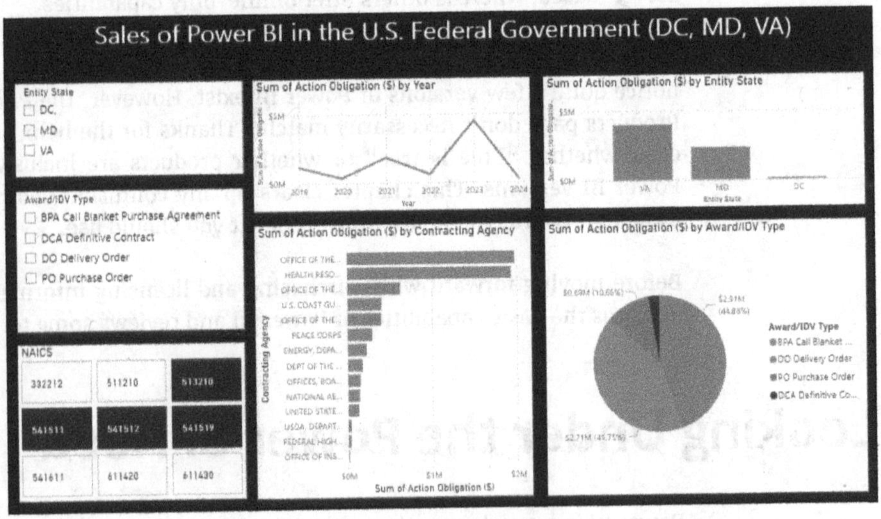

FIGURE 9-1: Example of Power BI output.

As I mentioned earlier in this section, Power BI isn't just a single source application. It has desktop, online, and mobile components. The following sections cover the smaller apps and services you will encounter when working with Power BI.

Posing questions with Power Query

With Power Query, Power BI meets the need for a more robust query editor than is provided by Excel. With the Excel editor, you can extract data from only a single data source, whereas with Power BI Power Query, you can extract data from numerous data sources as well as read data from relational sources such as SQL Server Enterprise, Azure SQL Server, Oracle, MySQL, DB2, and a host of other platforms. If you're looking to extract data from unstructured, semi structured, or application sources — such as CSV files, text files, Excel files, Word documents, SharePoint document libraries, Microsoft Exchange Server, Dynamics 365, or Outlook — Power Query makes that possible. And, if you have access to API services that map to specific data fields on platforms such as LinkedIn, Facebook, or Twitter, you can use Power Query to mine those platforms as well.

Whatever you have Power Query do, the procedure is always pretty much the same: It transforms the data you specify (using a graphical user interface as needed) by adding columns, rows, data types, date and time, text fields, and appropriate operators. Power Query manages this transformation by taking an extensive dataset, which is nothing more than a bunch of raw data (often disorganized and confusing to you, of course) and then creates some business sense by organizing it into tables, columns, and rows. You can then transfer this output to a portable file, such as Excel, or something more robust, such as a Power Pivot model (see the next section).

Modeling with Power Pivot

The Power BI data modeling tool is called Power Pivot. With this tool, you can create models such as star schemas, calculated measures, and columns and build complex diagrams. Power Pivot uses another programming language called the Data Analysis Expression language — or DAX, for short. DAX is a formula-based language used for data analysis purposes. You soon discover that, as a language, DAX is chock full of useful functions, so stay tuned.

Visualizing with Power View

The visualization engine of Power BI is Power View. The idea here is to connect to data sources, fetch and transform that data for analysis, and then have Power View present the output using one of its many visualization options. Power View gives users the ability to filter data for individual variables or an entire report. Users can slice data at the variable level or even break out elements in Power View to focus like a laser on data that may be considered anomalous.

Mapping data with Power Map

Sometimes, visualizing data requires a bit more than a bar chart or a table. Perhaps you need a map that integrates geospatial coordinates with 3D requirements. Suppose that you're looking to add dimensionality to your data — perhaps with the help of heat maps, by gauging the height and width of a column or basing the color used on a statistical reference. In that case, you want to consider Power BI's Power Map feature set. Another feature built into Power Map is the use of geospatial capabilities using Microsoft Bing, Microsoft's external search engine technology that includes capabilities for mapping locations. A user can highlight data using geocoordinate latitude and longitudinal data as granular as an address or as global as a country.

Interpreting data with Power Q&A

One of the biggest challenges for many users is data interpretation. Say, for example, that you've built this incredible data model using Power Pivot. Now what? Your data sample is often pretty significant in terms of size, which means that you need some way to make sense of all the data you've deployed in the model. That's why Microsoft created a natural language engine, a way to interpret text, numbers, and even speech so that users can query the data model directly.

REMEMBER

Power Q&A works directly in conjunction with Power View.

A classic example of a situation where Power Q&A can be enormously helpful would involve determining how many users have purchased a specific item at a given store location. If you want to drill down further, you could analyze a whole set of metrics — asking whether the item comes in several colors or sizes, for example, or specifying which day of the week saw the most items sold. The possibilities are endless as long as you've built your data model to accommodate the questions.

Power BI Desktop

All of these Power BI platforms are great ideas, but the truly stupendous idea was bundling together Power Query, Power Pivot, Power View, and Power Q&A to form

Power BI Desktop. Using Power BI Desktop, you can complete all your business intelligence activities under a single umbrella. You can also develop BI and data analysis activities far more easily. Finally, Microsoft updates Power BI Desktop features monthly, so you can always be on the BI cutting edge.

Power BI Services

Over time, the product name for Power BI Services has evolved. When the product was in beta, it was called Power BI Website. Nowadays, you often hear the product referred to as Power BI Online or Power BI Services. Whatever you call it, it functions as the Software as a Service (SaaS) companion to Power BI. Accessible at `https://app.powerbi.com`, Power BI Services allows users to collaborate and share their dashboards, reports, and datasets with other users from a single location.

REMEMBER

The version of Power BI you have licensed dictates your ability to share and ingest data in Power BI Services.

Knowing Your Power BI Terminology

Whether Microsoft or another vendor creates it, every product you come across has its own terminology. It may seem like a foreign language, but if you visit a vendor's website and do a simple search, you're sure to find a glossary that spells out what all these mysterious terms mean.

Microsoft, unsurprisingly, has its own glossary for Power BI as well. (Those folks refer to terminology as *concepts*, for reasons clear only to them.) Before you proceed any further on your Power BI journey, let's establish the lay of the land. In Microsoft Power BI-speak, some concepts resonate across vendors no matter who you are. For example, all vendors have reports and dashboards as critical concepts. Now, do all other vendors adopt Microsoft's practice and call dataflows a type of workflow? Not quite. They all have their names for these specific features, although all such features generally work the same way.

TIP

Microsoft has done a pretty good job of trying to stick with mainstream names for critical concepts. Nevertheless, some of the more advanced product features specific to AI/machine learning and security adopt the rarefied lingo of Microsoft products such as Azure Active Directory or Azure Machine Learning.

Capacities

What's the first thing you think about when it comes to data? Is it the type, or is it the quantity? Or do you consider both? With Power BI, the first concept you must be familiar with is *capacities*, which are central to Power BI. Why, you ask? Capacities are the sum total of resources needed in order for you to complete any project you may create in Power BI. Resources include the storage, processor, and memory required to host and deliver the Power BI projects.

There are two types of capacity: shared and dedicated. A *shared* capacity allows you to share resources with other Microsoft end users. *Dedicated* capacities fully commit resources to you alone. Whereas shared capacity is available for both free and paying Power BI users, dedicated capacity requires a Power BI premium subscription.

Workspaces

Workspaces are a means of collaborating and sharing content with colleagues. Whether it's personal or intended for collaboration, any workspace you create is created on capacities. Think of a workspace as a container that allows you to manage the entire lifecycle of dashboards, reports, workbooks, datasets, and dataflows in the Power BI Services environment. Figure 9-2 shows a My Workspace, a particular example of a Power BI workspace.

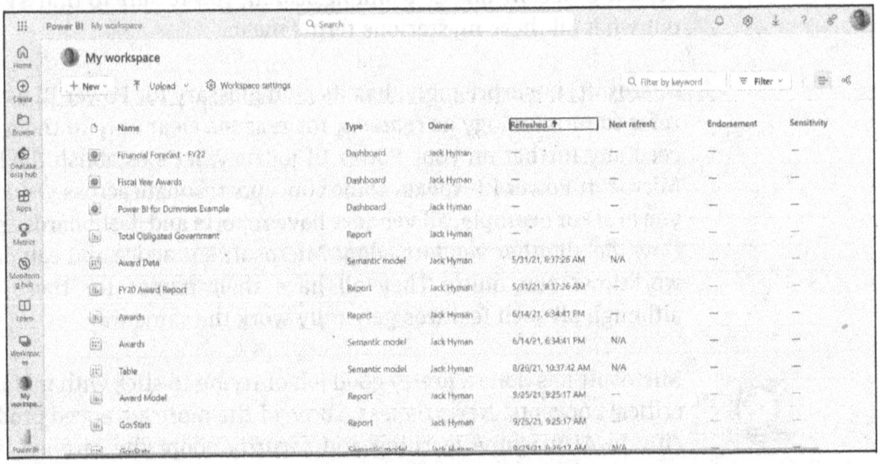

FIGURE 9-2: My Workspace in Power BI Services.

REMEMBER The My Workspace isn't the only type of workspace available. Power BI also has an option called Workspace, which is meant for group collaboration and sharing. If you want to collaborate, you have no choice but to upgrade to a Power BI Pro or Premium plan, as you can't go beyond the My Workspace unless you have a

Premium version of Power BI. Features that come with collaboration include the ability to create and publish Power BI-based dashboards, reports, workbooks, datasets, and apps with a team.

TECHNICAL STUFF

Looking to upload the work you've created using Power BI Desktop? Or perhaps you need to manipulate the work online without collaborating with anyone? If the answer to either question is yes, My Workspace is all that is necessary. You only *require* the use of the Power BI Online Free License. As soon as you want to collaborate with others, you need to upgrade to a paid Pro or Premium subscription.

So now you know that your work is stored in a workspace. Next question: What happens with the data in that workspace? The answer is twofold: There is what you see as the user, and then there's what goes on behind the scenes as part of the data transformation process. Let's start with the behind-the-scenes activities.

A *dataflow* is a collection of tables that collects the datasets imported into Power BI. After the tables are created and managed in your workspace as part of Power BI Services, you can add, edit, and delete data within a dataflow. The data refresh can occur using a predefined schedule as well. Keep in mind that Power BI uses an Azure data lake, a way to store the extremely large volumes of data necessary for Power BI to evaluate, process, and analyze data rapidly. As a service, Azure Data Lake also helps with cleaning and transforming data quickly when the datasets are voluminous in size.

Unlike a dataflow (which, again, is a collection of tables), a dataset should be treated as a single asset in your collection of data sources. Think of a dataset as a subset of data. When used with dataflows, the dataset is mapped to a managed Azure data lake. It likely includes some or all the data in the data lake. The granularity of the data varies greatly, depending on the speed and scale of the dataset available.

The analyst or developer can extract the data when building their desired output, such as a report. Sometimes, there may be a desire for multiple datasets, in which case dataflow transformation might be necessary. On the other hand, sometimes multiple datasets can leverage the same dataset housed in the Azure data lake. In this instance, little transformation is necessary.

REMEMBER

After you've manipulated the data on your own, you have to publish the data you've created in Power BI. Microsoft assumes that you intend to share the data among users. If you intend to share a dataset, assume that you need a Pro or Premium license.

Reports

Data can be stored in a system indefinitely and remain idle. But what good is it if the data in the system isn't queried from time to time so that users like you and me can understand what the data means, right? Suppose you worked for a hospital. You needed to query the employee database to find out how many employees worked within five miles of the facility in case of an emergency. That's when quickly (not warp speed though) you can create a summary of your dataset using a Power BI report. Sure, there could be a couple of hundred records or tens of thousands of records, all unique of course, but the records are all brought together to help the hospital home in just who can be all hands on deck in case of an emergency whether it is just down the block, five miles away, or fifty miles away.

Power BI Reports translates that data into one or more pages of visualizations — line charts, bar charts, donuts, treemaps — you name it. You can either evaluate your data at a high level or focus on a particular data subset (if you've managed to query the dataset beforehand). You can tackle creating a report in a number of ways, from taking a dataset using a single source and creating an output from scratch to importing data from many sources. One example here would be connecting to an Excel workbook or Google Sheets document using Power View sheets. From there, Power BI takes the data from across the source and makes sense of it. The result is a report (see Figure 9-3) based on the imported data using predefined configurations established by the report author.

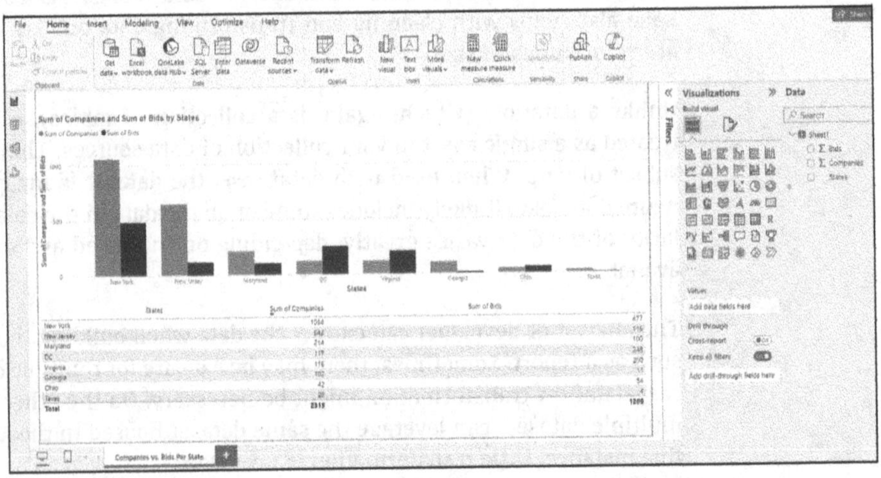

FIGURE 9-3: A sample Power BI report.

TIP

Power BI offers two report view modes: Reading view and Editing view. When you open a report, it typically opens in Reading view by default. If you have been granted Edit permissions, you can switch to Editing view to make changes to the report. In a workspace, users with admin, member, or contributor roles can edit reports, provided they have the appropriate permissions.

TECHNICAL STUFF

In Power BI, privileged users can design, build, and share reports within the Edit view, while users with Read-Only access can interact with these reports but cannot modify them. These reports are accessible under the Reports tab in a Power BI workspace and may contain multiple pages of visualizations, with each page potentially drawing from one or more datasets. Reports are not limited to a single-page visualization and can include various interactive elements based on multiple data sources.

Dashboards

If you've had any experience with Power BI whatsoever, you already know that it's a highly visual tool. In line with its visual nature, the Power BI dashboard, also known as Canvas, brings your data story to life. If you're looking to take all the pieces of your data puzzle and capture a moment in time, you use the dashboard. Think of it as a blank canvas. As you build your reports, widgets, tiles, and Key Performance Indicators (KPIs) over time, you pin the ones you like to the dashboard to create a single visualization. The dashboard represents the large dataset that you feel covers your topic at a glance. As such, it can help you make decisions, support you in monitoring data, or make it possible for you to drill down in your dataset by applying different visualization options.

To access a particular dashboard, you must first open a workspace. All you need to do then is click the Dashboards tab for whichever app you're working with. Keep in mind that every dashboard represents a customized view of an underlying dataset. To locate your dashboards, go to your My Workspaces and then choose Dashboards from the Filters Menu to see what's available (see Figure 9-4).

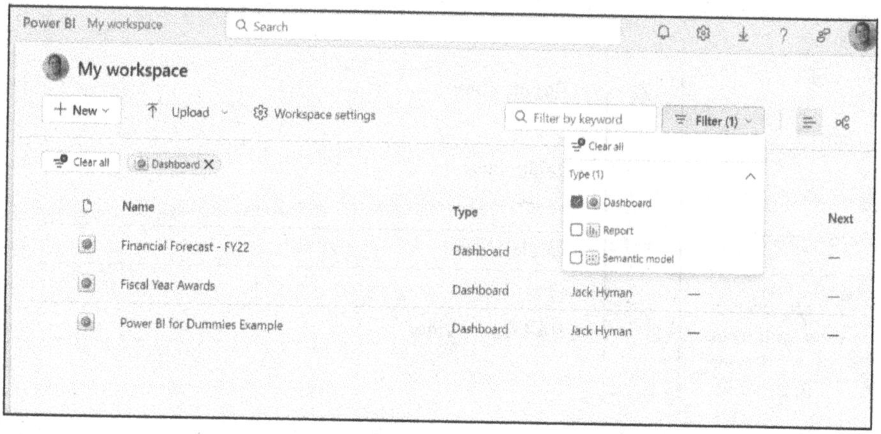

FIGURE 9-4: Locating your dashboards.

REMEMBER

If you own a dashboard, you have permission to edit it. Otherwise, you have only read-only access. You can share a dashboard with others, but they may not be able to save any changes. Keep in mind, however, that if you want to share a dashboard with a colleague, you need, at minimum, a Power BI Pro license.

Views

Core to Power BI Desktop is your ability to model and visualize your data before *publishing*, which is when the files created using Power BI Desktop are saved to Power BI Services. On the left side of the Power BI Desktop are four icons representing views for one's data (see Figure 9-5):

- **Report View:** The Report View is where a user can create their visualizations.
- **Table View:** With the Table View, a user can display the data in a matrix, or tabular format, with rows and columns visible. The user can then review and compare detailed data and values rather than visualize their data.
- **Model View:** In the Model View, a user can visualize all the tables, columns, and relations in the data model. You will find this view especially helpful when trying to build complex relationships with many tables yet show them in a single report.
- **DAX Query View:** The DAX Query View enables users to interact with and manipulate data within a Power BI semantic model by writing and executing Data Analysis Expressions (DAX) queries. This view supports advanced data analysis, filtering, and calculation, providing users with the flexibility to create complex insights and custom metrics directly within the data model.

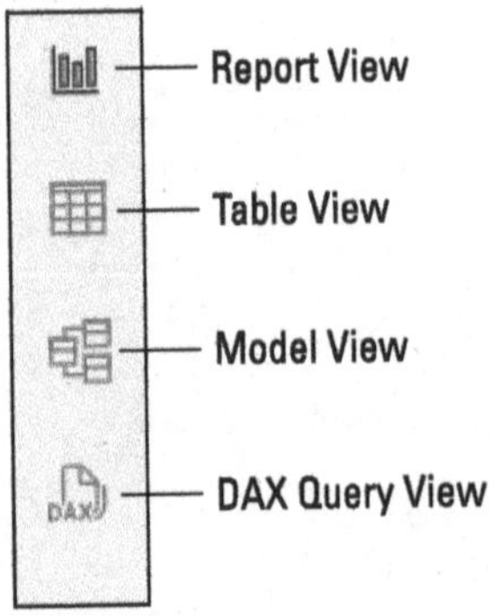

FIGURE 9-5: View options in Power BI Desktop.

Canvas

In Power BI, the canvas is the main work area where visualizations are created and arranged (see Figure 9-6). You'll find the term often used to describe the space within Power BI Desktop or the Power BI service where someone can drag and drop visual elements to create their reports or dashboards.

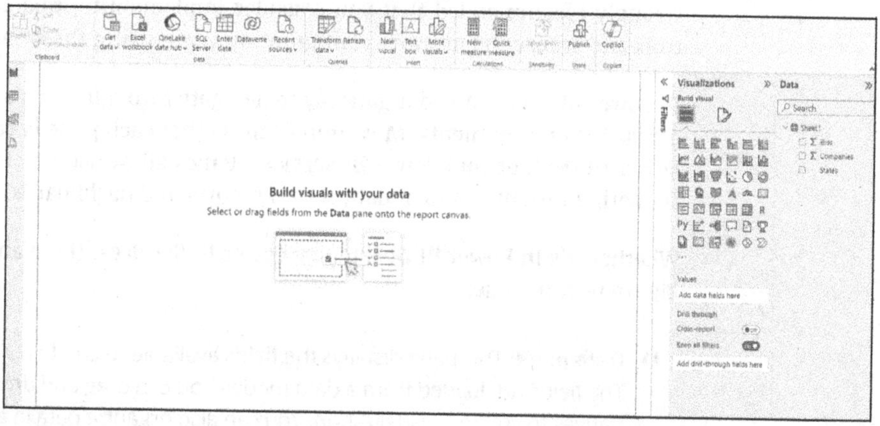

FIGURE 9-6: A blank canvas area in Power BI Desktop.

With respect to reports, the canvas is the area where a user can add, organize, and visualize their charts, graphics, tables, and maps. Each visualization is positioned by the user in a location they desire. You can have one visualization, or many on a canvas when building a report.

Dashboards can only be created in Power BI Services. A user can pin various reports on a canvas, which in this case, is a single page to provide a snapshot across different datasets.

DirectQuery

For enterprise users who need access to data in real-time, you'll want to choose DirectQuery versus Import. With import, you pull the data into Power BI one time and must refresh the dataset manually. DirectQuery allows a user to have a direct connection to data sources, enabling real-time querying capabilities. Instead of importing data into Power BI, it remains in the source system, such as Dataverse, and Power BI directly queries this data whenever the visualization source is refreshed. The DirectQuery approach is especially beneficial for working with large datasets or scenarios where data updates frequently. You are ensuring that users always see the most current data.

WARNING

While getting data refreshed in real-time may seem ideal, using DirectQuery certainly has its drawbacks. Users will experience performance issues depending on the underlying data source and its complexity. If the data source is slow or being taxed by heavy user capacity, there will certainly be delays in data retrieval. You also need to consider the security implications. DirectQuery involves making live queries to a data source. You must make sure that the data source is properly secured, as unauthorized access can impact the integrity of the dataset. It's strongly recommended that you consider implementing role-based access controls and secure the network configuration when using DirectQuery.

In Power BI, *panes* are your gateway to navigate through various features available across the environments. Most important is that each pane is consistent between Power BI Desktop and Power BI Services. Panes allow users to manage and interact with different layers of data across reports and dashboards.

Whether it's in Power BI Desktop or Power BI Services, the main panes, shown in Figure 9-7, include:

- **Data pane:** This pane displays the fields available to create a visualization. The fields are loaded from a data model. You can drag and drop fields onto a Canvas to create a visualization. You can also organize data in a table to create calculations with DAX (see the "Views" section, previously in this chapter, for more about DAX).
- **Visualizations pane:** You can select one of 20+ visualization types such as charts, graphs, and maps to create a report. You can also set visualizations using properties and establish formatting to tailor the presentation if the visualization.
- **Filters pane:** When you need to restrict a dataset to a targeted subset of characteristics, such as a specific location or active/inactive state based on stored columns, you can apply filters to the entire report or a subset of a visualization within a report.

Power BI Services has several other panes, accessed as shown in Figure 9-8. The following panes are specific to Power BI Services, whereas the panes listed previously are available in both Power BI Desktop and Services.

- **Create pane**: The Create pane allows users to initiate the creation of new reports, datasets, and dashboards inside Power BI Service.
- **Browser pane**: The Browser pane helps users navigate between different reports, datasets, dashboards, and other content available exclusive to Power BI Service.
- **Workspace pane**: The Workspace pane provides access to workspaces where users can organize, share, and collaborate on reports, dashboards, and datasets. There are two types of workspaces, a shared workspace and a personal workspace called *My Workspace*.

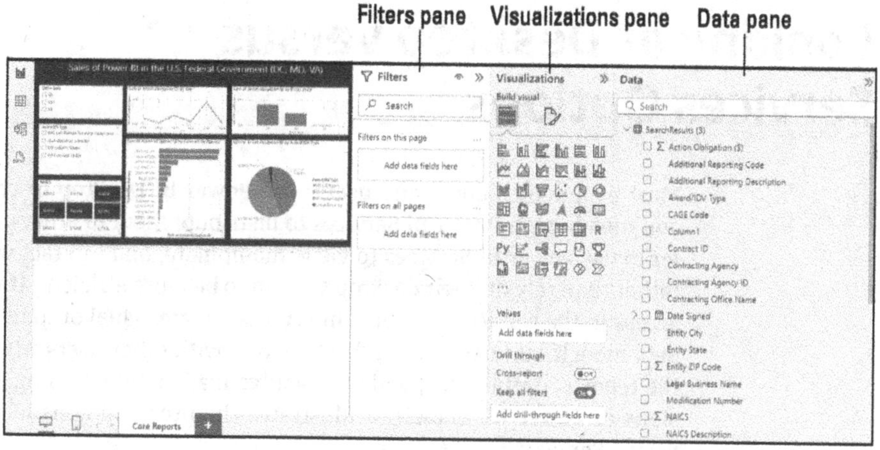

FIGURE 9-7: The Power BI main navigation panes.

- **Apps pane**: The Apps pane displays all accessible Power BI apps, which aggregate multiple dashboards and reports into a unified experience. (Access this pane by clicking the ellipsis.)
- **Monitor pane**: The Monitor pane offers tools for overseeing and managing the usage, performance, and health of reports, datasets, and dataflows within one or more workspaces. (Access this pane by clicking the ellipsis.)

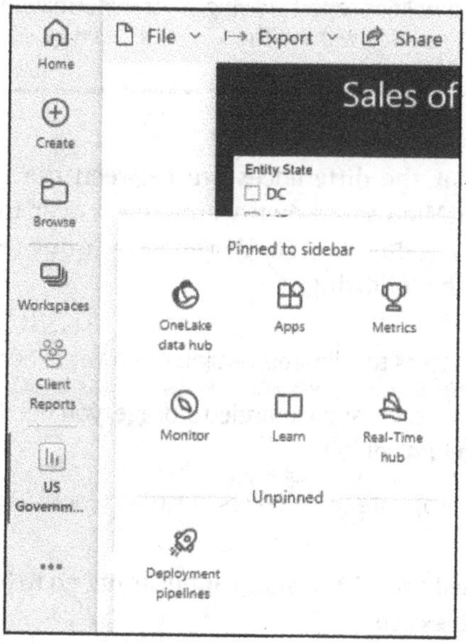

FIGURE 9-8: Power BI Services navigation panes.

Looking at Desktop versus Services Options

Most people (designers and users) use Power BI Desktop to create their reports and then hop on Power BI Services to distribute them to others. Some people prefer to use Power BI Services to view, manipulate, and interact with reports online rather than rely on their desktop version to be more efficient. If you have adequate access to the service, you can edit reports, create visual outputs based on existing data models and datasets, and collaborate with other users who require access to the reports, dashboards, and KPIs you've made without going between both versions of Power BI. Table 9-1 illustrates the pros and cons of Power BI Desktop versus Services.

TABLE 9-1 **Key Pros and Cons of Power BI Desktop and Power BI Services**

Platform	Pros	Cons
Power BI Desktop	Comprehensive data modeling and report-building capabilities. Supports offline access so users can work without an Internet connection.	Must be downloaded and installed, which can be limiting for those using multiple devices.
Power BI Services	Allows for seamless sharing and collaboration directly in the cloud. Being cloud-only simplifies report viewing, dashboard interaction, and KPI tracking without the need for local files on a user's Desktop.	Offers fewer data modeling and transformation tools than Power BI Desktop.

ON THE WEB

If you want to learn what the differences are between the Power BI Desktop and Power BI Services in Microsoft's own words, head over to `https://learn.microsoft.com/en-us/power-bi/fundamentals/service-service-vs-desktop`. There you find the following:

- Microsoft offers free access to a limited version of Power BI Services.
- For robust collaboration tools and expanded storage, you need a minimum of either the Pro or Premium edition.
- Use cases that are appropriate to both versions of Power BI.

To download a copy of the Power BI Desktop application, go to `https://powerbi.microsoft.com/en-us/desktop`.

Managing updates

The beauty of Software as a Service (SaaS) is that anytime a vendor wants to add a new feature to a product, it can do so with little effort. When vendors issue updates by SaaS cloud delivery, users see new features instantly and can start using them right away. Except for Power BI Desktop and Power BI Report Server, all other versions of Power BI fall into the cloud delivery model commonly referred to as Services, as each version is delivered as SaaS.

SaaS cloud delivery allows Microsoft to auto-update features regularly and deliver the product over the Internet using a web browser such as Microsoft Edge, Google Chrome, or Apple Safari. In case of a technical issue, Microsoft doesn't have to wait for the end-of-the-month software release to update the code — it does so immediately. SaaS Delivery ensures continuous access to the latest features, faster resolution of issues, and improved overall user experience without the need for manual updates or downtime.

With downloadable software such as Power BI Desktop, it's up to you to keep track of updates. Cloud-based solutions may be updated as often as daily, but vendors typically update downloadable software much less frequently. Microsoft provides cumulative updates for Power BI Desktop each month, with all the features and functionality available on the Services platform.

TECHNICAL STUFF

If you want to make sure you have the latest edition of Power BI Desktop, you have three options:

- Check the Microsoft website to see if an update is available.
- Watch for in-app notifications indicating that a new version can be downloaded.
- Configure automatic update notifications by choosing File ⇨ Options and Settings ⇨ Options ⇨ Updates. Click on the check box to Display update notifications for Power BI Desktop.

Comparing features

Table 9-2 describes the features that are available in Power BI Desktop and Power BI Services, and indicates which features are common to both.

TABLE 9-2 Power BI Desktop and Power BI Services Features

Power BI Desktop Features	Common Features	Power BI Services Features
More than 100 data sources	Reports	Limited data sources
Data transformation	Visualizations	Dashboarding
Data shaping	Security	KPI management
Data modeling	Filters	Workspaces
Measures	R visuals (big data outputs)	Sharing and collaboration
Calculated columns	Bookmarks	Hosting and storage
DAX	Q&A	Workflow/data flow
Python		Paginated reporting
Themes		Gateway management
Row Level Security (RLS) creation		Row Level Security (RLS) management

IN THIS CHAPTER

» Defining the types of data sources Power BI supports

» Exploring how to connect and configure data sources in Power BI

» Working with shared datasets

» Importing and connecting to datasets

» Finding and working with common data sources

» Identifying cleansing needs based on anomalies, properties, and data quality issues

Chapter 10
Working with Data

Enterprise software vendors such as Microsoft have built data source connectors to help organizations import data into applications such as Power BI. You quickly realize that connecting to data sources isn't necessarily the tricky part — it's often the data transformation that takes a bit of time. After you figure out which method is best to prep and load the data into Power BI, you're well on your way to analyzing and visualizing the data in your universe.

In this chapter, you learn the methods you can apply to prep and load data using Power BI Desktop and Services. Then you see how to detect anomalies and inconsistencies, check data structures and column properties, and put data statistics to use.

Getting Data from the Source

Without a data source, it's hard to use Microsoft Power BI. You can connect to your data source or use one of the many connectors Microsoft makes available to users as part of Power BI Desktop or Services. Before you begin loading data, you must first grasp what the business requirements are for your data source. For example, is the data source local to your desktop with occasional updates? Is your data perhaps coming from a third-party data source that supplies real-time feeds? The requirements for both scenarios are vastly different.

REMEMBER

Microsoft continually adds data connectors to its Desktop and Services platform. Don't be surprised to find at least one or two new connectors released monthly as part of the regular Power BI update. As a result, Power BI offers well over 100 data connectors. The most popular options include files, databases, and web services.

ON THE WEB

You can find a list of all available data sources at

`https://docs.microsoft.com/en-us/power-bi/connect-data/power-bi-data-sources`

To correctly map your data in Power BI, you must determine the exact nature of the data. For example, would you use the Excel Connector if the document type were meant for an Azure SQL database? That wouldn't produce the results you're looking for as a Power BI user.

ON THE WEB

Throughout *Microsoft Power Platform For Dummies*, you find references to XLS and CSV data sources. The data is curated from a specific publicly accessible data source called FPDS, the Federal Procurement Database (`https://fpds.gov`). To access the data sources used for the examples in this book, enter **Power BI** in the search box on the home page. Then click Go, and select the CSV button on the right side of the window once the queried results appear. You can then download the dataset to your Desktop as a file called `SearchResults.csv`, which is the default filename created by `fpds.gov`.

To import the data, follow these steps:

1. **Open the Home tab in Power BI Desktop, and choose Get Data ⇨ Text/CSV (see Figure 10-1).**
2. **In the Open window, navigate to the `SearchResults.csv` file, click to select it, and then click Open.**

   Power BI displays the data source in a Navigator Page. Figure 10-2 shows the Navigator Page for `SearchResults.csv`.

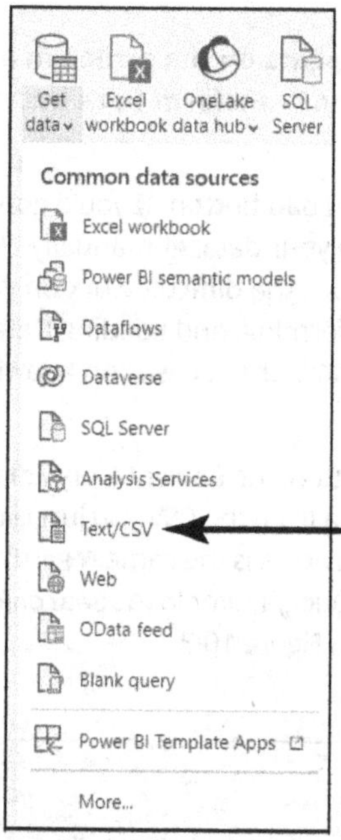

FIGURE 10-1: Finding the CSV Connector in Power BI Desktop.

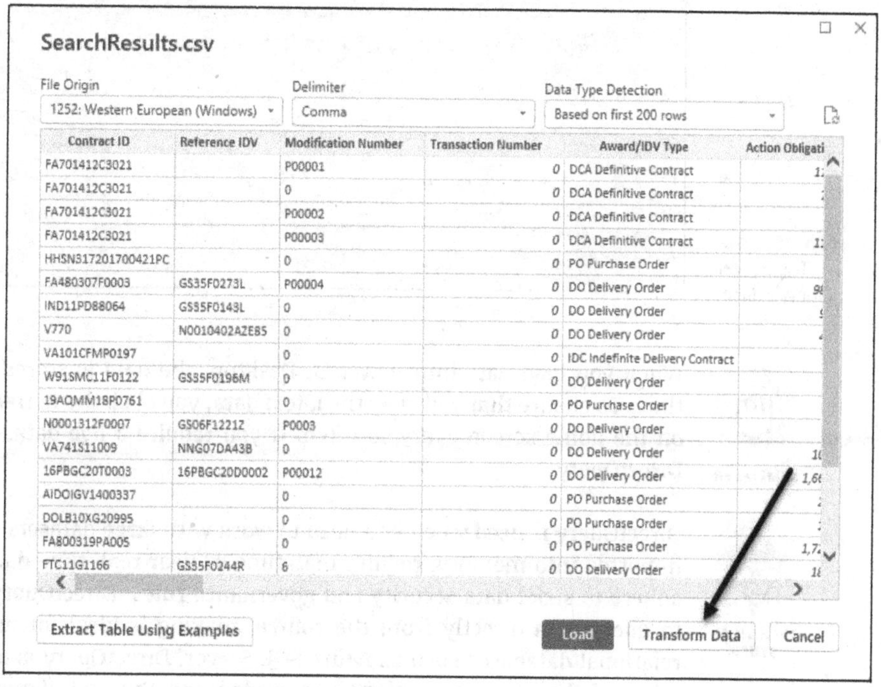

FIGURE 10-2: The Power BI Navigator Page.

3. **With the file open, the dataset appears on the screen in a window that is titled SearchResults.csv. Click the Transform Data button (refer to Figure 10-2).**

   You also have the option to click the Load button. If you'd gone with Load, you'd have to make modifications to your dataset manually. When you choose Transform Data, Power BI does the difficult work on your behalf. (The upcoming section "Cleansing, Transforming, and Loading Data" covers more about data transformation, but for now, the focus is on knowing how to prepare and load data.)

   After you click the Transform Data button, the Power Query Editor appears. The Power Query Editor loads the data from the CSV you just clicked on from the previous Power BI screens. This process is the same regardless of data source. For this example, the Power Query Editor loads `SearchResults.csv`, and the interface appears as shown in Figure 10-3.

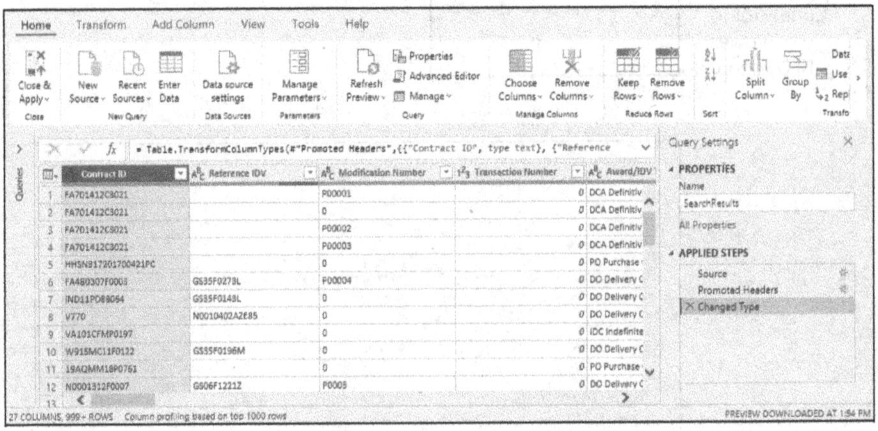

FIGURE 10-3: The Power Query Editor.

REMEMBER

When you load data into Power BI Desktop, the data is stored as a snapshot in time. To ensure that you view the latest data, you click the Refresh Preview button on the home screen every so often. If you require a live dataset, you must pick DirectQuery.

TECHNICAL STUFF

DirectQuery is used when you need to work with large datasets that can't be fully imported into memory, require real-time or near real-time data access, or must adhere to strict data security and governance rules. DirectQuery allows Power BI to query data directly from the source, making it ideal for environments with relational databases such as Azure SQL Server. DirectQuery is also suitable when minimal data transformations are needed and the underlying data source can handle query loads efficiently. When fast performance or complex data transformations are required, use Import mode instead.

Loading folders with data inside them can present a few unique challenges. Although you can select a folder and *ingest* (load data from) just about any type of file, it's another matter to replicate a folder structure using the Power Query Editor. When you load data in Power BI stored inside a folder, you should ensure that the same file type and structure exist.

For example, you might want to work with a series of Microsoft Excel or Google Sheets files that have similar structures or layouts. To ensure that data is consistently formatted, be sure to follow these steps, which work with the Premium version of Power Platform:

1. **Click to open the Home tab on the Ribbon, and click the Get Data button.**
2. **Choose All ⇨ Folder from the menu that appears.**

   Want to try another way? Go to the Home tab on the Ribbon, click New Source, choose More from the menu that appears, and then choose Folder.
3. **Whichever way you select Folder, your next step is to click the Connect button (see Figure 10-4).**

   Pressing the Connect button enables access to a single data source.

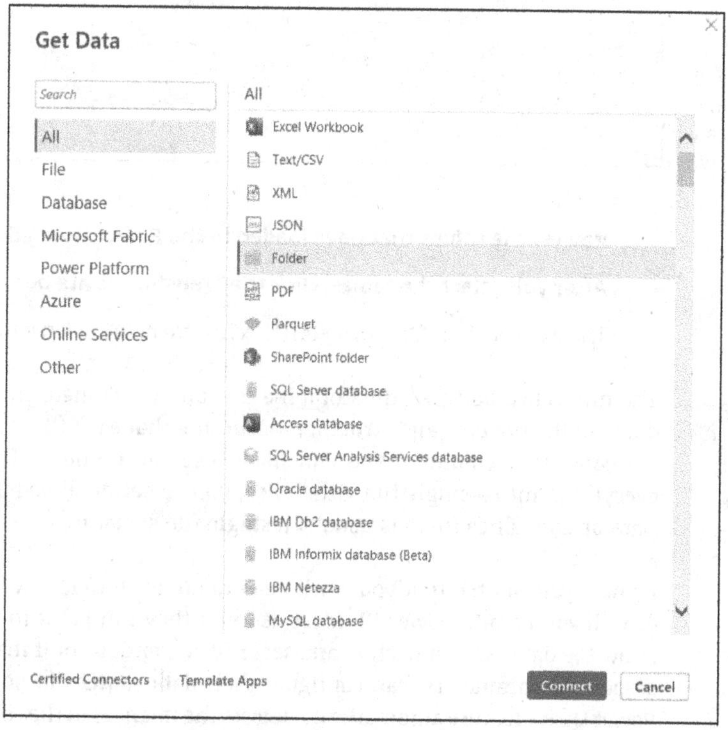

FIGURE 10-4: Selecting Folder from Get Data.

4. **Locate the folder path specific to where you've stored files on your desktop, and then browse to the location where you placed the file, similar to `C:\PPFD\Datafiles\`**

   The files from the folder you just selected load into the Power Query Screen, as shown in Figure 10-5.

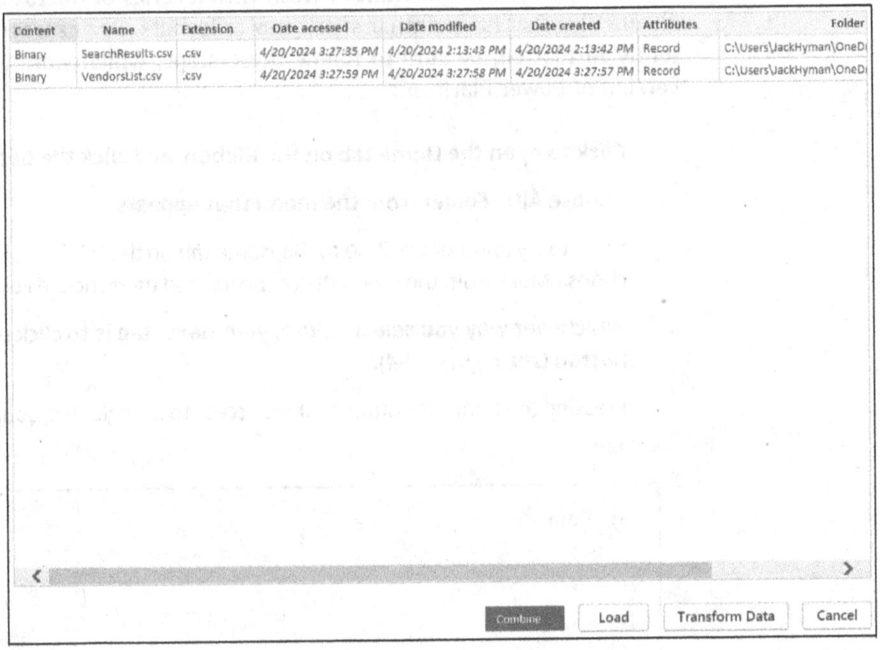

Content
Name
Extension
Date accessed
Date modified
Date created
Attributes
Folder
Binary
SearchResults.csv
.csv
4/20/2024 3:27:35 PM
4/20/2024 2:13:43 PM
4/20/2024 2:13:42 PM
Record
C:\Users\JackHyman\OneD
Binary
VendorsList.csv
.csv
4/20/2024 3:27:59 PM
4/20/2024 3:27:58 PM
4/20/2024 3:27:57 PM
Record
C:\Users\JackHyman\OneD
Combine
Load
Transform Data
Cancel

FIGURE 10-5: Files from a folder load into Power BI.

5. **Review the tables that have loaded in the Power Query Screen.**
6. **After you select the tables, click the Transform Data button.**

   The datasets from `TrainingNAICS.xlsx` are now loaded into Power Query Editor.

TIP

The difference between the Combine Button and Transform Data options comes down to the file type and structure. Assuming that each file is similar and can create consistent columns, you can likely use the Combine Data option to bring everything into a single file. Otherwise, you're better served using the Transform Data option, since there is usually a single file structure.

By now you can tell that you don't need to do much to load a file, folder, database, or web source into Power BI. Most users, if they can point to the file path, if they know the database connection and security credentials, or if they know the URL and associated parameters, can configure their data sources in no time. The Power BI Power Query feature automatically detects the nuances in the connection and applies the proper transformations. To find out more about Power Query, see Chapter 9.

Managing Data Source Settings

Commonly, your dataset requirements change over time. That means if the data source changes, so will some of the settings that were initially loaded when you configured Power BI. Suppose you move the folder PPFD from `C:\Desktop` to `C:\Documents` with two files in that PPFD folder. Such a change in folder location would require you to modify the data source settings pointing to those data files. You can go about making these changes in one of two ways:

1. **Select each query under DAX Queries on the left.**
2. **Locate Edit Query by right-clicking the imported table in the Data pane.**
3. **Under Applied Steps, click Source, as shown in Figure 10-6.**

   Doing so brings up a window pointing to the file path and file source. Note that the folder window will pop up if you click the gear icon next to Source. Otherwise, assume that you'll have to double-click the word *Source*.

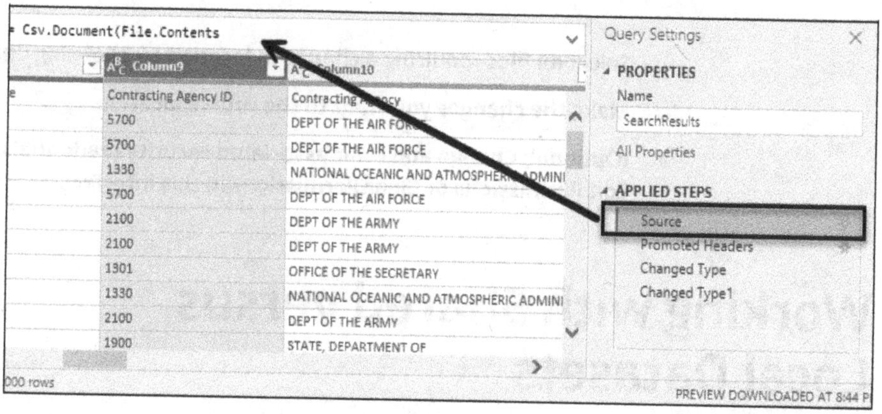

FIGURE 10-6: Using the Applied Steps area to update the data source settings.

4. **Make the updates necessary to match the new requirements.**

   Change the file type or path of the original file for each query with this option.

Though the steps outlined here may seem easy at first blush, they might become laborious because you need to make a change to each file listed for each query. That process can be pretty time-consuming, and if you have a lot of queries, you're bound to make errors, given the tedious nature of the work. That's why you want to consider an alternative option — one where you can change the source location in one fell swoop rather than tackle each query independently with this option. Follow these steps for the other method:

1. **On the Power Query Editor's Home tab, click the Data Source Settings button. (It's the one sporting a cog — see Figure 10-7.)**

   A new window opens to make the source location change.

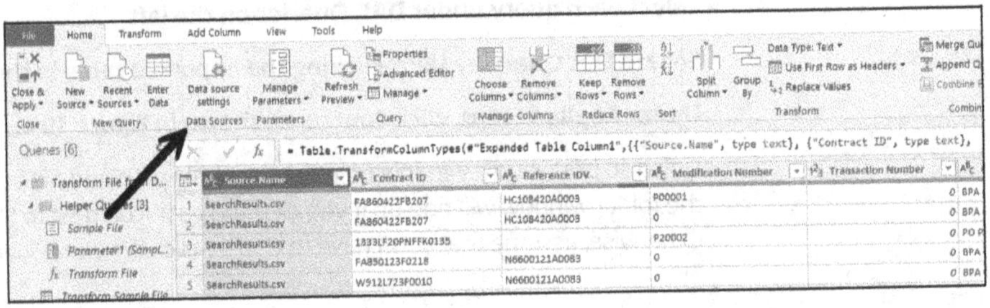

FIGURE 10-7: The Data Source Settings button.

2. **Select all files requiring a change in location by choosing Change Source.**
3. **Make the changes you want to the source location.**
4. **(Optional) Change and clear associated security credentials by selecting Edit Permissions or Clear Permissions in this interface.**

Working with Shared versus Local Datasets

So far, this chapter has focused on local datasets that you create and manage by using Power BI Desktop. After the dataset is published and shared with others using Power BI Services — by way of either your My Workspace or the shared workspace — the dataset is referred to as a *shared dataset*. Unlike with Power BI Desktop, where you have to continually update the dataset on the local hard drive, a shared dataset is stored on the cloud, which means that regardless of whether it's stored in your workspace or with others, updates can be more consistent each time you click Publish.

You can find many other benefits to using a shared dataset over a local dataset, including

- Consistency across reports and dashboards
- Reduction in dataset copying due to centralization of a data source
- The ability to create new data sources from existing sources with little effort

TIP

To connect to a published dataset in Power BI Services, you must have Build permission, or you must be a contributing member of the shared workspace where the dataset exists. Make sure the owner of the dataset provisions your access according to your business need.

You can connect to a shared dataset by using either Power BI Desktop or Power BI Services. To do so, follow these steps:

1. **Open the Home tab in Power BI Desktop, and choose Get Data ⇨ Power BI semantic models (see Figure 10-8).**

   The data is transferred from Power BI Desktop to Power BI Services for you to share with others, or access online versus from your Desktop.

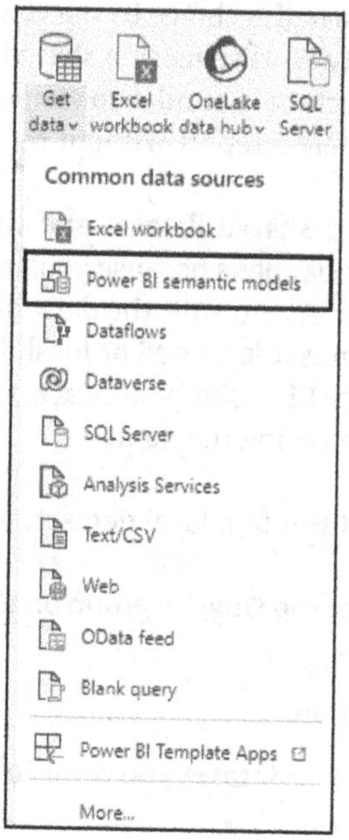

FIGURE 10-8: Choosing a dataset from Power BI Desktop.

2. **With Power BI Services, you would first go to the workspace you've published your data to and then choose New ➪ Report, as shown in Figure 10-9.**

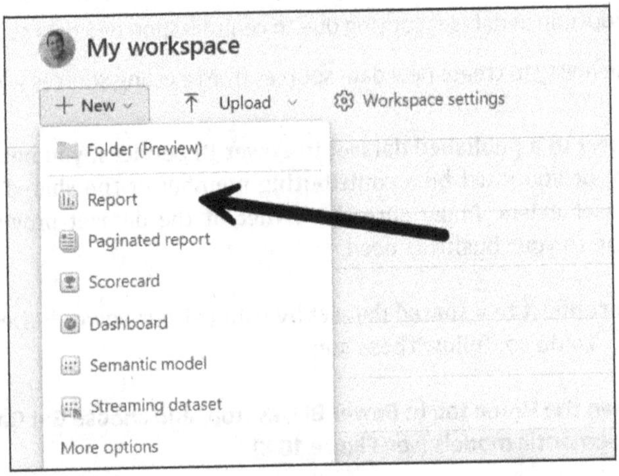

FIGURE 10-9: Connecting to a shared dataset in Power BI Services.

Whether you're using Power BI Desktop or Power BI Services, your ability to connect to a dataset without having to worry about data refresh issues or version control becomes a bit easier. You also have the choice to select Save a Copy in the Power BI Service next to any report in My Workspace or a shared workspace without having to re-create a dataset. This action is similar to connecting to a dataset using Power BI Desktop because you create a report without the base data model.

WARNING

Don't be alarmed if you decide to use a shared dataset and then some buttons become inactive in Power BI Desktop. It happens because you're no longer able to make changes using Power Query Editor. As a result, the data view is also no longer visible. You can tell whether your dataset is shared or local, however, by looking in the lower right corner of the Power BI Desktop interface, where you can find the name of the dataset and the user accessing the data.

If you need to change from a shared dataset to a local dataset, follow these steps:

1. **Click the Transform Data label from the Queries group on the Home menu.**
2. **Select the Data Source Settings option.**
3. **Modify the data source settings to the dataset you want to connect to instead of the shared dataset.**
4. **Click the Change Source button once complete.**

Selecting the Right Storage and Connection Mode

As you may have already guessed, you can consume data in many ways using Power BI Desktop and Power BI Services. The most common method is to import data into a data model. By importing the data into Power BI, you're copying the dataset locally until you commit to a data refresh. Although data files and folders can only be imported into Power BI, databases allow you to use a connection that supports more flexibility.

You can connect to a database in two ways:

- **Import the data locally.** This supports data model caching as well as the ability to reduce the number of connections and lookups. By importing the model, a user can use all Desktop features offered with Power BI. Importing locally leads to improved performance, faster report generation, and a more streamlined data analysis experience.
- **Create a connection to the data source with DirectQuery.** With this feature, the data isn't cached. Instead, the data source must be queried each time a data call is required. Most, but not all, data sources support DirectQuery. The key benefit of using DirectQuery is that it enables real-time data retrieval without caching, ensuring that the most up-to-date information is queried when a user seeks to retrieve data from the data source.

You can use one of two other methods. One is called *Live Connection*. With this method, the goal is to use the analysis services integrated with Power BI Desktop or Power BI Services. Live Connection also supports calculation-based activities that occur within a data model. The key benefit to using Live Connection is that it allows real-time access to complex, prebuilt multidimensional models without importing or replicating data. Choosing between Live Connection and DirectQuery boils down to the purpose of the data connection. With Live Connection, you are connecting to multidimensional models like SSAS, whereas DirectQuery is used for relational databases, querying data as needed using sources like Azure SQL Server.

The second alternative uses composite models. Now, suppose that a user must combine both importing data and DirectQuery, or there is a requirement to connect to multiple DirectQuery connections. In that case, you apply a composite model. You face some risks, though, when dealing with model security. For example, you might open a Power BI Desktop file that is sent from an untrusted source. If the file contains a composite model, the information that someone retrieves from a single source using credentials from a user opening the file can be sent to another data source as part of the newly formed query. Therefore, it's vital to ensure that your data sources are correctly assigned to only those who need access to the sources.

TECHNICAL STUFF

The four storage modes — local storage, DirectQuery, Live Connection, and composite models — have data housed in a single location. It's either local to the user or bound to a server on a network in a data center or the cloud.

Dual mode isn't a hybrid mode; rather, it allows a table to operate in both import and DirectQuery modes. This means a table can be cached for fast retrieval (imported) but also queried directly from the source as needed (DirectQuery). If another storage mode is used for other tables, you aren't restricted to using Direct-Query across all tables. Dual mode is especially useful when you need to work with tables that are available in DirectQuery but want the flexibility to treat them similarly to imported tables when necessary.

Data Sources Oh My!

Data can be a bit complicated at times. Admittedly, uploading a single file containing a few spreadsheets or perhaps a feed with a single stream of data to load and transform is child's play. What happens, though, when you have a dataset housed in a corporate-wide enterprise application that continually has transactions written to it? That scenario is quite different. And corporations should be concerned (for good reason) with the integration and output of business intelligence (BI) results. With Power BI, organizations don't need to worry about complex technical manipulations when it comes to their data systems or their communications with third-party data feeds. As you can see in this chapter, the integration is fluid — Power BI has the power to use a standardized connection process, no matter the connectivity requirement.

Getting data from Microsoft-based file systems

This section covers integration with Microsoft-based applications such as OneDrive for Business and SharePoint 365, both of which are Microsoft 365-based applications.

REMEMBER

When using OneDrive, you need to be logged in to Microsoft 365. As long as you're logged in, you can access files and folders as though you're accessing your local hard drive. The only difference is that your hard drive is Microsoft OneDrive.

On the other hand, SharePoint 365 offers a variety of options for document management and collaboration. The first option is to search a site collection, site, or subsite (referred to in Power BI as a SharePoint Folder). In this case, you must enter the complete SharePoint site URL. For example, if your company has an intranet, the site might be http://<*asite*>.sharepoint.com.

You can also collect, load, and transform one or more SharePoint lists in Power BI. (In SharePoint, a *list* looks like a simple container — kind of like an Excel spreadsheet — but acts more like a database.) Using a list lets users collect information — especially metadata — across a SharePoint site where documents might be collected. With a list, data is gathered in rows, with each row represented as a row item similar to a database or spreadsheet item. To load a SharePoint list, you must know the URL path of the SharePoint site collection, site, or subsite. Once a user is authenticated, all available lists are loaded for that person.

TIP

When you're first starting with Power BI, you might be tempted to keep all your files on the desktop as a way to manage your data. After a while, though, dealing with numerous versions of the same dataset becomes unmanageable. That's why you should use a cloud option such as OneDrive or a SharePoint site to manage your files and datasets, reports, dashboards, and connection files. It helps keep all of it streamlined.

Working with relational data sources

Many organizations use relational databases to record transactional activity. Examples of systems that typically run relational databases are enterprise resource planning (ERP), customer relationship management (CRM), and supply chain management (SCM)-based systems. Another type of system might be an e-commerce platform. Each of these systems has one thing in common: All can benefit from having a business intelligence tool such as Power BI evaluate data by connecting with the relational database instead of extracting individual data files.

Businesses rely on solutions such as Power BI to help them monitor the state of their operations by identifying trends and helping them forecast metrics, indicators, and targets. You can start using Power BI Desktop to connect to virtually any relational database available in the cloud or on-premise on the market.

In the example shown in Figure 10-10, Power BI is connected to an Azure SQL Server, Microsoft's web-based enterprise database. Depending on your relational database solution, you have a few choices. One would be to choose the Get Data ⇨ More . . . command from the Ribbon's Home tab, then look for Database. Here you will find Microsoft-specific databases. Otherwise, if you are looking for another type of data source, choose Get Data ⇨ More . . . and look for Other. You'll find 40+ alternate database options under this section.

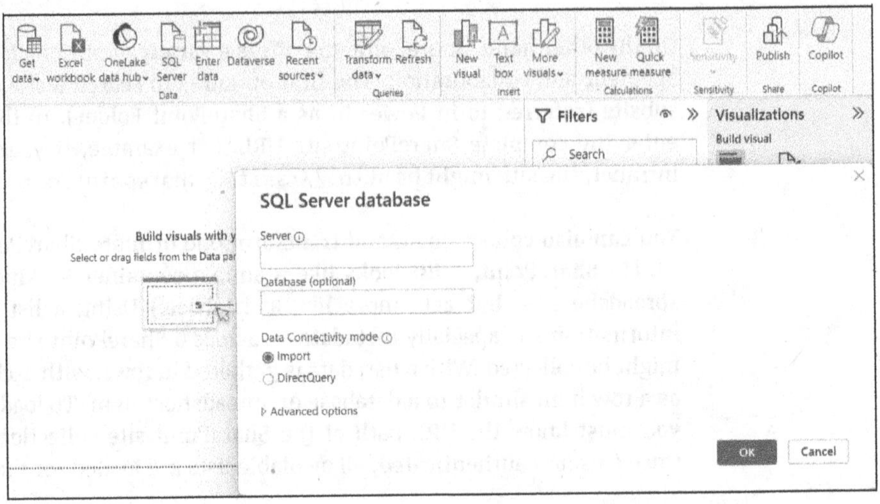

FIGURE 10-10: Azure SQL database location.

In this case, because the selected solution is a Microsoft Azure-based product, you can either search for the product in the Search box or click the Azure option after selecting More.

After you select the database source type under Get Data, you must enter the credentials for the relational database. In this case, you enter the following info:

- Server name
- Database name
- Mode type — Import or DirectQuery

Figure 10-11 gives an example of the fields you would need to fill out. (You don't need to add unique command lines or SQL query statements unless you're looking for a more granular data view.)

REMEMBER

In most cases, you should select Import. The circumstances where you select DirectQuery are for large datasets. The data updates are intended for near real-time updates.

After you've entered your credentials, you're prompted to log in with your username and password using your Windows, database, or Microsoft account authentication, as shown in Figure 10-12.

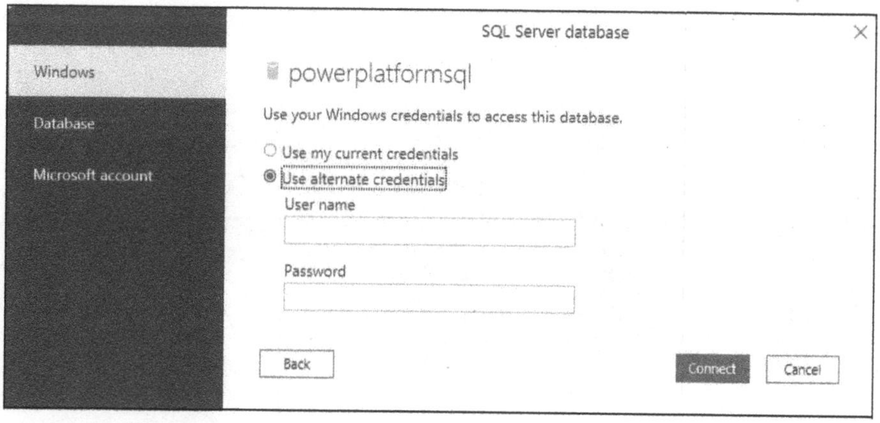

FIGURE 10-11: Entry of credentials for relational database.

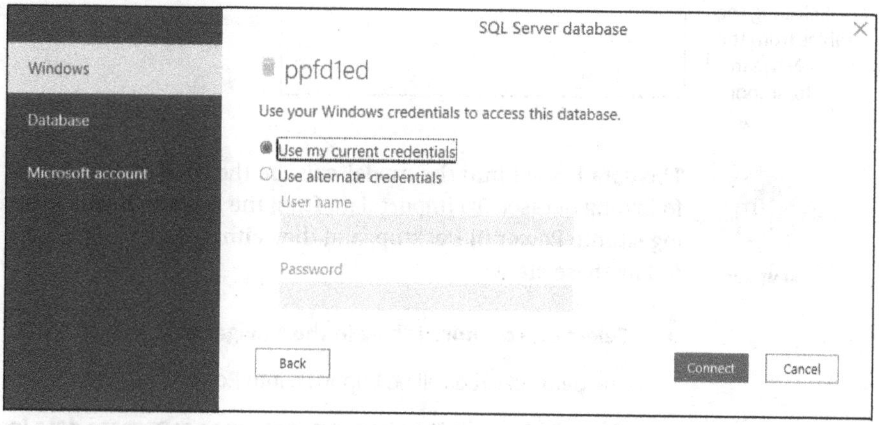

FIGURE 10-12: Selecting the authentication method to connect.

Relational databases

Connecting to the data source is often tricky because you need to make sure your database source and naming conventions are just right. However, once you get past these two facts, it should be smooth sailing — well, at least until you need to pick the data to import. Then you might become overwhelmed if the database has a lot of tables.

After you've connected the database to Power BI Desktop, the Navigator displays the data available from the data source, as shown in Figure 10-13. In this case, all data from the Azure SQL database is presented. You can select a table or one of the entities to preview the content.

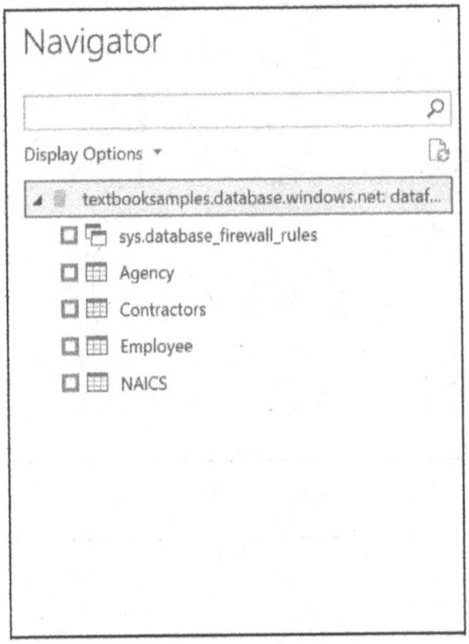

FIGURE 10-13: Selecting the tables from the Navigator for import.

REMEMBER

The data loaded into the model *must* be the correct data before moving on to the following dataset. To import data from the relational data source that you want to ingest into Power BI Desktop, and then either load or transform and load the data, follow these steps:

1. **Select one or more tables in the Navigator.**

   The data selected will be imported into Power Query Editor.

2. **Click the Load button if you're looking to automate data loading into a Power BI model based on its current state with no changes.**
3. **Click the Transform Data button if you want Power BI to execute the Power Query engine.**

   The engine performs actions such as cleaning up excessive columns, grouping data, removing errors, and promoting data quality.

Nonrelational databases

Some organizations use nonrelational databases such as Microsoft Cosmos DB or Apache Hadoop to handle their myriad and significant data challenges. These databases don't use tables to store their data. Data might be stored in a variety of ways in the case of nonrelational (NoSQL) data. Options run the gamut from document, key-value, wide-column, and graph. All database options provide flexible schemas and scale effortlessly with large data volumes.

You still must authenticate with a username and password to the database, but the querying approach is a bit different. For example, with Microsoft Cosmos DB, the NoSQL database created by Microsoft that is complementary to Power BI, a user must identify the endpoint URL and the Primary key and Read-Only key so that a connection can be created to the Cosmos DB instance in the Azure portal. To connect to the Cosmos DB, follow these steps:

1. **Open the Home tab in Power BI Desktop, and choose Get Data ⇨ More . . . .**
2. **In the submenu that appears, locate the Azure submenu and then click once.**
3. **Click to select the Azure Cosmos DB option, as shown in Figure 10-14, allowing you to create a nonrelational database connection.**
4. **Enter the URL of the Cosmos DB in the URL field, and then click OK (see Figure 10-15).**

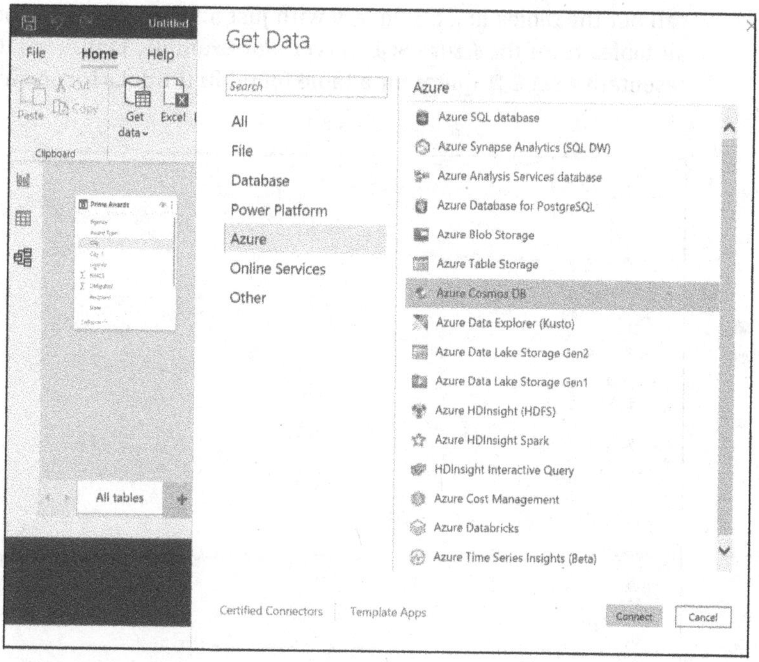

FIGURE 10-14: Selecting the Cosmos DB data source.

WARNING

When you're using a NoSQL database, you need to know the keys to authenticate. For Cosmos DB, you can find those keys in the Azure portal under the Cosmos DB Instance Settings, Key Link. Be sure to copy down the primary and secondary read-write keys and the primary and secondary read-only keys.

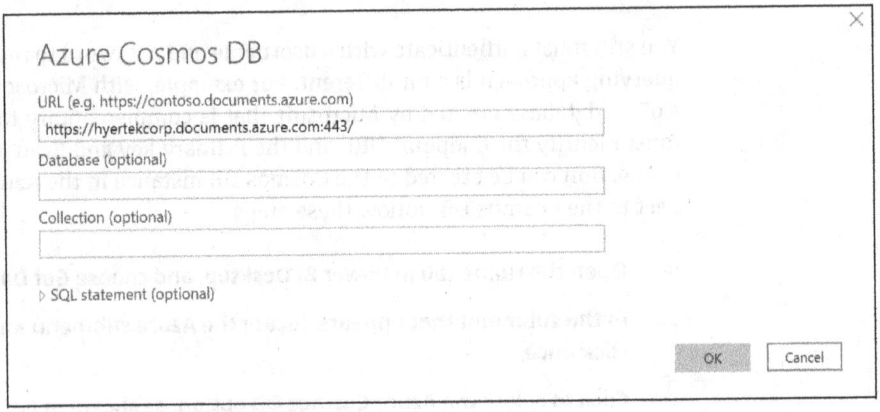

FIGURE 10-15: Connecting to the Cosmos DB, a Microsoft NoSQL database.

Using the SQL query

Power BI has an intelligent SQL query editor. Suppose you know precisely which tables you require from the Azure SQL database. In this case, all you need to do is call out the tables in a SQL query with just a few keystrokes, rather than request all tables from the Azure SQL Server. For example, Figure 10-16 presents a representative `SELECT` query for a table found in the `dataforpowerbi` database.

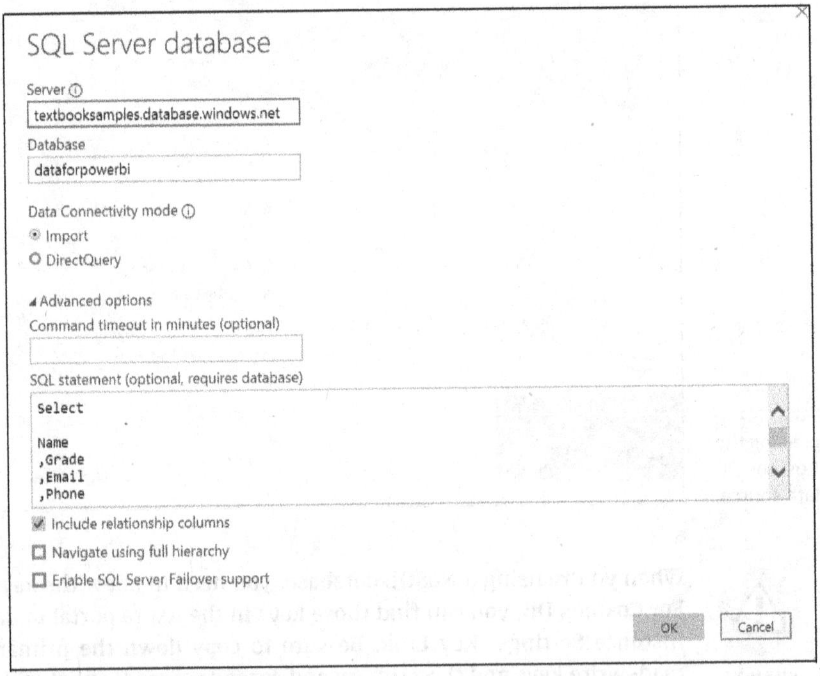

FIGURE 10-16: Representative query data from Azure SQL Server.

JSON files

JSON files don't look at all like structured data files. Why is that the case? JSON — short for JavaScript Object Notation — is a lightweight data-interchange format. Neither structured nor unstructured, the JSON file type is referred to as *semistructured* because the file type is written by default as a key-value pair. With JSON-based records, the data must be extracted and normalized before becoming a report in Power BI. That's why you must transform the data using Power BI Desktop's Power Query Editor.

If your goal is to extract data from a JSON file, you transform the list to a table by clicking the Transform tab and selecting To Table in the Convert group. Another option is to drill down into a specific record by clicking on a record link. If you want to preview the record, click on the cell without clicking on the link. Doing so opens a data preview pane at the bottom of Power Query Editor.

Need to get a bit more in the weeds? You can click on the cog wheel next to the source step in Query Settings, which opens a window to specify advanced settings. There you can specify options such as file encoding in the File Origin drop-down list. When you are ready for show time and your JSON file is transformed, click Close and Apply to load data into the Power BI data model. In the example found in Figure 10-17, employee records have been transformed from the JSON file.

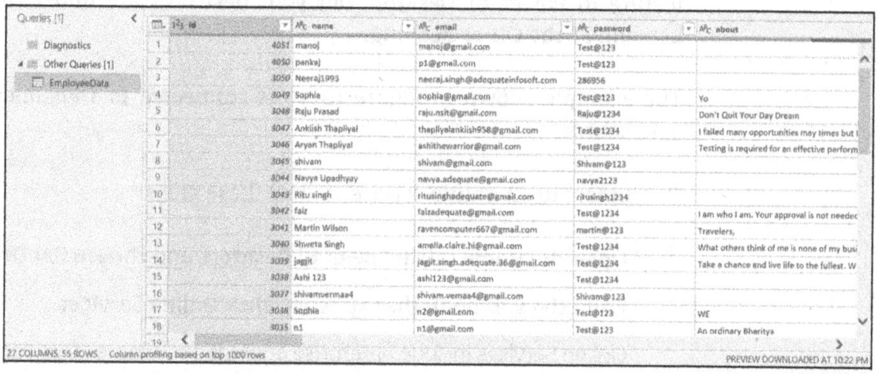

FIGURE 10-17: JSON file, transformed by the Power Query Editor.

After the Power Query Editor has transformed the file, you might still need to edit specific fields. In this example, the Country field has all null entries, so it's a prime candidate for field deletion. Such a choice is easily carried out with the help of the drop-down menu, as shown in Figure 10-18, where you can drill down and delete specific records.

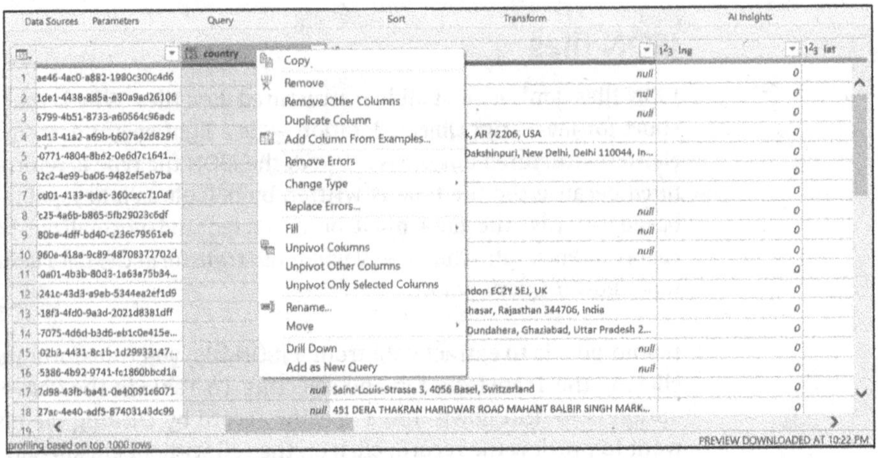

FIGURE 10-18: Modifying a JSON file using the Power Query Editor.

Online sources

Enterprise applications and third-party data feeds are widely available in Power BI. Microsoft has over 100 connectors to applications developed and managed by other vendors, including those by Adobe, Denodo, Oracle, and Salesforce, to name a few. Of course, Microsoft also supports its enterprise application solutions, including those in the Dynamics 365, SharePoint 365, and Power Platform families. Online sources can be found across several categories using the Get Data feature in Power BI Desktop, but your best bets are under the Online Services heading or the Other heading.

The example shown in Figure 10-19 is connected to Dynamics 365 (Dataverse) data source.

To connect to an online service, follow these steps:

1. **Open the Home tab in Power BI Desktop, and choose Get Data ⇨ More . . . .**
2. **From the submenu that appears, click Online Services.**

   Online Services include enterprise applications, where large datasets are available (assuming user credentials are accessible).
3. **On the right side of the Get Data menu, click Dynamics 365 (Dataverse).**

   Doing so allows for a connection to Microsoft's Data Repository specific for Power Platform and Dynamics 365.

4. **You will be asked to log in with a username and password to the data source. Once you've successfully authenticated, click Connect on the lower-right of the CommonDataService window.**

   A connection to Microsoft Dataverse is established.

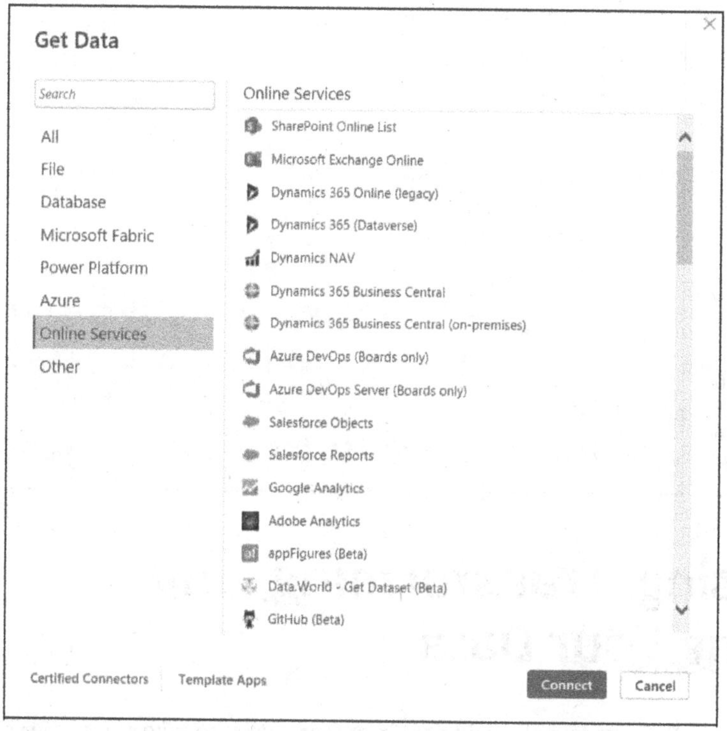

FIGURE 10-19: Connecting to an online service in Power BI Desktop.

You're then asked to enter your online organizational credentials if you haven't already authenticated with Power BI Desktop and the targeted data source. Generally, this part is already prepopulated because it's your Single Sign-On login associated with Azure Active Directory.

Once you authenticate a session, all data available from the database for the specific source is loaded in the Navigator pane within the Power Query Editor, as shown in Figure 10-20. Power Query transforms the data before loading it in Navigator. In this case, the data that will be transformed comes from a Dynamics 365 Dataverse instance called HR System.

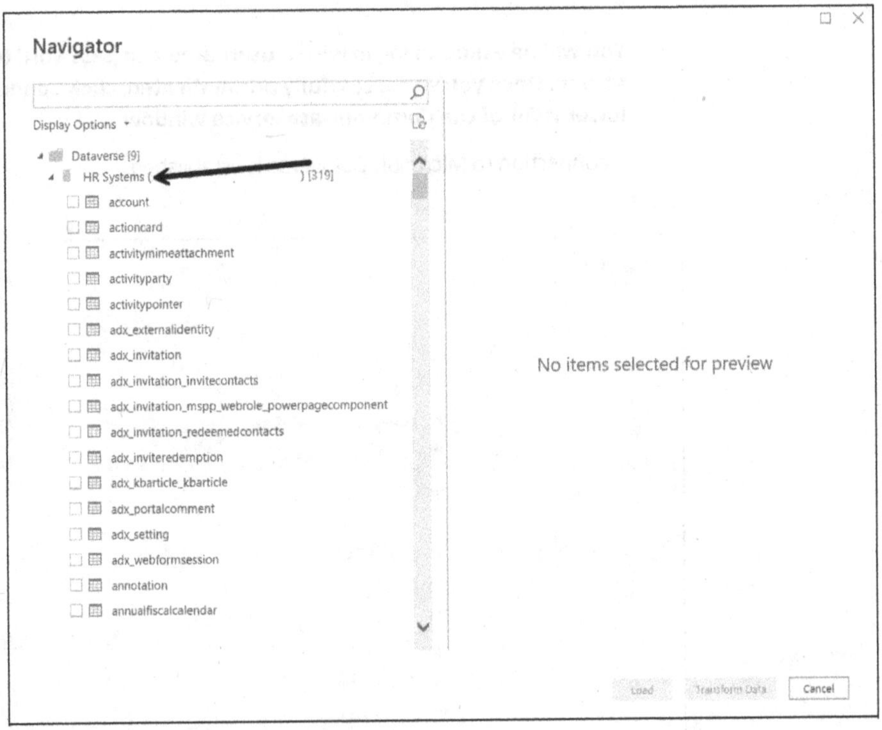

FIGURE 10-20: Data displayed in the Navigator pane within the Power Query Editor.

Cleansing, Transforming, and Loading Your Data

For any data cleansing and transformation to take place, your organization needs analysts and engineers — and detectives. The idea here is that you must first analyze the data before entering the system or after it exists in its intended data store. Simply glossing over the data alone doesn't cut it. You need to follow a rigorous process as you look for those needles in your data haystack. Without a rigorous process, you can't ensure data consistency across all columns, values, and keys. By following a meticulous analysis process, you can engineer optimized queries that help load the data into the system without issues.

The following sections describe the activities Power BI professionals perform that support this analysis process, which include cleansing, transforming, and loading data.

Detecting anomalies and inconsistencies

Anomalous data comes in many flavors. Using Power Query, you can find unusual data trends that you might be on the lookout for — even those slight ambiguities you'd have trouble catching on your own. For example, you can see how an out-of-context dollar amount or error can be traced back to missing values that skew the data results. These are all real-life scenarios that you can address using Power BI.

The easiest and most obvious way to spot errors is to look at a table in the Power Query Editor. You can evaluate the quality of each column by using the Data Preview feature. You can, among each column, review data under a header value in order to validate data, catch errors, and spot empty values. All you need to do is choose View ⇨ Data Preview ⇨ Column Quality from the Power Query main menu. In Figure 10-21, you notice right off the bat that the Agency column has data missing, as shown by the <1% number reported as empty. Such behavior is consistent with data anomalies.

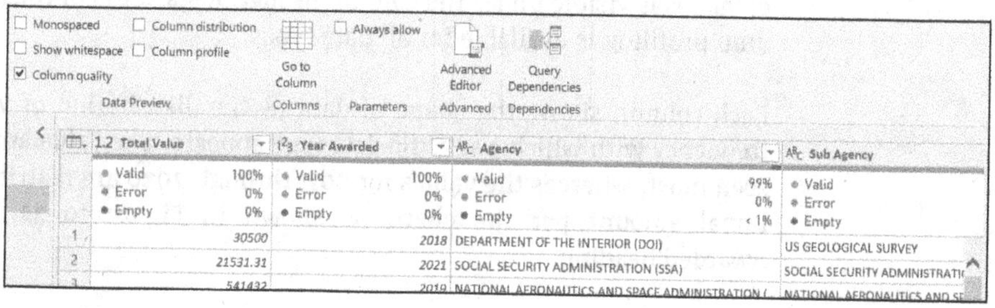

FIGURE 10-21: Addressing column quality issues.

Notice that all columns except for the Agency column have 100 percent validity. In this case, that <1% means you have either a null value or mistaken data. The purpose of investigating data quality issues using Power Query is best exemplified with this sampling because all other columns show an error percentage of 0. You learn how to correct such ambiguities later in this chapter.

Checking data structures and column properties

Evaluating data goes beyond column quality. Another measurement you can use to better identify data structure issues involves *column value distribution*, which is a measure of all distinct values in the selected column as well as the percentage of rows in the table that each value represents. You enable this measurement in the Power Query Editor by choosing View ⇨ Data Preview ⇨ Column Distribution. In Figure 10-22, notice that the Total Value columns have a high number of distinct and unique values.

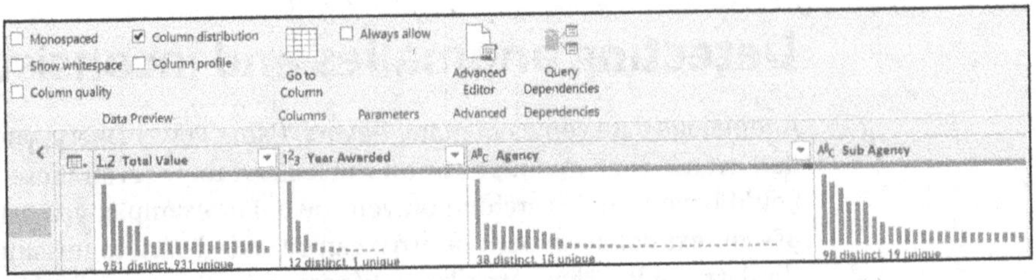

FIGURE 10-22: A look at column distribution.

Here's what *distinct* and *unique* are telling you:

- **Distinct number:** The number of different values in a column when duplicates are omitted
- **Unique number:** The number of values that occur precisely one time

By using the Column Distribution command, you can determine the number of distinct and unique values in each column. As noted, the distribution of columns of values is visible under the column header. Regardless of the analysis goal, column profiling is available for all data types.

Each column shows the shape of data — the distribution of values, say, or the frequency with which a specific data type appears. The value 2021, for example, is seen most, whereas the values for 2011 through 2020 are distributed in a proportional amount per the chart, as shown in Figure 10-22, under the Years Awarded heading.

TIP

If you want to evaluate the data outside of Power BI and the Power Query Editor, right-click the columns of choice and then select Copy Value Distribution from the menu that appears. You're supplied a list of distinct values and the number of times the data appears in the columns.

REMEMBER

Column distribution is a valuable utility: If certain columns offer little business value, you can omit the columns. An example might be where you have a limited number of distinct values. Removing columns as you conduct analysis can build more powerful queries because you're getting rid of clutter by deleting unwanted datasets.

Modifying data properties quickly

After you import data from your online targeted data source, or for that matter any data source, into Power BI, you need to make sure that the data properties are correctly assigned within the dataset. You don't want a set of values to be cut off and improperly displayed because a trailing zero exists in the dataset, or misassigned data types to throw your data visualization into chaos.

Ideally, you change these behaviors when you are loading the data and when you modify the data model under the Data Model view. You might discover, for example, that you need to switch a numeric field to a string field value, as is the case in Figure 10-23.

To modify a column's data properties once the data is loaded into Power BI, follow these steps:

1. **Open the Power BI Home tab and click Transform Data.**

   Your dataset appears on-screen next to the Queries Pane.

2. **Find the column where the data type is inaccurate.**

   For example, in Figure 10-23, the column called Transaction Number appears to be a numerical value, but the data type should be a Text data type instead, as some elements resemble strings.

3. **Select the icon on the left side of the column header. It's currently noted as 123 (indicated by A). Switch the value Whole Number to Text (clicking the option indicated by B).**

4. **After you review all the columns and apply the necessary changes to your data properties, click Close & Apply from the left side of the Power Query Editor.**

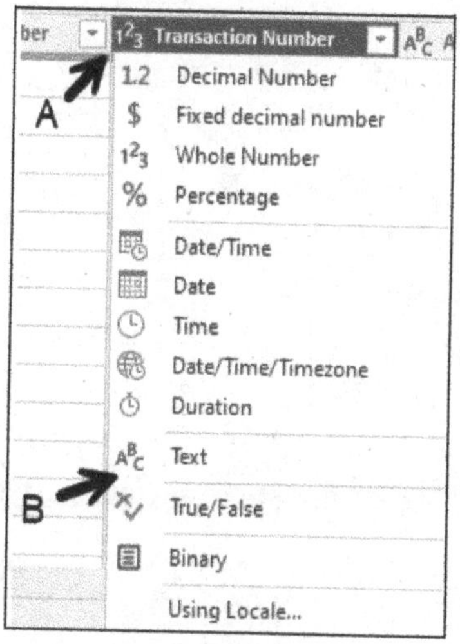

FIGURE 10-23: Modifying the properties of a column.

IN THIS CHAPTER

» **Mastering data modeling foundational concepts with Power BI**

» **Knowing data optimization strategies for data visualization**

» **Exploring data management techniques in Power BI**

» **Publishing your data model**

Chapter 11
Mastering Data Modeling for Visualization

Creating visualizations in Power BI starts with building a strong data model. After importing data into Power BI Desktop, you need to refine the data by defining types, designing tables, creating hierarchies, and establishing relationships. This preparation ensures the data is accurate and efficient for analysis, leading to meaningful visualizations.

In this chapter, I show how data modeling in Power BI Desktop leads to effective visualizations. As you refine your data using the data modeling tools available in Power BI, you can be assured that your data model is well-structured. This involves defining data types, formatting, and managing relationships and tables. Once the data model is ready for prime time, you can create detailed reports and compelling visualizations in Power BI Desktop. These visualizations can then be shared through Power BI Services, where you can create interactive dashboards that compile multiple reports and datasets, providing a comprehensive view of your data for analysis and decision-making.

Creating a Data Model Masterpiece

Creating visualizations requires a data model — it's just one of those things. Your data source also needs to be correct, specific, and well-crafted. Power BI can indeed do some amazing things, such as transforming data across multiple datasets through its ETL (extract, transform, and load) framework, to support development and design activity. After the data is safely in the Desktop application, though, the accessible data still needs your attention. You need to take some specific actions to prepare the data so that the model can be crafted and work as a well-oiled dataset for visualization and reporting. A well-defined dataset helps you analyze the data as well as gain prescriptive and descriptive insights.

REMEMBER

Model creation doesn't stop at data ingestion. It requires defining data types, exploiting table design, creating hierarchies, crafting joins and relationships, and classifying the data in the model.

Working with Table view and Modeling view

After importing data into the Power BI Desktop environment, your goal is to now manipulate the data so that it works the way you need it to for your models. The first stop on your journey is to explore the Table View tab and the Model View tab. The difference between the two is that the Table View tab presents all data imported into the data model. In contrast, the Model View tab is the visualization of the model based on what Power BI believes the model is at a point in time.

You are responsible for updating the model after importing the data. You can do this on either the Table View tab (by viewing all data instances) or the Model View tab (by reviewing the model itself). An example of the output on the Table View tab is shown in Figure 11-1; Figure 11-2 shows the output on the Model View tab.

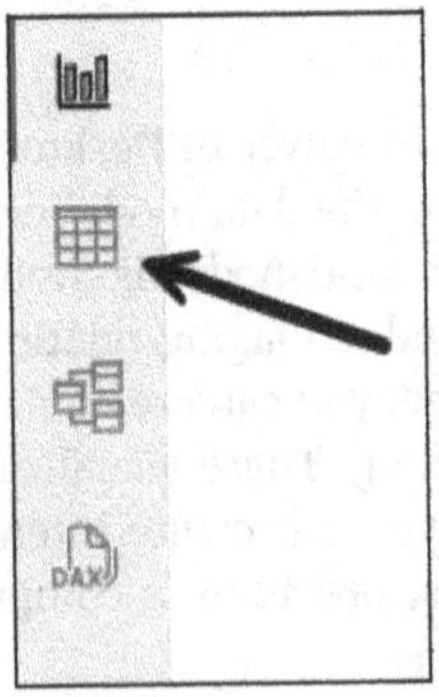

FIGURE 11-1: The Table View tab.

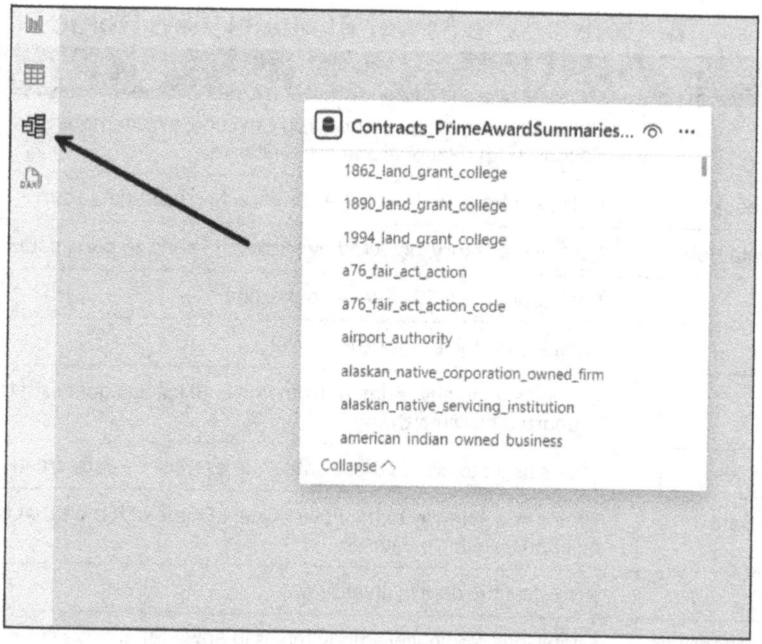

FIGURE 11-2: The Model View tab.

The Home Ribbon for the Model view is considered the cockpit for managing many of your data actions, no matter which view you're in within the Power BI Desktop. As you can see in Figure 11-3, the Home Ribbon for the Model view is broken into distinct areas: Data, Queries, Relationships, Calculations, Security, Q&A, Sensitivity, and Share. Each area has its own set of features, as listed in Table 11-1.

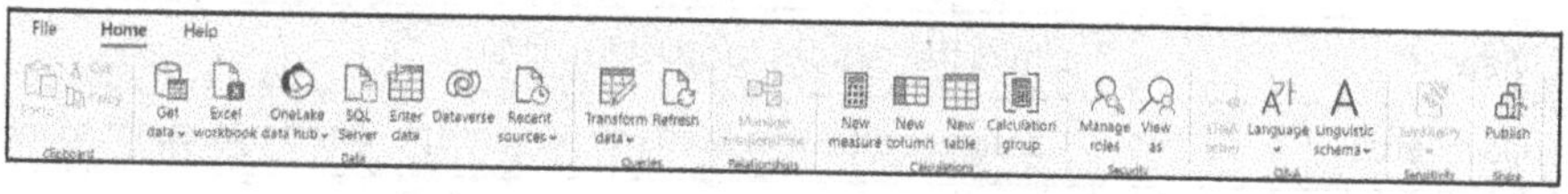

FIGURE 11-3: The Home Ribbon in Model view.

The Power Query Editor shares many of the same features shown in Table 11-1, although it also has (unsurprisingly) specific features for query editing, as shown in Figure 11-4.

A noticeable difference between Model view and Power Query Editor is that Power Query Editor allows you to change the data source settings, manage parameters, configure editor parameters, configure rows and columns, group by, sort by, and handle data types. It also focuses on artificial intelligence features for text analytics. As you begin to manage the design of your datasets, you'll likely venture into row and column management because configuring rows and columns to behave as you see fit is integral to dataset behavior. Therefore, as you probably guessed, you have a few more bells and whistles to play with under the Power Query Editor because you are manipulating queries versus model building.

TABLE 11-1 Buttons on the Power BI Model View Home Ribbon

Button	What It Does
Get Data	Gets data from a data source. You can choose from more than 100 data source options, both relational and nonrelational.
Excel Workbook	Gets data from an Excel file, a common Microsoft data source
OneLake Data Hub	Central repository, powered by Microsoft Fabric, to bring data into Power BI
SQL Server	Gets data from a SQL Server connection
Enter Data	Creates new tables inside Power BI
Dataverse	Connects to an environment from Power BI using a query string, including those supported by DirectQuery
Recent Sources	Allows users to access those data sources most recently created in Power BI
Transform Data	Serves as a gateway to the Power Query Editor with tools that can be found to edit and transform datasets
Refresh	Refreshes the data in an easy way
Manage Relationships	Establishes cardinality among tables in Power BI
New Measure	Creates a new calculated measure using the Formula bar
New Column	Creates a new column for a specific table
New Table	Creates a new table
Calculation Groups	Create reusable dynamic measures
Manage Roles	Determines who should be able to view specific data models
View As	Limits the dataset to specific users
Q&A Setup	Configure question & answer engine, powered by Copilot to interact with datasets
Language	Choose between English and Spanish
Linguistic Schema	Allows you to enhance the language schema using your own datasets via import or export
Sensitivity	Allows users to label data using a sensitivity classification such as general or confidential. Meant for data governance.
Publish	Publishes the dataset to Power BI Services

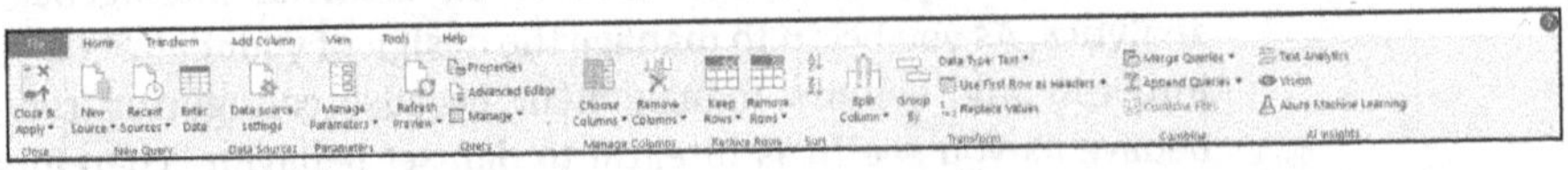

FIGURE 11-4: The Power Query Editor Ribbon.

Importing queries

It never hurts to practice importing one or more Excel files to establish fresh queries. Keep in mind that you can import your queries into Power BI Desktop using one of several import options. Start by using the Navigation pane on the left side of the screen to switch to Table view, where all existing tables are available. If you want to start fresh, open a new file by choosing File⇨New from the main menu. If, however, you want to import from one of 100+ data sources available to you, follow these steps:

1. **Click Get Data, and then select the type of file or source you want to import into Power BI.**

   Once you select your data source, the Navigator window opens, as shown in Figure 11-5.

2. **To load data, pick one or more datasets and then click the Load button.**
3. **To transform data, pick one or more datasets and then click the Transform Data button.**

In the example shown in Figure 11-5, I've selected Dataverse as a data source and a single table.

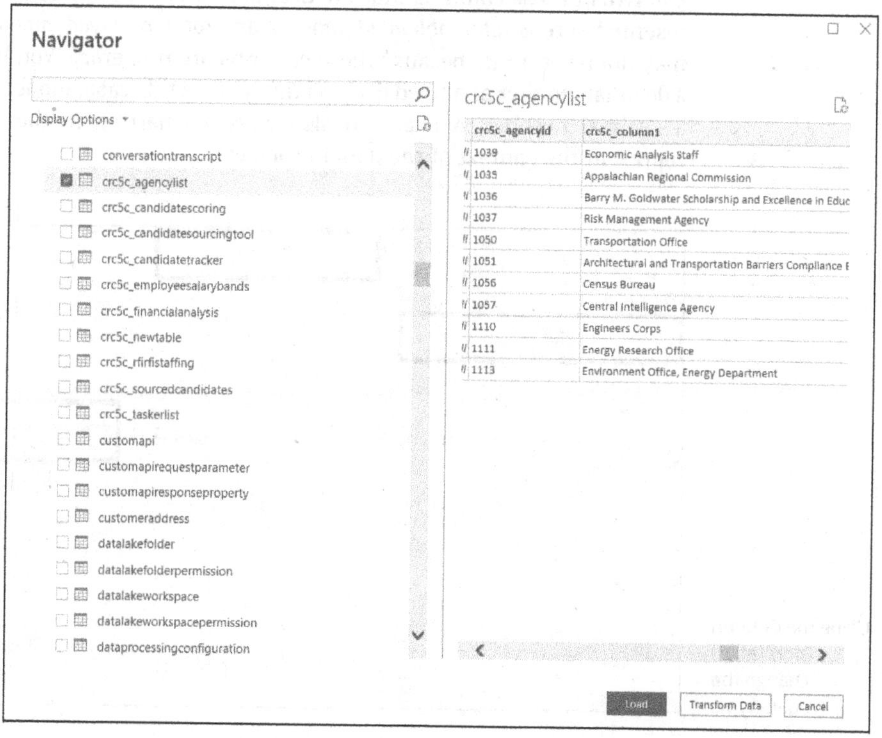

FIGURE 11-5: The Navigator window in Table view.

REMEMBER

If you choose Load, that means the data won't be mapped to a specific data type. If you choose Transform Data, Power BI does its best to map against the proper data type based on ETL properties. You have the opportunity to make changes to the data model with Transform Data.

TECHNICAL STUFF

Although Table view might look like the Power Query Editor, keep in mind that only a sample of your data is shown in the Power Query Editor, whereas all data is available in Table view after it's imported into the data model. In Table view, you're working with your entire dataset, and modifications are made live with the dashboard requirements and specifications. Both Table view and the Power Query Editor can handle the creation of calculated columns in real-time, though.

After the data is loaded, you can manipulate it, add queries, add or delete columns, or manage the existing relationships between one or more tables or columns within a single table. The following sections explain in detail how to complete each of these activities.

Defining data types

When Power BI imports a dataset, it defaults to a specific data type. For example, in Figure 11-6, you can see that the Prime Contracts table has several columns, and two of these columns indicate decimal numbers as options. The column represented here is *total_obligated_amount* and *total_outlayed_amount*. The data type may not be accurate because these columns are monetary. You have the choice of a decimal number or a fixed decimal number. In this case, monetary values require a decimal number. A user can also place formatting in the column to better represent the context of the data in each cell.

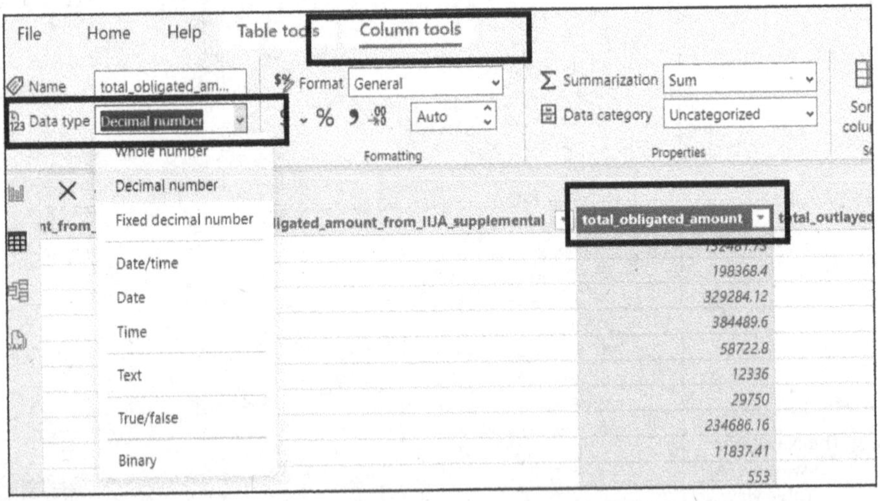

FIGURE 11-6: Using the Column Tools tab to change the data type.

To review the data types for a given column, follow these steps.

1. **Open Table view.**
2. **With the data source you just imported, select the column you want to review and highlight it.**
3. **Make sure you're on the Column Tools tab (refer to Figure 11-6).**
4. **On the Column Tools tab, check the Name property.**
5. **Verify that the Data Type drop-down menu (refer to Figure 11-6) is set to the correct data type.**

   In this case, it's set to Decimal Number.
6. **Switch the option to Fixed Decimal Number.**

This process is consistent throughout Power BI for modifying data types, whether you're trying to change numerical data to text or text to numeric.

Handling formatting and data type properties

Depending on whether the column is text or numeric, you can use the Format drop-down menu on the Column Tools tab to also apply specific properties to a column to ensure specific behaviors. In the preceding section, the Currency format is applied to the columns. If the column is numeric, you can also apply other behaviors, including decimal numbers, whole numbers, percentages, and scientific number formatting. (See Figure 11-7.)

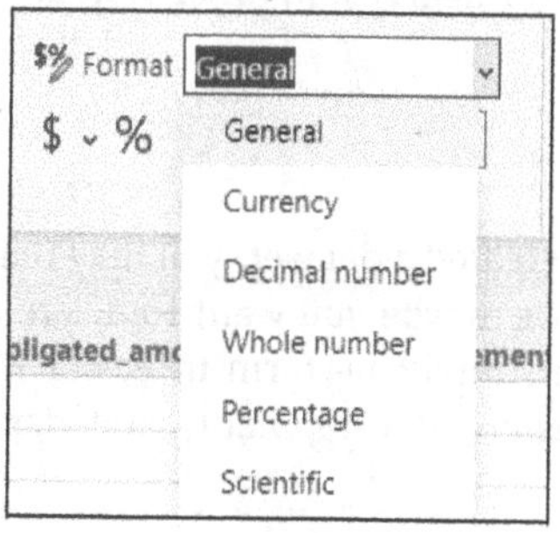

FIGURE 11-7: Numeric formatting options.

Suppose you're looking to apply properties such as Measures, Geographic markers, or Mathematical Behaviors against a column. In that case, you can apply a *summarization* (a way to further evaluate data mathematically) or a data category (a way to classify geographically based data). Summarization options for the Column Tools tab are shown in Figure 11-8, and the Data Category options are displayed in Figure 11-9.

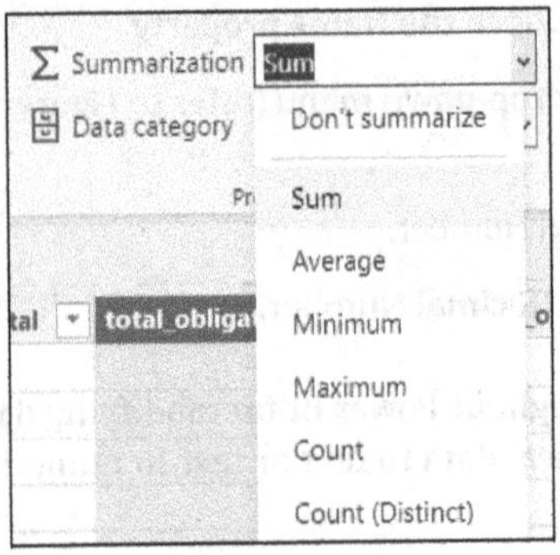

FIGURE 11-8: The Summarization options on the Column Tools tab.

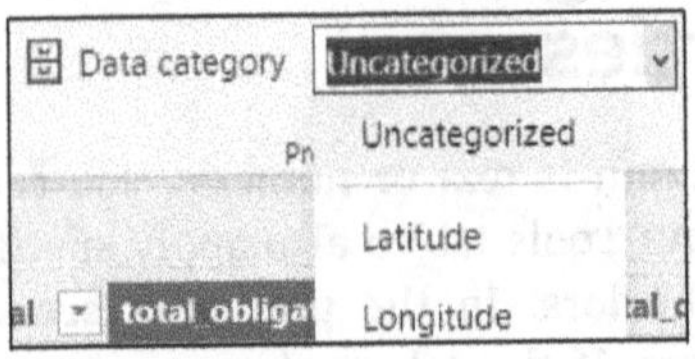

FIGURE 11-9: The Data Category options.

REMEMBER

Summarization options allow for any column of numeric data in a table to be summarized as a single value. Data Category options are applicable for Power BI mapping — latitude and longitude or degrees, in other words.

Managing tables

After you've imported a table and created a dataset, you may realize that you need to change the name of the table. Or maybe you want to delete a table. These are common actions that a data expert might perform in Power BI Desktop as they work their way through the design, development, and deployment of their data model.

Adding tables

There may be times when you need to add one or more tables to your data model after you've imported the dataset into Power BI Desktop. Perhaps you want to create an additional fact table for the transactional activity or a dimension table to support a new lookup. Both scenarios are standard, but luckily, adding a table is straightforward. You'll still need to do a bit of configuration after you set the column names, though.

In any event, here's how you add a table:

1. **In Model view, click the Enter Data button on the Home tab of the Model View Ribbon**, as shown in Figure 11-10.

   The Create Table Interface appears.

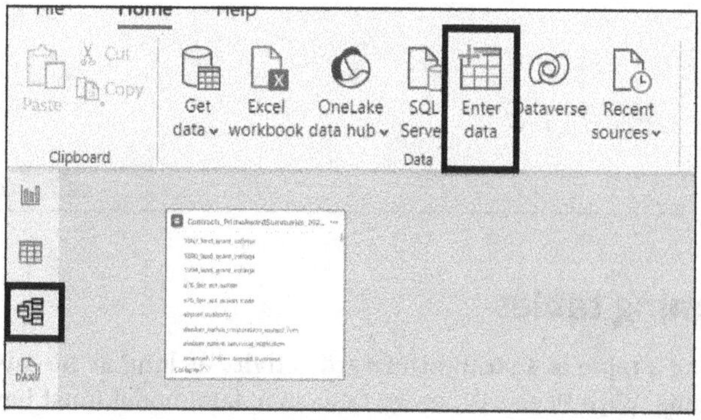

FIGURE 11-10: The Enter Data button.

2. **Enter the column names and data corresponding to the columns into the appropriate table cells.**
3. **Enter a table name in the Name field.**

   The table should look something like the one shown in Figure 11-11.

4. **Click Load once you are finished creating your table.**

The result is a brand-new table that appears as part of the data model you can access in Table view as well as in Model view.

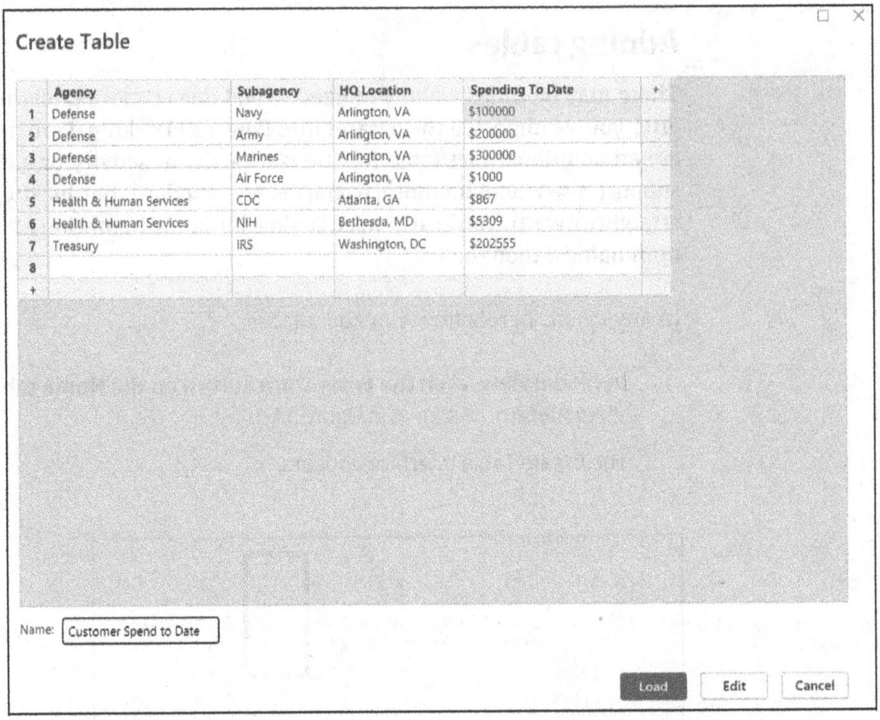

FIGURE 11-11: Creating a table.

Renaming tables

Renaming a table is a straightforward activity as long as no table already has the same name. With Power BI, every table in a data model must have a unique name. For example, two tables cannot have the name Product.

To rename a table in Power BI Desktop, follow these steps:

1. **In either Table view or Model view, locate the Data pane.**
2. **Right-click the table name you want to change.**
3. **Choose Rename from the menu that appears (see Figure 11-12).**
4. **Enter a new name for your table in the highlighted field and then press Enter.**

   The table name will refresh within 30 seconds.

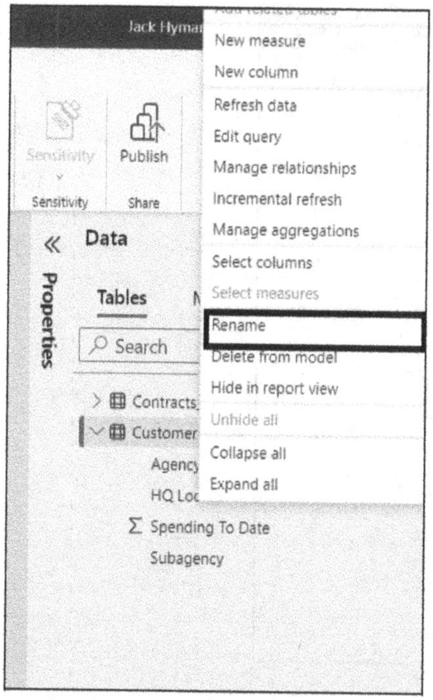

FIGURE 11-12: Updating the table name in Model view.

Deleting tables

If you want to delete a table from a model, you face a few risks. If relationships are associated with the table, those relationships will break. In addition, if calculated fields are embedded within a report, those too will disappear. That said, removing a table, like moving a column, is a relatively simple process. To remove a table, follow these steps:

1. **In either Table view or Model view, locate the Data pane.**
2. **Right-click a table to remove, and then choose Delete from Model from the menu that appears (see Figure 11-13).**

   A prompt appears, asking whether you're sure you want to delete the table, as shown in Figure 11-14. Once you click Yes, this change is not reversible.
3. **Click Delete.**

   The table is deleted from the model.

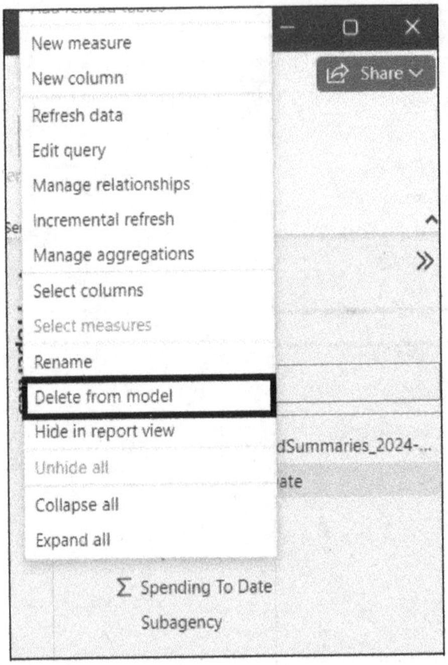

FIGURE 11-13: Removing a table.

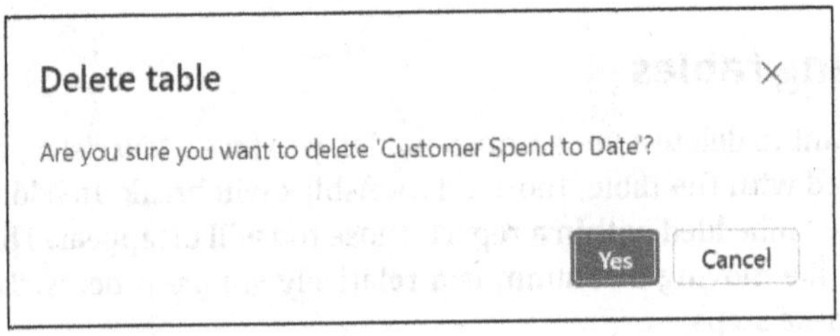

FIGURE 11-14: Confirming whether the table should be deleted.

Renaming and deleting columns

Renaming or deleting a column follows the same practice as renaming or deleting a table. The only caveat is that when dependencies such as key enforcements occur, deleting a column can result in potentially broken relationships.

To rename a column, follow these steps:

1. **In either Table view or Model view, locate the Data pane.**
2. **Right-click the column name you want to rename.**
3. **Rename the column.**

   The column name refreshes automatically.

   If relationship updates require updating, those are revised accordingly.

When the column is deleted, you'll notice that the link is broken if a relationship exists between two tables. Figure 11-15 shows a column that is requiring a name change to *Agency*. Once the name is changed, a relationship between the two tables will form.

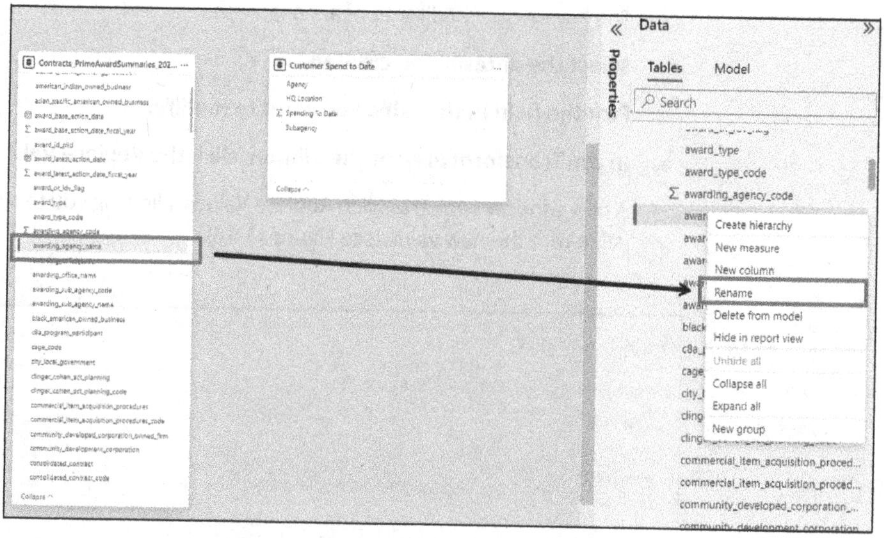

FIGURE 11-15: Changing a column name to form a relationship.

To delete a column, follow these steps:

1. **In either Table view or Model view, locate the Fields pane.**
2. **Right-click the column name, and then choose Delete from Model from the menu that appears.**

   You're alerted that the column is about to be deleted.
3. **Click Delete.**

   The column is deleted, and the model updates automatically.

   If relationships are broken, the links between the tables are updated accordingly.

Adding and modifying data in tables

At times, you may want to add or modify data in an existing table. This process is one of the less transparent ones because it requires a user to go into the Power Query Editor to complete the action. If you've created the data within Power BI, the process for adding or modifying is a bit more simplistic than datasets that have been imported using a file or ingested using Direct Query. To add rows or modify cells to rows of tables you've created yourself, follow these steps:

1. **Navigate to the Queries area on the Home tab of the Model View Ribbon, and click the Transform Data button.**

   The Power Query Editor appears onscreen.

2. **Select the dataset you created.**
3. **Pick the field in the table you want to modify.**
4. **In the Transform area of the Ribbon, click the Replace Values button.**

   A new window appears called Replace Values, allowing you to replace the old value with the new value (see Figure 11-16).

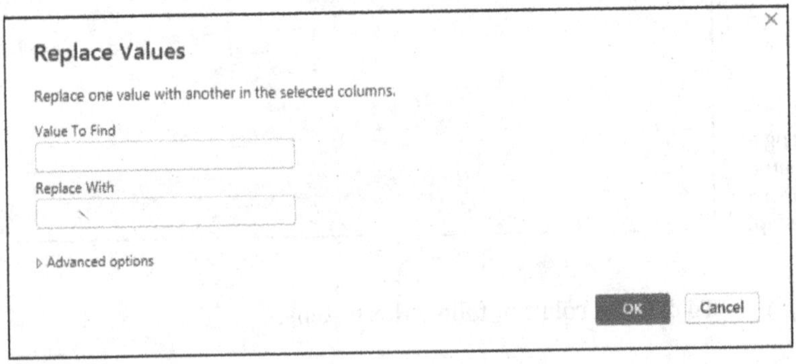

FIGURE 11-16: Changing table data.

Managing Relationships

When two tables are connected by a common bond, it often signifies that a relationship exists by way of a key. It can be a primary-primary key or a primary-foreign key relationship. In certain circumstances, a table may even be joined together in a single field. That single field can map to another table with a like-kind field, creating a lookup. This section covers the value of relationships in designing and developing the data model.

Creating automatic relationships

Power BI recognizes that, when data is transformed, a relationship exists. For example, if you have two tables with a numeric data type and they're named similarly, they're considered to be in a relationship. Power BI detects these relationships as part of the ETL process. The automatic detection helps reduce the manual work that goes into identifying the relationships yourself. Also, you can reduce the risk of errors from occurring between tables.

To see how Power BI views relationships between datasets, follow these steps:

1. **Open the Home tab of the Model View Ribbon.**
2. **In the Relationships area, click the Manage Relationships icon.**

   Relationships that exist when the datasets are imported are automatically matched.
3. **(Optional) If you want the systems to autodetect the relationships, click the Autodetect button.**

Creating manual relationships

Sometimes the names of primary and foreign keys may not match but you know that the data between them creates a relationship. For example, LocationID and CityID might be one and the same or perhaps StateID and StateAbbreviation. All these are examples where data analysts need to manually map the relationship between two tables even though Power BI should have been able to pick up the pattern. To manually establish relationships between tables and keys, follow these steps:

1. **Open the Home tab of the Model View Ribbon.**
2. **In the Relationships area, click the Manage Relationships icon.**
3. **Click the New Relationship button.**
4. **The New Relationship window appears, as shown in Figure 11-17.**
5. **Select the two tables that are in a relationship.**
6. **Using the Cardinality and Cross-Filter Direction drop-down menus, choose the settings you want.**
7. **Click Save when you finish.**

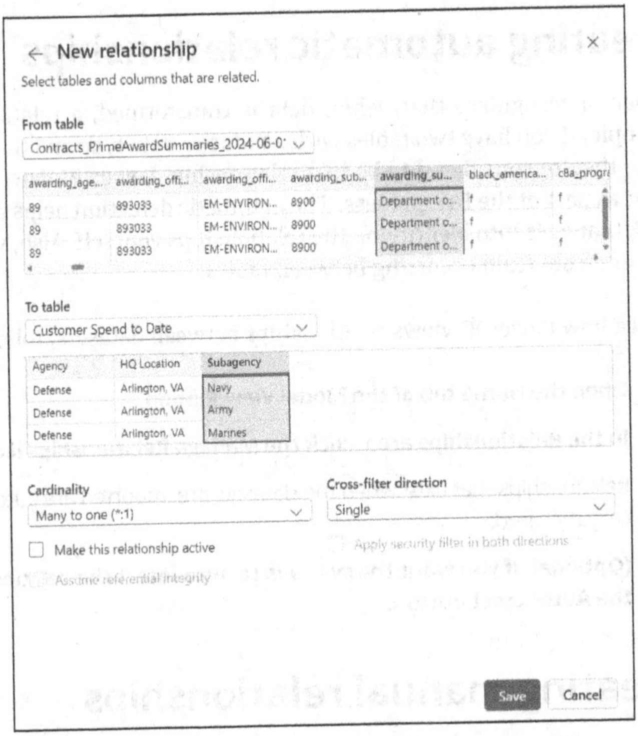

FIGURE 11-17: The New Relationship window.

Deleting relationships

Deleting relationships occurs in one of three ways. You're either removing the field in one of the two tables that sets up the join between the two tables or using the Manage Relationships interface to disconnect the relationship the same way you created the interface. You'd uncheck the Active box. Then you'd click Delete. A warning appears, showing a break in the relationship. You'd acknowledge the relationship to be broken and then click OK.

The easiest way to break a relationship is to open Model view and right-click the link. Choose Delete. You're prompted to acknowledge that the relationship will be broken.

Classifying and codifying data in tables

As you build your data collection in Power BI over time, it is important to add context so that any user who accesses those datasets you've begun to create can put the puzzle pieces together. Whether your descriptive data is tied to a single dataset or to many, it's an ongoing activity for the person responsible for managing the data. A way to help any user who comes across your data better understand exactly what they are reviewing is to add *metadata* — data better describing your data, in other words — within each table or column property.

To add metadata to each table or column, you follow these steps, depending on whether it's a table or a column:

1. **Open Model view.**
2. **Click to select the table (to describe an entire table) or a column inside the table. (You'll need to select the specific column among tables.)**
3. **In the Properties pane, enter a description in the Description box.**

   This can be an extended sentence regarding the specific item.
4. **Enter synonyms that can also describe the table or column name.**

WARNING

Be careful not to confuse data categories with data types. Data *categories* are a way to group data in a model, whereas data *types* are specific to help qualify if the data is text, numeric, or mixed. Think of Cities as a data category and the data type as Text.

Arranging Data

Arranging data in a dataset is different from what you experience when data is transformed in visualizing data. Arranging data in Power BI can be classified in a few different ways: Sort By, Group By, and Hide Data. The next few sections drill down into the specifics of each kind.

Sorting by and grouping by

You can easily be confused by Sort By and Group By. Sort By sorts data in ascending order (A–Z) and descending order (Z–A) on a column basis. To ascend or descend the data in a dataset, you need to open the Power Query Editor to complete any form of sort-by action. You can sort by only one column at a time.

Data Groups, the equivalent of Group By, allows users to create logical groupings of data points within a field. This feature, often referred to as *Grouping*, helps simplify and summarize large sets of data by categorizing them into smaller, more manageable segments. As an example, Figure 11-18 shows a data group called Executive Agencies. All agencies that report to the Executive Branch of the U.S. Government are listed in this Group By scenario.

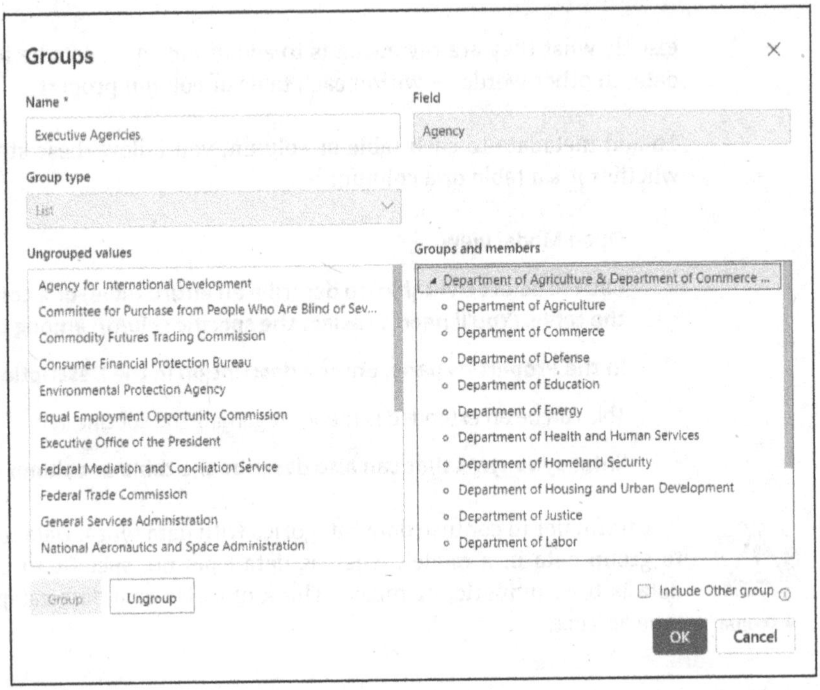

FIGURE 11-18: Using Data Grouping to better organize a large dataset.

Hiding data

At times, you may want to suppress column data from a table. Perhaps the column offers little value in the dataset when presenting results, or maybe the data adds too much complexity to the visualization. It might be that the column, when included in the dataset, actually provides inaccurate data. You might choose to hide data for any number of reasons. Hiding data, rather than deleting a column outright, ensures that you can still access the data later if you need it.

To hide a column, as shown in Figure 11-20, follow these steps:

1. **In Model view, click the table that contains the column you want to hide.**
2. **Click a column you want to hide.**
3. **Locate the Properties pane.**
4. **Locate the Is Hidden slider.**
5. **Slide the option from No to Yes.**

   An eye with a line through it appears in the field (shown in Figure 11-19), indicating that the field has been hidden.

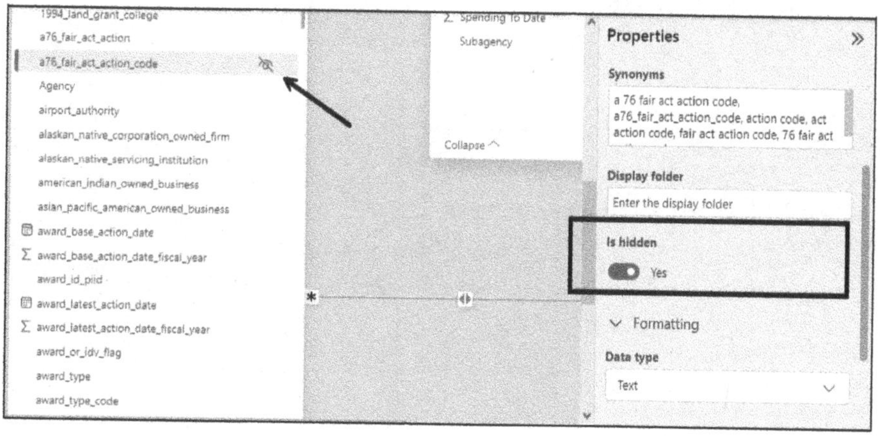

FIGURE 11-19: Hiding data.

If at any point you want to unhide the column, repeat these steps, but this time, slide the Is Hidden slider to No.

Publishing Data Models

When a data model is ready to be published to Power BI Services, the process is as easy as clicking a button — if you've set up your online account with Microsoft's Power BI Services at `https://app.powerbi.com/`. You're asked to supply your username and the email address that logs you into all Power Platform / Office 365 applications. Depending on the type of license you have, your model's data volume and refresh vary.

To publish your model, open the Home tab on the Power BI Desktop, and click Publish (see Figure 11-20).

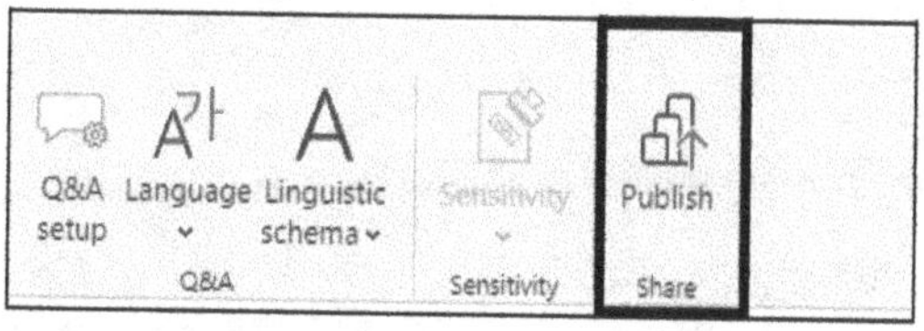

FIGURE 11-20: Clicking the Publish button deploys the data model and reports to Power BI Services.

TIP

There are hundreds of techniques to refine data and the Power BI data model. My book *Power BI For Dummies* (published by Wiley) covers additional techniques you can use to transform data models for visualization magic. Also, check out Microsoft's collection of articles and training videos on data modeling for Power BI. Go to `https://learn.microsoft.com`, and search for **data modeling**.

IN THIS CHAPTER

» Mastering the various visualization options available in Power BI

» Deciding when to use specific visualization techniques

» Learning how to craft powerful reports and dashboards

Chapter 12

Visualizing Data in Power BI

You've probably heard the adage, "A picture speaks a thousand words." One of the reasons so many people use Power BI is to create pictures of data. After you import the data, perhaps millions of records, you can use Power BI to create visualizations to help understand what the data says. A visualization is a bit easier for most people to understand than a large, complex dataset or a single-page report.

In this chapter, I show how to access the visualizations available in Power BI and help you determine which visualizations are best suited for the data experiences you want to create. The chapter also delves into reports and dashboarding, which help tell the story you want to create with your visualizations.

Looking at Report Fundamentals and Visualizations

Visualizations are basically pictures of data. A visualization can be as simple as a chart or graph that shows one or more data points within a dataset. When you work with visualizations in Power BI, you use Power BI Desktop to create a data model and visualizations, and Power BI Services to deploy datasets, *reports* (a single visual that tells a distinct story), and *dashboards* (a collection of reports) to the web.

In other words, if you want to share your data with other users, you must become familiar with Power BI Desktop and Power BI Services. You can manipulate visualizations or update them from within Services. You can collaborate with other users in Power BI Services exclusively, whereas you can make edits on your own to your reports using either version of Power BI. Nevertheless, because there are more opportunities for data modeling, most of your visualization manipulation occurs in Power BI Desktop, not in Power BI Services.

Creating visualizations

Assume that you have a dataset stored in Power BI Desktop and you want to share it as a visualization. First, head over to the Report tab by clicking the Report View tab on the left-side navigation (see Figure 12-1). The visualization interface appears. You can use this interface to drag and drop a visualization type from the Visualizations pane on the right side to the Visualization canvas. Figure 12-2 presents an example of Report view in Power BI Desktop. This view is where visualizations are created and edited.

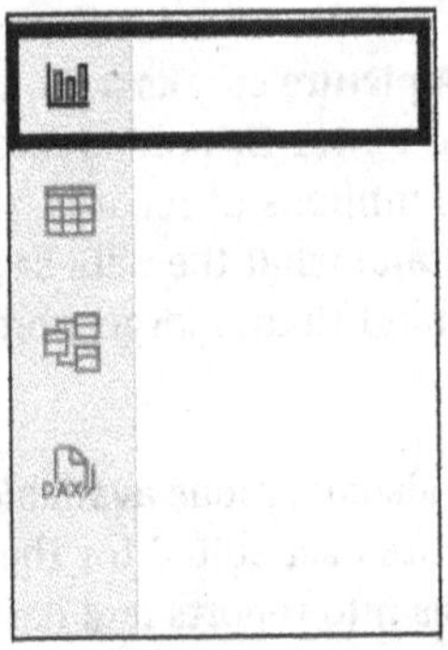

FIGURE 12-1: The Report View button.

In Report view, you can complete several activities associated with visualization, such as

- Selecting a visual icon from the Visualizations pane.
- Selecting the data fields to be used in the visualization.

- Dragging fields from the Data pane to the canvas for visualization creation.
- Using the Ribbon is a quick way to access various commands, tools, and features for managing your data, creating visualizations, and customizing reports.
- Interpreting the results of the visualizations by using the Q&A editor.

You can enhance reports by integrating text boxes, custom shapes, and images. For visualizations within multipage reports, you can add buttons, bookmarks, and page navigation to the visualizations.

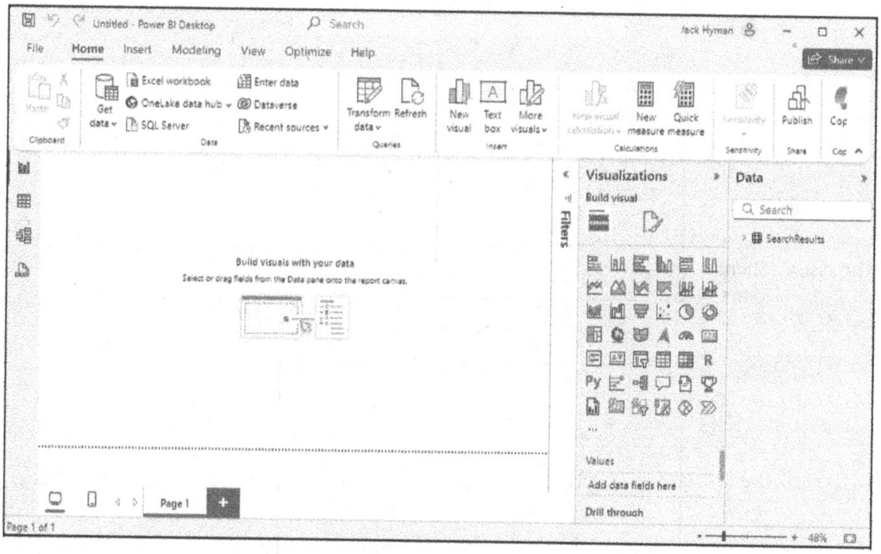

FIGURE 12-2: Power BI Desktop Report view.

Choosing a visualization

The Visualizations pane of Power BI Desktop's Report view hosts more than 20 visualization options that you can drag to the canvas. Each visualization requires a user to select one or more fields from the Data pane after dragging the visual to the canvas. A user must select the check box to include the field from the Data pane for a visual. Figure 12-3 provides you with an example of the Visualizations pane, and Figure 12-4 illustrates the associated Data pane.

TIP

Limit the number of check boxes you select, or else you may create a poor visualization. Select only those variables from the Data pane that are relevant. Use those fields that contribute to the report's specificity. Keep in mind that "The more, the merrier" doesn't necessarily apply to visual elements you include in visualizations since too many details can result in confusion and clutter.

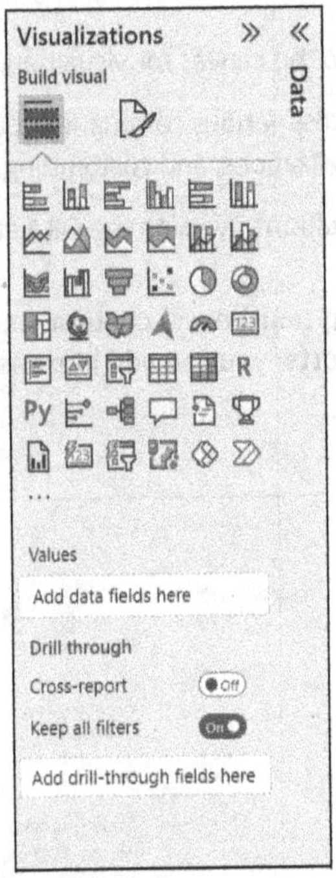

FIGURE 12-3: The Visualizations pane.

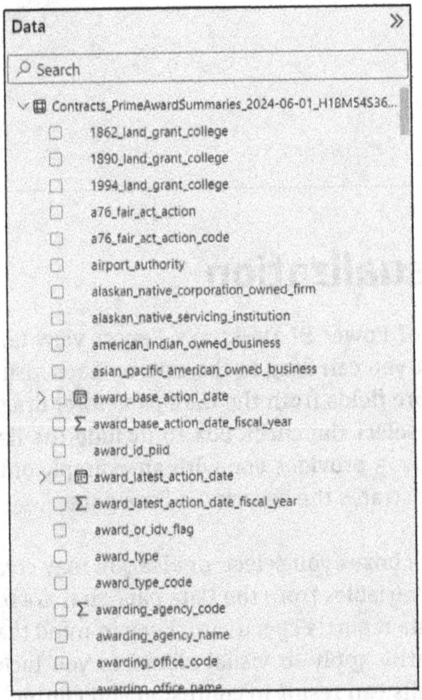

FIGURE 12-4: The Data pane.

Filtering data

You will often need to filter data while crafting a visualization. When you select a new field to incorporate into a visualization, the field appears as another value that can be filtered. Depending on the size of your dataset for a specific value, you may want to narrow the focus.

Suppose you select a value named *funding_agency_name* as a choice from the Data pane. Under *funding_agency_name*, you have a list of agencies to filter from, including Select All. In Figure 12-5, you'll see that several filters have been placed in the pane, but none of have been manipulated just yet. You'll run into instances where reducing a dataset based on a value significantly reduces the dataset. In the case of Figure 12-6, only those entries associated with the subagency selected will appear in the visualization.

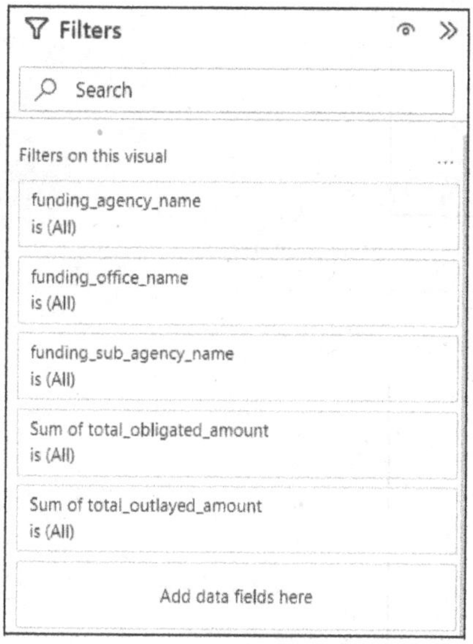

FIGURE 12-5: Filtering pane with several fields from the Data pane.

TIP

Users can filter the data on just the specific visualization or across all visualizations by using the Filter On This Page or Filter On All Pages options within the Filter pane, as shown in Figure 12-7.

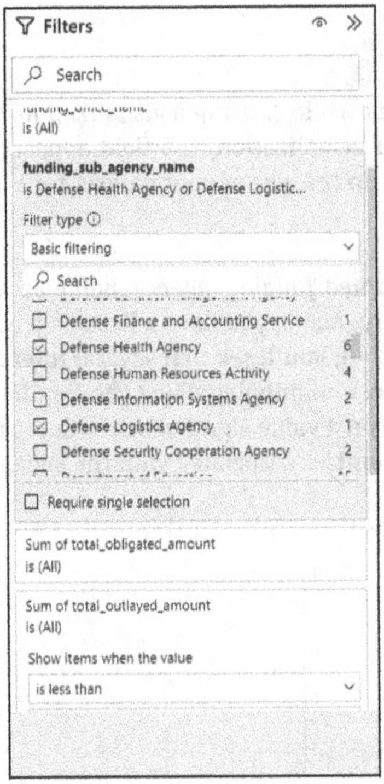

FIGURE 12-6: Setting up filtering conditions with quantitative data.

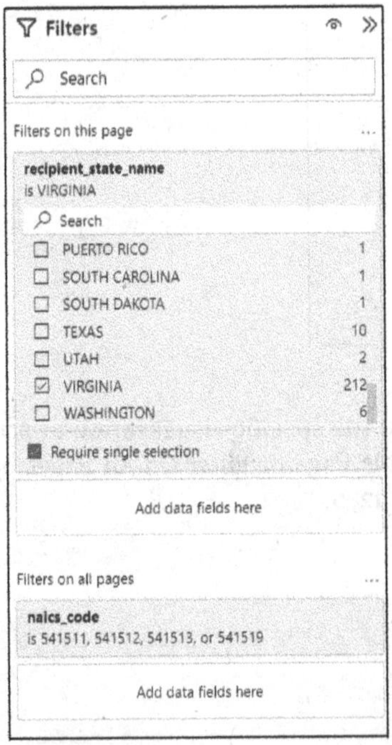

FIGURE 12-7: The Filter On This Page and Filter On All Page options.

Choosing the Best Visualization for the Job

Selecting the appropriate visualization type is key to creating effective and insightful Power BI reports and dashboards. When choosing a visualization, it's essential to consider the nature of your data and the story you want to convey in your presentation choices. Bar charts, line charts, scatter plots, and treemaps are just a few examples of the diverse options available in Power BI.

Working with bar charts and column charts

Power BI offers several varieties of the bar chart and column chart. Each one allows you to summarize and compare two or more values within a focused data category. You would use a bar chart or column chart for comparisons because they offer a snapshot of a dataset.

Stacked bar charts and stacked column charts

The stacked bar charts and stacked column charts are best used when trying to compare categories against a standard quantitative variable. The bars are proportionally displayed based on the values displayed — horizontally for stacked bar charts, and a vertical alignment for stacked column charts. One axis of a chart presents a category for comparison, and the other is the focused value.

TIP

You usually begin by comparing just two variables, but should you have more, Power BI supports the breakout of datasets into finer-grained details. For example, in Figure 12-8, you see a stacked bar chart with a single data category, obligated amount. The obligated amount is then broken into segments with the value assigned to the different award type. The proportionality of the bars is the contract type. In this case, it's either a small business being awarded a contract (red) or a large business (blue).

If you add a second dimension for the x-axis, you can see that the stacked bar charts are broken out even further as an aggregate of values. It combines the outlay and obligated amounts for each award type (see Figure 12-9). There may be only one status with some stacked bars, and several in others.

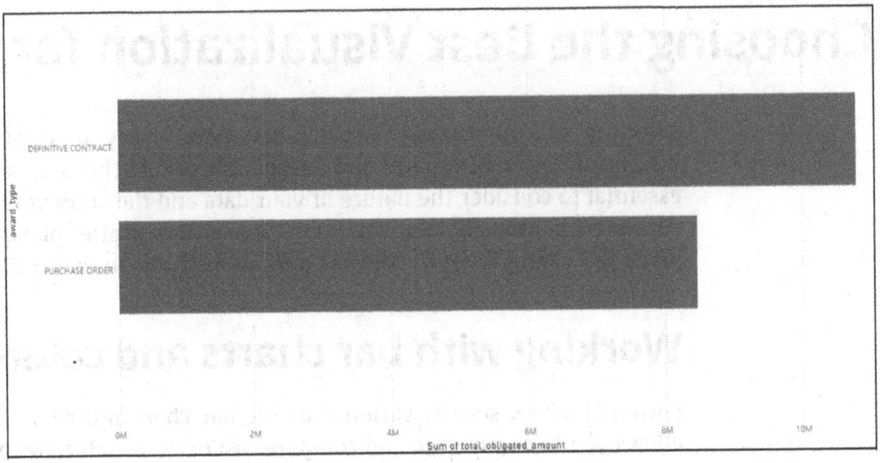

FIGURE 12-8: A stacked bar chart.

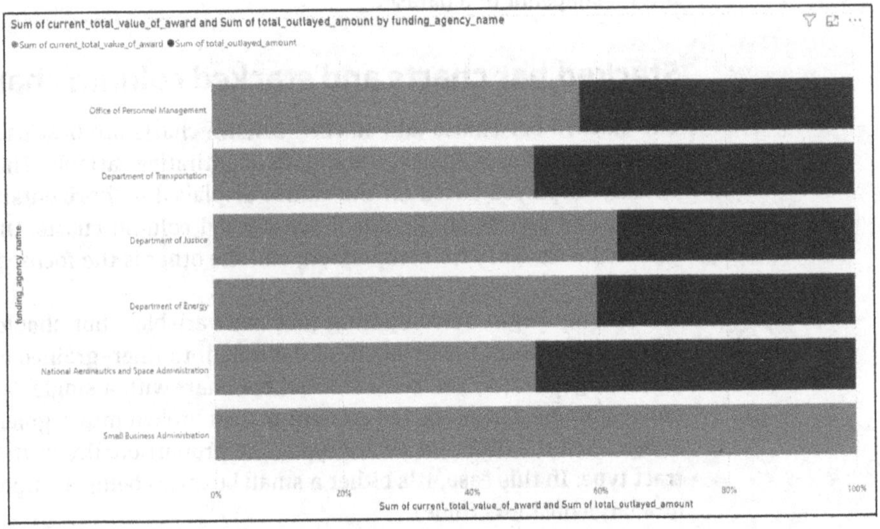

FIGURE 12-9: Using multiple dimensions in a stacked bar chart.

A stacked column chart changes the direction of the data from horizontal to vertical. There is no actual difference in the summarization of data — only the visualization of the dataset. Figure 12-10 shows conceptually the same data as shown in Figure 12-8 for definitive contracts (an award type), but this time displayed vertically. The same is true for the multiple dimensions shown in Figure 12-11. In the example shown in Figure 12-11, a different dimension was used. The x-axis factors in agency. The y-axis combines obligations and outlays across different award types.

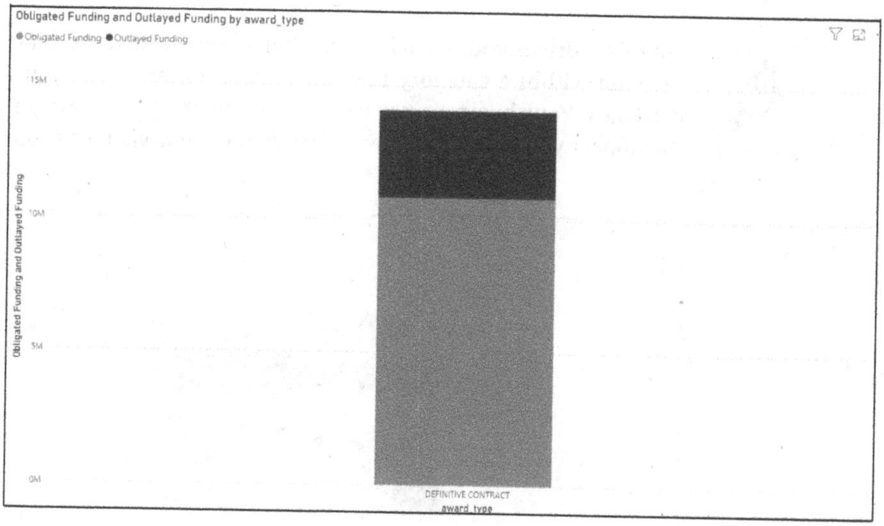

FIGURE 12-10: A stacked column chart.

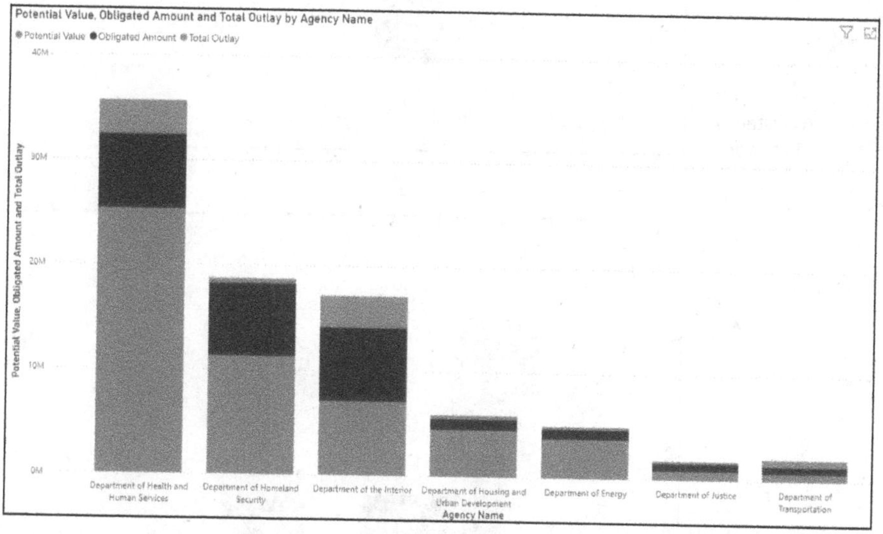

FIGURE 12-11: Using multiple dimensions in a stacked column chart.

Clustered bar charts and clustered column charts

Unlike stacked bar charts and stacked column charts, where the data is compressed into a single bar or column per category, the data is broken out more discretely in clustered bar charts and clustered column charts. It's easier to discern values as larger or smaller when the values are broken out into their discrete bars. Think of this as your typical compare scenario. In the case of Figure 12-12, you have a comparison of obligated versus outlaid funding for three contract types. For the clustered column chart in Figure 12-13, you'll find that each of the columns compare obligated and outlaid funding aggregated for award types. The mere difference is the placement of the bars.

Your data drives your visualization choice. Sometimes you may want to show how the data within a category is consistent. At other times, you may want to show extremes. Your business use case, the number of data categories and fields, and the impact you hope to achieve must dictate your visualization choices.

REMEMBER

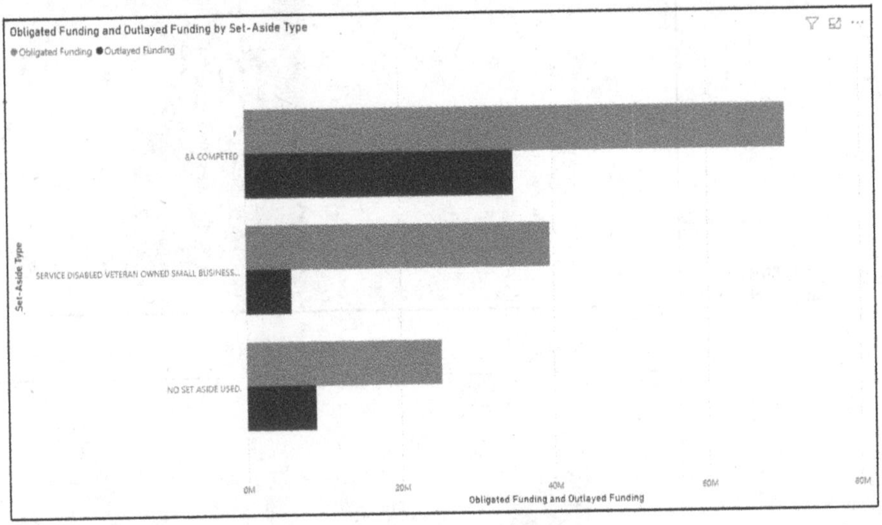

FIGURE 12-12: A clustered bar chart.

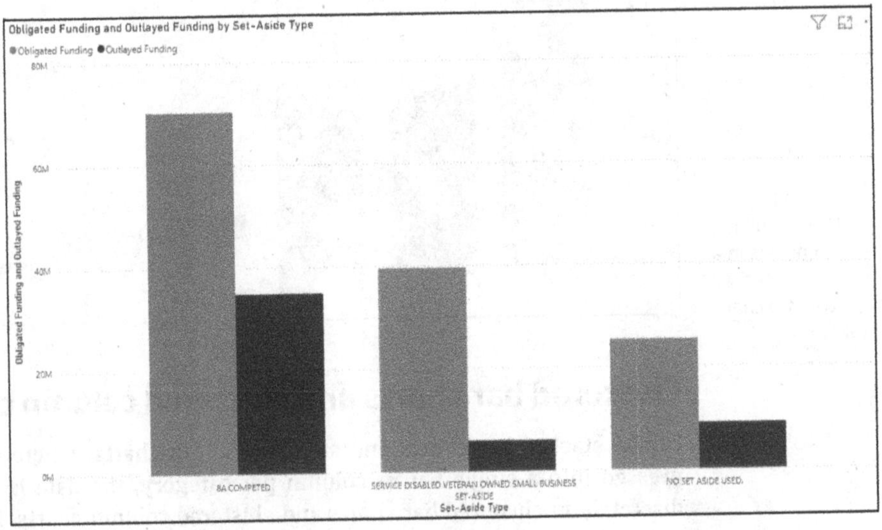

FIGURE 12-13: A clustered column chart.

TIP

There is another type of bar and column chart called the *100% stacked bar and 100% chart*, which shows the relative proportion of different categories within a grouping. Each grouping totals 100%, and each bar may contain several categories, and of course, the total appears as a whole bar. In addition, several bars may be compared within each category. The sum of parts within a bar, regardless of whether the graphic is a bar or column, totals 100% in value.

Using basic line charts and area charts

When trend analysis over a period is your goal, consider using a line chart or an area chart. For both chart types, you assign the x-axis a numerical value while the y-axis acts as a key measure. A line chart connects specific data points by using a straight-line segment. The area chart is more proper when you're looking for changes in a dataset. Though both adhere to a trend, the area chart is filled with a particular color or texture to show data variation.

In the examples shown in Figures 12-14 (line chart) and in 12-15 (area chart), you see a snapshot of obligated funding trends over a period of several calendar years. It's expected that in 2024, the highest amount of spend will be realized at around $250 million. On the other hand, spending was almost flat from 2010 – 2020.

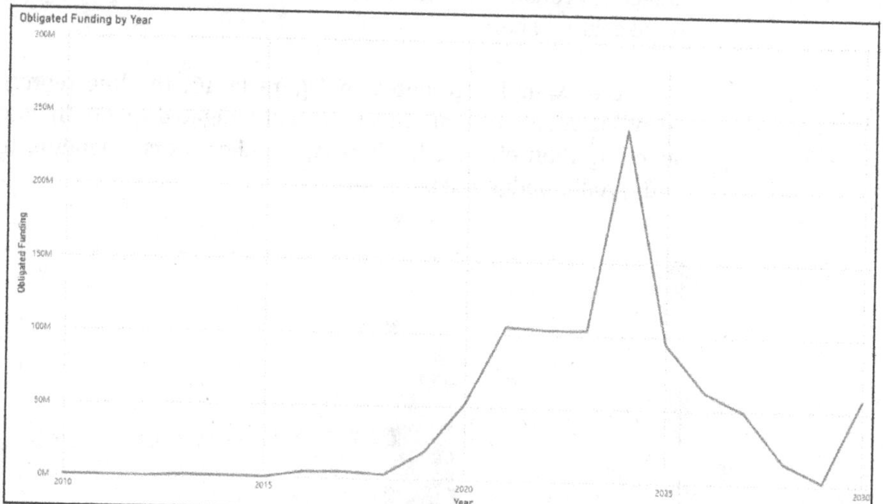

FIGURE 12-14: A line chart.

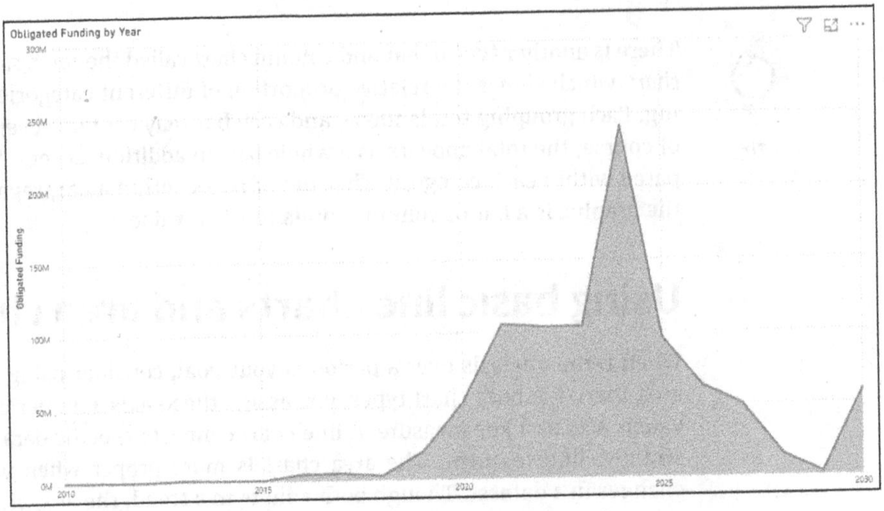

FIGURE 12-15: An area chart.

Combining line charts and bar charts

There might be times when you're trying to complete an analysis for multiple trends. When the dataset is significant, and you want to put as much information as possible into a single visualization, combining chart types is a possibility. Two choices to consider are the line and stacked column chart, and the line and clustered column chart.

Take the example presented in Figure 12-16; the line represents total current spending versus the columns represent obligated spend. In 2023, there was more spending than obligated, whereas, in other years, spending tends to be in line with proper budgeting behaviors.

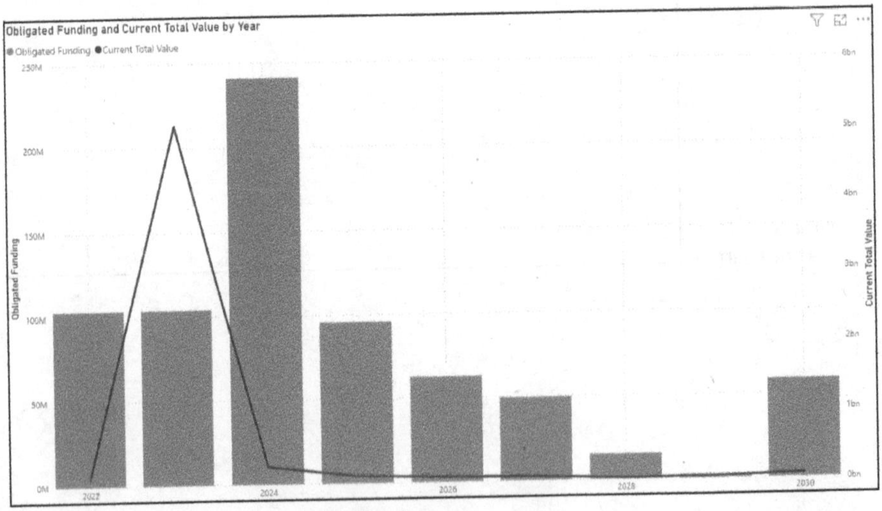

FIGURE 12-16: A line chart and a stacked column chart.

REMEMBER

When you're trying to create comparisons for joint charts, make sure they're relevant to one another. The data comparison shouldn't be too ambiguous, because you don't want to dilute the value of your report. Also, be sure not to add too many comparison layers.

Working with ribbon charts

Should you want to see the values in the order in which they appear as items in a legend, your best choice is to consider the ribbon chart. A *ribbon chart* orders items based on which item has most of its measures in a particular axis. When a category has multiple values being evaluated, each category type is represented differently.

In Figure 12-17, the products and services evaluated indicate the most awards issued by the government were to disadvantaged companies called *8a* organizations. The least were set aside for HUBZone enterprises.

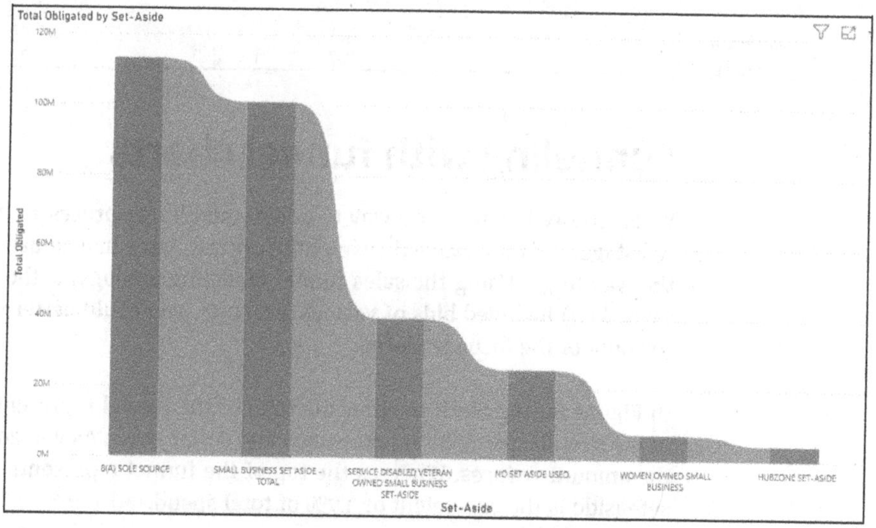

FIGURE 12-17: A ribbon chart.

Going with the flow with waterfall charts

When comparing the strength or weakness of a given value from its start and understanding how the value transforms based on one or more other conditions, consider using a Waterfall chart. A classic use case for a waterfall chart is a cost analysis or checking account balance. You have intermediate actions displayed in the chart that show positives and negatives.

In the example shown in Figure 12-18, the last column represents the total of spending ($300 million). Each of the waterfall bars represent a part of the 300 million dollars.

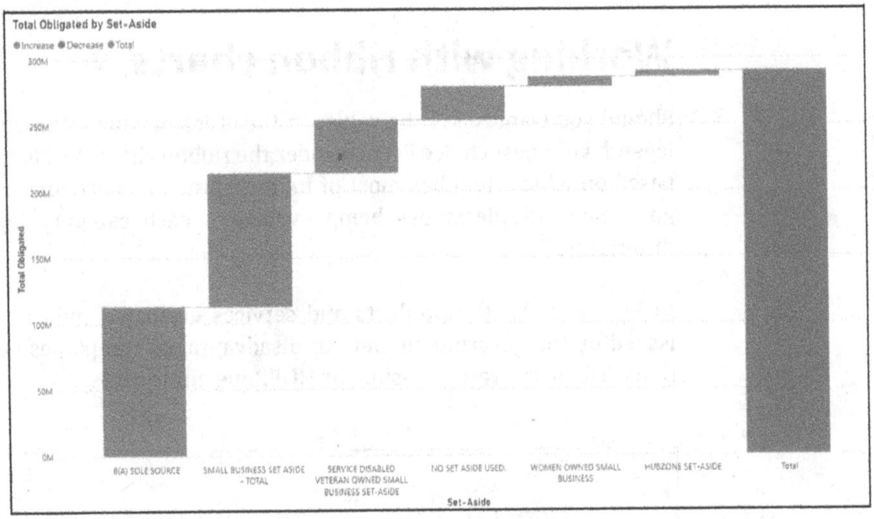

FIGURE 12-18: A waterfall chart.

Funneling with funnel charts

When you're looking for a way to understand linear processes, visualize sequential stages, or rationalize the weight of critical items in a dataset, a funnel chart is the way to go. Using the sales funnel modeling analogy, if the pipeline (all your sales data) included bids of various amounts, you could better understand where the bulk of the focus is placed.

In Figure 12-19, you'll see that the total of the funnel represents the largest part of the overall spend, both percentage and dollar-wise. As you go down the funnel, the amount reduces. Whereas the top of the funnel represents 100%, the bottom set-aside is the equivalent of 3.7% of total spend.

TECHNICAL STUFF

You've probably noticed that some of the reports described in this chapter become specific when it comes to filtering. Much of the specificity correlates to field association in the Visualizations pane. Regardless of the visualization, you may need to tailor the following areas under Formatting in the Visualizations pane:

- **Categories:** Represented on the horizontal axis in bar charts (or vertical axis in column charts). You can include multiple categories and enable drill-down to explore deeper levels of data.

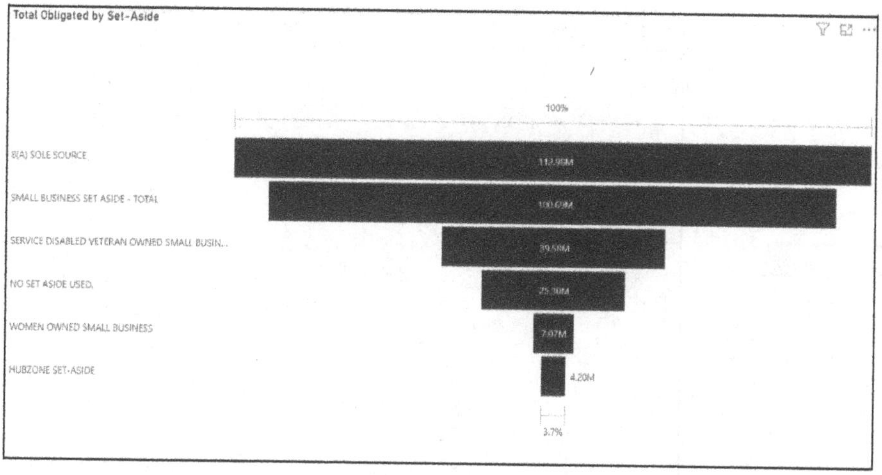

FIGURE 12-19: A funnel chart.

- **Breakdown:** Allows you to show changes between categories.
- **Values:** Designates the key numerical field that will be plotted.
- **Tooltip:** Adds field descriptions automatically as a user hovers the mouse cursor over a bar or column in a visualization.

Scattering with scatter charts

Suppose you have an extensive dataset where you want to find the relationship between one variable found among two axes and then decide the *correlation* — the similarity or lack thereof. In that case, a scatter chart is a decisive choice to consider. In Figure 12-20, you'll see each dot in the State of Maryland or District of Columbia represents an award. Each dot corresponds to the amount obligated to a contract award versus the amount spent to date.

Sweetening the data using pie charts and donut charts

Pie charts are circular graphics that break the values from an individual category into slices (or percentages). The whole piece adds up to 100 percent. The *donut chart* is an extension of the pie chart in that it displays categories as arcs with a big hole in the center. The values are precisely the same — it's more about aesthetic design.

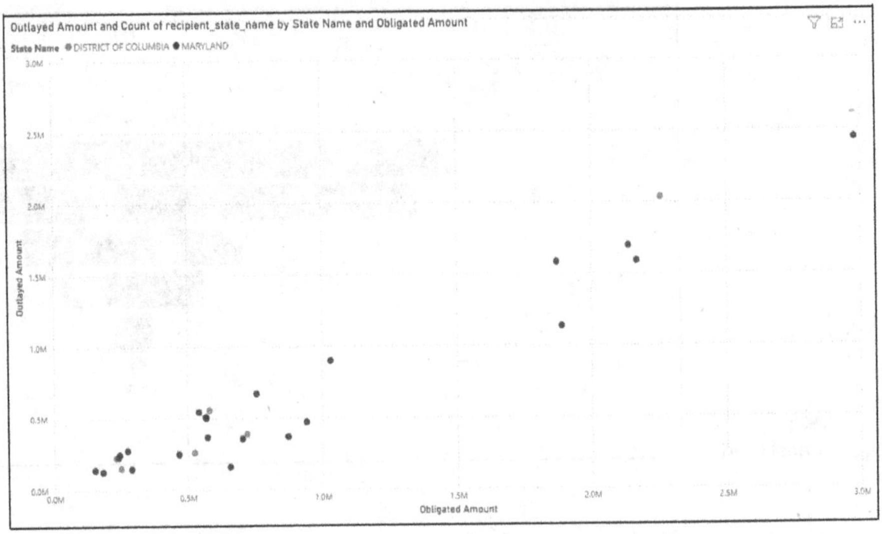

FIGURE 12-20: Scatterplot.

In Figure 12-21 (pie chart) and Figure 12-22 (donut chart), you see a breakdown of the contract types for a specified product purchased by the government over some time. The bigger the segment of the pie or donut, the more contracts were issued.

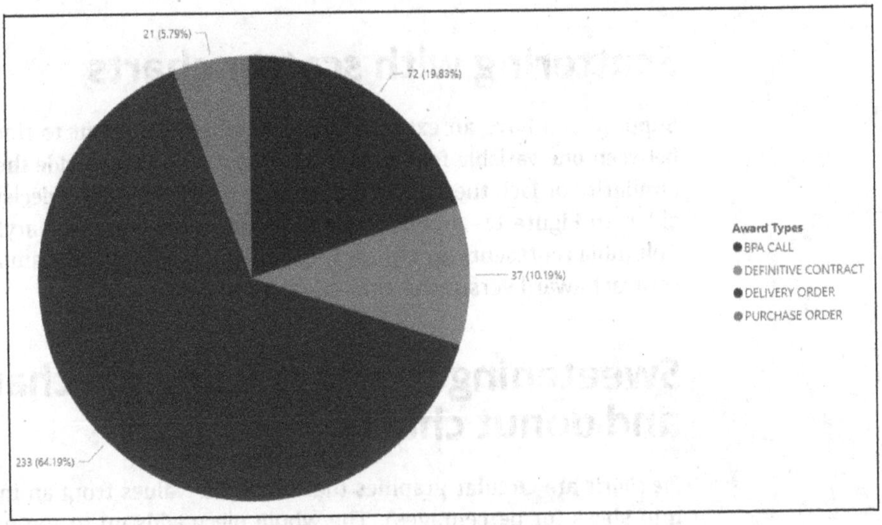

FIGURE 12-21: A pie chart.

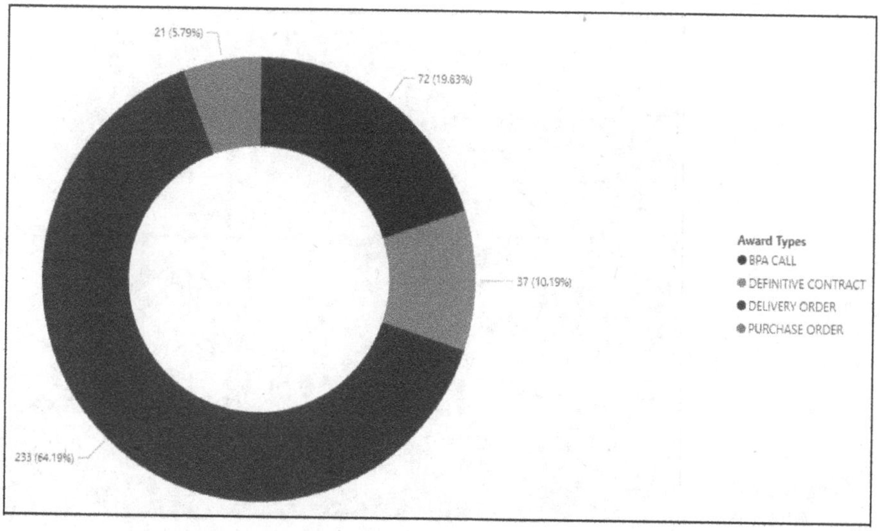

FIGURE 12-22: A donut chart.

Branching out with treemaps

Weight and proportionality require that a user have a better understanding of data from a hierarchical perspective. The treemap, with its series of nested rectangles of various sizes, offers such a perspective. Corresponding to the summarization of values or frequency, more prominent representations show more activity. In contrast, smaller rectangles represent a smaller subset of data within a branch. The data volume on the left side of a treemap is always proportionally greater than that on the right, as though you're reading a book by its cover from left to right to tell a story.

The treemap in Figure 12-23 illustrates a few measures. First, it measures the distribution of contracts across three locations: Virginia, Maryland, and District of Columbia for a specific product. Virginia has the lion's share of product and service sales. Next, within each state, the division of contract types is illustrated. Across each location, delivery orders were the most popular contract vehicle used.

Keying in on Indicators

Whenever you're trying to measure the effectiveness of a business goal, you want to compare one or more like-kind measures. Power BI offers *Indicators*, or *Key Performance Indicators* (KPIs), to help you measure the value your business provides against one or more variables. Several types of critical performance indicator visualizations are available.

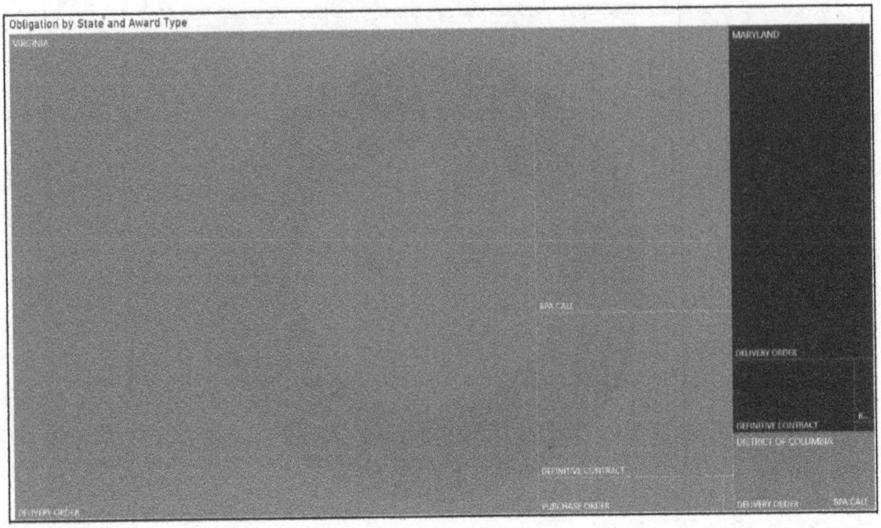

FIGURE 12-23: A treemap.

Gauges

When you think of KPIs, a *gauge* is often used as a quick way to display a data point comparing a value to a target range. Suppose you're tracking budget financials. In Figure 12-24, the total fiscal obligations for a specific product across five years (2019 – 2024) is $637 million.

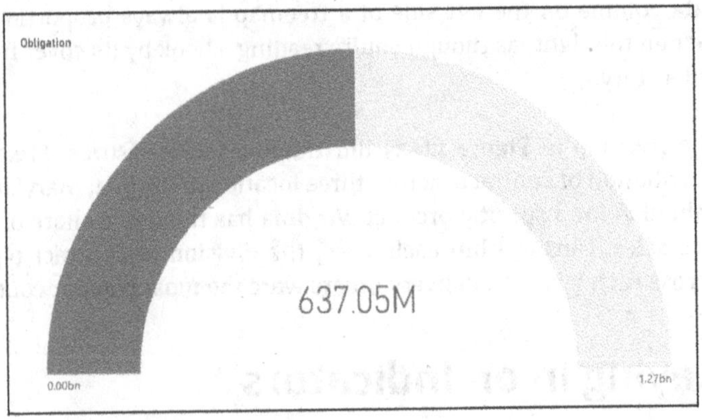

FIGURE 12-24: Using a gauge.

Cards and multi-cards

Suppose you're looking for a single number to help you address a specific statistic. In that case, the Card indicator can help you track your data. Examples of card uses are total sales, market share, or, as shown in Figure 12-25, the obligated dollar amount like the gauge in Figure 12-24. The multi-card example shows a breakout of the spend across the three states (see Figure 12-26).

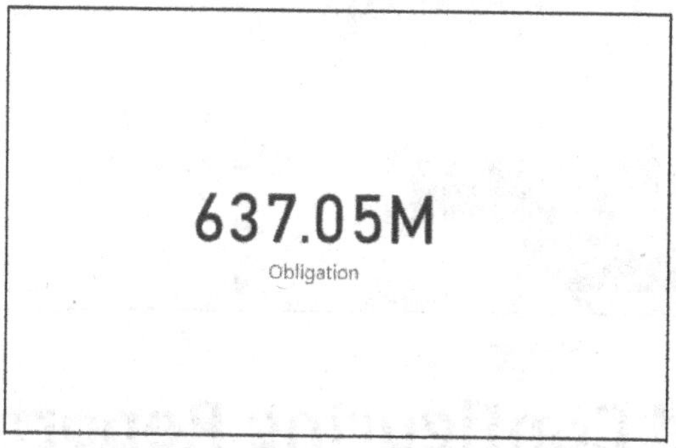

FIGURE 12-25: A card example.

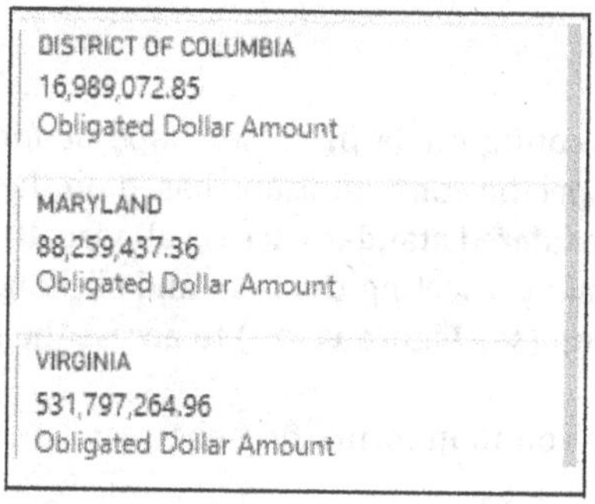

FIGURE 12-26: A multi-card example.

Zeroing in with slicers

Suppose you want to create a visual drill-down filter for a large set of table data so that the user can sort and filter to their needs. In that case, a *slicer* — a dashboard-style tool that can be integrated directly into the report, letting users select values as they analyze the data — may be just what you need. You can choose dashboards, drop-down, or check box slicers. An example of several slicer types can be found in Figure 12-27, along with an example of tabular data.

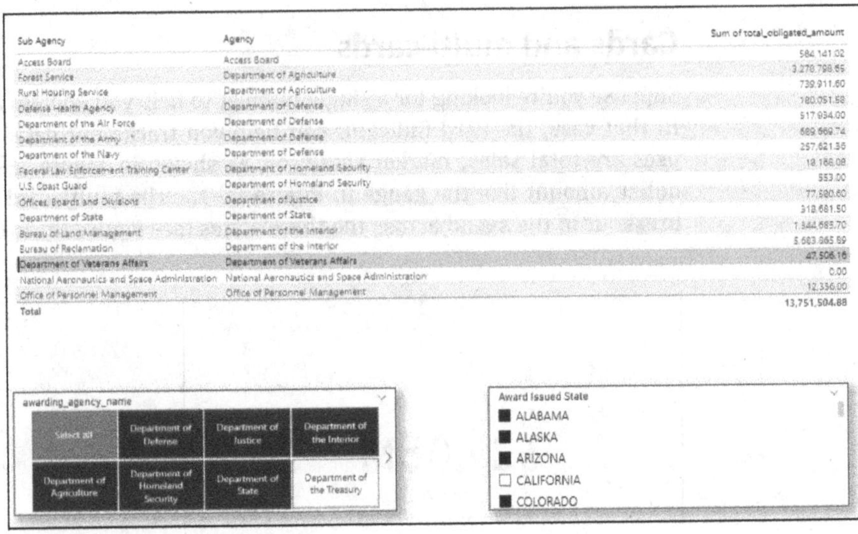

FIGURE 12-27: A slicer and table example.

Formatting and Configuring Report Visualizations

All visuals in Power BI are configurable in some shape or form. Though some visualizations have report-specific configurations based on their predefined criteria, many items can be considered standard across all visualizations. No matter what, you can format a visual by selecting the item and clicking the Visualization pane's handy Paint Roller icon (see Figure 12-28) to access the formatting tools.

Here's a description of some common formatting choices:

- **General formatting:** Here's where you can select the *x*-position, *y*-position, width, height, and *alt text* — the description used for accessibility options.
- **Title:** Format the title text, text and word wrapping, color (font and background), and text features (alignment, font size, and font face).
- **Background:** Set the page and visualization background.
- **Lock aspect:** Lock a visual element based on the proportion of the specific object on the canvas.
- **Borders:** Format the border colors and radii of your visuals.

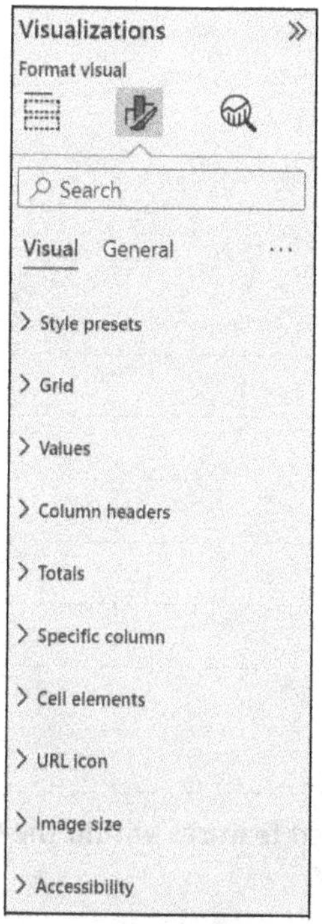

FIGURE 12-28: Formatting features found in the Visualizations pane.

- **Shadow:** Set the shadow color and position.
- **Tooltips:** Format any default or report-specific tooltips (descriptors).
- **Headers:** Hide or show headers based on conditions.

REMEMBER

Many other options are available, depending on the visualization. The preceding list covers only the options that are available across all visualizations.

Configuring the report page

Formatting a report page isn't much different from formatting a visual element, except that a report may have multiple visuals. To handle this, go straight to the Visualizations panel. Once there, click the Paint Roller icon. On the screen that appears, you should then go to the General tab. Here is where you can standardize the report configuration, including titles, properties, and icons for a report (see Figure 12-29).

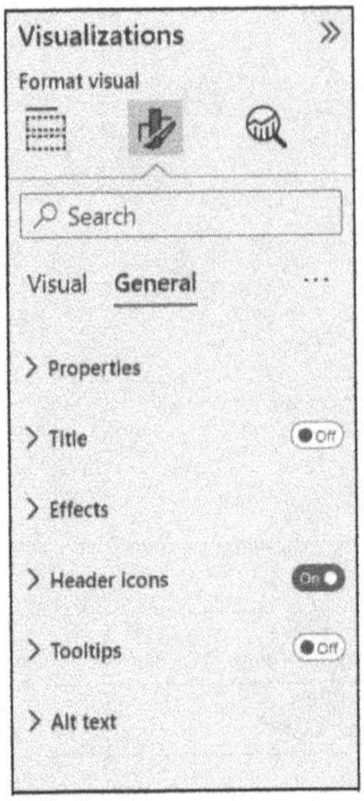

FIGURE 12-29: Configuring report properties on the General tab.

You can format the following page-related features within the General tab under Properties:

- **Page information:** Modify the report's name, turn tooltips on and off, and enable Q&A across an entire page, not just a specific visual.
- **Page size:** Pick the size factor for your visualization, which then impacts the paper type and page size (see Figure 12-30).
- **Page background:** Configure the background color of the report page.
- **Page alignment:** Decide whether to make the content of your reports flush-left top or flush-left center on a page.
- **Titles:** Brand a report with a specific look and feel for the title of your report (see Figure 12-31).
- **Object-level design aesthetics:** Change the background color, add a visual border, or apply a shadow to the report object, not just the page (see Figure 12-32).

REMEMBER

The best way to ensure consistency when it comes to report formatting is to create a page once and duplicate the page configuration multiple times. That saves you the wasted effort of re-creating the wheel several times over.

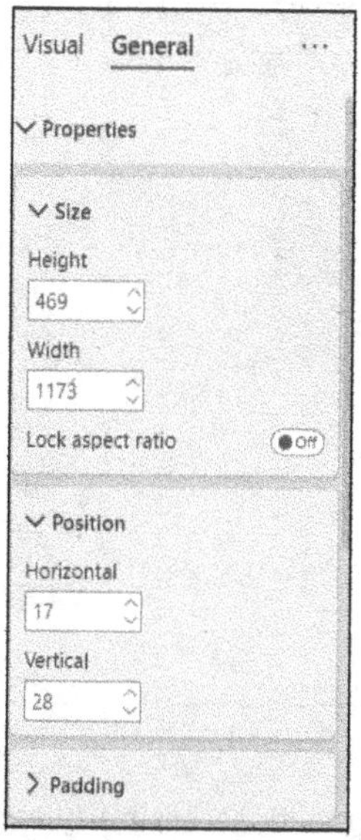

FIGURE 12-30: Page layout properties.

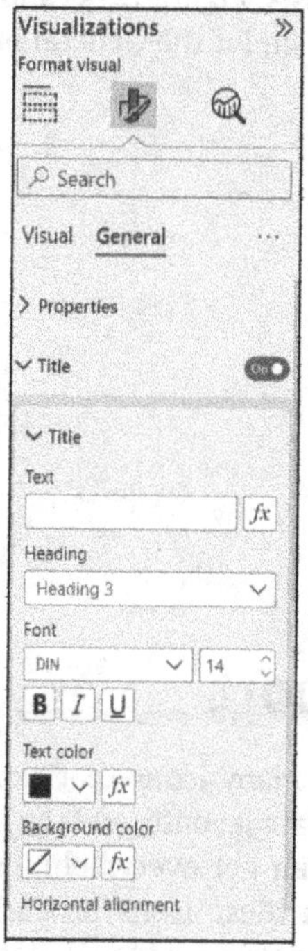

FIGURE 12-31: Example of branding for a report.

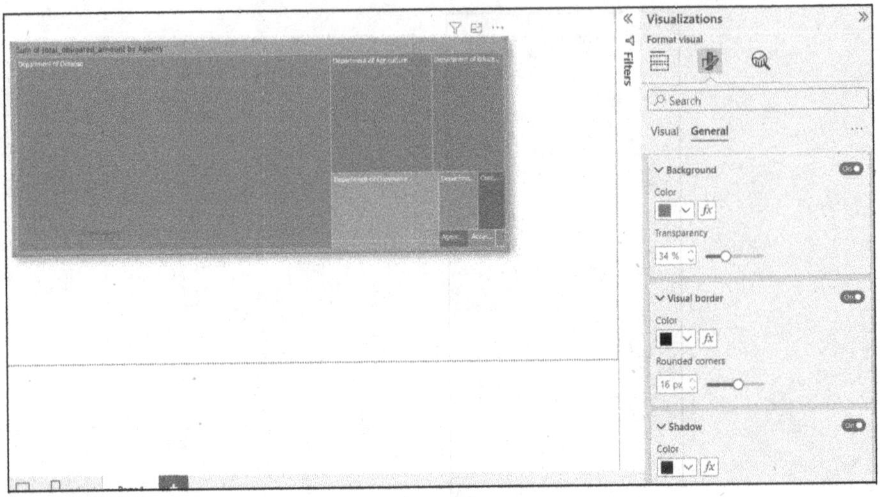

FIGURE 12-32: Object-level design for a report.

TIP

For those looking to ensure your report meets accessibility compliance requirements, there is an option to add *alt text* (a way to describe things for those requiring accessibility support) on a per-object basis. Figure 12-33 shows an example of the Alt Text editor. You can find this option under the General pane as well.

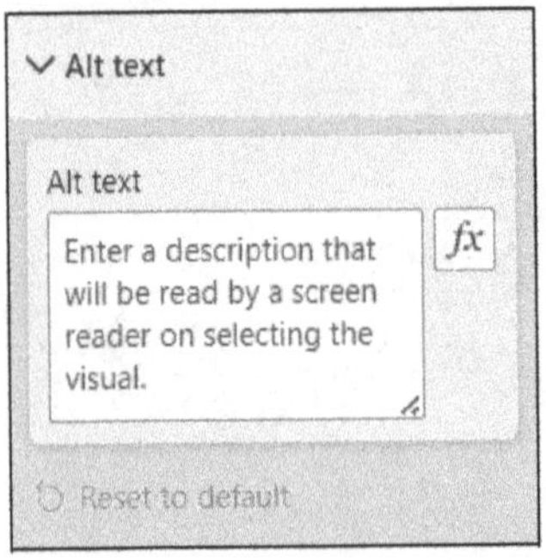

FIGURE 12-33: Alt Text editor.

Removing icons in a report

Throughout a Power BI report, you'll find many icons that control functionality within the report — pinning, focus mode, data layouts, and the list goes on. Power BI can be a powerful tool, but the icons can get overwhelming if you want the visualization to shine on its own. To turn these icons on and off, click on the report object. Then head over to the Formatting pane. Under the General tab, locate the Icon option under the Header Icons drop-down list. Here you can turn on or off a dozen plus (and growing) features that are likely embedded within your Power BI report, as shown in Figure 12-34. Examples include Visual Warnings and Visual Errors.

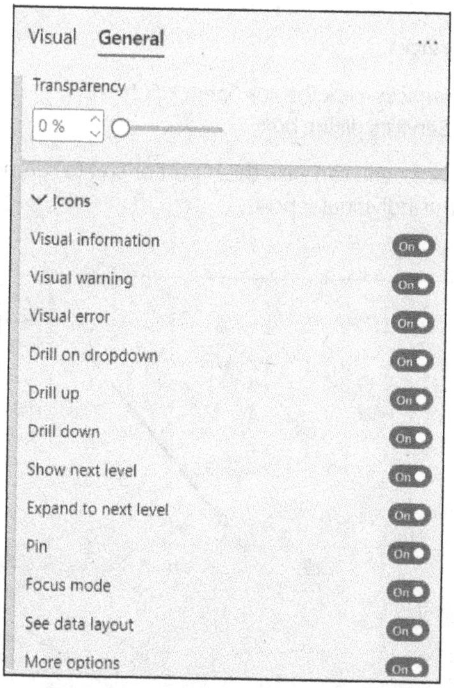

FIGURE 12-34: Managing the icons on a Power BI report.

Publishing Your Report from the Desktop to the Web

It's showtime! Once you've made all the changes to your report page using Power BI Desktop, you'll want to find the Publish button on the top toolbar within the Home tab, and follow these steps:

1. **Click the Publish button.**

   Power BI prompts you to save the Power BI Report to your desktop locally. This renders a PBIX file. The Power BI Service interface appears.

2. **Select the workspace where you want to save the report for viewing and distribution within Power BI Services (see Figure 12-35), and then click Save.**

   Power BI notifies you that the report has reached its destination workspace for viewing. You can read more about workspaces in Chapter 13.

3. **Open Power BI Services.**

   To open Power BI Services, click the link Open *<file name>* in Power BI from the Power BI Services dialog box.

   From Power BI Services, you can view the report or create compelling dashboards from the individual reports.

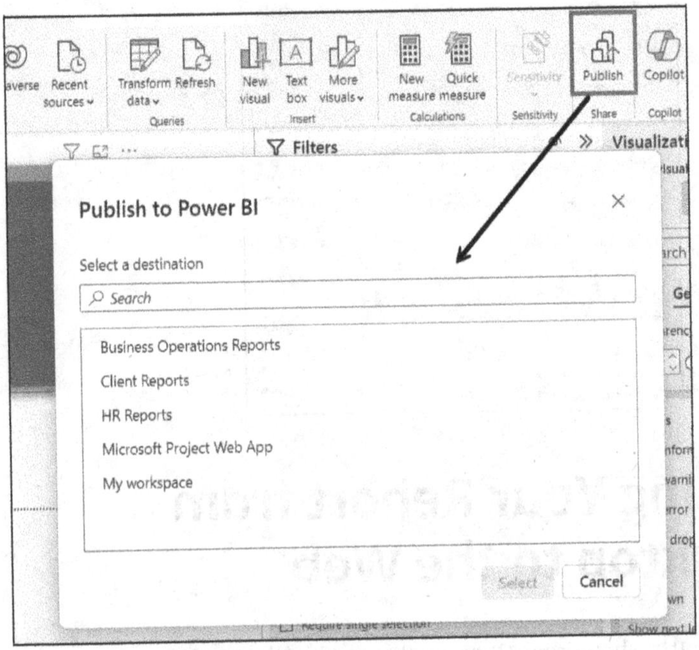

FIGURE 12-35: Publish a report from Power BI Desktop to Power BI Services.

Diving into Dashboards

Picture this: a mixture of pictures and text neatly organized like a beautiful canvas. It tells you that everything in your organization is running smoothly, but then one of the visuals changes. Alarm bells go off — figurative ones, at least — causing many phones to ring and SMS messages to be sent. The person responding to the emergency doesn't have to dig too deep because the organization has collected a series of datasets, available in the form of a single user experience, not a collection of ad hoc reports.

The datasets on a single canvas all give real-time access to the current state of operations. The dashboard may appear to be a big mush of data, but it's meaningful data presented in a way that those who have mastered the intricacies of the dashboard can immediately see what's wrong. This section introduces you to the mysteries of dashboarding using Power BI Services.

Before your initiation into the mysteries, here are a few critical principles regarding dashboarding with Power BI:

- **You can only create a dashboard using Power BI Services.** To truly experience the full breadth of dashboarding, you need a Pro or Premium license.
- **A dashboard is meant to fill a business void.** A report can contain only a single dataset. Though it's perfectly okay to use just one dataset in a dashboard, using dashboards to present multiple datasets is far more common.
- **A dashboard is a compilation of many objects.** It manages that compilation by limiting itself to only one screen.
- **Each visual in a dashboard is referred to as a *tile*.** In reports, visuals are referred to as *outputs*.
- **Power BI Services is a web-based service.** Power BI Desktop doesn't require an Internet connection. Data alerts are only available using Power BI Services.

Configuring dashboards

A *dashboard*, in its simplest form, is merely a collage of many data objects that can be pinned to a single page. Most times, the items are visual; at other times, the content contained in the dashboard may have text, video, audio, or navigation to other dashboards and data sources. Dashboards can integrate resources using reports, Excel workbooks, insights, Q&A results, and multimedia across content providers.

Creating a new dashboard

If you're logged into Power BI Services, you should ensure that you have a dataset and some visuals that can be placed on a dashboard. If you've never created a dashboard, follow these steps:

1. **In Power BI Services, open My Workspace or the workspace you want to add the Dashboard for consumption.**
2. **Click New at the top of the workspace window.**

3. **Choose Dashboard from the menu that appears, as shown in Figure 12-36.**
4. **Enter the name of the new dashboard and then click Create.**

   A blank canvas is set up for you to begin porting and pinning reports,

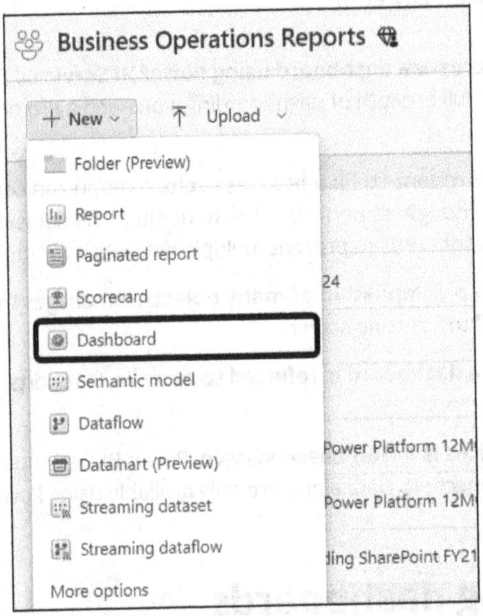

FIGURE 12-36: Creating a dashboard.

Enriching your dashboard with content

You need to keep a couple of points in mind when trying to integrate an object on your dashboard canvas. The first thing to consider is what type of objects are needed to accentuate a planned report compilation on a dashboard. The second has to do with the layout and number of objects you intend to pin to the canvas.

At this point, you can add a few different items beyond the reports proper:

- **Web content:** HTML-based web content
- **Images:** Publicly accessible images exclusively
- **Text boxes:** Static text that can be formatted

» **Video:** Videos that can be embedded either on YouTube or Vimeo

» **Custom streaming data:** Real-time data coming from an API, Azure Stream, or PubNub source

TECHNICAL STUFF

You may be familiar with most of the content sources described in the preceding list, but if you are interested in extremely large datasets being presented in a dashboard, consider using Azure Streams or PubNub. Azure Stream is the abbreviated name for Azure Stream Analytics, a real-time analytics and complex event-processing engine designed to analyze and process high volumes of (usually live) data from multiple sources simultaneously. PubNub, like Azure Streams, is another real-time analytics streaming service focused on delivering content using a real-time publish/subscribe messaging process, primarily for Internet of Things (IoT) devices.

To add content-based objects to the canvas — *tiles*, in Power BI-speak — follow these steps:

1. **On the dashboard canvas, go to the Edit menu.**
2. **Choose Add a Tile.**
3. **From the new menu that appears, choose one of the listed object types.**
4. **Customize the object as desired on the dashboard canvas.**

WARNING

All the content you place on a dashboard must be publicly accessible. Even if authentication or uploading is necessary for a user to view the data, Power BI doesn't presently support such features.

Pinning reports

Creating a report visualization tile, the objects that reside on the dashboard, is a slightly different process from other content additions. With dashboards, you pin the existing report visualization you've created in Power BI Desktop and ported over to Power BI Service as individual objects. A collection of reports is then brought together to create a singular dashboard. To pin a report visualization, follow these steps:

1. **Go to a workspace that contains a report, including one or more visualizations you'd like to include in a dashboard.**
2. **Locate the Pin to a Dashboard option in the Visual header of each chart visual (see Figure 12-37).**

3. **On the Pin to Dashboard screen that appears, click a radio button to specify whether the visualization will be part of a new dashboard or added to an existing dashboard (see Figure 12-38).**

   You'll add the visualization to an existing dashboard, so you should choose that option. You then use the drop-down menu to select the dashboard you want.

4. **After making your selections, click Pin.**

   Repeat Steps 1–4 for as many visualizations as you want to include on your dashboard. The result is a dashboard like the one that appears in Figure 12-39.

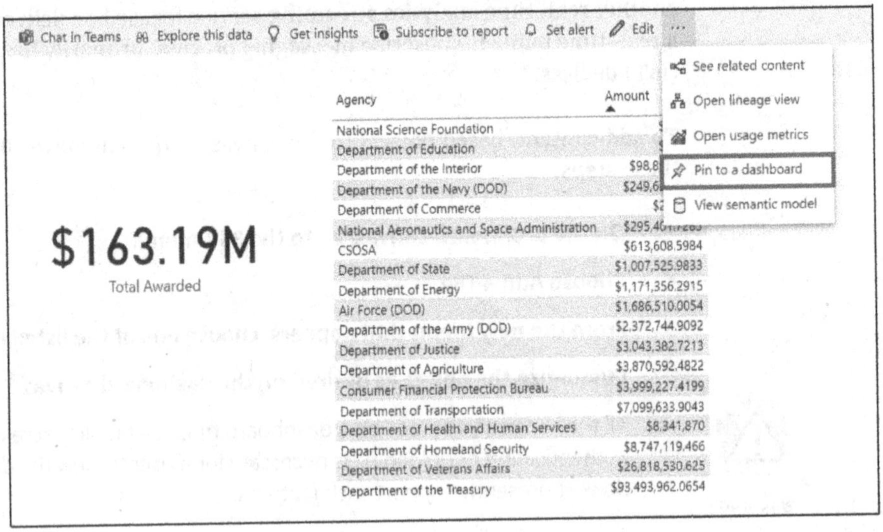

FIGURE 12-37: The Pin to a Dashboard option.

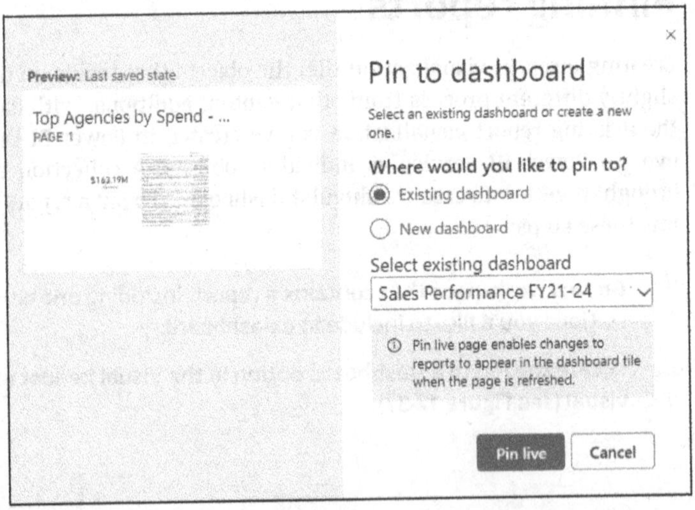

FIGURE 12-38: Opting for a new or existing dashboard.

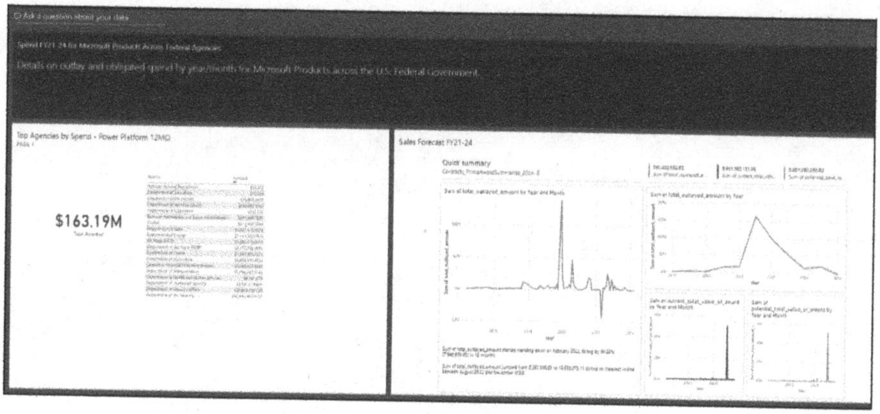

FIGURE 12-39: A finished dashboard with a text tile.

REMEMBER

Pinned visualizations aren't interactive. Updates are visible only after you refresh the dataset from which the visualization was derived. If you're looking for real-time data, you use the Custom Streaming Data tile.

IN THIS CHAPTER

» Setting up sharing and collaboration with Power BI Services

» Accelerating business operations with monitoring and performance tools

» Troubleshooting data online by viewing a data lineage

Chapter 13 Sharing and Collaborating with Power BI Services

After experiencing the entire data lifecycle across data sources, building visualizations, and publishing reports, your next step is to share the data from your desktop with everyone who is a stakeholder in your business. To do that, you have to switch gears and move to the web because you're unlikely to want users mangling your Power BI Desktop data. Instead, they should be using Power BI Services to carry out activities using a workspace, which is a crucial feature for collaboration and sharing. In this chapter, you learn about workspaces and how you can collaborate, share, and accelerate your business operations with monitoring tools, all available using Power BI Services.

Working Together in a Workspace

Picture yourself in an art museum. You can explore visuals and read anecdotal tales about each work by yourself or with others by your side. A Power BI workspace, available in Power BI Services, is analogous to curating content for a museum, but of course, it's data! A workspace is created by a Power BI designer to manage a collection of dashboards and reports. Think of a workspace as a file cabinet. The designer can share the workspace with users based on roles, responsibilities, and permissions. The designer can even build an app by bundling together targeted collections of dashboards and reports and distributing them to their organization, whether that involves just a few users or an entire community. These apps, called *template* apps, are distributable on a variety of devices, including desktops and smartphones.

Defining the types of workspaces

The idea behind a Power BI workspace is that it should contain all content specific to a singular app. You might even consider creating multiple workspaces based on the type of user or report. For example, you may want one workspace exclusively for PBIX files and another for paginated reports. When designers create an app, they bundle all the content assets necessary for use and deployment they might embed in an app, or utilize standalone in a workspace. The content can include anything from datasets to dashboards to reports.

REMEMBER

A workspace may not necessarily include all content types. It may contain reports, datasets, or dashboards exclusively. It depends on the business purpose and how the designer wants to share and collaborate with other users.

The workspaces shown in Figure 13-1 are intended for sharing and collaboration using a collaboration scheme with others. You access them via your My Workspace (see Figure 13-2), as it is your desktop on the Internet for Power BI. You can publish data from Power BI Desktop to Power BI Services. Then, you can organize, store, and share those assets just published online to one or more workspaces that you might intend to use for collaboration. In Figure 13-3, you find assets that were created in Power BI Desktop now available in a workspace. For this chapter, the project is referred to as the Pipeline Identification project.

You may wonder why you should bother to transition from Power BI Desktop to Power BI Services. As a sharing and collaboration feature in Power BI Services, workspaces allow you to do the following:

- Sustain focused collaboration among a small or globally dispersed team.
- Use workspaces to house reports and dashboards for one team or multiple teams.
- Streamline the sharing and presentation of reports and dashboards by housing them in a single environment.
- Maintain security by controlling access to datasets, reports, and dashboards.

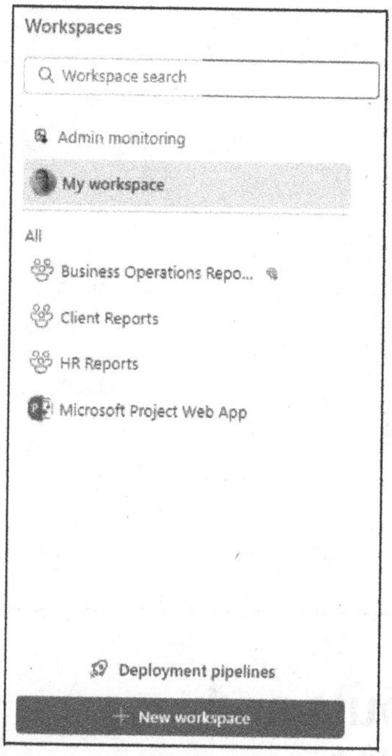

FIGURE 13-1: A list of workspace apps.

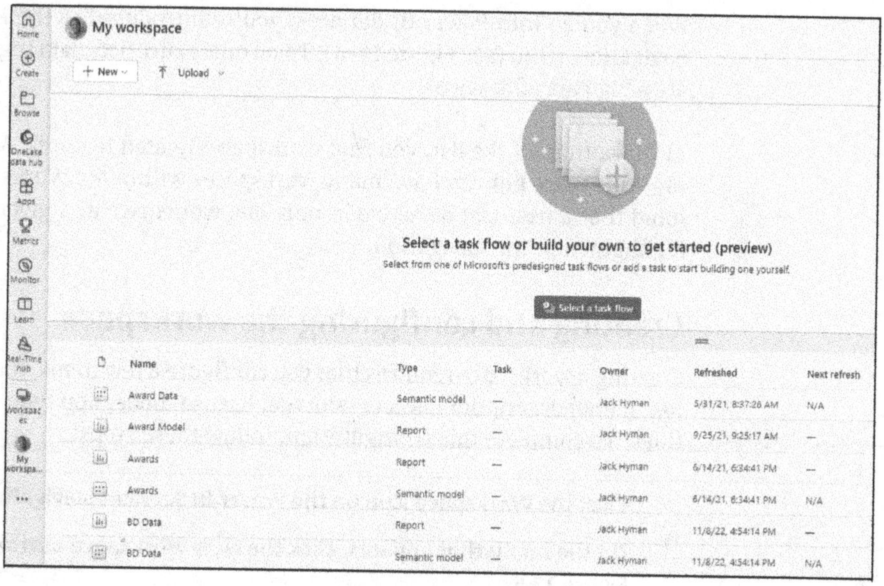

FIGURE 13-2: The My Workspace interface.

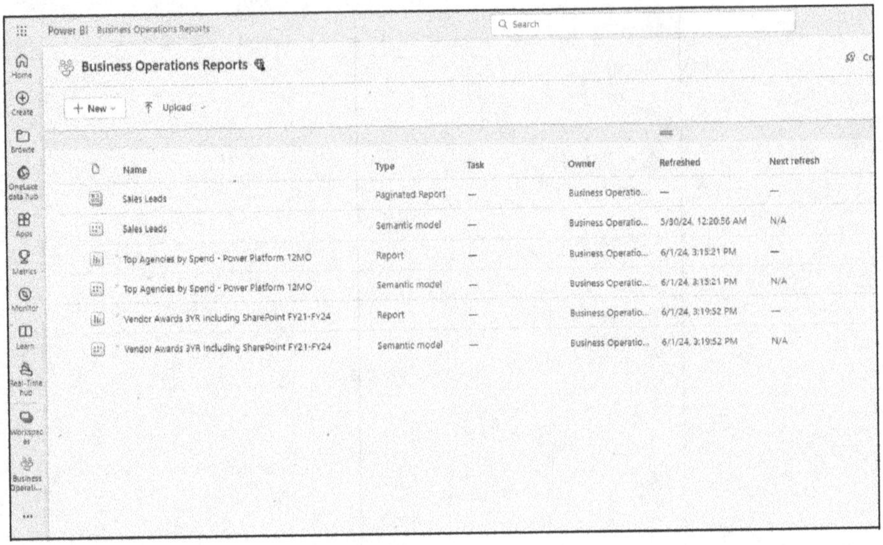

FIGURE 13-3: The content of a workspace in Power BI.

Figuring out the nuts and bolts of workspaces

When you go into Power BI Services, you're introduced to the Power BI Services navigation menu (see Figure 13-4). To no one's surprise, data ingestion and access are a big part of Services.

At the bottom of the list, you find workspace-related features. A user has a single My Workspace but can have many workspaces within My Workspace. Just keep in mind that a user can be active in only one workspace at a given time — the one highlighted in the navigation.

Creating and configuring the workspace

Creating a workspace requires that you configure a few items, including its branding, name, description, access, storage, license mode, app type, and security settings. To complete this configuration, follow these steps:

1. **Click the Workspace icon on the Power BI Services Navigation pane.**
2. **On the menu that appears, click the New Workspace button, shown in Figure 13-5.**

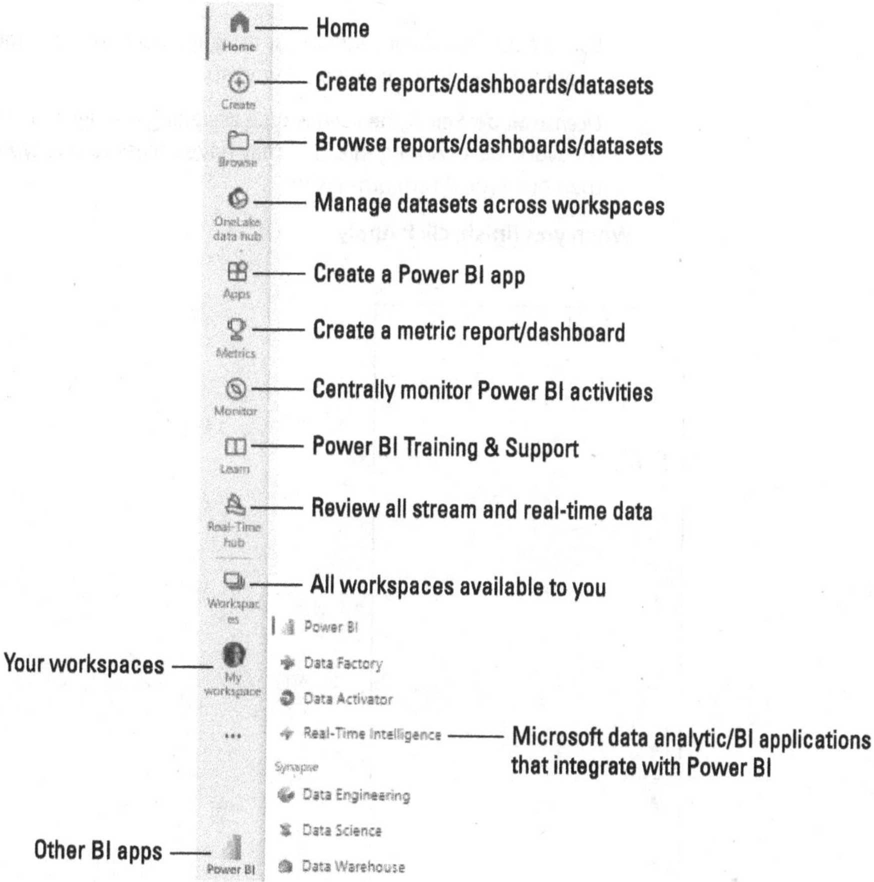

FIGURE 13-4: The navigation menu in Power BI Services.

3. **In the Create Workspace window that appears on the right side, use the settings to configure the new workspace.**

   Here are your options, divided between Standard (see Figure 13-6) and Advanced (see Figure 13-7):

   - *Name:* Name the workspace based on its content and datasets. Treat this name as you would for a file collection.
   - *Description:* Describe the purpose of the workspace.
   - *Upload:* Save a photo from your desktop to customize the workspace experience.

- *Contact List:* Workspace admins or assigned users receive notifications about updates in each Power BI workspace.
- *License Mode:* Select the license type assigning the right to access content in the workspace. An organization may have access to one type (Pro) or more than one type (Premium-based).

4. When you finish, click Apply.

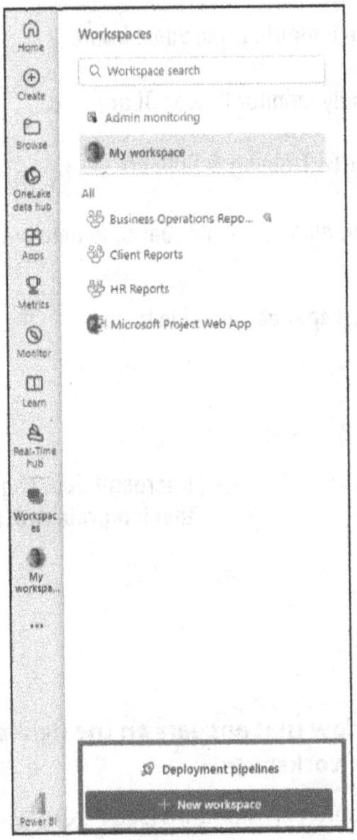

FIGURE 13-5: The New Workspace button.

Wandering into access management

A big part of sharing and collaborating starts with access management. You must configure who gains access to workspaces and each of the content assets inside the workspaces. You as the designer can assign four distinct role types: admin, member, contributor, or viewer. To change access, follow these steps:

1. Click the Workspace icon on the Power BI navigation pane.

2. Choose the workspace you want to modify from the menu that appears.

3. On the right side of the workspace label, select the three vertical dots.

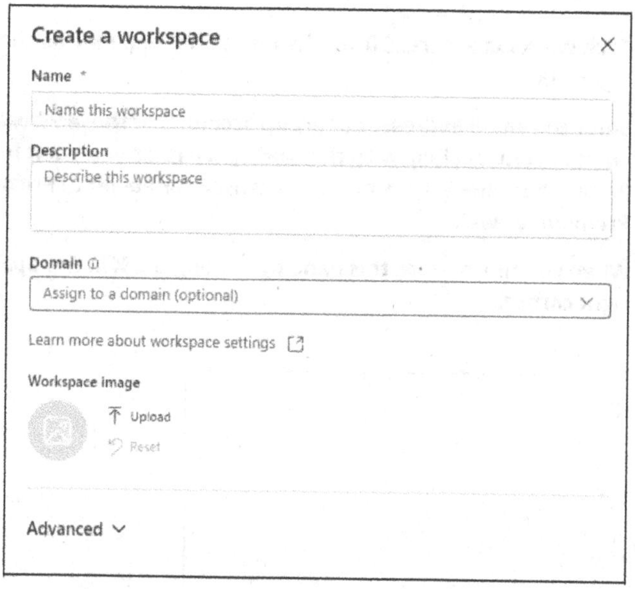

FIGURE 13-6: Configuring the standard features of a workspace.

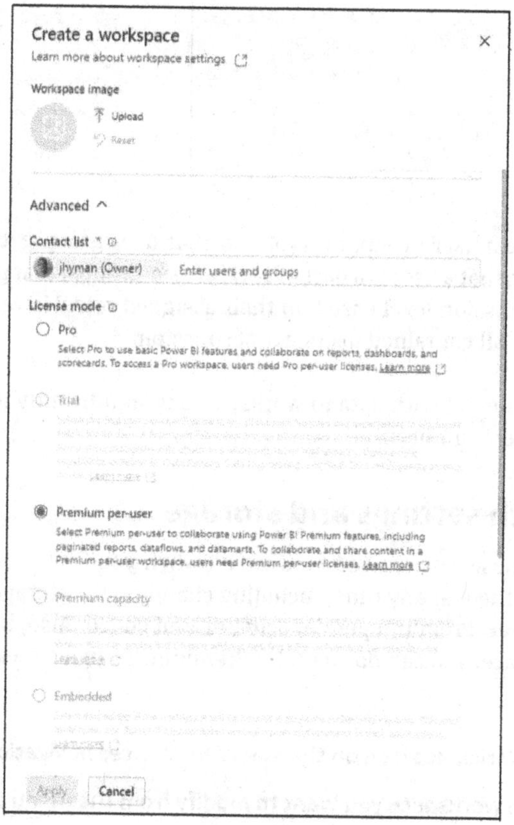

FIGURE 13-7: Configuring the advanced features of a workspace.

4. **Click Workspace Access from the menu that appears, as shown in Figure 13-8.**
5. **Enter the email addresses or group accounts of those whose access you want to control along with the workspace roles you want to assign them. Remember, these users must be licensed for Power BI Pro or Premium as well.**
6. **When you finish, close this pane by clicking the X in the upper-right corner.**

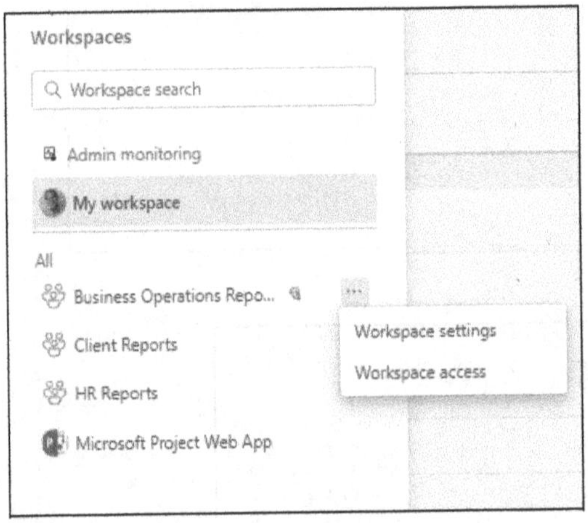

FIGURE 13-8: Assigning workspace access.

REMEMBER

When you create a user group, everyone in that user group gets assigned to the group. Assuming that a user is a part of several user groups, that person is assigned the highest permission level based on their assigned role. However, if you embed the user groups, all contained users get permission.

WARNING

Your ability to interact with data in workspaces is significantly limited unless you have a Pro or Premium license.

Dealing with settings and storage

Remember all those settings you configured when you first created a workspace? You can modify them at any time, including changing the storage type from Pro to Premium Per User, Premium per Capacity, or Embedded. Also, if you're looking to delete a workspace, you can do so under Premium. To make these changes, follow these steps:

1. **Click the Workspace icon on the Power BI Services navigation pane.**
2. **Choose the workspace you want to modify from the menu that appears.**

3. **On the right side of the workspace label, click the vertical dots.**
4. **Click Workspace Settings.**

   Doing so brings up the Workspace Settings pane on the right side of the screen.
5. **Click Premium (see Figure 13-9).**
6. **Select the capacity choice that best reflects your need.**
7. **When you finish, click Save.**

TECHNICAL STUFF

You may be wondering what exactly the Embedded option involves. Suppose that you've used an enterprise application or visited a website and seen analytics features embedded. In that case, Power BI might just be the solution behind the application or website. The Embedded choice allows you to build an app so that a customer does not need to authenticate.

WARNING

Depending on the type of Power BI license you own, this interface will vary. You may not have some of the features shown. For Figure 13-9, I assume that a user has Power BI Premium Per User.

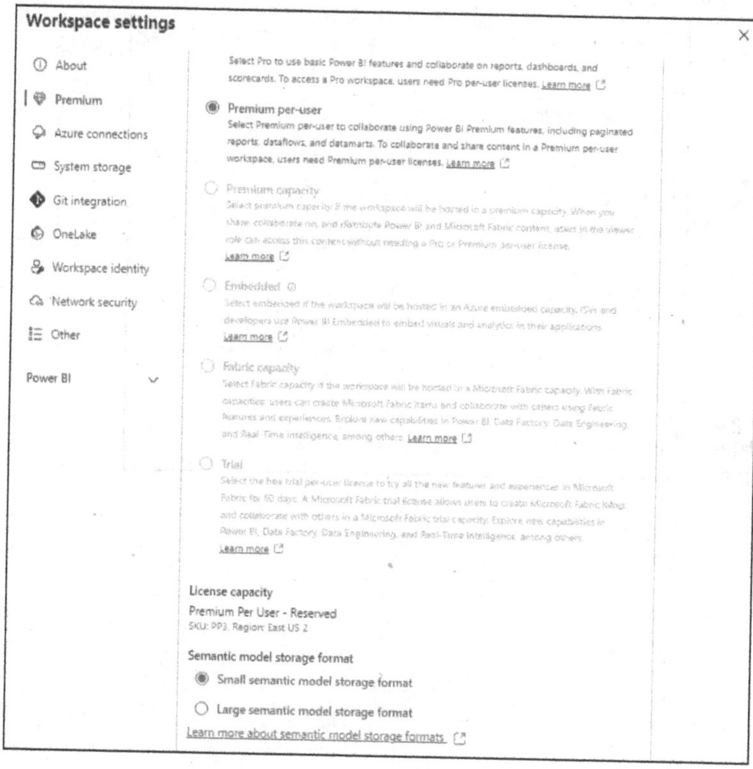

FIGURE 13-9: Workspace Settings pane.

Slicing and Dicing Data

As users consume your reports, dashboards, and datasets, you might want to know *how* they consume these content assets. That's why Microsoft has integrated monitoring and alternate data analysis tools within Power BI for those users who have Pro and Premium licensing to evaluate such metrics.

You can slice and dice usage data in several ways. Options include analyzing data in Excel as well as accessing a high-level view of your data with the Quick Insights report. You can also use metrics reports to understand who is accessing and viewing your reports and dashboards. Click the new button at the top of the page to create data outputs including reports, dashboards, and semantic models within a workspace (see Figure 13-10). If you want to create a report specifically for a semantic model, click the three dots, and then select a data output format (see Figure 13-11). Here you can analyze your data in Excel, create a report, or create a paginated report. You can also let Copilot analyze your dataset and auto-create a report for you.

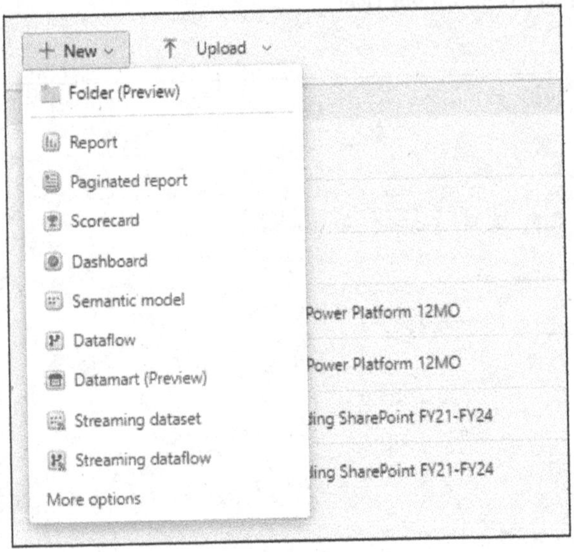

FIGURE 13-10: Creating a data-driven output.

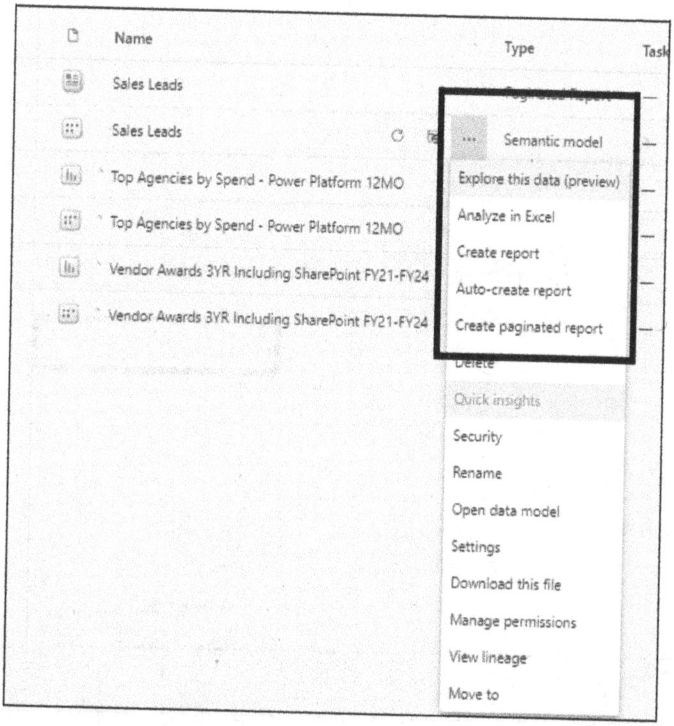

FIGURE 13-11: Various ways to create reports and analyze data.

Benefiting from Quick Insights

Perhaps you want a quick snapshot of a dataset. Or maybe you're looking for patterns, trends, and ambiguities in your data. The anomalies in the data can be challenging to find if you're first starting and don't know where to start looking. However, Power BI at least attempts to do the hard work for you using the power of Copilot for Power BI. With Copilot for Power BI using the Quick Insights report, you can identify critical trends, patterns, indicators, and anomalies in your data. To access Quick Insights, locate a data model that has several (at least 5–6 columns of data) with several hundred rows of data. Once you locate the semantic model, click on the three dots (or *ellipsis*), and select Get Quick Insights, as shown in Figure 13-12. This will produce an optimal synopsis for you, as shown in Figure 13-13. The dataset used in this example came from `usaspending.gov` and includes 278 columns worth of data. The specific query included 2,400 rows of data.

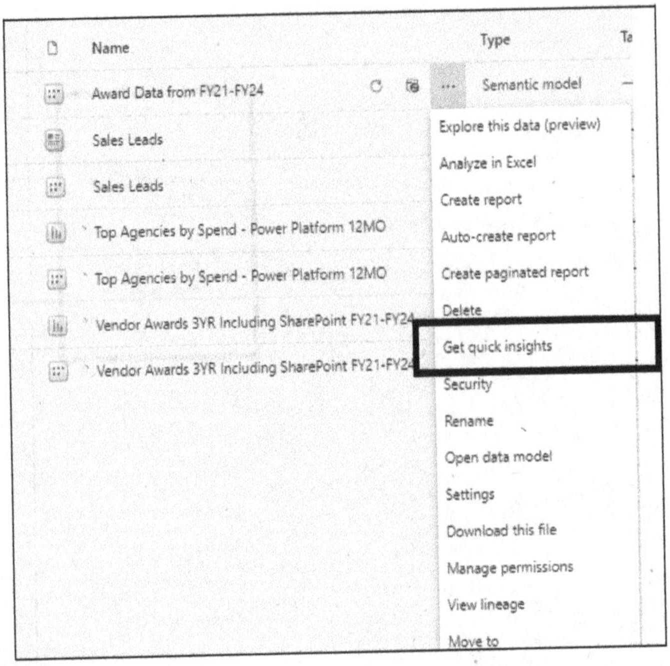

FIGURE 13-12: The Get Quick Insights menu option.

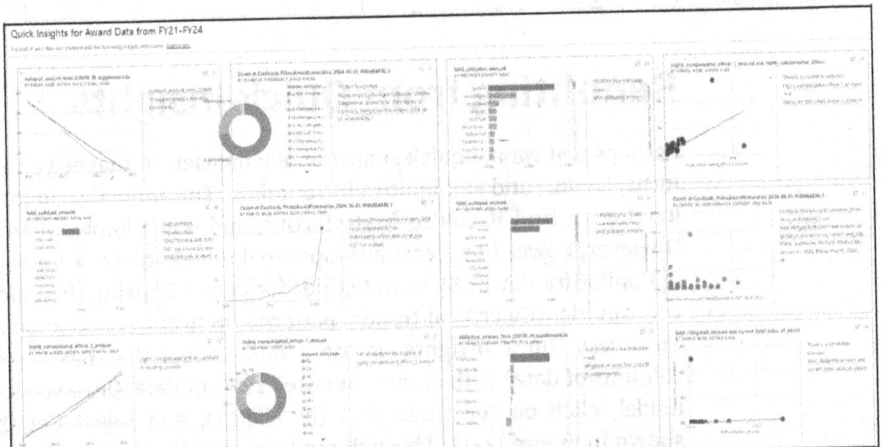

FIGURE 13-13: Example of Quick Insights output.

Using usage metric reports

Ever want to know how popular a report or dashboard is? Or perhaps who accessed an item in a workspace today, this week, or over time? Microsoft recognized that data access metrics help improve a designer's ability to deliver best-in-class analytics. A usage metrics report can help users analyze data points, including distribution types, views, viewers, viewer rank, views per day, and unique views per day, as shown in Figure 13-14.

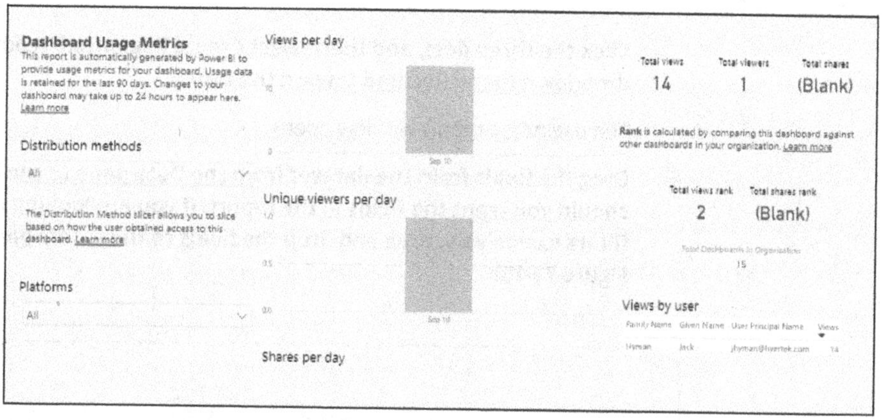

FIGURE 13-14: A usage metrics report.

Working with paginated reports

Earlier in this chapter, you see how to create, update, and delete reports as standalone content assets in Power BI Desktop and Services. The standalone report is optimized for data exploration and interactivity, but these reports are not printable. You are bound by the first page only. That's where the paginated report comes in handy, as it is a report type that can be distributed to users in several formats where the data continuously flows. In other words, the data doesn't break at the end of page one. You do, however, have limits as to how the report is laid out.

Unlike web-based reports, paginated reports are meant for print. That means they're formatted to fit well on paper. You might call the presentation of these reports "pixel-perfect." Suppose that you're looking to render a highly sophisticated PDF. An example might be a year-end report or profit-and-loss statement. In that case, a paginated report is an excellent choice.

To create a paginated report, follow these steps:

1. **Open the workspace that contains your target dataset.**

   In this case, the workspace is Business Operations Reports (refer to Figure 13-3).

2. **Select the semantic model (dataset) that you would like to use to build your paginated report and then locate the three dots (ellipsis) next to the model name.**

   In this case, the semantic model is called Sales Leads.

3. **Click the three dots, and then select Create Paginated Report from the dropdown menu (located toward the top).**

   The paginated report window opens.

4. **Drag the fields from the dataset from the Data pane to the Build pane should you want the fields in the report. If you are looking to use fields as filters exclusively, drag and drop the fields to the Filters pane (see Figure 13-15).**

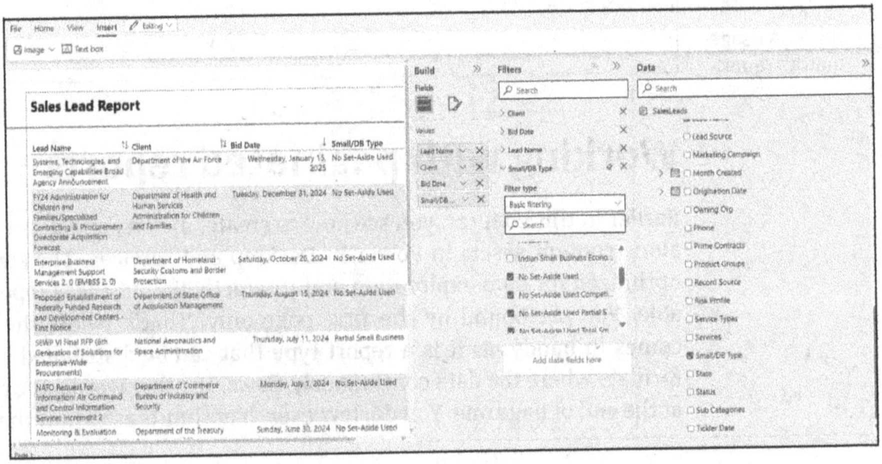

FIGURE 13-15: Building a paginated report.

5. **Your report begins populating with the relevant columns.**
6. **Modify the header and footer with images or textboxes, as desired. Format the columns by changing the fonts and aligning the text as you see fit.**
7. **Once you are done editing the paginated report, choose File ⇨ Save, and enter a name for your report.**

   In this case, the report has been saved as Sales Leads.

Any user who has access to this report, either by subscription or via collaboration with this workspace can now download and distribute the printer and download-friendly report.

REMEMBER

Though viewing a paginated report is possible as a Pro or Premium user, publishing requires a Premium license.

Troubleshooting the Use of Data Lineage

Business intelligence projects can get complex pretty quickly. Following the flow of data from one source to its destination might even be a challenge. Suppose that you've built a relatively complex, advanced analytical project that contains several data sources and maintains numerous reports and dashboards. Each of these assets has a variety of dependencies. As you review these assets, you might come upon questions such as, "What will happen to this report if I make a change to this data point?" Or you may want to better understand how a change you might make will reflect in a dataset.

Data lineage simplifies many complex processes by breaking down processes into more manageable steps. Think of it as your little detective! With data lineage, you can see the path your data takes from start to completion, which is crucial when you're scratching your head, having hit many roadblocks. Whether you're managing a workspace with a single report or dashboard or one with many, make sure that the impact of a single change in a dataset is recognized by referring to the data lineage to track those changes. A bonus is that you can resolve many data-refresh concerns with data lineage as well.

To access data lineage information, follow these steps:

1. **Go to the workspace you're targeting.**
2. **Open the item you are looking to review the lineage.**
3. **Choose Lineage from the menu that appears (see Figure 13-16).**

   Lineage view appears, as shown in Figure 13-17, for all data sources in the Business Operations Reports workspace tied to the item you've selected.

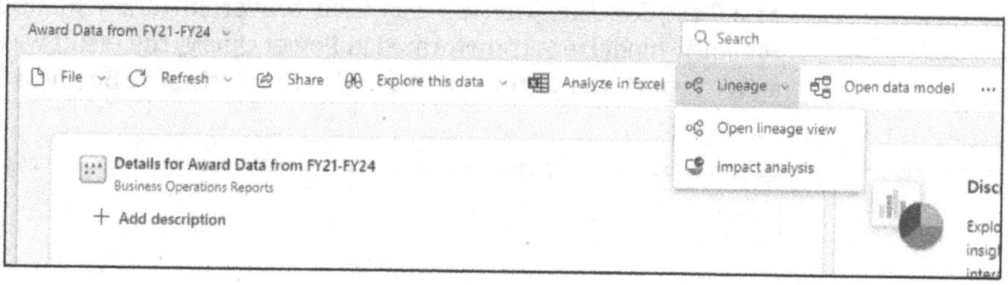

FIGURE 13-16: Gaining access to data lineage.

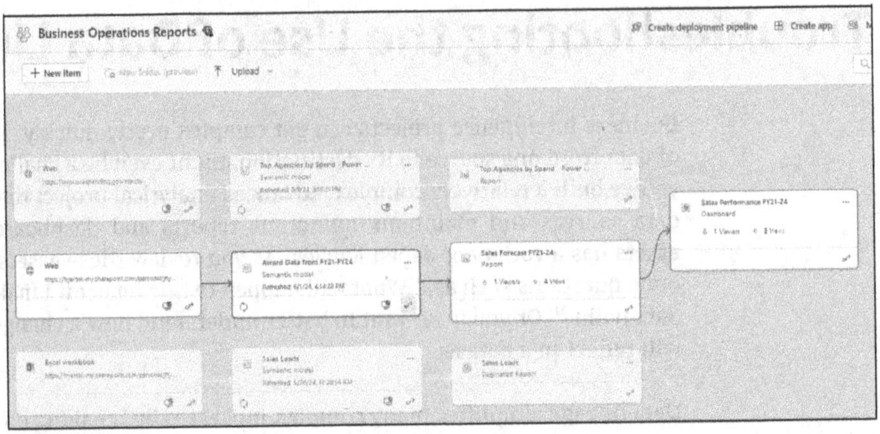

FIGURE 13-17: An example of workspace lineage.

As with other workspace features, only specific roles can access the Lineage view. You must be an admin, a contributor, or a member to see the Lineage view. Also, you must have a Power BI Pro or Premium license using an app-based workspace to make use of the view.

Once you select Lineage, the view of all items found within the workspace appears on the canvas. Figure 13-17, for example, shows the data lineage for the Business Operations Reports workspace project discussed throughout this chapter.

Lineage view provides a synopsis of all artifacts found in your workspace — datasets, dataflows, reports, and dashboards, for example. As shown in Figures 13-18, each of the cards on the canvas as represented in the Lineage view is a separate asset. The arrows between each of the cards explain the dataflows among assets. Data flows from left to right, letting you observe data as it goes from the source to the destination. Generally, the flow tells a story. In the case of Figure 13-18, the data started from the Web and was ported into Power BI Services as a Text/CSV file. The file was then converted to a semantic model. Once the semantic model was transformed in Power Query, the result was a Power BI Interactive Report (not paginated), posted to the workspace Business Operation Reports.

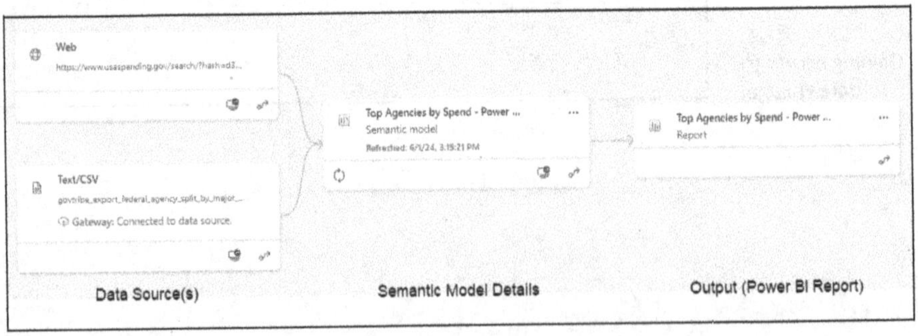

FIGURE 13-18: Example data lineage.

Datasets, Dataflows, and Lineage

It's not uncommon for datasets and dataflows to be associated with external sources. Some examples may include databases or datasets found in external workspaces. You see that — when reviewing the Semantic Model card, as shown in Figure 13-19 — a user can drill down to evaluate different factors by choosing one of these four commands. Each command reveals a different aspect of the dataset:

- **Refresh Now**: Refresh the dataset immediately, without waiting for a regularly scheduled cycle.
- **Show More:** This command displays all reports available for an associated dataset or dataflow.
- **Show Impact Across Workspace:** This command provides you with an impact analysis of how the dataset or dataflow impacts workspace activity.
- **Show Lineage**: This command provides you with a micro-level view of the dataset.

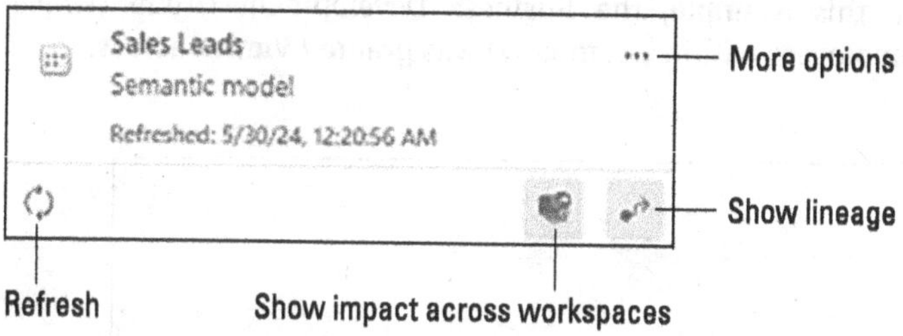

FIGURE 13-19: Drilling down into a Semantic Model card.

Step to Managing Workspace and Report Security in Power BI

Security can be configured many ways in Power BI. You can secure the workspace, the report, and the dataset. If you want to get even more granular, you can get down to the row level using row-level security. The following sections show how you can quickly secure data online.

Securing a workspace

When creating a workspace, you'll want to secure the Workspace. You'll secure the workspace by going to the Power BI Service.

1. **Choose Workspaces ⇨ New Workspace.**
2. **Name your workspace and configure the foundational settings.**
3. **Assign the relevant role to those users who are licensed for Power BI.**

   REMEMBER

   Users without licenses cannot access Power BI Services, only Power BI Desktop.
4. **To set up the security in the workspace settings, click the three dots next to your workspace, and then click Workspace Access (see Figure 13-20).**

   The Manage Access panel appears (Figure 13-21).
5. **Add users and assign them roles.**

   Options to assign access include Admin, Member, Contributor, and Viewer (see Figure 13-22).

In this example, the Business Development Group (which contains several employees within a company) was granted Viewer access.

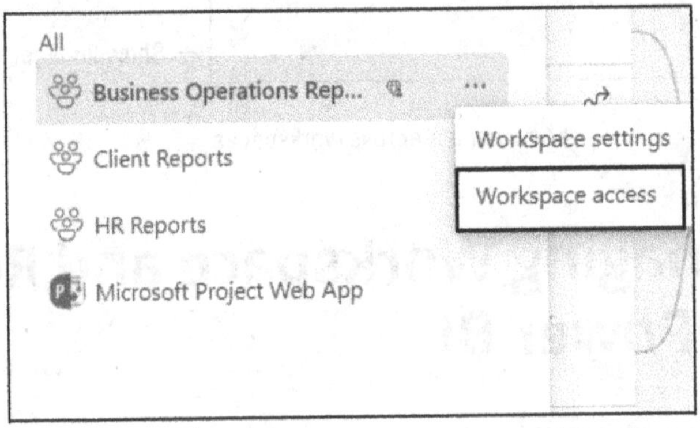

FIGURE 13-20: The Workspace Access option.

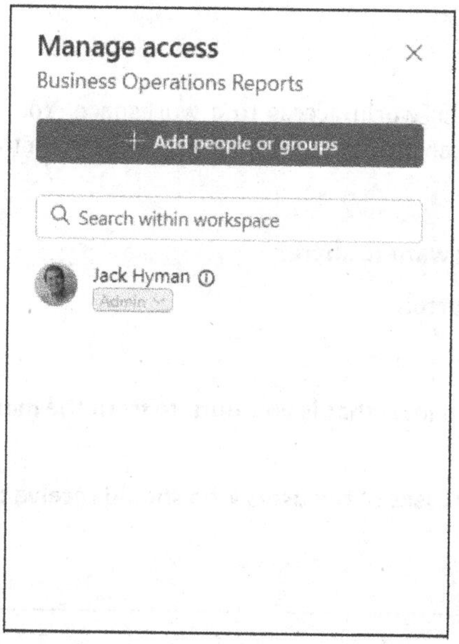

FIGURE 13-21: The Manage Access panel.

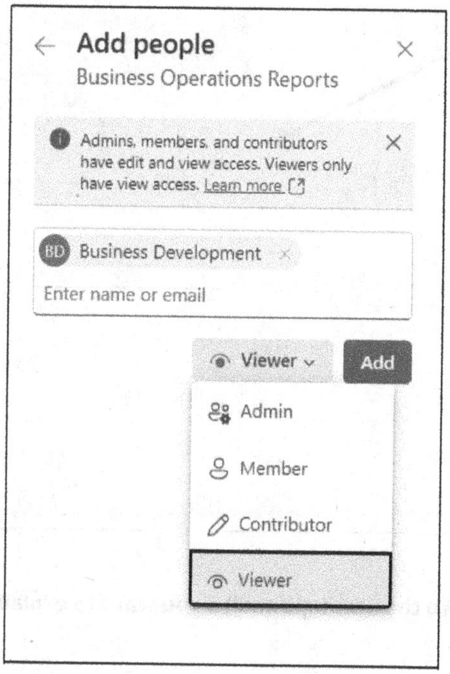

FIGURE 13-22: Assigning users and groups to a Power BI workspace.

Share reports

You don't have to give the world access to a workspace. You can give targeted users access to reports in a workspace without exposing them to all the data. Follow these steps:

1. **Open the report you want to share.**
2. **Click on the Share button**

   The Send Link window appears.
3. **Select the permission level that is appropriate from the menu above the email address field.**
4. **Enter the email addresses of the users who should receive the report (see Figure 13-23).**

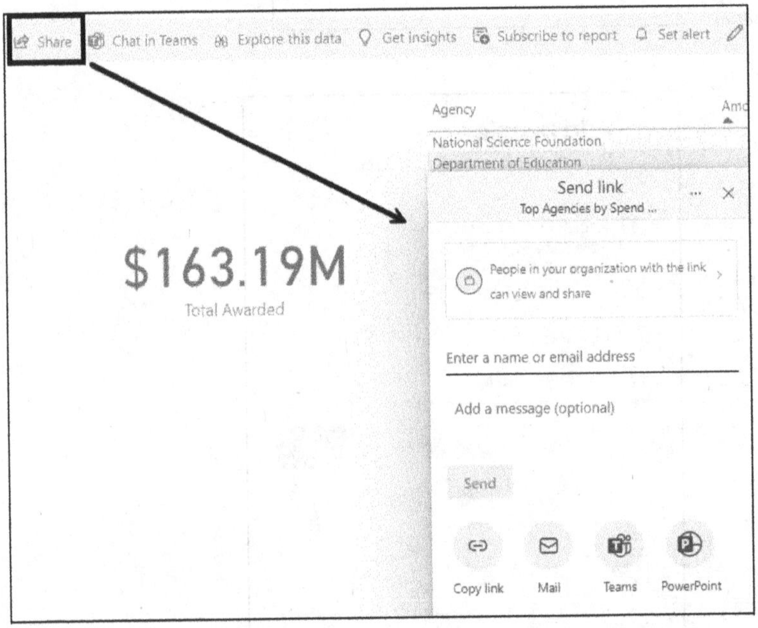

FIGURE 13-23: Sharing a Power BI report.

5. **Enter a message to the user (optional) if you want to explain the report's purpose.**
6. **Select the method in which you'd like to distribute the report link by clicking on one of the delivery options, such as Copy Link, Mail, Teams, or PowerPoint.**
7. **Click Send to distribute.**

You must make sure the user is part of the organization; they must be licensed or else they will not be able to access the report. You can grant access to users that have existing access (common), specific users (most restrictive), or people in your organization (least restrictive).

TECHNICAL STUFF

There is another type of security that is even more restrictive called row-level security (RLS) in Power BI. RLS restricts data access for certain users by defining roles and rules that limit the data they can view within a report based on their role and conditions set on a row-by-row basis. Data might not be exposed to certain users, for example, when personally identifiable information such as a social security number is present. In this case, only certain users would be granted access. To learn more about how to configure row-level security, go to `https://learn.microsoft.com/en-us/fabric/security/service-admin-row-level-security`.

4

Simplifying Workflows with Automation

IN THIS PART . . .

Understand the different types of workflows available in Power Automate.

Craft cloud-based and desktop flows using common connectors.

See how to optimize workflows using techniques including branching, triggers, and logic.

Design workflows that require an approval process.

IN THIS CHAPTER

» Understanding flow types

» Constructing flows using Power Automate Online

» Building and executing desktop flows

Chapter 14

Understanding Automation Basics

If you've read trade publications or listened to industry leaders, you may have heard predictions that automation could lead to massive job losses. However, that's not the full story. While automation is indeed transforming the workplace, it's not necessarily a job killer. Instead, it helps reduce the time workers spend on mundane tasks and can significantly speed up complex processes, turning processes that once took hours, weeks, or even months into processes that take mere minutes — especially when those processes are repeatable. Power Automate, a key component of Power Platform, facilitates workflow automation, robotic process automation, and process mining. With Microsoft's advanced AI solutions, everyone — from individuals to large corporations — is looking at how repetitive tasks can be automated with just a few clicks or a scheduled process.

This chapter covers the fundamentals of automation design, focusing on cloud-based and desktop automation using Power Platform. I steer clear of more advanced topics like robotic process automation and process mining, as these areas are typically more complex and costly. By the end of this chapter, you'll have a solid grasp of creating foundational cloud and desktop flows, setting you on the path to harnessing the full potential of automation in your daily work.

Getting to Know Power Automate

Microsoft Power Automate, formerly known as Microsoft Flow, is a cloud-based tool designed to enable users to create and automate workflows between various applications and services without requiring programming skills or developer assistance. Power Automate also has a desktop companion to support like-kind automation for offline and online consumption. These automated workflows, called *flows*, enable you to specify actions that should occur automatically when certain events are triggered or conditions are met.

You can use Power Automate to generate simple notifications or perform complex workflows that involve multiple steps and decision points. The Premium version of Power Automate also integrates robotics process automation and AI functionality.

Many people use Power Automate to trigger notifications, such as alerting sales representatives via email or text when a new lead is added to a CRM such as Dynamics 365 or collaboration portal such as SharePoint Online. Power Automate can also facilitate file management by automatically copying files from one location, such as Dropbox or OneDrive, to another, such as SharePoint, whenever a new file is added to a defined storage space or even sent to your email address based on a predefined schedule and other criteria. It also offers data collection capabilities, such as capturing social media mentions about a brand and storing them in a database for further analysis.

Power Automate integrates with Microsoft's suite of Power Platform and Microsoft 365 products, as well as with a vast array of third-party applications and services called *connectors*. These connectors act as bridges between Power Automate and external apps, allowing it to communicate with and interact with other platforms. They enable Power Automate to send data to, receive data from, or trigger actions in external systems. As of this writing, Power Automate supports well over 250 connectors.

Grasping key concepts

Before you begin this foundational journey on how to use Power Automate, you should be familiar with concepts that are mentioned throughout Chapters 14 and 15. Table 14-1 describes some terms that developers and non-developers can use to describe how they create and manage their flows, regardless of type, when using Power Automate and, more generally, Power Platform.

TABLE 14-1 Power Platform Terminology

Term	What It Means
Flow	Automated workflow that connects apps, services, and data by automating repetitive tasks. Can be triggered manually, on a schedule, or initiated by an event.
Trigger	An event that starts a workflow. Can be time-based or action-based.
Action	A step in a workflow that performs one or more tasks. A workflow will consist of one or more actions that are executed in a sequence.
Condition	A logical expression that evaluates a condition as true/false or yes/no, whereby the workflow action is directed by the action-based outcome.
Expression	Function to manipulate data within a workflow such as string manipulation, date formatting, or calculations.
Dynamic content	Data from previous workflow steps that are reusable in a workflow.
Connector	Acts as a bridge for Power Automate to external data sources. Can act as both an action and a trigger to interact with services.
Variable	Stores data temporarily within a workflow's execution.
Approval	A workflow type that is used to obtain user content. Generally used with applications such as Outlook and Teams.
Loop	Repeat set of actions that are called multiple times until a condition is met.
Scope	Group of related actions within a workflow that aid an organization in all steps of the lifecycle including error handling and troubleshooting.
Error handling	Actions and settings that help manage errors during a workflow's execution.
Gateway	Connects Power Automate to on-premises data sources, enabling data interaction behind a firewall.

Navigating the Power Automate home page

This book focuses on Power Automate Online, except for the section "Discovering Desktop Flows" later in this chapter. Power Automate Online offers a wealth of features for users who have the free version. If you upgrade to the premium edition, you unlock most of the features associated with robotics process automation and a trove of third-party connectors.

WARNING

Even the premium edition of Power Automate is not complete. If you want to use Robotics Process Automation (RPA) or support bots unattended, you must also purchase the RPA add-on for Power Automate on a per-process basis.

The interface that you are welcomed to upon logging into Power Automate is divided into three sections: navigation (a), Copilot (b), and training (c). (See Figure 14-1.)

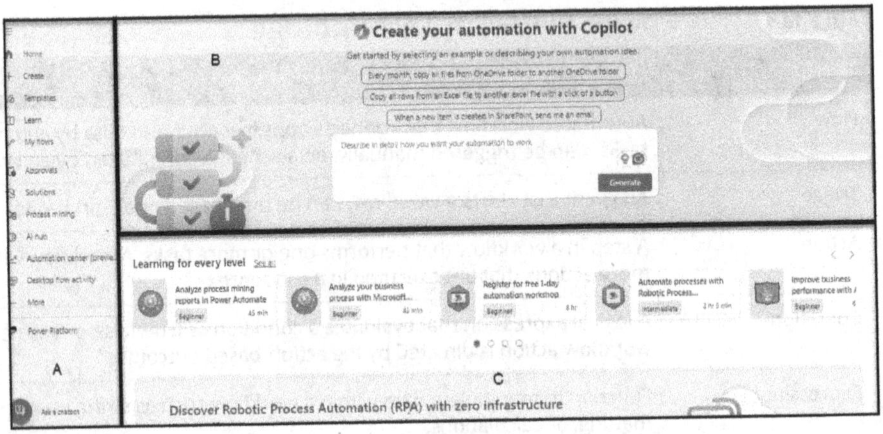

FIGURE 14-1: Power Automate home page.

Section A introduces you to a wealth of options that you can access, many of which are beyond the scope of this book. You can use Power Automate navigation to go to the following destinations:

- **Home:** Opens the Power Automate home page.
- **Create:** Your starting point for creating a new flow.
- **Templates:** A place to generate ideas for popular flows, and not just Microsoft flows either. You have access to hundreds of connectors to other vendors' products that have pre-built capabilities with Microsoft-based applications such as SharePoint, Outlook, Teams, and OneDrive.
- **Learn:** Power Automate Training in one central location.
- **My Flows:** Any flow you create resides right here.
- **Approvals:** Your one-stop location for managing approval and business process flow activity.
- **Solutions:** Just as you manage a solution in Power Apps, you can access solutions in Power Automate to integrate flows within your project. (For more information about solutions, refer to Chapter 2.)
- **Process Mining:** Enables you to analyze and visualize existing business processes by uncovering real-time patterns, bottlenecks, and inefficiencies. The tools offered by Power Automate provide detailed insights into how processes are carried out, allowing you to identify areas for improvement and automation.
- **AI Hub:** A low-code, no-code capability designed for business users within Power Automate (although available for other Power Platform applications) to integrate AI models such as form processing and text recognition into workflows and apps without requiring deep technical expertise.
- **Automation Center:** A centralized hub for monitoring, managing, and optimizing all automation workflows, including cloud flows, desktop flows (RPA), and AI-driven processes developed using Power Automate. Automation Center

provides insights into performance, usage metrics, and tools for troubleshooting to help users efficiently oversee and scale their automation initiatives.

- **Desktop Flow Activity:** A central location for accessing any flows that integrate between Power Automate Online and Power Automate Desktop.
- **More:** Access to shared resources between Power Automate and other Power Platform Applications, including Tables (Dataverse) and Connections (All Power Platform Applications).

Section B is a launchpad for non-developers to build flows using Copilot (via plain language prompts), and Section C offers a variety of training options for users to learn how to automate workflows of all sizes.

Taking Copilot for a ride

Copilot takes center stage on the Power Automate home page. Creating automated workflows can be challenging for non-developers. With Copilot, you can indicate what you want to automate by typing a request in plain English. After you enter your request in the Copilot box, click Generate, and Power Automate produces automation that you can then configure. As you type your requirements in the box, Microsoft suggests parameters that can be incorporated into the automation (see Figure 14-2). For example, as you type **Save a PDF**, Copilot recommends a variety of workflows that indicate where a PDF will be saved in real-time.

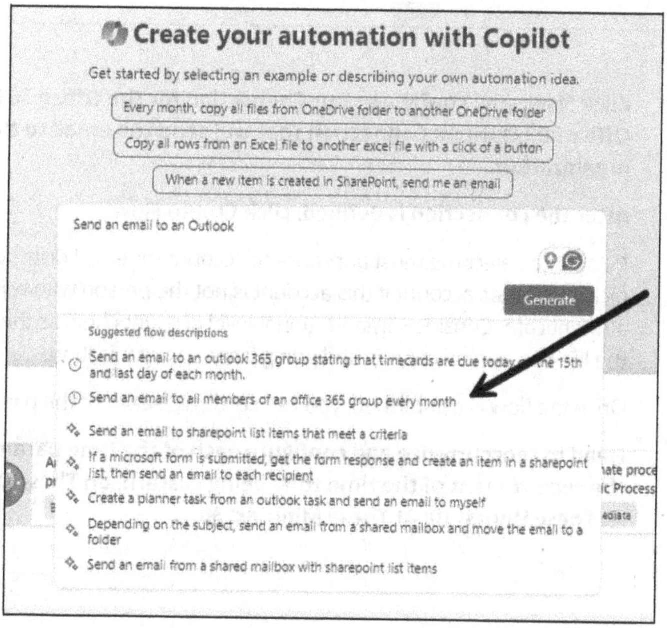

FIGURE 14-2: Using Copilot to generate a Power Automate flow recommendation.

Suppose you want to email an Outlook Group weekly, say on a Friday at 10:30 AM EST. Here is how you can create automation so administrative personnel is not responsible for this mundane activity:

1. **In the Copilot box, enter** Send an email to an Outlook.

   A list of options appears.

2. **Select the option: `Send an email to all members of an Office 365 group every month`, and click Generate.**

   Power Automate displays a prototype flow, as shown in Figure 14-3.

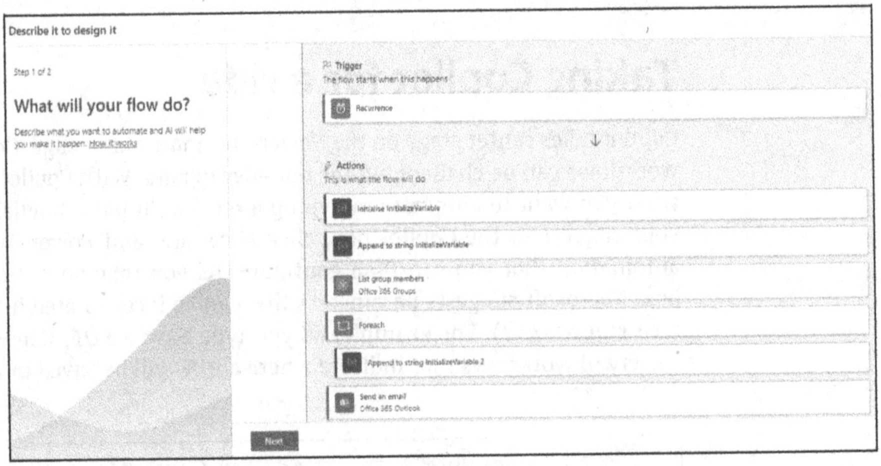

FIGURE 14-3: Prototype flow created by using Copilot.

3. **Click Next, and configure your Connection for the Office 365 Groups and Office 365 Outlook Connection that will send the email to the organization.**

4. **After the connection is defined, click Create Flow.**

   TIP

   Be sure to select the most appropriate account for email distribution. Don't pick your email account if this account is not the person who will ultimately authenticate. Consider organizational-level accounts first, as these last beyond the life of a person coming and going from an organization.

   Once the flow is established, you can customize each of the parameters.

5. **Head to reoccurrence and configure each of the time parameters to meet the requirement of the time zone being Eastern; on These Days: Friday; At These Hours: 10; At These Minutes: 30.**

6. **Navigate to the Append to String InitializeVariable step to complete the configuration. Enter the value: "Timecard." Repeat this for Append to String InitializeVariable2.**
7. **From List Group Members, select the appropriate Outlook Group Distribution list. If you do not have one, you'll need to create one.**
8. **Enter your email requirements in the Send an email step. Include the To (the distribution list), the email body, and the From address (the email address that the timecard reminder will be sent from), as shown in Figure 14-4.**

   An email is created based on the Copilot-generated flow, as shown in Figure 14-5.

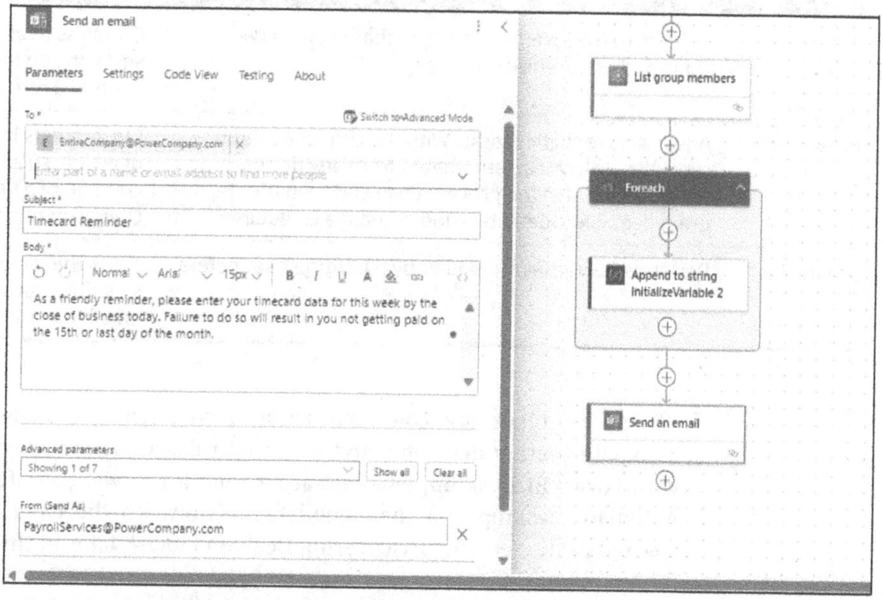

FIGURE 14-4: Example configuration of email requirements.

FIGURE 14-5: Example email output produced from the Copilot-generated flow.

Understanding flow types

Power Automate is meant to automate repetitive tasks. However, the process by which automation is done can vary widely based on the type of task that requires automation. Most flows in Power Automate use *cloud flows* A cloud flow is an automated flow that allows the user to connect various online services and applications to automate tasks such as sending notifications, collecting data, and managing approvals all from a web browser. Table 14-2 describes the types of cloud flows available in Power Automate.

TABLE 14-2 Types of Cloud Flows

Type	What It Does	Targets
Automated Flow	Triggers events when connectors share data between cloud and on-premises services.	Events such as an email arrival, social media mention, or the creation of a new database record.
Instant Flow	Automates repetitive tasks. With the click of a button, a repetitive task can be automated from any device. A developer creates the process once and then the steps are repeatable indefinitely until a change is required.	Most targets involve some form of action, such as an approval, creation of a new record, or change in record state.
Scheduled Flow	Performs flows that are bound by date/time parameters.	Tasks that are derived on a schedule, such as sending an email to a distribution list.

Other flow types are commonly used with Power Automate. Desktop Flows automate routine desktop activities using robotic process automation (RPA). As with Power BI Desktop, when creating complex flows, you often start in Power Automate Desktop and then publish the flows to the cloud. These flows are covered in the section "Discovering Desktop Flows" later in this chapter.

The other flow type is a Business Process Flow. These flows are embedded in model-driven apps. These structured flows guide users through multi-step processes to capture and process data. Business Process Flows are discussed in Chapters 6 and 7.

Working with Cloud Flows

You can create a flow in Power Automate by starting from a blank canvas, giving you full control over designing a custom workflow from scratch. Alternatively, you can choose from one of Microsoft's pre-built templates, which provide ready-made solutions for common automation tasks that you can easily modify to fit your needs. Another approach is to base your flow on a specific connector, allowing you to automate processes between different applications or services, such as linking Outlook, SharePoint, or third-party apps. Each of these methods offer flexibility and customization, catering to a wide range of use cases and technical expertise.

Choosing a Cloud Flow type

If you choose Start From Blank from the Create tab in the left navigation pane, you have six options, as shown in Figure 14-6.

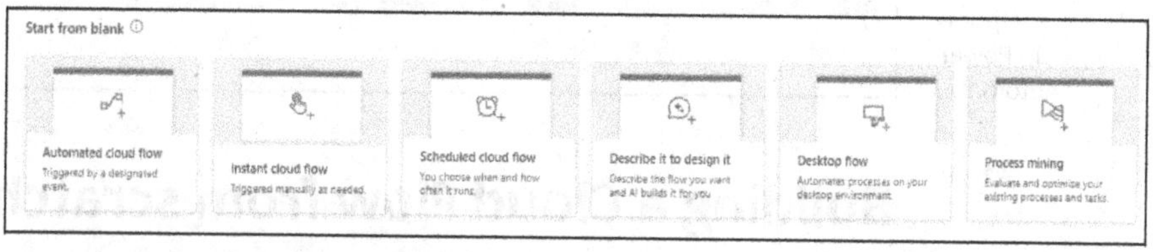

FIGURE 14-6: The Start From Blank options.

Starting from a template provides a gallery of the most common templates, broken down into categories including Top Picks, Remote Work, Email, Notifications, Save to Cloud, and Approvals. Admittedly, most of these templates emphasize using Microsoft 365 or Power Platform tools over other vendors, as shown in Figure 14-7.

FIGURE 14-7: Template Gallery Automate options.

Figure 14-8 shows the entry points to the most popular connectors. You can find a list of every connector available across all variations of Power Automate at `https://learn.microsoft.com/en-us/connectors/connector-reference/connector-reference-powerautomate-connectors`.

WARNING

As you review the following sections, don't be alarmed if the connectors mentioned differ slightly. The free version of Power Automate has a limited number of connectors available, while the Premium version is continually evolving. You may even see slight changes in the names of key connectors.

FIGURE 14-8: Connectors Option in Power Automate.

Building a Cloud Flow from scratch

Regardless of which Cloud Flow option you choose, you initiate the creation process the same way — by clicking the Create button and selecting the Cloud Flow type you'd like to create. The next screen asks you to name your Cloud Flow. From here, the steps to creating a flow vary as follows:

- **Automated Cloud Flows**: You are asked to select the trigger that will kick off an automation.
- **Instant Cloud Flow**: You are asked to select how to trigger the flow.
- **Scheduled Cloud Flow**: You are asked to set the time/data parameters for the flow to run.
- **Describe to Design:** Consistent with the Power Automate home page's use of Copilot, users are presented with a friendly way to create flows by describing tasks in non-techie speak (natural language).
- **Desktop Flow:** You are asked to provide the name of the Flow. On the next page, you establish the parameters that connect the Desktop Flow with the online environment.
- **Process Mining:** A way to help users analyze how business processes are executed across cloud services by examining data from this workflow. These flows are often based on pre-defined business models, such as finance and supply chain.

In this chapter, you learn about topics relevant to Power Automate Free, not the Premium licensing model. If Premium options are covered, they are highlighted as a feature worth considering. The three main areas covered are Automated Cloud Flows, Instant Cloud Flows, and Scheduled Cloud Flows.

Starting from Blank with an Automated Cloud Flow

An automated flow is appropriate if you want to free yourself from repetitive work by connecting an app and its data source to Power Automate, whereby the result of an output can trigger an output such as an alert, report, or task. Examples may be to generate a notification if you receive an email from an important client, or perhaps generate a report based on a flagged event.

The following example shows how to create an email notification when an item is added to a SharePoint Site Folder.

1. **From the left navigation pane, click Create to open the Power Automate Create Page, and then click Automated Cloud Flow.**
2. **Enter the flow name.**

   For this example, the flow name is Save Notification By Email About File.
3. **In the search box, type** File SharePoint Added.

   By narrowing the search parameters to the targeted action, you can identify the flow trigger in the system.
4. **Select the trigger.**

   For this example, the trigger is `When a file is created in a folder (deprecated)`.
5. **Click Create.**

   Figure 14-9 shows the Build an Automated Cloud Flow configuration window.
6. **Double-click the trigger, `When a File is Created in a Folder`, and fill in the relevant site and folder.**

   You'll need to enter the Site Address and Folder ID at minimum. Review the Advanced Parameters section to select the frequency of checking for new content.
7. **Click the plus sign (+) and add the next step.**

   In this case, the next step is to add an action. The action you select is `Office 365 Outlook`.

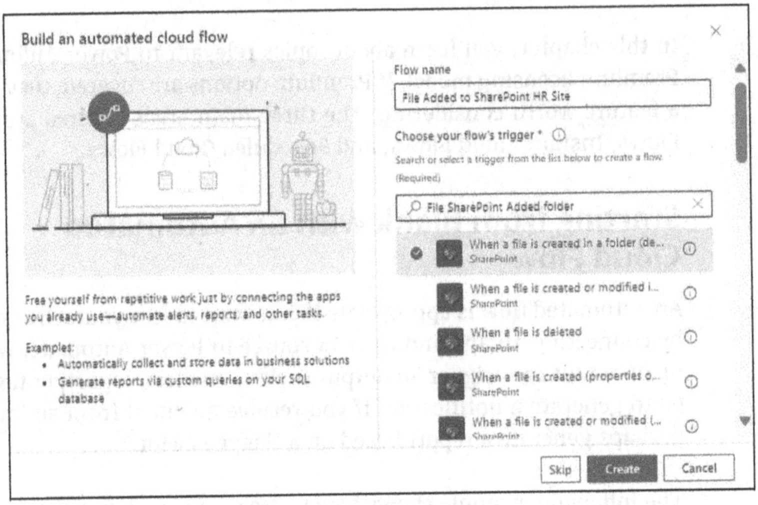

FIGURE 14-9: Creating an Automated Flow.

8. **When prompted, select the action** `Send an email (V2)`**.**

   You select the action based on the specific outcome you are looking to achieve. In this case, each time a new file is added to the folder in Step 6, an action to send an email is triggered in Step 8.

   Another window appears and prompts you to configure the action. Field data will vary based on your organization's requirements (see Figure 14-10).

9. **After you make all the changes, save the flow by clicking the arrow (Collapse) on the right.**

10. **Click Save in the toolbar.**

    Assuming there are no errors, the flow will begin to run immediately.

Starting from Blank with an Instant Cloud Flow

People often find that tasks they often repeat may seem to take a few moments of their time here and there, but when they add up the time, the repeated effort amounts to a significant amount.

Suppose that you spend some time organizing PDF files received via email. Sorting through hundreds of emails is undoubtedly overwhelming, especially when locating a specific PDF from a customer buried in a long email thread. These common time-consuming tasks surely impact productivity. Instant Cloud Flow can resolve this problem by automating the process, streamlining repetitive tasks, and enabling you to take immediate action with a single button-click. Once the button is clicked, a triggering action is set off based on predefined conditions between the saved file and the email sent out.

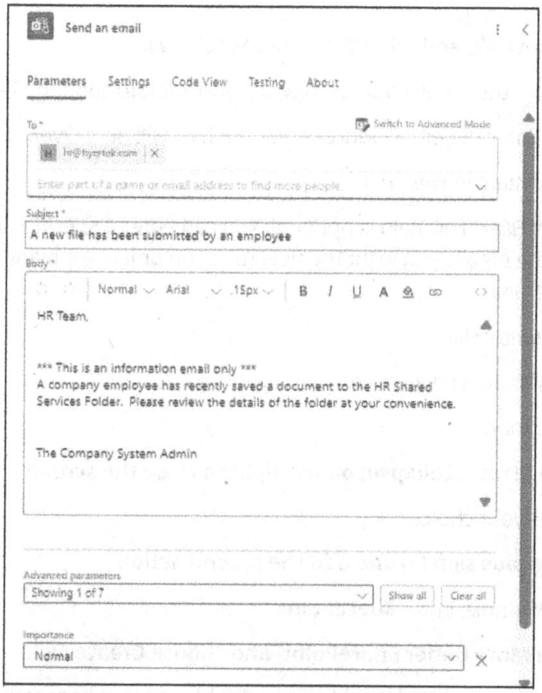
Send an email
Parameters
Settings
Code View
Testing
About
To *
Switch to Advanced Mode
Subject *
A new file has been submitted by an employee
Body *
HR Team,
*** This is an information email only ***
A company employee has recently saved a document to the HR Shared Services Folder. Please review the details of the folder at your convenience.
The Company System Admin
Advanced parameters
Showing 1 of 7
Show all
Clear all
Importance
Normal

FIGURE 14-10: Entering an email communication for an Automated Flow.

The following steps show how to extract all attachments from a specific email address and store them in a SharePoint Document Library.

1. **From the Power Automate home page, choose Create ⇨ Instant Cloud Flow.**
2. **Enter the name of your Cloud Flow, and click Skip at the bottom of the page.**

   An example flow name is *Extract Files from Outlook 365.*
3. **Click Add a Trigger.**

   A window appears, prompting you to select a trigger type.
4. **Select `Office 365 Outlook`.**

   Power Automate displays a list of triggers available in Office 365 Outlook.
5. **Choose `When a new email arrives (V3)`.**

   A window appears, prompting you to enter the parameters to send the email notification (see Figure 14-11).

6. **Select Show All, and fill in the fields as follows:**

   - *To:* Enter the email address to which you want to send the files
   - *From:* Enter the email address that the files will be delivered from
   - *Include Attachments:* Yes
   - *Subject Filter:* This field is optional. You can enter a specific subject line to filter the emails you want the flow to act on or leave it blank to apply to all email
   - *Importance:* High
   - *Only with Attachments:* Yes
   - *Folder:* Inbox

7. **Click the arrow (Collapse) on the right to close the screen.**

   This saves your choices.

8. **Press the plus sign (+) and add the second action.**

   For this example, enter **SharePoint.**

9. **Click See More under SharePoint, and choose Create File.**

10. **Pick the SharePoint site address and folder path where you want the files to be saved.**

    Assuming you have a SharePoint site, you'll navigate to your SharePoint Site address, and then select the folder within the SharePoint site to which the files will be saved.

11. **Enter the filename and file content by selecting the appropriate dynamic fields from previous steps in the flow (see Figure 14-12).**

    Dynamic fields, a popup during your flow configuration, automatically pull data like the email attachment's name (for filename) and the file itself (for file content), saving you from manually entering this information.

12. **Press the plus sign (+) and add a third action.**

    For this example, enter **Microsoft Office 365 Outlook.**

13. **Choose `Send an Email (V2)`.**

    You've now added a new trigger to the flow canvas.

14. **Fill in the fields, including the To, Subject, Body, and Importance.**

    These fields that you populate for this Send an Email action are different from the ones you populated in Step 6; the business objective is to get a confirmation email, not pull the PDF into the SharePoint site.

15. **Click Save.**

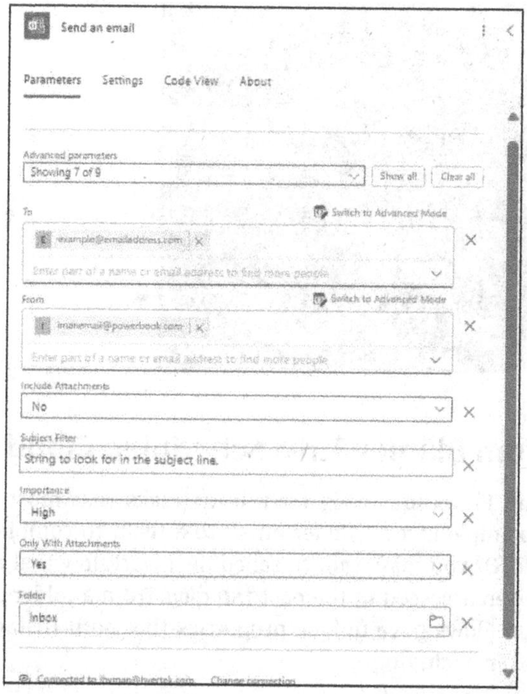

FIGURE 14-11: Email parameters for an Instant Cloud Flow.

16. **Go to the SharePoint site and verify that the file has been added. Also, verify that you've received a confirmation email.**

    Figure 14-13 confirms that the files `50States.xlsx` and `Demo Agenda.xlsx` sent by the target email were posted to the SharePoint site (A). An email also confirms that the files were posted to the SharePoint site (B). This process will occur instantaneously any time an email with attachments comes in from targeted addresses.

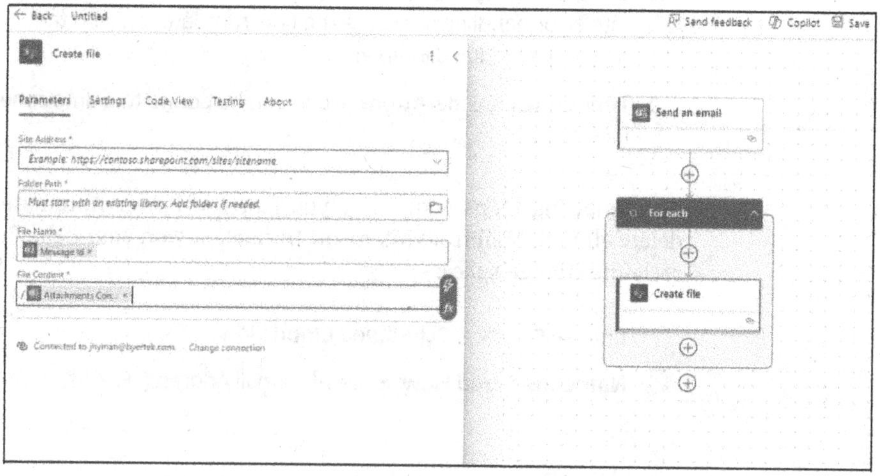

FIGURE 14-12: Configuring SharePoint to accept attachments from Outlook 365.

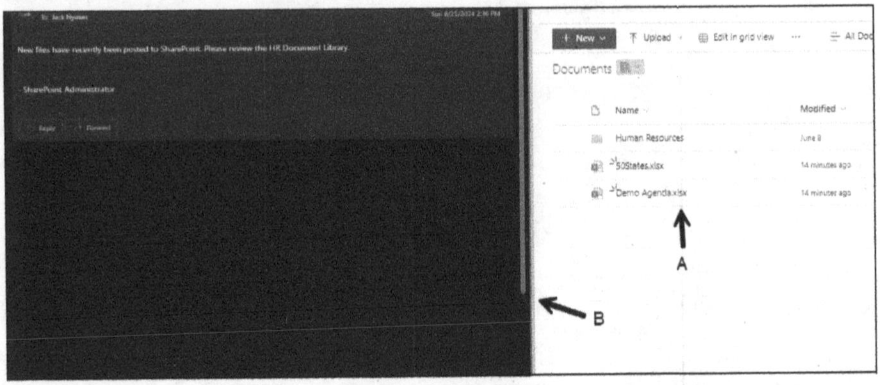

FIGURE 14-13: Confirmation of SharePoint attachment extraction from Outlook using an Instant Flow.

Starting from Blank with a Scheduled Cloud Flow

Scheduled Cloud Flows are made for routine tasks that must be executed on a schedule. An example is a reminder email to a team to complete their time and expense reports. Or you may want to schedule a workflow that deletes all records that have not been accessed in the past 180 days from a folder or an email inbox. Scheduled Cloud Flows have unique properties that both Instant and Automated Flows do not offer, including:

- **Time-based triggers:** You can schedule a flow to run once, daily, weekly, monthly, or at custom intervals.
- **Flexible recurrence patterns:** You can specify the recurrence pattern, whether daily, weekly, monthly, or yearly. You can even set the flow to trigger to start at a specific hour and minute.
- **Automated actions:** Once the flow triggers, you can be hands-off unless a modification to the schedule is required.
- **Error handling and retry policies:** If the flow errors or fails, you can incorporate error handling to ensure the flow runs later on, and then resumes at its regularly scheduled interval.
- **Time zone considerations:** Flows can be bound to a time zone, not the local time.

The following steps show how you can use Power Automate to automatically delete all Junk Mail from Microsoft Outlook 365 on your behalf so that your inbox reclaims storage space:

1. **Choose Create ⇨ Scheduled Cloud Flow.**
2. **Name the Cloud Flow:** Erase All <Email Address> Emails.

3. **Set the parameters under `Run this flow` to a schedule you are comfortable with, as shown in Figure 14-14, and click Create.**

   The reoccurrence trigger is now on the canvas.

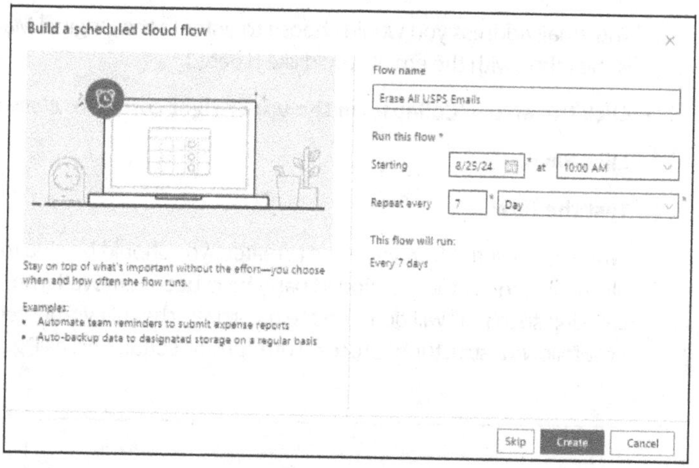

FIGURE 14-14: Build a Scheduled Cloud Flow window.

4. **Click plus sign (+) to add another action.**

   Another action is added to the flow canvas when you click plus sign (+) and select Add an Action.

5. **Enter** Office 365 Outlook **in the Search box.**
6. **Click the See More link. Then select `Get Emails (V3)`.**
7. **Click the Show All button. Enter an appropriate From and To. If the subject is repetitive, also enter the subject.**

   REMEMBER

   As in other sections describing the workflow process for emails, creating the process is highly customized based on the procedure to get and send emails. You should fill in the fields that are marked as required. All others are deemed optional.

8. **Click the plus sign (+) again to add an action, and select Control.**
9. **Double-click the control and set the parameter where `FROM` equals `FROM = `*`<targeted email address>`*`.`**

   An example would be `FROM = jack@powerco.com`.

10. **In the Yes box under TRUE, click the plus sign (+) and select Add an Action from the menu that appears.**
11. **Select the action: `Delete email (V2)`.**

12. **Click the action, `Delete email (V2)`, and enter the parameters as follows:**
   - *Message ID:* Use the Dynamic Fields and select `Message ID`.
   - *Advanced Parameters:* Select `Original Mailbox Address`.

   The email address you would choose to enter in the Original Mailbox Address is the Inbox with the emails you'd like deleted.
13. **Click the arrow (Collapse) in the upper-right corner to close the window.**
14. **Click Save.**
15. **Test the flow.**

   When you test the flow you've just created, you should be able to confirm that all emails sent by the mentioned party have been removed from your inbox. Deleting such mail will occur on the recurring schedule you've set. The complete flow follows a structured process with specific conditions, as Figure 14-15 shows.

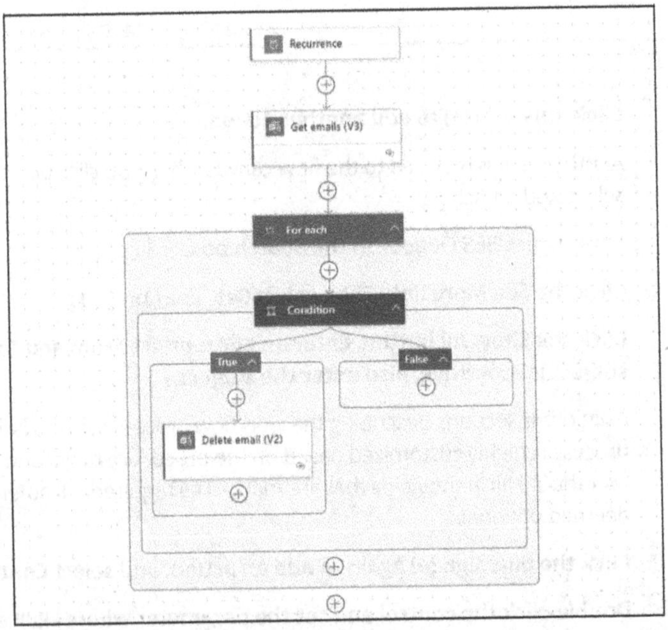

FIGURE 14-15: A sample Scheduled Cloud Flow.

Automating Using Templates and Connectors

Conceptually, the starting point for using a template and connector is the same. For templates, you'll find that common work activities are associated with connectors, some of which are Microsoft, but not all. Templates are discrete tasks, often one or two steps. When dealing with connectors, the focus is more targeted on technology, which can open the doors to complex workflow design.

TIP

Creating a flow using a template provides a quick and easy way to automate common tasks by using pre-built workflows with predefined triggers and actions, ideal for beginners. Flows using a connector allow for more customization and flexibility, enabling users to build tailored workflows from scratch that can handle complex automation needs by integrating various services and applications.

Using a template to automate a task

If you like information, you'll love using templates. Almost all templates are designed to help end users gain insights through notifications, messages, or tasks. Most templates bring together two or three applications to accomplish mundane tasks. If done independently, these tasks would take someone like you or me a while to accomplish. With Power Automate, the time to complete a task is compressed to mere seconds or minutes once a flow is built and successfully executed.

A common task almost any administrative team faces is sending reminders to a team to complete repetitive activities. Instead of an operations specialist having to complete the task weekly, why not have Power Automate do the work for you?

The following steps show how you can use the template "Get Daily Reminder in Your Office 365 Email Account," accessible under email, to create a Scheduled Flow that automates this common task. Here are the steps:

1. **Click the Create tab on the left navigation.**
2. **Scroll down to `Start from a Template` (Template Gallery).**

   On the Create Page, Microsoft provides several pre-built workflow types. The gallery is located at the bottom of the page.
3. **Click the Email tab.**

   The Template Gallery has six tabs: Top Picks, Remote Work, Email, Notifications, Save to Cloud, and Approvals. For this example, you select the Email tab.
4. **Choose the template, "Get Daily Reminder from Your `Outlook.com` email."**

   Scroll through the gallery to find this option. Or you can use the Search box to locate this template option quickly.

5. **From the screen that pops up, confirm the required connections. For this example, you require access to Office 365 Outlook (a premium connector) and Office 365 Users (a premium connector).**

   For this connector, you must specify an email address for authentication. The other connectors are automated on your behalf, as shown in Figure 14-16.

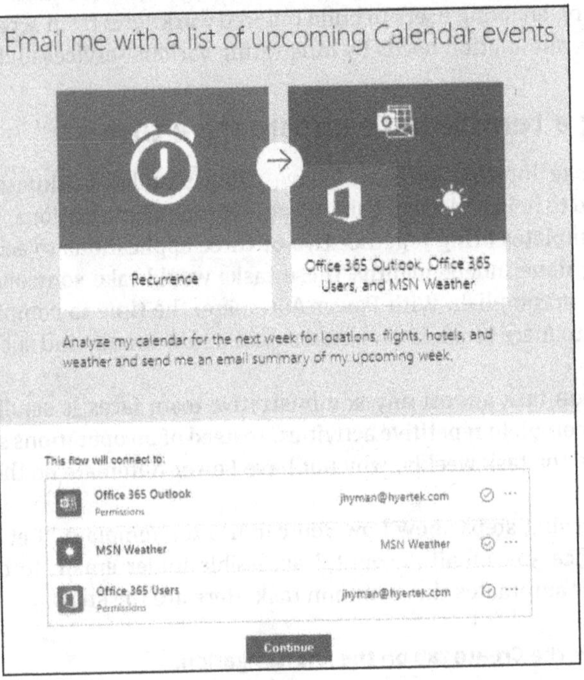

FIGURE 14-16: Establishing authentication parameters for your connectors.

6. **Once you are satisfied with the requirements listed for your environment, click Continue.**
7. **Click the top action in the flow. This action is the recurrence action.**

   By default, the recurrence action is set to every day. You can adjust this as you see fit.

8. **Click the Send `an Email (V3)` action.**

   Here you establish who you will send the recurring notification to at a scheduled interval. At first, Power Automate will indicate invalid parameters because you must provide the To and From parameters to complete the flow.

9. **Update the To: and Body fields of the Send `an Email (V3)` action.**

   In the *To:* field, specify the parties to whom you want the notification sent. The *From* is the email address from which you want the email to come.

10. **Click Test.**

11. **Save the flow.**

You've now created a reminder email similar to others you've developed in previous sections. In this case, though, the reminder was built by applying a fraction of the steps given that the task is far more discrete, all because you had a template created on your behalf.

Using connectors to automate a task

Microsoft has introduced a new way for users to create flows by shifting the focus from individual actions or devices (such as clicking a button, sending an email, or approving a request) to a more technology-based approach. Instead of centering on the specific task or device, this view organizes flow creation around the underlying technologies and services used, such as Microsoft 365, SharePoint, or third-party integrations. Organizing flows this way allows users to think about which systems and applications need to interact rather than focusing only on the individual tasks or devices involved.

Microsoft has curated a set of common tasks that integrate seamlessly with partner technologies from vendors such as Google, Salesforce, and HubSpot. These tasks are available as Connector templates, which Microsoft designed to give developers — whether beginners or experts — a head start in building automation by using pre-built actions through defined templates.

REMEMBER

The process of building a Connector-based workflow doesn't change one bit from what you've already learned when starting from a Blank or using a Template.

Discovering Desktop Flows

Similar to Power BI Desktop, Power Automate has a Desktop companion application to support Robotics Process Automation (RPA) and workflow design activities that work just for personal computers. You read that right: Not everything is online. An activity you create on the Desktop can surely be moved from the Desktop to the web, but the automation starts at the Desktop for repetitive administrative activities such as organizing your file systems. If you want to build processes that are repetitive at the PC level where Desktop applications are a prerequisite, you should use Power Automate Desktop to build such workflows. Power Automate Desktop Flows are ideal if you are looking to

- Quickly organize documents by a specific file and folder structure
- Extract data from a website and then store it in a file using automation

- **»** Apply automation capabilities that can be put on autopilot with repeatability using consistent metadata attribution

To get started, you need to download Power Automate to your computer and log in using your personal or organization account.

Understanding Desktop Flow types

Desktop Flows automate tasks on your Desktop or within any Windows application. Power Automate works with two primary types of Desktop Flows:

- **» Attended Desktop Flows:** Require human interaction. These flows run on the user's machine while the user is logged in and interacts with their Desktop. These flows are ideal for tasks such as data entry that require user approvals or decision-making.
- **» Unattended Desktop Flows:** Can be implemented without human intervention. These flows run in the background on a dedicated machine, continuing their tasks even when the user is not logged into their computer. They are perfect for back-office tasks like processing bulk data, data transfers, or automating repetitive tasks. Both flow types use the Robotic Process Automation (RPA) capabilities of Power Automate, providing powerful automation solutions for legacy applications and repetitive tasks that lack your API integrations.

Crafting an Attended Flow

Attended Flows require user interaction, such as clicking the Run button in Power Automate Desktop, to trigger an action. With Power Automate, you create the flow once, and it orchestrates all the tasks automatically after they are initiated. You must understand logical operators such as If, Else, and End to build more complex Desktop Flows.

For the following example, I created an Attended Flow to delete specific files from a folder named `Review To Be Deleted` that I created on my Desktop, allowing me to trigger the file deletion process with a single click. Figure 14-17 shows the complete flow that accomplishes this and where I'd press Run.

Following are the steps to create the flow shown in Figure 14-17:

1. **Open Power Automate Desktop.**

   Launch Power Automate Desktop from the Start menu or a Desktop shortcut. If prompted, sign in using your Microsoft account.

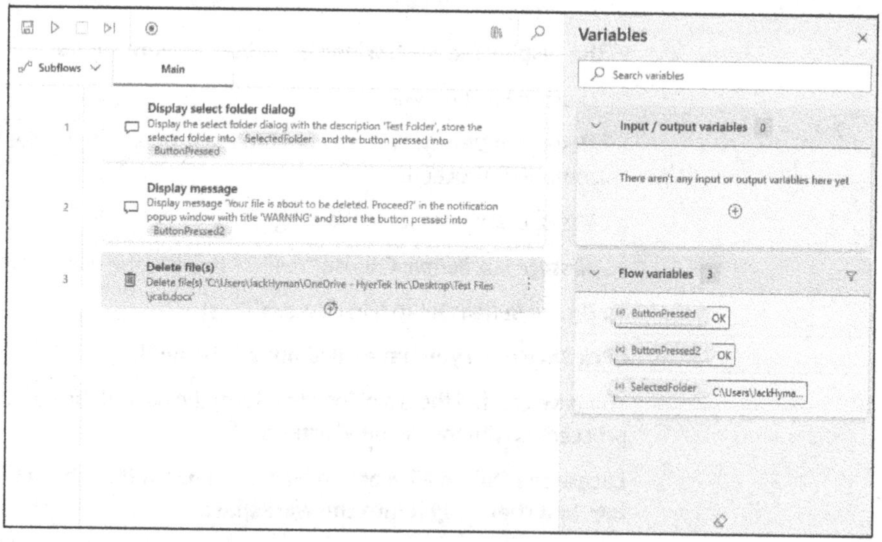

FIGURE 14-17: Example of an Attended Flow with a Run button.

2. **Click Create a New Flow.**

   In the toolbar, click the New Flow button. A window will appear, asking you to name your flow.

3. **Enter a name for the flow, and click Create.**

   For this example, name the flow **Delete Files on Desktop**.

4. **In the actions search bar, search for the Display Select Folder Dialog action. Drag this action into the workspace.**

   Completing this action allows the user to select the folder where the files will be deleted.

5. **In the new window that appears, give the dialog a name (for example,** Select Folder to Delete Files From).

   For the Initial Folder field, specify a folder path to guide the user to access the folder where the files will be deleted. For this example, the file is in a folder called `Test Folder`.

6. **When you finish filling in the fields, click Save.**

Next you need to add a message box to alert the user that their files will be deleted. To do so, head back to the actions search bar and follow these steps:

1. **Locate the Display Message action by searching for it in the actions search bar. Drag the action into the workspace to create a popup warning message before any files are deleted.**

2. **In the Display Message window, fill in the following fields:**
   - *Message Box Title:* Warning!!!
   - *Message to Display:* You are about to erase one or more files from your computer. Proceed?
   - *Message Box Icon:* Set to Warning.
   - *Message Box Button:* Choose "Yes-No" to allow the user to confirm or cancel.
   - *Default Button:* Set to "First Button" (Yes).
3. **Click Save once you have filled out all the fields.**

   You have created the dialog box to inform the user of the consequences of proceeding with the intended actions.
4. **Locate the Delete Files action by searching for it in the actions search bar, and then drag it into the workspace.**

   The Delete Files window appears, where you are asked to select the file(s) you want to delete. For this example, select the file called `Test File`.docx.
5. **Select the file you want to delete in the targeted folder, and click Save.**

   You've pointed to a file that will be deleted if it meets the criteria in the workflow each time you click Run.

Your flow is now complete. Now you can test the flow by pressing the Run button in the toolbar to validate the flow. If the files you placed in the folder meet the flow criteria, the file is permanently deleted.

Running Unattended Flows without any assistance

Pretend for a moment that you do a task every Friday at 3:00 p.m., such as emailing your entire organization reminding them to submit timecards by Monday at noon. What happens when you want to take a vacation? Instead of logging in at 2:55 p.m. to send that email, Power Automate allows you to automate the task, so it's done for you — even if you're not at your computer.

Unattended Flows can run without human intervention, automatically triggering actions like sending emails, and don't require your computer to be on. However, Unattended Flows is a premium feature that requires both bots for RPA tasks and a Power Automate Premium license.

While Attended Desktop Flows require a user to be signed in to perform actions, Unattended Desktop Flows can't run if the Windows user session is active, even if the session is locked. To avoid this issue, you can run Unattended Flows on a *virtual machine* (software-based emulation of a physical computer that runs an operating system and applications in the cloud), which allows all physical devices to remain available.

For an Unattended Desktop Flow to run, the following conditions must be met:

- All users must be signed out.
- A locked screen should be displayed to keep actions hidden.
- A gateway should sync with user sign-in details or a connection through the Power Automate Machine Runtime App.
- The user must be running Windows 10/11 Pro or Enterprise.

TIP

You can run multiple Unattended Desktop Flows in sequence on the same device by manually managing the run queue. However, flows that don't start within three hours of the request will time out. If multiple flows are triggered, they run one after the other unless the queue exceeds three hours.

REMEMBER

Microsoft Power Automate allows multiple Unattended Flows to run simultaneously on a single device as long as each flow uses a different user account. This feature helps organizations reduce infrastructure costs by connecting to a gateway via multiple user accounts on one device.

To create an Unattended Flow, follow these steps:

1. **Open Power Automate Online.**
2. **Select Instant Cloud Flow as the type of flow to create.**
3. **Choose Manually Trigger a Flow.**
4. **Click Create.**

   Your first flow step is now defined on the design canvas.
5. **Select the plus sign (+) to add a step.**
6. **Choose `Run a flow built with Power Automate for Desktop`.**
7. **Connect a flow you've created using Power Automate Desktop.**

   In this case, use the flow, Review To Be Deleted.
8. **Assign the flow type.**

   Assign the flow as an unattended if you want to have a bot run the routine for you, and attended to execute the flow upon pressing a button. No parameters need to be assigned on this screen (see Figure 14-18).
9. **Click the Save button to save the flow.**

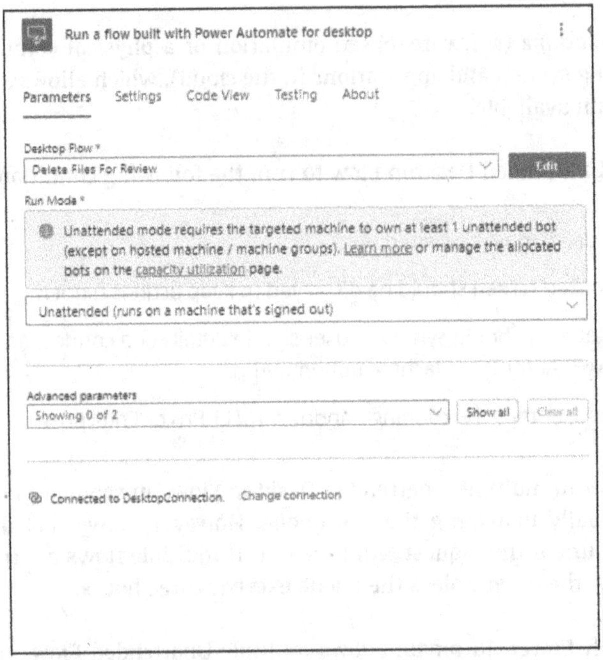

FIGURE 14-18: Configuring an Unattended Flow.

WARNING

If you don't have a Premium license, this exercise can't be completed beyond this point. Furthermore, if you want to run a flow unattended, you must configure your system to not only run Power Automate on your Desktop but also the Machine Runtime. This feature is accessible under settings using Power Automate Desktop. Finally, you need a premium RPA add-on to run any bot processes. Process automation is costly and can add up quickly!

ON THE WEB

To learn more about the RPA add-on bot, including configuring the bot for use with Unattended Desktop Flows, go to `https://learn.microsoft.com/en-us/power-platform/admin/power-automate-licensing/add-ons`.

Recording Flows

Recording Flows leverage attended-based processes to record actions within Power Automate Desktop. These flows are helpful to users who complete mundane tasks repetitiously and want to simply cut to the chase and press a button to get the work done versus go click happy.

For example, if you download an Excel spreadsheet every week to look for specific data trends, and then create variations of the dataset for data analysis review, you may be interested in streamlining this task. Instead of spending a few hours sifting, sorting, and saving the data, you can record the action once and then, using a template, the routine can run independently on a weekly schedule.

Suppose that you have an Excel spreadsheet that was downloaded from a Premium Government Bid Website. The request was to download all federal contracting opportunities mentioning "Power Platform" in the past 12 months under a classification starting with "541;" 291 records were found. The organization has its analyst extract data weekly, looking for trends based on two parameters: *pre-solicitation* and *no-set aside used.* That is a great deal of work for a person to do manually.

Instead of opening the Excel spreadsheet each week, an analyst can simply copy and paste the dataset into this workbook's assigned columns and click Run (the triangle). The result is a compressed dataset that goes from 291 records down to 43 records. To accomplish the tasks, the developer simply clicks the Record button and steps through their normal routine, clicking once versus going click-happy, having to take ten-plus steps each week to get the same results (see Figure 14-19).

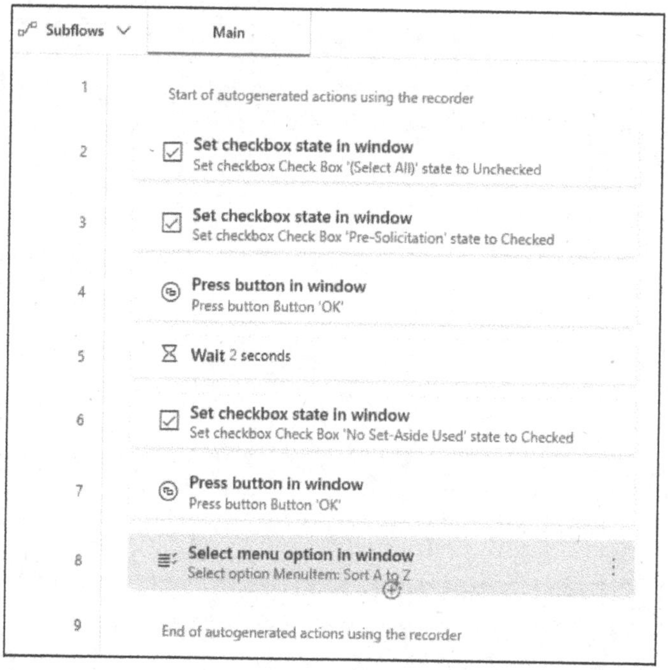

FIGURE 14-19: Recorded script of sorting and sifting through Excel data.

IN THIS CHAPTER

» Exploring the New Cloud Flow Designer

» Optimizing flows using triggers, conditions, and loops

» Using approvals in your workflows

Chapter 15
Diving into Advanced Automation

This chapter considers the practical aspects of designing automation workflows, focusing specifically on workflow optimization. The chapter first provides a deep-dive into the Cloud Flow Designer toolset. Then you see how to use built-in optimization tools to implement workflows that minimize unnecessary steps. You also discover how you can implement advanced techniques such as parallel branching and conditional logic. By the end of this chapter, you will know how to craft high-performing workflows that automate routine tasks and adapt dynamically to meet changing business needs.

Delving into the New Cloud Flow Designer

Creating a Cloud Flow from the Power Automate online navigation pane involves selecting conditions, actions, and triggers (see Chapter 14). This section delves further into the New Cloud Flow Designer interface, which offers abundant testing and optimization tools. The interface looks simple enough, but as you can see in Figure 15-1, the New Cloud Flow Designer contains 13 sections to explore as you build more robust cloud flows. Most sections contain tools to test and refine your flows. The following list describes what each numbered section in Figure 15-1 represents.

TIP

You should be familiar with two workspace types: Classic and New Experience. At the upper-right side of the Power Automate window, you can switch between the two user experience types. Throughout the book, we've dipped into the New Cloud Flow Designer. In this chapter, the only designer used is the New Cloud Flow Designer.

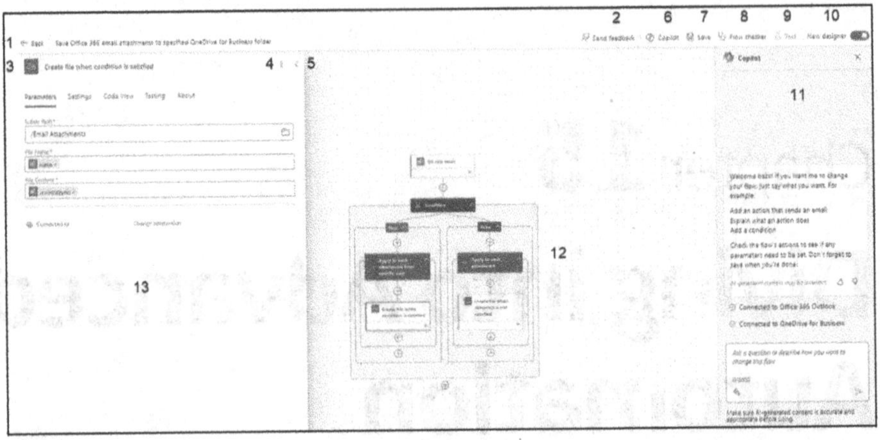

FIGURE 15-1: The New Cloud Flow Designer.

- **Left Arrow button (1):** Click this button to return to the previous page.
- **Send Feedback button (2):** Microsoft is always looking for product feedback, particularly about its AI features. Click this button, and tell them what works and what needs fixing.
- **Action/Trigger name (3):** Whether you create your own flow name or use a Template or Connector, the workflow name, described as the *Action/Trigger name,* appears in this location.
- **More commands (4):** The three ellipses expand to allow a user to add a note about a workflow or delete the workflow. It's all or nothing here!
- **Collapse/Expand Button (5):** If you want to hide the Actions Configuration pane, click this button. Click it again to show the pane. The button appears as › for show hidden, or ‹ for hidden.
- **Copilot (6):** Displaying the Copilot pane while working on a flow allows you to view a description, courtesy of Copilot, of what your flow is attempting to do. You can use this information to further refine your flow.
- **Save (7):** Click this button to save your workflows.

- **Flow Checker (8):** Flow Checker provides detailed messages about errors or warnings, allowing users to quickly identify and fix issues to ensure their flows run smoothly and correctly.
- **Test (9):** Once a flow is ready and before you unleash it to the world, it's a good idea to test it manually. The test function allows users to run a flow manually to check its functionality and ensure it performs as expected.
- **New Designer (10):** Microsoft offers a Classic Cloud Flow Designer and a New Cloud Flow Designer. By default, users are presented with the New Cloud Flow Designer.
- **Copilot pane (11):** The Copilot pane appears each time you click the Copilot button (Callout 6 in Figure 15-1). It is central to AI functionality in the New Cloud Flow Designer.
- **Flow Designer (12):** When you build your workflow, you do so on a canvas-like experience called the Flow Designer, much like you create your Canvas Apps in Power Automate.
- **Action Configuration pane (13):** Each item in the Flow Designer has specific parameters and settings associated with the action, condition, or trigger. Behind each configuration is the logic that determines how the action behaves. When you select an object in the Flow Designer, the configuration pane updates to display the relevant settings and options for the selected action, condition, or trigger.

Working with parameters in the Action Configuration pane

You manage parameters from the Action Configuration pane (refer to Figure 15-1). Parameters play a crucial role in defining and refining the behavior of automated workflows. Each control, condition, trigger, or loop has its own set of parameters.

Parameters are variables that users can set to dynamically control the input values, conditions, and execution logic of a flow. They allow for customization and flexibility, enabling flows to handle different scenarios and data inputs without requiring manual adjustments. Parameters vary widely depending on the control, but inevitably, each control enables users to create sophisticated, dynamic workflows that can adapt to various business needs and data environments.

Control-based parameters to set a condition (see Figure 15-2) are vastly different from connector-based parameters (see Figure 15-3), which require Power Automate to save files to OneDrive from Outlook.

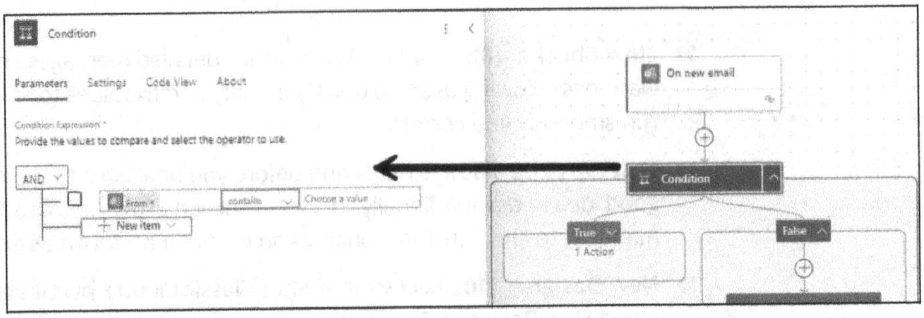

FIGURE 15-2: Control-based parameters.

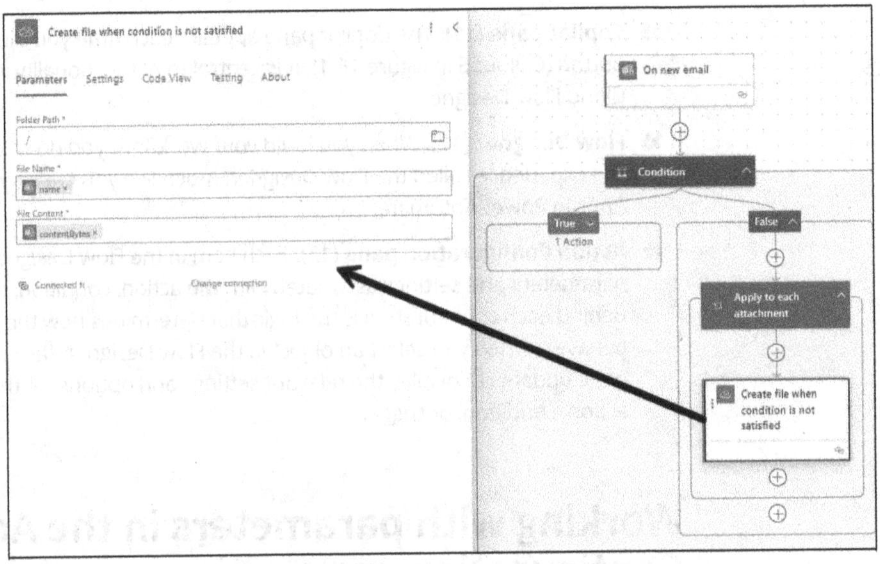

FIGURE 15-3: Connector-based parameters.

Addressing settings in the Action Configuration pane

The settings vary widely in the Action Configuration pane depending on whether you're using a control- or action-based connector. Generally, the base parameters on the Settings tab cover action time-out, network retry policy, how an action should run, secure input and output, and tracking properties within the general, networking, security, and tracking settings. Various options are available, depending on the connector type or if the control manages logic, such as triggering loops or conditions. Table 15-1 describes these settings, and Figure 15-4 shows an example of a Settings tab for an action associated with a connector.

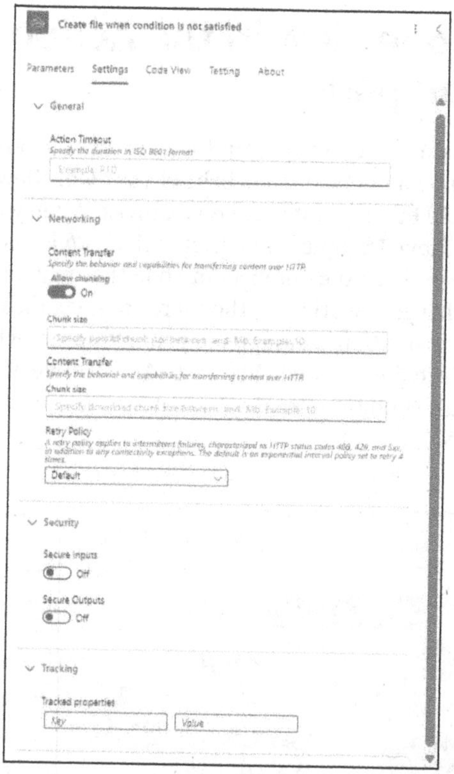

FIGURE 15-4: Settings tab illustrating a connector configuration in the Action Configuration pane.

TABLE 15-1 **Control and Connector Settings Managed in the Action Configuration Pane**

Setting	What It Does
General	Set the maximum time an action can wait for retries and responses. This does not affect the time-out of a single request.
Networking	Choose a retry policy for handling intermittent failures. The default is an exponential retry up to four times. You can customize the interval or choose the Retry Policy.
Run After	Define how an action should proceed based on the result of previous actions (success, timeout, skip, or failure).
Security	Toggle options to secure input and output data, hiding sensitive information.
Tracking	Set key-value pairs for tracking specific properties in the flow.

Reviewing Code view in the Action Configuration pane

Whether you have a single action or condition, or even twenty on your Flow Designer, you have some amount of code behind your workflow. Each control or connector is represented by a separate card on a canvas. When you select an action or condition on the Flow Designer and then select Code view in the Action Configuration pane, you'll see the snippets of code that make the workflow run. The more you customize your workflow, the more complex the code snippets get. Furthermore, for every additional parameter you add to an action or condition, those changes are reflected in the Code View tab. An example of the Code view for the OneDrive Connector condition `Create File When Condition Is Satisfied` appears in Figure 15-5.

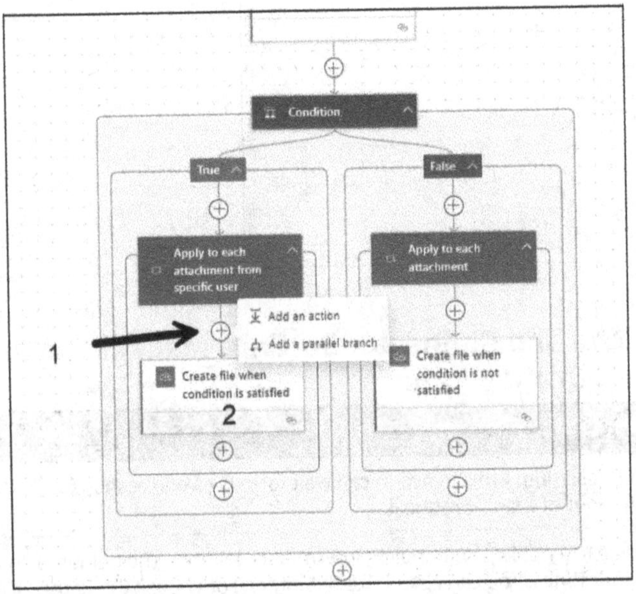

FIGURE 15-5: Code view.

Tackling Triggers and Approvals

A *trigger* is an event that initiates a cloud or desktop flow. As discussed in Chapter 14, which covers triggers in greater detail, receiving a file from an email address can trigger a notification or save a file to a SharePoint Document Library. But as you'll quickly realize, creating a workflow incorporates one or more triggers, and tweaking a trigger to operate precisely is more complex.

Tweaking triggers in an existing workflow

Setting up a workflow is a piece of cake compared to editing a workflow with an existing trigger. You need to make sure that a new trigger is put in place before you remove the old trigger. Otherwise, you'll lose all the steps in your workflow logic. The following steps show how to edit a flow by replacing a new trigger and then deleting the existing trigger.

1. **Click on My Flows in the sidebar. Locate the flow you want to modify, and click its name to open it.**
2. **Click the Edit button (a pencil icon) at the top of the workflow.**

   The Flow Designer opens, and you can begin editing the flow.
3. **From the Flow Designer, click the + New Step button to add a new action, condition, or trigger.**

   As in other examples, you use the search bar that appears to find the trigger you want to add. As an example, if you enter **When a new item is created** in the Search box, many options follow that phrase. In this case, you would identify the option that represents the most appropriate business requirement from the list, and click it. The Flow Designer would then add the option you chose to the top of the workflow.
4. **Modify the step's parameters.**

   Double-click the action, condition, or trigger, and modify its parameters in the Action Configuration pane.

   Your configuration requirements will vary widely depending on the step. For example, you may need to set up specific fields, such as specifying a mailbox for email triggers or a prescribed schedule.
5. **Locate the step you want to remove in the flow. Click on the ellipsis (three dots) next to the old step, and from the dropdown menu, select Delete.**

   You can now remove the old step from the flow without breaking the workflow and its logic.

   REMEMBER

   If the step you are removing has conditional operators associated with it, it may still break the flow. Before removing a step where conditionals are part of the flow, make sure to consider all dependencies, including remapping the flow.
6. **After configuring the new step and removing the old one, click Save at the top of the page to apply your changes.**

   You have now removed and then added a step in an existing workflow.

Customizing triggers while using conditions

Almost all modern programming languages incorporate some form of expression that addresses conditional states. You may receive 100 emails a day, but only those emails that contain attachments will trigger. The trigger then copies the file to a target location.

The use of conditions, specifically expressions and loops, can help streamline flows and reduce the number of unnecessary runs a flow must make. When fewer limits are imposed on a flow, consumption increases. More runs mean more spending if an organization is bound to a per-flow plan. To combat these challenges, consider using the expressions in Table 15-2 and the loops in Table 15-3.

TABLE 15-2 Key Expressions that Optimize Conditions

Expression	What It Does
AND	Returns true if both arguments are true
OR	Returns true if either argument is true
EQUALS	Returns true if two values are equal
LESS	Returns true if the first argument is less than the second
LESSOREQUALS	Returns true if the first argument is less than or equal to the second
GREATER	Returns true if the first argument is greater than the second
GREATEROREQUALS	Returns true if the first argument is greater than or equal to the second
EMPTY	Returns true if the object, array, or string is empty
IF	Returns one value if the expression is true and another if it is false
NOT	Returns the opposite of a Boolean value

TABLE 15-3 Key Conditionals and Loops

Action	What It Does
`If`	Runs a block of actions if the condition is met
`Else if`	Runs a block of actions if the preceding 'If' conditions aren't met, but the specified condition in this statement is
`Else`	Runs a block of actions if none of the preceding `If` or `Else if` conditions are met

Action	What It Does
`Switch`	Dispatches execution to different parts of the switch body based on the value of an expression
`Case`	Runs a block of actions if the specified case condition is met
`Default Case`	Runs a block of actions if no case expression in the switch body is met
`Loop`	Repeats a block of actions a specified number of times
`For each`	Iterates over items in a list, data table, or data row, executing a block of actions repeatedly
`Loop Condition`	Repeats a block of actions as long as a specified condition is true
`Exit Loop`	Terminates the loop, resuming flow at the next action or statement
`Next Loop`	Forces the next iteration of the loop, skipping any remaining actions in the current iteration

ON THE WEB

To see code snippets and examples on how to use conditions and loops head over to `https://learn.microsoft.com/en-us/power-automate/desktop-flows/actions-reference/conditionals` for conditionals and `https://learn.microsoft.com/en-us/power-automate/desktop-flows/actions-reference/loops` for loops.

Playing the approvals game

Approvals are essential to organizational workflows, whether for obtaining written acknowledgment from one or more stakeholders. Power Automate offers an approvals capability that allows you to automate sign-off requests and integrate human decision-making into workflows in four ways. Common scenarios for using approvals include approving leave requests, purchase requisitions, or document signoffs. When a flow submits an approval request, the designated approvers are notified and can review and act on the request, ensuring a streamlined and efficient approval process.

Actions in Power Automate approvals dictate what events your flow should perform once triggered. For example, you can configure a flow to trigger an approval when a new item is added to a Microsoft SharePoint List, prompting someone to review the item if they receive a notification by email or SMS. For this flow type, the most appropriate option is to use `Start and wait for an approval`. This action allows you to specify the details of the approval request and designate the approvers who will receive it. The flow then waits for the approvers' response before completing its run. Table 15-4 describes the four types of approvals available, followed by an example that shows how to create an end-to-end `Start and wait for an approval` process.

TABLE 15-4 Approval Types

Flow Type	Description
Approval/Reject – Everyone Must Approve	All approvers must approve or reject; the flow completes after all responses are collected or after a single rejection.
Approve/Reject – First To Respond	Approval or rejection by any approver completes the request; the flow completes after the first response.
Custom Responses – Wait for all Responses	All approvers must respond for the process to be complete based on your customer conditions.
Custom Responses – Wait for one response	The process completes after any approver provides a response based on custom conditions.

Building a common Approval Flow

Approval Flows are useful for when an item is added to a SharePoint Document Library or List, a Word document requires review, or a document must be circulated for approval before it is distributed. You may need only one person to sign off at one time, while many people will be required to sign off at other times. Sometimes, a particular order may apply in which the sign-off occurs.

The following steps show how to create a common approval workflow that can apply any approval types listed in Table 15-4 while interacting with SharePoint Online and Microsoft Office 365 Outlook.

1. **Click Create from the left navigation panel on the Power Automate homepage.**
2. **On the Create page, select Automated Cloud Flow to start a flow triggered by an event.**
3. **Name your flow and select the trigger `When a file is created`.**

   In this case, several options exist for where the file can be stored. Select either OneDrive or OneDrive for Business (based on the type of license you own).

4. **Click Create.**

   Next you create the framework for the approval workflow.

5. **From the Flow Designer, click the trigger and then select the folder where the file will be saved.**

   For this example, you can select a Test Folder in the OneDrive root directory.

6. **Add the approval action by clicking the plus sign (+) and then choosing `Create an Approval` from the list of available actions that appears in the search bar.**

   This action establishes the approval process, allowing you to request approval when the workflow is triggered.

7. **Open the `Create an Approval` action, and select an approval type. For this example, select `First to Respond` (see Figure 15-6).**

   Remember, this menu offers four approval types (refer to Table 15-4). Selecting the correct approval type ensures the approval workflow matches your decision-making process.

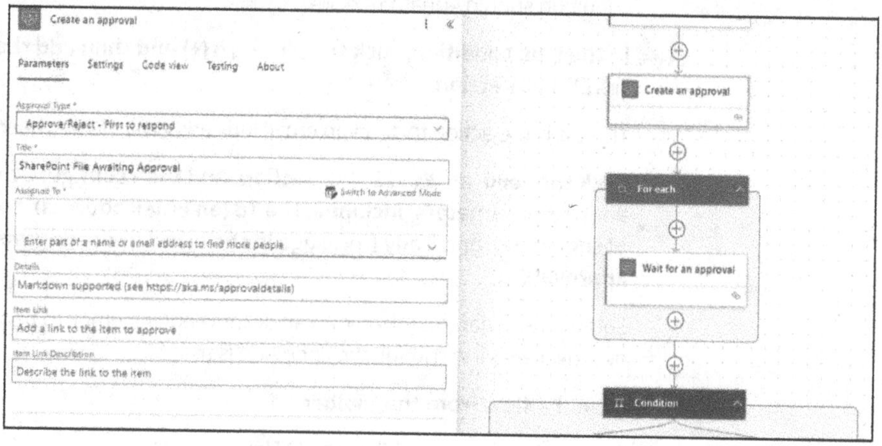

FIGURE 15-6: Selecting the appropriate approval type.

8. **Fill in the approval details, such as the title, and assign to fields that are mandatory. You can also fill out additional fields such as notifications, reassignments, and custom messages.**

   These fields control how the approval request is communicated to approvers.

9. **From the Flow Designer, click the plus sign (+) again to add another approval action. This time, you will add an approval action to Wait for an Approval.**

   In this step, you are creating a pause in the workflow so that the flow stops until the approval is executed. During this step, you'd use Dynamic Content on the entry form to automate key parts of the approval process in fields such as Approval ID or Approver Name.

10. **Return to the Flow Designer and click the plus sign (+) again after inserting the second approval. Here you want to add a condition action.**

    In this case, you are adding true/false logic to indicate if the approval is approved (true) or not approved (false) for the workflow requirement.

11. **Configure the condition to branch the workflow based on whether the file was approved. You do so by filling in the conditions with dynamic content.**

    The first value should point to the value from the approval condition `When a file is created`. Set that condition to `Approver item`. The second condition should point to the approval condition, `Wait for an outcome`. That condition should equal, `Outcome`.

12. **In the true condition, click the plus sign (+) and then add the `Send an Email (V2)` action.**

    This adds the action to send an email indicating the file has been approved.

13. **Click the `Send an Email (V2)` action, and then configure the email address parameters, including the To (an email address), Subject (subject of the email), and Body (message in the email indicating workflow approval).**

    Setting these parameters allows an acknowledging email to be sent as an approval email, assuming the condition is true.

14. **Save the flow from the toolbar.**

    This saves the approval flow to My Flows.

15. **Test the flow by saving a new document to the targeted folder.**

    The workflow should then trigger as expected within minutes. The flow will result in the following: A user must approve or decline the submission each time a file is added to a specific OneDrive folder. If approved, the user will receive an email indicating that the file was approved for upload. Only one user had to approve the file submission. Figure 15-7 shows this flow in its entirety.

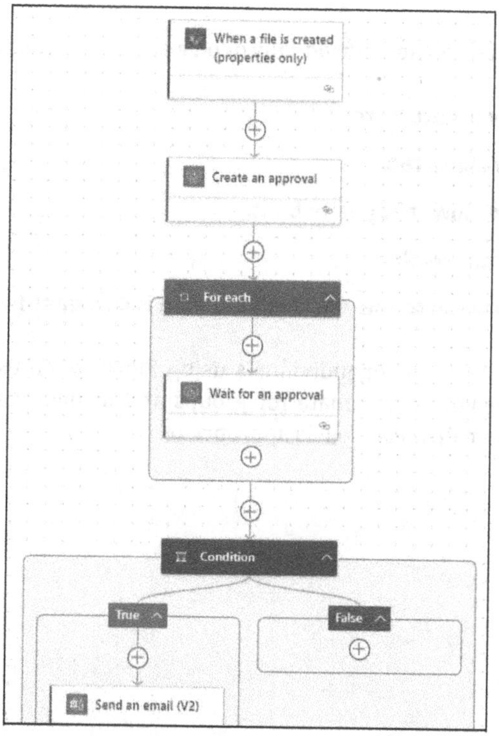

FIGURE 15-7: An example of an approval workflow.

Understanding Automation Licensing Limitations

While Microsoft provides all users with a free version of Power Automate as part of their Microsoft 365 license, this version is limited in its features. Many connectors, including those that enable certain triggers for flows, require a Power Automate Premium license. Flows built using Power Apps and using standard Microsoft connectors are free, but premium connectors or enterprise features — whether from Microsoft or third-party vendors — require a Premium license. While Power BI has its own licensing model, automating Power BI tasks using Power Automate may also require a Premium license when using advanced or premium connectors.

ON THE WEB

Licensing is always a dicey area as every organization has its own unique requirements. Go to Microsoft's Power Platform definitive licensing guide, found at `https://go.microsoft.com/fwlink/?linkid=2085130` to understand what is free and what is premium.

To find out if you are licensed individually or on a per-flow plan, follow these steps:

1. **Sign in to Power Automate.**
2. **Select the My Flows tab.**
3. **Select a Cloud Flow that you've built.**
4. **Go to the Details section.**
5. **Check the View tab to see whether your plan is Owner or Per Flow.**

TIP

An owner's plan is meant for individuals using Flows when using Power Automate. When using Power Automate for groups and teams, using the enterprise licensing construct called *Per Flow* is appropriate.

5
The Part of Tens

IN THIS PART . . .

Discover best practices for building end-to-end solutions within the Microsoft Power Platform.

Find additional recommended training and resources online to learn Power Platform.

IN THIS CHAPTER

» Optimizing your Power Platform experience

» Discovering development and deployment protocols to consider in the Power Platform

» Exploring business practices that can help accelerate your solution development

Chapter 16

Ten Best Practices When Developing Power Platform Solutions

If you've come to this chapter, you are probably looking for those nuggets of wisdom to help you get a much-needed jolt for your new Power Platform project. Or perhaps you are looking to refine your journey in low-code development. Whether you are a seasoned business analyst, a citizen developer, or a master application developer, the practices described throughout this chapter are foundational in ensuring that your use of Power Platform remains efficient, robust, and secure no matter what stage in the development and deployment lifecycle you may find yourself in. And remember, development is only one part of the journey; also included are planning, governance, policy, and continuous improvement.

Focusing on the Essential Business Needs

It's no secret that the IT folks can sometimes get carried away with gold plating and scope creep when developing solutions. When building a low-code or no-code solution, it's easy to assemble a product by tucking in a few extra bells and whistles along the way.

When you are trying to analyze a business problem, focus on the specific need for the application in the development of the application. Build for those features exclusively, and nothing more. Be creative when planning for what-if scenarios, asking questions such as "What will it take for the application to grow later?"

For example, would you create 20 individual reports using Power BI when you could simply use a slicer control to filter the data among the twenty different report options? Probably not unless it is a business requirement. Alternatively, would you vary the color of an interface to reflect the type of user logging into the application? I hope not, but if it is a business requirement to create color-dependent interfaces, that's when you implement the feature. These are examples where you want to think about maximizing for low code and process optimization, not giving away everything in the kitchen sink.

Don't Over-Engineer Processes and Data Models

Simplicity and efficiency make for the best-designed applications, easiest reporting instruments, and most accommodating workflows to manage. In other words, avoiding the temptation to make processes and data models complex or convoluted can save you time later, and save you money along the way.

- **Processes:** Intricate processes should only be implemented when the business requires such a need. It's important to address all necessary steps in a process, but not add any extras or conditional branches "just because" as having to manage and maintain extra leads to more work later. Simplified process management ensures smoother execution and easier troubleshooting across all applications.
- **Data models:** Every application in the Power Platform suite is equipped with some form of data model. Over-engineering your data may include adding too many tables, overcomplicating relationships, creating unnecessary fields, establishing too many branches in workflows, or even adding too many filters in a report. The result is increased complexity and decreased performance.

Therefore, keeping processes and the data models supporting those models in check to meet business essential needs can help create solutions that are easier to build, manage, and adapt over time.

Keep Data Squeaky Clean

The old saying that the quality of a system is only as good as the data in the system rings true with the Power Platform. When building tables, you want to avoid adding unnecessary table columns, because that only leads to confusion and adds to your data expenses. When populating lookup tables with data, only put options in the lookup columns that provide value and nothing more. For example, how many states are in the United States: 250 or 50? The latter, of course. Would it be helpful to search through a list of 100+ data entries? Not at all. Because the dataset would not only be faulty when producing reports but also slow to load in the application; you want to keep the dataset to just the required values.

Actively managing and maintaining the quality and integrity of your data to ensure efficiency, compliance, and effective decision-making is integral to optimal application design and performance. This practice is essential for enhancing user experiences, optimizing operations, and ensuring data-driven decisions are based on accurate, consistent, and reliable information. In summary, data cleanliness underpins the success of applications, workflows, and analytics within the Power Platform ecosystem.

Automate Processes Intelligently

If there is an easier way to do a task that requires manual input, automate the task. For example, if an application requires a user to input data across multiple tables, automate it. If there is a requirement to validate the value in a dataset without having to manually check the application: automate the process. You can accomplish most of these automation steps intelligently using Power Automate or a virtual agent courtesy of Microsoft Copilot. Remember though, automation must be addressed in the context of the data and its processes. Therefore, making decisions based on more than just static inputs is key. Intelligent automation focuses on evaluating trends, pattern recognition, and predictive analysis, not just on an activity that occurs at a single moment in time.

TECHNICAL STUFF

Power Automate is adaptive because it learns based on real-time data, feedback generated, and conditions evaluated over time. As workflows continue to be optimized for efficiency and effectiveness, so do the processes.

Develop a Center of Excellence

Assembling a Power Platform solution requires a bit of planning. Once developed and then put into production, then what? Is your work over? Can an organization take a victory lap and claim total success? Not quite. The next step is establishing a Power Platform Center of Excellence (CoE). A CoE is an organizational hub that consolidates expertise, governance, best practices, and support across the entire application suite so that all developers can further enhance the application in future iterations, focusing on innovation, efficiency, and quality.

REMEMBER

As your organization matures, a CoE will not only take existing assets and archive them but also build new ones, with particular emphasis on training, guidelines, and policy documentation to promote secure and compliant use of the Power Platform for all skill levels.

Optimize for All Platforms

Optimizing for all platforms comes with some caveats. If you are building an application for a specific device type, then all your focus should go into designing the user experience that meets the end-user requirements. For example, a mobile interest calculator built using a canvas app in Power Apps should be optimized for what: a smartphone or tablet exclusively. Will a desktop user access the application, unlikely. However, an HR application meant for gathering payroll data and project data across different device types, including desktop, tablet, and phone should be treated much differently. Think about what functionality and features are necessary to ensure the user can accomplish their business objective, and nothing more.

Implement Version Control and Application Lifecycle Management

First-time developers build once and call their development effort a success, but is that the best approach to developing with Power Platform? Not really. When dealing with enterprise-class applications, knowing when to convert an application from unmanaged to managed, and a way to limit unlimited changes to an application once mature is just as important as version control and application lifecycle management (ALM), as discussed in Chapter 4.

Enterprises should deploy applications in stages. First, the development team should develop a feature in one environment (development). Next, once the development is proven to be mature enough, the feature is promoted to another environment for testing (user acceptance). Once the end-users approve of the feature, the application can be deployed to its final home in production. Each time a team iterates through these stages, a new application version should be notated, leading to collaboration among the team that requires code collaboration and validation.

When developing Power Platform solutions, a developer and their team will want to use the built-in support for version control and ALM through Power Apps integration with GitHub or Azure DevOps. It's essential to also use the Power Platform environment and solution manager to bring all like-kind project assets together. Additionally, as a project matures, implementing a Center of Excellence (CoE) for each implementation helps isolate tools and guidelines to ensure repeatable processes are in place for continued scalability and business efficiency.

ON THE WEB

To learn more about Application Lifecycle Management (ALM), go to `https://learn.microsoft.com/en-us/power-platform/alm`.

Constantly Monitor and Optimize Power Platform Functionality

Just when you think you are finished with your Power Platform masterpiece, you'll be surprised to know that your journey has just begun. Why? That's because Microsoft regularly releases platform updates across the suite that may impact your solution's performance. You need to evaluate the application and its components for usage and performance issues. That's not all, you should also get feedback from users to enhance application performance. At first, you may not have any issues, but with so many ongoing enhancements in the platform, over time, it will be inevitable that a benign product change will cause an application bug. Therefore, keeping up with the latest resources and then optimizing the application through ongoing adjustments is essential when trying to be a good development steward.

ON THE WEB

If you want to keep up with every new feature Microsoft is releasing across the Microsoft Power Platform, head to the Release Planner website at `https://releaseplans.microsoft.com/en-US/?app=Power+Apps`.

Focus on Least Privileged Security

Just because applications are low-code in the Power Platform does not mean you can forget about security and compliance, an often sticky subject to broach with citizen developers. When dealing with security and auditing, organizations must address safeguarding sensitive data and ensuring compliance with local government regulations. That begins with implementing data protection measures across data sources being used including encryption, role-based access controls, data loss protection policies, and adhering to the use of authentication such as Microsoft Entra ID.

WARNING

The last thing you'll want to deal with is unauthorized access or a data breach. Securing data for just those who need access to ensure the integrity and confidentiality of your data is paramount. You'll want to follow the security principle of least privileged access, even with Power Platform applications.

If your application contains any form of personal data, then you'll want to implement an authentication and authorization mechanism. Not only that, but implementing multi-factor authentication should be considered to ensure a user's identity is verified, not once but twice. Organizations must also address granular authorization policies. That means creating security groups, not just assigning a single user to an application as part of the application identity management platform. Each group should assign users only to the minimum access levels based on the roles and responsibilities, and nothing more.

Leverage Modular Design Approaches

Having a "build once" to scale, maintain, and reuse mentality can enhance the life and usefulness of your applications and their associated components. Here are four tactics to follow as you plan, design, develop, and execute your development in the Microsoft Power Platform:

» **Componentize:** The very first step in your development is to componentize every application function. If the capability can be made repeatable, create an application component; don't make a developer reinvent the wheel many times. By componentizing, you can standardize UI elements, improve application user experience consistency, and speed up development.

» **Connectors:** If your application will interact with external systems, connect to at least one data source, or require some business logic, leverage the use of custom connectors. A custom connector is a way to abstract the complexity of a data source or interact with APIs independently. A connector allows you to encapsulate reusable logic by applying consistency in how apps interact with external systems.

- **Make it a service:** Most novice Power Apps developers embed complex logic directly into their apps, forcing a one-time usage of a Power Automate Flow. Instead, why not encapsulate logic with a flow using cloud services (Chapter 14) and allow the flow to be called from several apps if the process is reusable? Again, the goal is to promote reuse and simplify maintenance of repeatable activities.
- **Data source abstraction:** Hard-coding data is unavoidable for most developers at some point, but seldom should it be done anymore with the use of Power Platform. Instead, a better approach is to abstract data sources for an application through *data centralization.* That means isolating data into one location by using sources such as Dataflows or Dataverse (as discussed in depth in Chapters 2 and 3). By applying data abstraction alternatives, you effectively decouple your apps and their components from specific data sources. Any time you need to switch or update the source, it's transparent to the application, not a hard dependency.

By adopting a modular design strategy, your organization will be able to build a robust application without much overhead and simplification ahead.

IN THIS CHAPTER

» **Exploring key online training platforms to extend your Power Platform knowledge**

» **Discovering online forums and in-person events**

Chapter 17 Ten Useful Power Platform Resources

Whether you go on any major search engine such as Google or Bing or head straight to the Microsoft website, you are likely to find a trove of information on Power Platform. Like me, you'll review the first set of results and then close your browser. It's not an uncommon reaction as the Internet is inundated with questionable information from many unreliable sources.

For this chapter, I've curated a list of indispensable resources for anyone wanting to learn Power Platform as a beginner to intermediate user.

Microsoft Learn

When you begin your journey with any Microsoft product, your first stop should be the Microsoft self-instruction portal, Microsoft Learn, found at `https://learn.microsoft.com`. Microsoft Learn helps beginners and others looking to refresh their knowledge about Microsoft products and services, including all areas of Microsoft Power Platform. The Learn curriculum is structured using a task-based, interactive learning style. Each product line contains a series of individual courses. Microsoft has also curated lesson plans based on your role in the product lifecycle.

Learn provides various curricula for Microsoft Power Platform, including Microsoft Dataverse, Power Apps, Power Automate, Power BI, Power Pages, and Copilot. As of this writing, the Learn website offers over 80 hours of free training specific to Microsoft Power Platform.

Microsoft Documentation

To find the most up-to-date reference on anything Microsoft Power Platform from the vendor, check out Microsoft's online documentation site for Power Platform, found at `https://learn.microsoft.com/en-us/power-platform`.

Microsoft's documentation is the most comprehensive resource provided for Power Platform. If you search for help using the Help functionality in-app, you're taken right back to the official documentation website. Because the product is constantly evolving, the documentation is always being updated. Having access to this official source, which includes structured learning and relevant tutorials, is invaluable to the citizen and professional developer.

REMEMBER

For those of you who are looking to take a Microsoft certification, the most reliable source to acquire the requisite knowledge for the exams is the Microsoft official documentation, not a textbook.

WARNING

The documentation for Power Platform is robust, but you may need to sift through other product lines to find the details you need for complex integration scenarios. For example, Microsoft Power Platform works seamlessly with Microsoft 365, Dynamics 365, and Azure. In some instances, the Power Platform documentation explains an integration pattern with the complementary product. In other instances, you may find the integration covered in the complementary products documentation.

The Power Platform Community

The Power Platform Community, sponsored by Microsoft, is the largest public forum for developers and enthusiasts to engage on any of the Power Platform products with users globally. The community offers thousands of discussion forums, in-person and virtual event sessions, targeted user groups, and online resources to help expedite your learning journey. As of mid-2024, there are almost 1 million users, 500 thousand user groups, 100 thousand independent solutions, and 150 thousand discussion forums actively running. Talk about a vibrant community.

REMEMBER

The community may be self-managed by end users, but Microsoft does incorporate support through participation from its product marketing and development teams. These participants provide blogs and article support as Microsoft insiders. Articles delve into product updates, instructional tutorials, best practices, and ways to create innovative applications using the Power Platform.

Power CAT Live

Microsoft has an A-team within the product engineering group, called the *Power Customer Advisory Team (Power CAT)*. This elite squad of professionals works with Microsoft's key enterprise customers (think of the top 50–100 enterprises globally) to ensure they succeed when adapting Power Platform and Dynamics 365. Because product engineering is all about knowledge sharing, Power CAT created an online YouTube channel to share their knowledge with the world. On this channel, called Power CAT Live, found at `https://www.youtube.com/@powercat8566`, you can review case studies from around the world that highlight how others have tackled challenging scenarios with each of the Microsoft Power Platform applications.

Redmond Channel Partners

Keeping up with Microsoft and any other comings and goings in the tech industry can be dizzying to say the least. The most reliable industry news source outside of Microsoft is Redmond Channel Partners, found at `https://rcpmag.com`. Redmond Channel Partners is an online website that serves *Microsoft Partners* (third parties that sell products and services on behalf of Microsoft).

Redmond Channel Partners provides news analysis, business strategies, and product insights, including future roadmap opportunities across each major product line, like Power Platform. You'll find the content ranges from product and service updates to strategies on how to use Microsoft technologies in conjunction with its partner ecosystem.

The site also provides a list of the most reliable service providers and events to attend worldwide.

WARNING

Redmond Channel Partners is not affiliated with Microsoft. Most of the information provided by the site is spot on and has been vetted by the editors, but the final source of truth for any product update is Microsoft.

Podcasts

There are hundreds of podcasts on platforms such as Apple iTunes, Spotify, Soundcloud, and YouTube. A *podcast series* is a digital audio or video series available to stream or download from the Internet. One or more subject matter experts serve as hosts for the series, and the content covers a niche topic for a targeted audience. Users subscribe to the podcast series via its corresponding platform and are notified when new content is made available. Podcast creators update their content with frequencies ranging from several times a week to once a month. Podcasts have grown in popularity due to their digital portability as well as the personal touch they offer, as the hosts often build a direct connection with their audience.

Following are three popular and long-running Power Platform podcasts. You can search for each podcast by name on the corresponding podcast service, or access the podcasts directly by using the links provided in the following list:

- Microsoft Business Applications Podcast
  `https://player.fm/series/microsoft-business-applications-podcast-2936583`
- Low Code Approach
  `https://open.spotify.com/show/0NHHn4KmLe206Cd6CYrGu0`
- Power Platform Boost
  `https://open.spotify.com/show/02dmQ6wZQqr93WUdI16Tw8`

Online Videos

The Power Platform YouTube channel may come as a surprising resource as most people don't often associate Microsoft with Google. Guess again! Power Platform has a vast social media presence. There are well over 600 videos dedicated to helpful hints and tricks, conference proceedings, product launch demos, tutorials, and community demos all on one site. To access the Microsoft Power Platform Community on YouTube, go to `https://www.youtube.com/@mspowerplatform`.

Training Platforms

Beyond the Microsoft Learning community, you can find thousands of free or low-cost training opportunities on platforms such as LinkedIn Learning, Udemy, and Pluralsight. Using these three platforms, you can graduate from novice to expert developer in no time. Most of these platforms have training to prepare you for Microsoft Power Platform certifications. Notably, Udemy's instructional platform is curated by many of Microsoft's Most Valuable Players (MVPs).

For each of the platforms listed, type one of the product names in the platform's search engine to access courseware from around the world.

- LinkedIn Learning
  `https://www.linkedin.com/learning`
- Udemy
  `https://www.udemy.com`
- Pluralsight
  `https://www.pluralsight.com`

Code Samples and Snippets

Microsoft touts Power Platform as a low-code environment. But the reality is that there will come a point when you'll want to get a bit creative and try your hand at developing a more sophisticated application. At that point, you'll need to get immersed in a bit of development. The code you develop will not be many pages long, but the logic requires structure and discipline. That's where open-source websites such as GitHub become the citizen and professional developers' best friend because generally, someone has already tried it out there. And guess what, they've posted how they've accomplished the tasks.

Here are two websites with thousands of code samples prepared specifically for Microsoft Power Platform:

- Power Platform Code Samples on GitHub
  `https://pnp.github.io/powerplatform-samples`
- Microsoft Learn Power Platform Code Samples
  `https://learn.microsoft.com/en-us/samples/browse`

Technical Conferences

While attending conferences in person can be a costly investment, it's worth noting that many major events make their presentation slides and key sessions available online for free after the event, either on their websites or through platforms such as YouTube or Vimeo. This is a great way to access valuable insights if attending in person isn't feasible. If you have the chance to attend a conference, the experience and networking opportunities are invaluable. Keep an eye on these events, as they often release post-conference content that can be incredibly helpful about 30–60 days post-event. Check out these particular events each year:

- Microsoft Power Platform and Microsoft 365 Conference
  `https://pwrcon.com`
- Microsoft Power Platform Community Conference
  `https://powerplatformconf.com`
- DynamicsCon
  `https://dynamicscon.com`

Index

A

B

C

D

E

F

G

N

O

P

Q

R

S

T

U

V

W

About the Author

Jack Hyman is the founder of HyerTek, a technology and training services firm based in Washington, D.C., that specializes in cloud computing, business intelligence, and enterprise application advisory services for federal, state, and private sector organizations. Before establishing HyerTek, he worked at Oracle and IBM. Jack is the author of *Power BI For Dummies, Azure For Dummies, 2nd Edition*, and *Tableau For Dummies, 2nd Edition*. He earned his PhD in Information Systems from Nova Southeastern University.

Dedication

To my children, Jeremy and Emily: I hope you always love learning as much as I do.

Author's Acknowledgments

Many folks were involved in making *Power Platform For Dummies* become a reality. Thanks to Executive Editor Steve Hayes and Senior Managing Editor Kristie Pyles for allowing me to write this book (and so many other *For Dummies* projects over the past five years). A great big thanks to Project Manager Colleen Diamond and Editors Colleen Diamond and Laura Miller for keeping me on track throughout this project — you've made this book a fantastic read! A hearty thanks to Technical Editor Jennifer Reed for ensuring that the content in the book was technically sound. Also, thanks to Carole Jelen of Waterside Productions for bringing me yet another exciting project to share with the world. And finally, thanks to my wife, Debbie, and kids, Jeremy and Emily, for allowing me to take on yet another book.

Publisher's Acknowledgments

Executive Editor: Steve Hayes

Project Manager: Colleen Diamond

Editors: Colleen Diamond and Laura Miller

Technical Editor: Jennifer Reed

Production Editor: Tamilmani Varadharaj

Managing Editors: Murari Mukandan and Kristie Pyles

Cover Image: © instamatics/Getty Images